KU-216-265

Winds of the Spirit

Winds of the Spirit

A Constructive Christian Theology

Peter C. Hodgson

SCM PRESS LTD

All rights reserved. No part of this publication may be reproduced, stored in a retrieval system, or transmitted, in any form or by any means, electronic, mechanical, photocopying, recording or otherwise, without the prior permission of the publisher, SCM Press Ltd.

Copyright © Peter C. Hodgson 1994

Biblical quotations, unless otherwise noted, are from the New Revised Standard Version of the Bible, copyright © 1989 by the Division of Christian Education of the National Council of Churches of Christ in the USA.

0 334 02575 3

First published in Britain 1994
by SCM Press Ltd
26–30 Tottenham Road London N1 4BZ

Printed in Finland by
Werner Söderström Oy

To Edward Farley and Sallie McFague—
Vanderbilt colleagues for twenty-five years

CONTENTS

PART 2. CONTEXTUALIZING

PART 3. REVISIONING

God: The One

Spirit: Freedom

PREFACE

This book has evolved from lectures given over the years in introductory courses on Christian theology at the Divinity School of Vanderbilt University. Those who have made the most direct contribution to it are the students who continually pressed for clarification and offered many original insights of their own. In preparing the work for publication, I have tried to stay fairly close to the lecture format and to make the book accessible to beginning students of theology. It is intended as an introduction to theology, but at the same time it is more than an introduction. It is an attempt to set forth a revisioning of Christian theology, and that has pushed me to the horizons of my own thinking. It will demand no less of students—but opening up new horizons is what education is all about.

I argue that theology requires a continual process of interpretation that constructs new visions of Christian faith and practice from resources provided by scripture, tradition, reason, and experience in the context of contemporary cultural challenges. The fundamental challenge of postmodernity seems to be the loss of any meaningful discourse about God. Yet out of the depths of the cultural crises of our time a new revelation of the divine may be appearing. To discern this I attend to three cultural quests or practices that embrace much of what is going on today: the *emancipatory*, the *ecological*, and the *dialogical*. I argue that a correlation exists between these quests and a triadic structure of the divine life, namely *freedom*, *love*, and *wholeness*. God is the One who creates out of love that which is radically different from yet deeply related to God, namely the world, and who liberates this world from its fallenness, fragmentation, and futility by drawing it into everlasting communion with God and empowering the endless struggle against evil. God is the One Who Loves in Freedom. God is not an isolated supreme being over against the world; rather, embodied by the world, incarnate in the shapes of Christ, God becomes a concrete, living, relational God, "Spirit." In this frame of reference, which can be described as a trinitarian holism, I offer a reconstruction of central themes of Christian theology: faith, reason and revelation, God, creation, nature, human being, sin and evil, Christ, Spirit, church, religions, history, and eschatology. A summary of the constructive argument is found on pages 46–50. The epilogue (chap. 20) provides some information on the theological orientation, personal experience, and social location of the author. Among other things it is worth noting that the sort of revisioning undertaken in this work claims to stand within the tradition of Reformed theology—a theology that at its best recognizes the need for continually reforming itself. New forms require new visions and vice versa.

Theology is drawn and driven by winds of the Spirit. Of course there is *one* prevailing wind, which simply *is* Spirit, or God as Spirit. A wind from God—the Spirit of God—swept over the face of the waters: so we are told at the beginning of the story of creation. And at the end of the story it appears that Spirit is the most adequate and encompassing of the symbols for God, the climax of a trinitarian vision of the whole God, which includes God and world together.

There are also *many* winds of the Spirit—winds that are God's messengers, says the Psalmist. God's presence and power in the world are configured in a multitude of ways by the contours of the world itself, just as the prevailing wind breaks into currents as it comes into contact with land and water, hills and valleys, heat and cold. Winds of the Spirit are sweeping through the world, scattering and gathering, leveling and lifting, overturning and setting free. This is God at work in the world. The task of constructive Christian theology is to hearken to these winds as they appear in its central themes—the creative energy of the triune God, the dynamics of the natural world, the glory and tragedy of human beings, the reconciling and emancipatory work of Christ, the ecclesial community with its word and sacraments, the plurality and interaction of world religions, the ebb and flow of history, the challenges of postmodernity, the quests for freedom, love, and wholeness. Today new winds are blowing and old winds are freshening. Theology's vocation is to catch these winds in its constructive sails and release their redemptive potential by envisioning them in new forms. Theological doctrines are themselves winds of the Spirit—or they are lifeless relics.

Lectures outlining the project were presented at Harvard Divinity School and Yale Divinity School; to the systematic theology section of the Wissenschaftliche Gesellschaft für Theologie in Germany; to the theological faculty and students of the University of Iceland; to the staff of the Theology and Worship Unit of the Presbyterian Church (U.S.A.); and to the Workgroup on Constructive Christian Theology. For the vigorous discussion and critique as well as hospitality provided in all these settings I am appreciative. Special thanks are due to Hanna Mariá Pétursdóttir and Sigurdur Árni Thordarson, who invited me to Thingvellir in Iceland, where in that powerful spiritual environment my thoughts about nature and spirit came into sharper focus. Thingvellir, site of the ancient Icelandic parliament, now a national park in a magnificent setting of volcanic plain and surrounding mountains, lies on the mid-Atlantic rift and thus at the point where two continents are joined. Its location may have been determined by an ancient number symbolism related to the goddess figure, signifying cosmic harmony; later it was the place where Christianity was accepted in Iceland. Just south of the park lies a lovely lake, Thingvallavatn. As I watched the wind sweep across its waters in a changing play of light and color, the title metaphor of this book began to form in my mind.

Several sections draw upon earlier writings of mine, and to some extent this book represents an attempt to reconceive and synthesize my own work in a new form. Where I could not improve upon earlier formulations, I adopted them. I am grateful for the permission granted by Fortress Press and Abingdon Press to make use of previously published material. Davis Perkins, director of Westminster/John Knox Press, has been a staunch supporter of this project from the start. The manuscript has been read by Rebecca Chopp, John Cobb, Edward Farley, Sallie McFague, and Lewis Mudge. I am deeply indebted to these colleagues and friends for their thoughtful comments and many helpful suggestions for improving the work. They pushed me to clarify and refine my thinking at numerous points, and they have reminded me how much theology is—or ought to be—a collaborative enterprise. Final revisions were made in the context of a seminar on the nature of theological construction with a group of perceptive and imaginative students. Financial assistance was provided by the Association of Theological Schools and the Vanderbilt University Research Council, permitting nearly a full year of leave during which the work was completed.

ACKNOWLEDGMENTS

The following publishers have given permission for the use of materials by Peter C. Hodgson and published by them in earlier versions:

For extracts from *Jesus—Word and Presence: An Essay in Christology*, copyright © 1971: Fortress Press.

For extracts from *New Birth of Freedom: A Theology of Bondage and Liberation*, copyright © 1976: Fortress Press.

For extracts from "Scripture and Tradition" (co-authored with Edward Farley) in *Christian Theology: An Introduction to Its Traditions and Tasks*, copyright © 1982, 1985, 1994: Fortress Press.

For extracts from *Revisioning the Church: Ecclesial Freedom in the New Paradigm*, copyright © 1988: Fortress Press. Used by permission.

For extracts adapted from *God in History: Shapes of Freedom*. Copyright © 1989 by Peter C. Hodgson. Used by permission of Abingdon Press.

The Crossroad Publishing Company has given permission to quote material from *She Who Is: The Mystery of God in Feminist Theological Discourse* by Elizabeth A. Johnson. Copyright © 1992 by Elizabeth A. Johnson. Reprinted by permission of The Crossroad Publishing Company.

The University of Chicago Press has given permission to quote material from *Systematic Theology* by Paul Tillich. Copyright © 1951, 1957, 1963 by The University of Chicago.

Brethren Press has given permission for quoting four lines from a poem in *Threatened With Resurrection* by Julia Esquivel. Copyright © 1982: Brethren Press. Used by permission.

British publishers of books cited in the bibliography are as follows:

Barbour, Ian, *Religion in an Age of Science*, SCM Press
Bultmann, Rudolf, *Theology of the New Testament*, SCM Press
Fiorenza, Elisabeth Schüssler, *In Memory of Her*, SCM Press
Fuller, Reginald H., *Foundations of New Testament Christology*, Lutterworth Press
Gadamer, Hans-Georg, *Truth and Method*, Sheed and Ward
Gutiérrez, Gustavo, *God of Life*, SCM Press
——, *The Power of the Poor in History*, SCM Press
——, *A Theology of Liberation*, SCM Press
Habermas, Jürgen, *Communication and the Evolution of Society*, Blackwell
——, *Theory of Communicative Action*, Blackwell
Heidegger, *Being and Time*, Blackwell
Hendry, George, *The Holy Spirit in Christian Theology*, SCM Press
Hick, John, *The Metaphor of God Incarnate*, SCM Press
Hick, John and Paul F. Knitter, eds., *The Myth of Christian Uniqueness*, SCM Press
Jüngel, Eberhard, *God as the Mystery of the World*, T. & T. Clark
Käsemann, Ernst, *Jesus Means Freedom*, SCM Press
Kelsey, David H., *The Uses of Scripture in Recent Theology*, SCM Press
Knitter, Paul F., *No Other Name?*, SCM Press
Küng, Hans, *The Church*, Search Press
McFague, Sallie, *The Body of God*, SCM Press
——, *Models of God*, SCM Press
Macquarrie, John, *Jesus Christ in Modern Thought*, SCM Press
——, *Principles of Christian Theology*, SCM Press
Moltmann, Jürgen, *The Crucified God*, SCM Press
——, *The Spirit of Life*, SCM Press
Monod, Jacques, *Chance and Necessity*, Collins
Niebuhr, H. Richard, *Christ and Culture*, Faber and Faber
——, *The Purpose of the Church and Its Ministry*, Hamish Hamilton
——, *Radical Monotheism and Western Culture*, Faber and Faber
Niebuhr, Reinhold, *The Nature and Destiny of Man*, Nisbet
Pieris, Aloysius, *An Asian Theology of Liberation*, T. & T. Clark
Polkinghorne, John, *One World*, SPCK
——, *Science and Providence*, SPCK
Rahner, Karl, *Foundations of Christian Faith*, Darton, Longman and Todd
Richardson, Alan, and John Bowden, eds., *A New Dictionary of Christian Theology*, SCM Press
Ruether, Rosemary Radford, *To Change the World*, SCM Press
——, *Gaia and God*, SCM Press
——, *Sexism and God Talk*, SCM Press

Schillebeeckx, Edward, *Ministry*, SCM Press
Sölle, Dorothee, *Thinking about God*, SCM Press
Tillich, Paul, *The Courage to Be*, Nisbet
——, *Systematic Theology*, SCM Press
Tracy, David, *The Analogical Imagination*, SCM Press
——, *Plurality and Ambiguity*, SCM Press
Troeltsch, Ernst, *Writings on Theology and Religion*, Duckworth

Part 1
INTERPRETING

1
THINKING THEOLOGICALLY

A Definition of Theology

Faith's Language about God

Theology is rather like sailing. It is in contact with powerful, fluid elements, symbolized by wind and water, over which it has little control and by which it is drawn and driven toward mysterious goals. The ship of theology has no foundation other than itself, no external prop, but only the structural integrity and interplay of its component parts, which enable it to float and sail. Occasionally the ship has to be taken into port for repairs and refitting. On the open water sailing can be an exhilarating and joyous adventure but also one filled with danger and disappointment. Truth, value, and beauty do not exist in the abstract but are created in the act of sailing through a symbiosis of ship and elemental forces.

I shall return to this metaphor as the project of revisioning Christian theology unfolds. Behind the metaphor and at the beginning of the project stands this little word, "theology." It is a compound composed of two Greek words and means in the most basic sense "language or thought (*logos*) about God (*theos*)." This simple etymology seems rather barren, but it contains valuable hints that might lead to a more adequate definition through a process of reflection.

In the first place the word "theology" tells us that the ultimate subject matter of theology—the "wind" that drives the ship—is *God* (*theos*). If theology is to be true to its name, it cannot rest content with any subject other than this one, despite its elusiveness, intangibility, and deep mystery. Theology's temptation is to look away from God to a multitude of other topics, not only because it recognizes the difficulty of talking about God, but also because it knows that we *can* talk about God only in relation to the world and ourselves. We cannot know God in and for godself apart from the world (as, presumably, God is capable of knowing God) but only in relationship to the world and as expressed by human language. Yet, what we know about God in relationship to the world does tell us something about the very being of God: God *is* in some sense an event of primordial and everlasting relatedness, both self-relatedness and world-relatedness. The fluid metaphors, wind and water, fire and light, are powerful representations of this relatedness. God's self-relatedness is not reducible to world-relatedness, and it is important to reflect on it as an independent theme if we are to understand God as in some sense a personal subject who enters into relations and is not merely relationality or process. Such an understanding seems to be required by religious experience, and I shall attempt to show that there are good theological reasons for affirming it. At the same time, world-relatedness is a constitutive feature of the divine life, and it is only on the basis of God's revelatory presence in the world that we are able to say anything about God's identity as "the One who loves in freedom."

In the second place, the word "theology" tells us that the proximate subject matter of theology—the "ship" that catches the wind—is *language* (*logos*). This is not any sort of language but the *language of faith*, which is called forth by God's self-revelation and self-presentation in the world. Most of the time in theology we do not talk directly about God but about faith's language about God. The language of faith is the "place" where God's self-revelation and self-presentation take place. There is for humans no wordless grasp of God, no word of God apart from human words. But—and this is equally important—language is always embodied and enacted; thus it is appropriate to speak not simply of "word" and "language" but of "word-event" and "language-event."[1] Language *is* a corporate, worldly event, an event of communication, the characteristically human form of activity. We must guard against the danger of disembodying language, of not recognizing that it is always embedded in a physical, social, and emotional matrix.

Language, properly understood, involves both speaking and acting, both word and praxis.[2] Praxis without word (the instrument of critical reflection and thought) is subhuman, mere labor; words without praxis are ideology or idle chatter. The "language of faith" includes both word and praxis; it is a form of "communicative action."[3] There are, of course, powerful nonverbal media of communication—painting, photography, music, dance, sculpture, signing, gesturing—but they all presuppose language and are inconceivable without it. When words are totally lacking, there is no access to God, self, or world; silence is a meditation upon words, feeling is a reverberation of words.[4] The ship of theology is a language-event.

The language of faith is irreducibly symbolic, imaginative, metaphorical, embedded in texts, stories, traditions; yet it is always pressing toward thoughts, concepts, doctrines. The metaphorical and symbolic character of language is not something to be avoided, not only because its richness and concreteness are irreplaceable but also because the *broken* character of the bond between the human and the sacred can best be expressed by the indirect language of faith.[5] Yet theology cannot simply remain within the symbolic mode; it must attempt to saturate the symbols of faith with intelligibility. The symbols themselves seek intelligibility: Symbols give rise to thought (Ricoeur). The heart has its reasons (Pascal). Faith seeks understanding (Anselm). The reason for this is that faith seeks meaning and truth, and claims about meaning and truth involve analysis, clarification, judgment, publicly available discourse. The concepts and doctrines with which theology works *incorporate* the metaphors of faith, but they seek to grasp or comprehend the whole of which a metaphor gives only a specific angle of vision or limited picture.[6] We may speak of God as a mighty whirlwind and as a still small voice—but what *is* God, and how do we reconcile these seemingly contradictory attributes? Constructive theology addresses such questions; to "construct" is to build up by fitting parts together. Thus theology must work with both the concrete symbols of religion and the abstract concepts of thought, granting a privileged or exclusive position to neither of these alone.

Every discipline has its lingo, and theology is no exception. Part of learning the discipline is getting in on the lingo. Theology (like sailing) has a lot of lingo because it is a very ancient discipline. But even new disciplines can build up a lingo with astonishing rapidity, as evidenced by computer science and aerospace technology. The lingo serves the purpose of communicating more rapidly and precisely, but there is also a "gamey" aspect to it. Humans love to play games with language. Theology is a language game, and the rules of the game are the proper use of terms and concepts. The rules are learned through disciplined practice. In the study of medicine, or law, or economics, people are expected to learn an astonishing amount of new vocabulary. Theological vocabulary is relatively simple by comparison, but it still demands a concentrated effort. The main technical terms used in this book will be defined as they appear, but its vocabulary and argument presuppose a willingness on the part of readers to work hard at the practice of theological discourse. Excellent theological dictionaries are available as well as other resources for beginning students.[7]

Faith's language about God provides the actual content or subject matter of Christian theology, stated in very broad terms. My treatment of the major themes of the language of faith—reason and revelation, the being and act of God, creation, the natural world, human being, sin and evil, Christ incarnate and risen, the Spirit and freedom, the church, religions, history, eschatology—are addressed in the third main part of this work (chaps. 9–19), under the rubric of "revisioning" and on the basis of a trinitarian model of God-world interaction. A summary of the constructive argument and an explanation of how these themes are related is provided in the last section of chapter 4.

Thinking about Faith's Language

The Greek word *logos* means not only "word" and "language" but also "reason," "thought," "understanding" (the English word "logic" is a derivative). I have already said that faith seeks meaning, truth, understanding. Anselm defined theology as *fides quarens intellectum*, "faith seeking understanding." This means that we must *think* about faith's language, and theology proper does not appear on the scene until thinking occurs. I shall argue that theology employs two closely related ways of thinking: interpretation and appropriation, or critical reflection and practical application. The reasoning involved in theological thinking is both theoretical and practical. These ways of thinking come together to form what I shall call theological "construction"—that is, the construction of new visions of the meaning of Christian language and practice from resources provided by scripture and tradition, on the basis of root/revelatory experiences of God, and in the context of contemporary cultural challenges. There is an interaction of revelatory experience, scripture and tradition, and situation or context in every theological construction, and thus theology is engaged in a continual process of reforming itself: *theologia semper reformanda.*[8] Critical and practical thinking moves back and forth among these elements that make up the circle of theological understanding, and binds them together. A closer look at this process is provided in the second section of this chapter, while the nature of theological construction is discussed in chapter 4.

Elaboration of the ways of thinking will help us to identify the resources (the sources, norms, and authorities) with which theologians work, as well as the major dimensions that order their work (historical, practical, and constructive theology). It is to this set of questions—the interplay of interpretation and appropriation in theological thinking, the resources and dimensions of theology, and the specific task of constructive theology—that I turn in the first part of this work, which is called "interpreting" (chaps. 1–4).

The method of theology is essentially one of "interpreting." To say this is slightly confusing since the word "interpretation" is being used in two senses. In the narrow sense, it describes one of the components (the critical, analytical, theoretical component) in the circle that makes up theological thinking. In the broad sense, the whole of theology is a project of interpretation—a construal of the meaning of Christian faith in light of a particular set of cultural exigencies and on the basis of a particular reading of texts and traditions. Theology (I have said) is a kind of ship, which has no foundation other than itself and no secure port; it sails on the open seas and is subject to the force of highly fluid elements, drawn and driven by the winds of the Spirit. No theology can claim to escape the always incomplete task of interpretation by grasping at the anchor of an authoritative scripture or a special revelation. The method of theology is in this broad sense interpretation and nothing but interpretation. It requires a constant "revisioning" of Christian faith. I prefer the term "revisioning" because it avoids an overly intellectualized way of understanding the task and content of theology. Revisioning is a matter of *seeing* things anew, and that involves insight, imagination, and practical engagement as well as theoretical reflection. Seeing is a gift of the Spirit, which is the light by which all things become visible.

Contextualizing Theological Thinking

Theological thinking does not occur in a vacuum but in specific cultural and religious contexts. These contexts contribute as much to the actual substance of theology as traditional sources and revelatory events, and because they are always changing theology itself changes.

In the second part of this work, "contextualizing" (chaps. 5–8), I argue that the central theological implication of late twentieth-century culture is the posing of a difficult yet inescapable question: "How is it possible to speak meaningfully of God's presence and action in the world today?" The fundamental challenge of postmodernity seems to be the loss of any meaningful discourse about God. Yet, out of the depths of the cultural crises of our time a new revelation of the divine may be appearing. The crises are not merely threats but opportunities: They are the winds of the Spirit sweeping away what is old and opening up new possibilities.

To discern this I shall attend to three cultural quests or practices that embrace much of what is going on today: the *emancipatory,* the *ecological,* and the *dialogical.* The first of these is present in the various branches of liberation theology (Asian and African, Latin American and Hispanic, African American, feminist, gay and lesbian), all of which arise out of a heightened awareness of human suffering and oppression and out of the conviction that conditions can in fact be changed, that classism, ethnocentrism, racism, sexism, homophobia, and other destructive practices are fundamentally unacceptable and must be resisted. Here God is experienced or sought as the power of *emancipatory freedom*. The second quest arises out of the ecological sensibility and new scientific cosmologies of our time, which articulate the sense of the interrelatedness of life and seek the harmonious dwelling of the human in the whole of the natural world. Here God is experienced as a *primordial love* or alluring power that draws all things together and into itself. The third quest arises out of the awareness of a plurality of religious traditions and seeks a dialogical encounter and transformation that will overcome religious provincialisms while honoring the particularity of many traditions. Here God is known as the power of *wholeness* or of *unity in diversity*.

The three quests interact and reinforce each other in various ways, and ultimately they are all variations on a single complex theme of profound religious significance, which has to do with the relationship between God and the struggle of life, human and nonhuman, to survive and even flourish on this planet. Our sense at the end of the twentieth century is that life is at risk and that God is involved in this risk.

The question surely will be asked whether it is appropriate to address the question of cultural context before that of theological content and to allow it to play such a major role in theological construction. The success or failure of such an approach can ultimately be judged only at the end, in light of its results. At the outset I offer a few observations: (1) Every study of the past, every appropriation of religious traditions originates out of a set of present circumstances, conditions, and needs. Experientially the present is what is immediate to us, and we cannot escape it although we may well attempt to conceal or distort it. (2) We shall already find ourselves engaged with the content of Christian faith as we address the question of speaking meaningfully about God's presence and action in the world today. In fact, I shall argue that the triadic scheme by which the third part of the work is structured is prefigured by the cultural analysis of the second part; the themes of oneness (wholeness), love, and freedom appear precisely in relation to the dialogical, ecological, and emancipatory quests. A correlation exists between the reality of God and the question about God. The implications of this correlation merit careful reflection. (3) Context and content are in fact always intertwined, and each presupposes the other. We cannot properly endorse the modern and postmodern critiques of the theological tradition without attending to that tradition and knowing it well. Nor can we responsibly reconstruct the central themes of Christian theology (God, creation, nature, human being, sin and evil, Christ, Spirit, redemption, eschatology, etc.) without constantly attending to the very issues raised by science and ecology, liberation struggles, and encounters among the religions.

The interplay of context and content makes for a certain complexity in the organization of a book such as this. One of my assumptions is that everything is related, and as a consequence several topics are treated more than once from different angles of vision, viewed first as contextual challenges and then as parts of a constructive agenda. In this way the second and third parts of the book are tied together but at the cost of some repetition of themes (which I have tried to hold to a minimum). Some materials lend themselves more to an analysis of context and others to a constructive argument, but alternative arrangements are certainly feasible. I do not claim that my choice of where to discuss specific materials is the best or only one. Of course the methodological questions addressed in the first part of this book are also ultimately inseparable from issues of context and content, and here too some repetition is unavoidable. Repetition is not necessarily a bad thing; it is as Kierkegaard observed a "forward recollection"[9] by means of which we discover what we know and learn how to live.

There is another aspect of context that is different from theology's cultural setting but just as important, namely, its relation to specific religious communities of faith and practice. Christian theology is among other things a practice of the Christian community. It should be evident that theology *is* an activity of a community of faith, not just isolated, individual stargazing or navel-gazing. It is dependent on a specific history and tradition, which is socially mediated, and it is the faith community's exercise at self-understanding and self-criticism. For this reason it is appropriate to prefix the adjective "Christian" to the word "theology" although this need not be done every time the word is used. Other religious traditions have theologies—Jewish, Muslim, Hindu, for example—and it is presumptuous of Christians to use this term as if it were theirs alone. Moreover, within Christianity itself there are many theologies, just as there are many Christian communities. The characteristics, limitations, and location of the particular Christian theology set forth in this book will become evident as it proceeds and are discussed more specifically in the epilogue.

Does this mean that one must be a believing member of a Christian church in order to "do theology"? Does it mean that theology becomes radically confessional in character and is applicable only to a particular cultural-religious community? Does theology have an obligation primarily only to its own community of faith? Or is it obligated as well to become an ecumenical Christian theology or even a global theology of religions, at which point its specifically Christian identity might be put aside in some way? These questions and others like them point to a more fundamental question: What does it mean to think theologically? It is to this question that I next turn.

Bringing these various reflections on the meaning of the word "theology" together yields a more comprehensive definition:

Theology, as a practice of the Christian community, is a constructive activity that requires critical interpretations and practical appropriations of faith's language about God in the context of contemporary cultural challenges and their theological implications.

The remainder of the book is simply an elaboration of facets of this definition, turning first to questions of method and interpretation, moving on to contextual challenges, and arriving finally at a reconstruction of central themes of Christian faith in the shape of a trinitarian vision of the whole.

Ways of Thinking: Interpretation and Appropriation

The Hermeneutical Circle

Here is a diagrammatic model of the "hermeneutical circle" in theology. It may appear rather daunting at first, but it helps to illustrate a number of connections that will be discussed in this and later chapters, and it should prove useful as a reference later on.

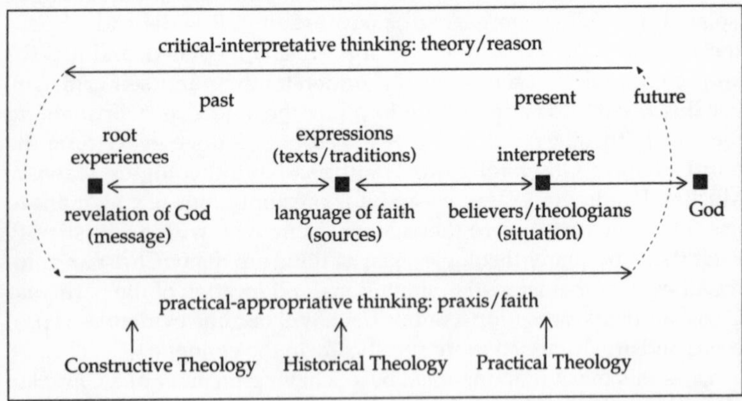

"Hermeneutics" is simply a technical term for "interpretation," referring especially to the science or principles of interpretation. Hermes was the messenger of the gods who interpreted the gods to humans and communicated between gods and humans. "Interpretation" can be used in both a broad sense to refer to the entire circle of understanding that constitutes hermeneutics and in a narrow sense to refer to one of the movements within this circle. It is used in both senses below.[10]

The model identifies three distinct elements that together make up the circle of understanding or interpretation: (1) the *root experiences*[11] of human historical existence, which might also be described as events in which a revelation or disclosure of ultimate being occurs; (2) the *expressions* of the root experiences in the texts and traditions that constitute the stream of culture; and (3) the situation of those who *interpret* the root experiences as they are mediated by texts and other cultural expressions. It is important in my view to distinguish the first element from the second, especially since they are frequently collapsed or combined. The theological meaning of a text does not reside *behind* the text (in the mind of its author or in its original setting) or *in* it (in its linguistic structure and semantic relations), but rather *in front of* it, in the subject matter or experience that is common to both text and interpreter and that is always constituted anew in the act of interpretation. For example, the theological meaning of the story of the exodus of Israel from Egypt is to be found neither in its original historical referent nor in the authorial intention and literary structure of Exodus 3—14 (although these, of course, contribute to an understanding of the text) but rather in the experience of divine deliverance that lies at the heart of true religion and is evoked in ever-new contexts. Thus there are *three* elements in the hermeneutical circle, not two: there is a pre-text as well as a text and a con-text, a message as well as a source and a situation. The ontological status of the pre-text (or "message") is tricky in the sense that we never have access to it directly but only as mediated through texts (or sources). An experience *is* insofar as it is expressed, but it is not reducible to its expressions.[12]

The third element, the con-text or situation, introduces another dimension of experience into the hermeneutical process—existential, immediate experience (both personal and social) as distinct from root experience. There is a sense in which interpretation goes between experience and experience—the experience that generates interpretation and the experience that is the object of interpretation. The latter does not always, or even usually, show itself as *root* experience. The *radical, root* character of experience is usually concealed in the mundaneness of everyday existence, as is the potentially revelatory power of experience. Nevertheless, the ultimate object of every interpretative act is precisely this dimension of radicality. It remains for the most part hidden in historical, aesthetic, and literary interpretation; it becomes more explicit in philosophical and especially theological interpretation. In religion the potential radicality of all experience is thematized in central root experiences by which everything else is illumined.

The model also identifies two movements or ways of thinking that connect the three elements. The first, which I am calling *critical-interpretative thinking* (interpretation in the narrow sense), entails a backward, questioning movement from the interpreter through the textual media to the root or revelatory experience, which is established as an object of critical scrutiny, a meant object. It is a movement of critical distancing and analysis, of explanation by means of concepts, of interpretative judgments.[13] It entails cognitive initiative on the part of the interpreter by which a range of experience is taken apart and constituted before the mind as an object of knowledge. It involves a flow of meaning from the interpreter through the medium to the experience. But then, in the case of *root* experiences at least, a strange thing happens: A *reversal* in the flow of meaning occurs, so that now experience discloses itself on its own terms and by its own power, through its own primary symbols, rather than having a constructed meaning imposed upon it.

This gives rise to the second way, that of *practical-appropriative thinking,* which entails a forward, answering movement from the root experience through the media to the interpreter, a movement to which we as interpreters belong and in which we experience something like a disclosure. We both appropriate this movement, make it our own, *and* are appropriated by it, caught up in it. This is a movement of application, of participatory praxis, which not only is oriented to concrete worldly situations but also helps to shape the preunderstandings that are the fundamental source of the conceptuality that makes critical thinking possible. No matter where we enter this circle of understanding, whether at the point of critical theory or of participatory praxis, we are in the middle of things, something is always presupposed, something always follows, and we must work our way through the circuit in disciplined fashion.

The hermeneutical event—the event of understanding made up of this interplay of interpretation and application—has a *temporal* aspect. In relation to the present of the interpreter, textual expressions have the status of being something past (whether the immediate past or the remote past is of no consequence). But the root or revelatory experiences they mediate are not simply past. They may indeed be associated with normative events of the historical past, but root experiences as such are oriented to the future. They mediate new possibilities of being and point to the power of new being. Human beings are intentional, future-oriented beings. We interpret out of the past, but we live toward the future. The past serves as the vehicle by which the future approaches, enters into the present. This is the fundamental significance of the past for the present. The past serves the future, interpretation serves application, theory serves praxis. This is why it is appropriate to grant the primacy to praxis in the work of theology.

The hermeneutical process has a *spatial* or social as well as a temporal aspect. Space and time intersect in the present moment: Interpreters are not isolated subjects but function only in a rich social matrix of meanings and interests. Textual expressions are products of interpretative communities, and root experiences are always socially mediated even if individuals play key roles in them. Sociality adds "thickness" to our hermeneutical model, prevents it from being a merely linear timeline. The corporate character of theological reflection is a theme that is insufficiently developed in the present work. Theologians have found it difficult to break the mold of the individual thinker who works in isolation from others. We know from experience that collaborative work is often time-consuming and frustrating. Yet the model of the hermeneutical circle presented here has an intrinsically social dimension. Theology is not a lone and narrow path but a broad vessel in which people live and work together.

The hermeneutical circle as I have displayed it might be thought of as a hermeneutical *ship*—a sailing vessel, that is, viewed from the top with its masts, bowsprit, tiller, etc. The ship has no foundation other than itself, no permanent port. It sails on the open seas and is subject to the force of highly fluid elements (wind, water). What supports it is solely its own structural integrity, the interplay of its elements (wood, iron, canvas, rope, fittings, crew). There is no Atlas god who carries the ship on his shoulders. This is why everything is always and only a matter of interpretation. The ship is a powerful antifoundationalist metaphor, but using it is by no means a counsel of despair or an embrace of conceptual relativism. On board the ship meaningful and ordered life goes on, purposes are accomplished, goals attained. Life on board the ship can be one of adventure, joy, fulfillment. But it is an illusion to think that the ship will someday arrive at a mythic island of paradise or absolute truth. The only truth we know is the truth we create as we sail the seas. Of course if the ship did not function in a symbiotic relationship with its environment it would not float and sail at all, so there must be a certain harmony between the truth of the ship and the truth of the whole. Later I will suggest (below, page 36) that the metaphor of the ship has implications when we think about the ultimate subject matter of constructive theology, God.[14]

The hermeneutical model presented thus far is of general validity for the humanities, including philosophy, history, and art and literature as well as theology. It is also increasingly recognized by the social and natural sciences (see the discussion of postmodern science in chap. 7). When we turn more explicitly to theology, we can say that the root experiences with which we are concerned have the character of the revelation of ultimate reality (God); the expressions of such revelatory experience have the character of the language of faith (scripture and tradition); and the interpreters of this language are believers and/or theologians. The same interplay of theory and praxis applies. This means that theology cannot simply be identified with the act of faith itself, but neither is it merely the critical analysis of Christian religious texts and experience. It stands between the two: It stands at the juncture of faith (or praxis) and reason (or theory), without either being sacrificed to the other. Theology is the "disciplined development of the reasoning that permeates faith," and it is the reasoned "critique of faith."[15]

The Interplay of Faith and Reason in Theology

Thus the theory-praxis correlation can be rethought, in more traditional theological terms, as the reason-faith correlation. Theology, as a rational activity, participates in a movement toward understanding already implicit in faith, a movement characterized by Anselm's description of theology as *fides quarens intellectum*, "faith seeking understanding." Theology is the explicit development of the quest for understanding implicit to faith. As such it participates in the act of faith itself and in the experience that gives rise to faith, namely, revelation. It participates in the event of appropriation. Rather than simply making revelation the object of critical scrutiny, theology engages in the sort of thinking called forth by the revelation of God; it is a thinking rigorously controlled by and directed toward its ultimate subject matter, God.[16]

At the same time the theologian's participation in the praxis of faith is of a special sort. It is more like the historian's empathetic participation in the life of a figure of the historical past than it is an immediate act of faith itself. Empathy means participation from without; and thus the theologian who is also a believer must learn to disengage her- or himself from faith as a confessional act in order to participate in it as a theologian. Theology requires a critical distancing from the shared experience as well as an empathetic appropriation of it. It is in this way that the dialectic of distanciation and appropriation, which is characteristic of all interpretation,[17] bears upon the work of theology.

This provides a basis for answering the question posed earlier, whether one must be a believing member of the community of faith in order to do theology. The answer is both "yes" and "no." If one does not belong to a community of faith in terms of one's personal convictions, one must enter into such a community empathetically in order to think theologically. If one is a member of such a community, one must distance oneself from it, bracket or suspend its claims, in order to examine them theologically, that is, to examine them in the mode of critical inquiry as opposed to the citation of authorities and beliefs. The latter is a confessional act, not an instance of theological thinking, although it often passes for it. Theology is neither a neutral descriptive science nor a quantum of faith.[18]

Theology is the *theory* of a praxis, and at the same time a *form* of praxis—it is a reflective praxis or critical praxis as distinct from confessional praxis or the actual living out of faith in the world. Perhaps the expression "critical praxis," or "critical engagement," best captures the two dimensions that seem to be essential to theological thinking: critical-interpretative and practical-appropriative. Rebecca Chopp refers to the method of liberation theology as that of a "critical praxis correlation."[19] As opposed to a "critical theoretic correlation," which understands theology to be essentially theory whose aim or goal, to be sure, is praxis, a critical praxis correlation emphasizes that theology itself is a form of praxis, and that praxis is not only the goal but also the foundation of theory. It is the foundation of theory in the sense that productive praxis issues in new theoretical insight; or, as I have put it, theological concepts are generated out of the preunderstandings shaped by praxis.

Of course, theory is also the foundation of praxis in the sense that critical inquiry evokes and perhaps also helps to release a fresh disclosure of the transformative power of religious symbols. But we cannot say that theory is the goal of praxis in the same sense that praxis is the goal of theory. The goal of praxis is to *change* the world, not merely *interpret* it. At this point the potentially vicious circle of interpretation is broken. Rather than circling around and around the same static point, theology as critical praxis spirals forward in the direction of new, richer, more powerfully transformative praxis, lured and empowered by the vision of communicative freedom, which in the terms of Jewish and Christian faith is the kingdom of God. Precisely for the sake of this praxis, the moment of theory, of critical inquiry, must be granted the autonomy and rigor that it requires. With the primacy of praxis, the hermeneutical circle becomes a hermeneutical spiral. Or, to vary the metaphor, our hermeneutical ship does not simply sail in circles; it is on a voyage toward a destination—a destination never attained on the seas of this world but a destination nonetheless.

Edward Farley is getting at a similar point about theory and praxis with his argument that the word "theology" *(theologia)* initially had two senses.[20] First, it referred to an actual cognition of God and things related to God, a cognition that attends faith and has eternal happiness as its final goal. Theology in this sense was *wisdom,* a *habitus* of the human soul; it was theology as a form of praxis although the praxis involved traditionally was not so much world-transforming as soul-saving. Second, theology was a term for a discipline of critical inquiry, a self-conscious scholarly enterprise of understanding, usually occurring in a pedagogical setting. Initially, these two senses of the word "theology" were closely related; but in modern times, Farley argues, they have fallen apart as the unitary discipline of theology evolved into an aggregate of special sciences (only one of which retained the name "theology") and as that aspect of theology offering wisdom was displaced by practical know-how and ministerial skills.

Thus a split occurred between "practical theology" and "academic theology."

Obviously, the proposal to understand theology as "critical engagement" is an attempt to heal this split and recover an older and more unified sense of the term. But the type of engagement or praxis that I have in mind is distinctly modern, informed by liberation theology as well as recent philosophies and hermeneutics of praxis.

The model of the hermeneutical circle presented here has a number of similarities to David Tracy's discussion of theological method.[21] Where I speak of a double correlation (critical and practical) of root experience, expression, and interpreter (or of message, sources, and situation), Tracy argues that theology establishes "mutually critical correlations between an interpretation of the Christian tradition and an interpretation of the contemporary situation." In this he is deeply influenced, as am I, by Paul Tillich's method of correlation.[22]

By "correlation" I mean bringing things into, or showing that they stand in, a mutual and reciprocal relation. These relations are not so much demonstrative as illuminative: Insight is obtained by seeing how things are connected. For example, insight into theological knowledge is obtained by seeing the correlation between interpretation and appropriation and between text, pre-text, and con-text; insight into faith is obtained by seeing the correlation between reason and revelation; and insight into revelation is obtained by seeing the correlation between postmodern quests and the triune figuration of God. One of the tasks of systematic or constructive theology is to explore these many overlapping correlations, not with the purpose of deducing one thing from another (as though one thing were foundational and another derivative), but of showing that truth occurs in terms of mutually interdependent relations. Everything is related and thus everything is a matter of interpretation.

Tracy makes the important point that contemporary theology shares with the humanities, the social sciences, and the natural sciences a turn to reflection on the process of interpretation itself. This is part of the postmodern sensibility, and with it comes the recognition that theology *is* a process of interpretation, from beginning to end. Any attempt to retreat from interpretation is a retreat into fundamentalism. Rather than retreat, Tracy argues that we must strive to create a *pluralistic* community of inquiry in which many different perspectives will be recognized, honored, and given voice.[23] The acceptance of pluralism challenges the logic of fundamentalism at a very basic level.

Teaching and Doing Theology

This is an appropriate place to say something about the teaching of theology. Basically I have taught constructive theology by *doing* theology, that is, by advancing proposals, building arguments, taking positions, attempting to shape a coherent and hopefully persuasive way of thinking about the meaning and truth of Christian faith. In effect, I have attempted to model the sort of critical praxis or critical engagement that I believe ought to characterize theological thinking. This is not a topic about which I can be neutral. I am caught up in it, struggling with it, arguing with myself and others, trying to deepen my understanding of Christian faith and commitment to it. I have invited students to do the same, to become apprentices in the project of theology, and to give expression to their own emergent theologies in the form of a credo.[24] The book that has emerged from my teaching of theology has the character of advocacy. It is not an account of classic and modern theological options, and for the most part it does not attend to the history of theological ideas.[25] This is one of its limitations. It is rather an exercise in constructive theology from a particular point of view and with reference to contemporary issues and authors.

I am committed to a theology of critical engagement that is "revisionist" in character.[26] "Revisionist" means here the necessity of "revisioning" all the central claims of Christian faith in light of the critical questions raised by the modern and especially now the postmodern world—revisioning them in such a way that their potential for redemptive transformation will be released anew. This means I am committed to the agenda of liberal theology as modified in the direction of liberation theology and pluralistic inquiry.

At many key points I find myself at odds with the agenda of evangelical or conservative theology—basically because I do not think it addresses with sufficient seriousness the critical, emancipatory, ecological, and dialogical questions raised by the modern/postmodern world. I recognize that evangelical theology is itself diverse and that a number of evangelical theologians *are* attempting to confront the critical and practical challenges of modernity.[27] Whether they allow their theological projects to be fundamentally affected by these challenges is the question. For example, Gabriel Fackre[28] recognizes that a hermeneutical circle exists between text and context. But for him text must retain priority, and the hermeneutical circle in fact becomes, in his image, a "hermeneutical arrow"—from text to context, not the reverse. His primary hermeneutical concern is with the dangers of over-contextualization and indigenization rather than of textual irrelevance. Thus, from my point of view, the balance between text and context that keeps the hermeneutical circle open and spiraling into new forms of faith and praxis is lost in his model. For this reason I prefer the image of the ship to that of the arrow.

"Revisioning" means seeing things anew, attaining a new vision of the whole, not just revising details here and there. It involves risks of distortion and loss, but it is the adventure to which we are called theologically. For me it is what is required by the concept of theology as *semper reformanda,*[29] and thus I regard my work as a contribution to a certain kind of Reformed theology. What is generally regarded as Reformed theology is in danger of thinking that the job of reforming needed to be done only once. But in fact we are never done with it. What is required today, I believe, is a fundamental revisioning of the relationship of God and world and of ways of understanding how God acts redemptively in nature and history. Insofar as Reformed theology has always focused on this question, from Calvin to Barth, the present project stands in the Reformed tradition. But in addressing this question I have drawn upon a broad range of resources and have sought to think theologically in an ecumenical, global, and plural framework rather than a confessional one.

2
THE RESOURCES OF THEOLOGY

"Resources" are something that lie ready at hand and can be drawn upon for use or assistance. The term suggests the basically pragmatic, functional approach to the tools of theological reflection that I am advocating. The sources are not sacred fonts of truth but *re*sources that work best when employed in combination with each other. As resources they function within an interpretative process rather than standing outside it. For purposes of analysis I distinguish between sources, norms, and authorities, but these are simply different aspects of the same reality, namely that Christian theology derives from a rich and variegated historical tradition. We are the beneficiary of a great cloud of witnesses (Heb. 12:1).

Sources

Scripture and Tradition as Vehicles of Ecclesial Process

Traditionally the Bible has been understood as the basic source of theology because it is the original document that bears witness to the revelatory events on which Christian faith is based and to which it refers. More often than not, the Bible has been *identified* with these revelatory events and endowed with the supernatural qualities of infallibility, inerrancy, inspiration, and—as the unique deposit of revelation—unchallengeable authority. Similar qualities have frequently been extended to the teaching authority of the church or "tradition" although for Protestants usually in a subsidiary sense. Such claims on behalf of scripture and tradition have been severely tested and largely discredited during the past two centuries on both critical and theological grounds. It is clear that these documents are very human products, sharing the insights and limitations of the cultures that produced them. Edward Farley has referred to this as "the collapse of the house of authority." In our chapter on "Scripture and Tradition" in *Christian Theology*,[1] he and I attempted to formulate an alternative way of understanding scripture and tradition as sources and authorities for theology.

Our basic thesis is that scripture and tradition are *vehicles (or media) of ecclesial process* by means of which the originative events (or root experiences) of Christian faith are able to endure as normative and to function redemptively in the transformation of human existence. Implicit in this thesis is a rejection of the traditional way of understanding the church as primarily a community of revelation that endures by means of deposits of revelation in scripture, dogmas, and institutions. Rather, ecclesial existence should be viewed as the redemptive presence of the transcendent, transforming any and all provincial human spaces in the direction of a universal community (see chap. 18, pp. 293–304). The church is a redemptive community, and the question is how such a redemptive community originates and endures, and what the vehicles of its duration are.

My intent is not to deny the reality of revelation as such but only certain ways of understanding how revelation is mediated, namely, in a supernaturally inspired, infallible, exhaustive, and immutable written vehicle. Revelation is not primarily a cognitive or verbal content that can be encapsulated in biblical and doctrinal statements. Rather it is an ongoing, transformative process—indeed a redemptive process—and as such a central category of any Christian theology (see chap. 9). Revelation is a continuing event rather than a past deposit of supernatural truths.

One implication of our way of understanding scripture and tradition is that a hard and fast line cannot be drawn between the first and second elements in the hermeneutical circle of theology—namely, the root experiences or revelatory events, on the one hand, and the expressions or media of such experiences, on the other. The experiences only become "root" or "paradigmatic" or "revelatory" to the extent that they are mediated to us in a redemptively transformative way. Conversely, the media do not point to themselves but to "something" that is borne by them and transcends them. Founding events and vehicles of duration *need* each other: They may be neither separated nor identified. It is precisely in the hermeneutical relation between root experiences and media of expression that revelation occurs. Revelation is a *relation*, not a truth, doctrine, deposit, or supernatural disclosure. Neither events alone nor sacred texts alone but *interpreted* events and *interpretative* texts are revelatory.

The Christian Kerygmatic Writings
(Christian Scripture)

Now, for Christian faith the paradigmatic figure Jesus of Nazareth is the decisive nucleus of the transition to ecclesial existence. Yet in order for this paradigmatic figure to be redemptively efficacious for subsequent generations, his story had to assume linguistic embodiment. This occurred first orally, in the apostolic witness, but then expanded to a body of writings whose function was to contribute to the upbuilding of ecclesia. Since its function is one of bearing a message and witness, this body of writings can be called *kerygma* (rather than *torah* or *dogma*).

The determination of what is properly to be included in this normative literature cannot be settled on the basis of an official canon of inspired writings. Canonization in any event came after the fact as a way of recognizing what had taken on the quality of kerygma. Rather, we have to look to the character of the writings themselves as constituting a unique witness to the originative event and as containing intrinsic literary and theological power to evoke a fresh disclosure of God and consequent redemptive transformations of human existence. Writings having these qualities came to be regarded as "scripture" within the Christian community, just as other writings have become "classics" for the wider human community.[2] A classic emerges when it functions in a hermeneutically productive way for an ongoing community. If a classic loses its power, no amount of canonization can restore it. Obviously no hard and fast line may be drawn between the writings called "scripture" and other early Christian literature, but this is not to say that distinctions are not possible and necessary.

The Literature of Israel
(Hebrew Scripture)

The writings of Israel are also an essential vehicle of ecclesial process because the faith of Israel is immanent in and constitutive of Christianity as well as of Judaism. Faith in Jesus Christ is not a substitute for Israel's faith but a new universal availability of divine presence—a universality already implicit in Israel's faith but hindered by the particular conditions of Israel's existence. (It is equally hindered, we should add, by the idolatries of Christian existence.) Yet it is clear that the literature of Israel, Hebrew Scripture, is a much richer resource on many of the central themes of faith—God, creation, providence, idolatry, sin, wisdom, worship, justice—than the literature that makes up Christian Scripture. The latter on its own could not function as an adequate scripture for a religious community. To call the latter "New Testament" and the former "Old Testament" reflects the old posture of Christian superiority, expressed in the notion that the old covenant has been "superseded" by the new. This supercessionist posture must be decisively repudiated if there is ever to be a healing of the rift between Christianity and Judaism. Christianity is *different* from Judaism (although much of the faith of Israel is immanent within it), but it is not *better* than Judaism. There are indeed differences: Christianity is not simply Judaism for Gentiles, nor is Judaism simply proto-Christianity; the two religions have distinct though related root experiences. The differences between them should be understood on a pluralistic rather than a hierarchical model.[3] The situation is complicated by the fact that the Hebrew Bible functions as sacred scripture for both religions.

Streams of Interpretative Tradition: Mainstream and Marginalized Streams

In addition to these two scriptures, there is the subsequent interpretative tradition. Communities are shaped not only by events of origin but also by the controversies, crises, and interpretations that make up their ongoing tradition. "Tradition" (*traditio*) means to deliver or hand over what has been given. But every handing over is an interpretation in which something new is added as well. In tradition there is both a fluid element and a sediment: both a traditioning process (*actus tradendi*), which is *living* interpretation, and sedimented or deposited traditions (*traditum*), which become part of the textual and doctrinal heritage of a community.[4] Once sedimentation has occurred, new interpretation is necessary. The Hebraic and Christian scriptures are the originative part of the sedimented tradition of Christian faith, and subsequent tradition is formed largely through the ongoing interpretation of the original tradition. It has been said that church history is the history of the interpretation of scripture. But it is more than that because of the role played by other factors in the life of the church—the history of culture and religions, the contemporary situation, personal religious experience.

It is important to recognize that "tradition" was at one time living interpretation; it does not simply "bear" truth but at one time was the living occurrence of truth, of revelatory disclosure and redemptive transformation. Likewise our own attempts at interpretation will one day become sedimented, part of the growing, ever-changing traditioning process. The great work of Paul Tillich, *Systematic Theology*, was until recently a living interpretation of Christian faith. For many years I used it as a primary text for the course from which this book has evolved. But now Tillich's work is in process of becoming sedimented since the contextual issues to which it spoke so powerfully, framed in terms of an analysis of existential estrangement and cultural fragmentation, are no longer precisely our issues. This is a great loss since no subsequent work in systematic theology is remotely comparable to Tillich's in originality, range, and analytic power. But Tillich's issues are still *close* enough to ours to cast considerable light on our own situation, and his theological genius helps to frame many issues with clarity. Thus from time to time I turn to Tillichian sediment as the soil out of which to begin the project of revisioning—beginning in fact with this discussion of theological resources.

We tend to speak of "tradition" in the singular, but Rosemary Radford Ruether forcefully reminds us that there are not one but many streams of interpretation—a mainstream or dominant stream (which is what we usually mean when we speak of "tradition") and numerous suppressed and marginalized streams.[5] This should not surprise us if tradition is formed out of the controversies, conflicts, and crises of living interpretation. The problem is that history is usually written by the victors (and these have usually been the patriarchs, the ruling-class males), who have a tendency to suppress their opponents and wipe out any memories of them. Sometimes they are so successful as to obliterate all traces. There is a pervasive historical amnesia. But these marginalized or heretical traditions—spiritual, mystical, and utopian sects, the writings of women and of free-thinkers—have at the same time displayed a remarkable survival power. They are not *quite* forgotten, and even if they do not survive in the memories of cults, they sometimes can be recovered through diligent research. Already in the nineteenth century, Ferdinand Christian Baur and Adolf Harnack[6] recognized that heresy makes just as important a contribution to the formation of tradition as orthodoxy—in fact more important since it is in the history of heresy that things *happen,* whereas in the history of orthodoxy presumably nothing ever changes.

Today we are becoming aware of our Eurocentric perspective and know that Western theology not only has suppressed deviant elements within its own history but also has ignored the presence of Christianity in other cultures, partly through ignorance and partly on the assumption of superiority. A tremendous wealth of Christian traditions is found both within the Euro–North American stream and outside it—in Asia, Australia, Africa, Central and South America; in Greek and Russian Orthodoxy as well as in the many forms of Catholicism and Protestantism. As we shift to a multicultural perspective, the study of theology becomes much richer and also much more complicated.[7] Most of us just have to acknowledge our very limited knowledge and keep ourselves open to an ever-widening world.

I do want to stress the importance of attending to these various streams of tradition and of taking them seriously as sources, not only of theological reflection, but also of preaching. Protestant preaching has almost always been based solely on biblical texts, but this reflects assumptions about the Bible that are questionable. Even churches that are relatively sophisticated in the study of scripture generally share a vast ignorance of even the mainstream of Christian theology throughout the history of the church. How many people, really, know anything about Origen and Augustine, Anselm and Aquinas, Luther and Calvin, Edwards and Bushnell, Schleiermacher and Kierkegaard, Barth and Tillich, Rahner and Gutiérrez, Ruether and Cone? There is, of course, even less familiarity with the nonmainstream traditions and global Christianity: the African American churches, feminist voices within the tradition, the ancient heretics and the modern sects, the churches of Asia, Africa, Latin America. All of this is a great impoverishment. Of course there is no canon of tradition, at least for Protestants, but canonical status finally does not resolve anything with respect to the meaning and truth of biblical texts either. There is no avoiding the risk, the conflict, and the interplay of interpretations. Truth is strong, and it will win out in such a process.

Other Religious Traditions

Tillich was one of the first to recognize that the history of religions is an important source of Christian theology. In his view, it provides a framework for understanding the specificity of Christian faith and for recognizing that redemptive truth in its totality is mediated through a great variety of religious traditions, although in the *Systematic Theology* Tillich maintained that Christianity contains the highest revelation and is the final truth.[8] We must now go beyond this point of view by insisting that the history of religions not only provides a *framework* but also contributes to the *substance* of Christian theology. It is as important for a minister or theologian to know in some depth at least one other religion, and to be committed to interreligious dialogue, as it is to know her or his own tradition and scriptures. In fact, we do not really know our own tradition without knowing others. Our own faith will be enormously enriched, deepened, and extended through dialogue with other religions, and through dialogue the religions will not remain the same. At the end of his life Tillich himself had become aware of this, and it is a point to which I return in considerable detail below.[9]

Cultural History and Theology

Tillich also identified cultural analysis, or "history of culture," as a contributory source of Christian theology. The task of a "theology of culture," he said, is to discover the "religious substance" behind all cultural expressions—that is, "to discover the ultimate concern in the ground of a philosophy, a political system, an artistic style, a set of ethical or social principles."[10] It is essential to attend to this because not everything of importance for theological reflection and praxis is by any means found in overt religious traditions, whether our own or others'. Much of the foundational and apologetic work of theology depends upon resources drawn from the humanities (philosophy, history, the social sciences, ethics, art, and literature) and perhaps also the natural sciences. Ruether, for example, identifies "critical post-Christian world views" as a contributory source of feminist theology. She has in mind predominantly political and social models: liberalism, romanticism, socialism in its various forms.[11]

This is one instance of a theology of culture, but there are many others as well. Culture infuses every theology that attempts to stay in close contact with other disciplines and to incorporate those resources into its own work. Much of the best theology being done today is interdisciplinary, involving discussions with, for example, literary criticism, social theory, economics, ecology, and professional studies (medicine, law, education), as well as the more traditional helping disciplines of philosophy and history.

Cultural Context (Situation, Location)

Should the situation, social location, or cultural context of the interpreter/believer also be considered a source of constructive theology? In Tillich's view, the situation is not a source but rather what must be *correlated* with the sources as that which generates the "questions" to which the sources give the "answers."[12] But insofar as the questions really are determined by the situation, and insofar as the actual content of theology results from the correlation of questions and answers, the situation is also a "source," and a very important one at that. Questions determine the content of theology as much as answers: Whoever controls the questions to a considerable extent also controls the answers. Analyses of the role of social location in constructing reality have underscored this point, as have black, liberation, and feminist theologies. The latter have helped us to appreciate that the "questions" by which tradition is interpreted always reflect particular interests and ideological biases. It seems to me that James Cone is irrefutable on this point.[13] Generally it has been the theological and ecclesiastical mainstream, the "establishment," that has determined these questions, rather than oppressed or marginalized groups. But it is precisely the questions that have risen out of the situation of these groups that have brought to light new meanings hidden in ancient texts, as well as aspects of human experience and existence that have not been thought about before. New streams of interpretation and experience—Asian and African, Latin American, African American, Hispanic, feminist, gay and lesbian—are flowing alongside the Western mainstream. They are mingling their waters with what was once thought to be a pure and holy source but had in fact become polluted, and they are having a cleansing effect.

Tillich thought about the "situation" in rather global terms as a condition of human existence that characterizes a particular age; for modernity it was the condition of existential estrangement (disruption, fragmentation, self-destruction, meaninglessness, despair), as expressed in art, religion, psychology, and philosophy. I will argue that for us the situation appears rather differently, as the heightened awareness of bondage on the part of oppressed and marginalized groups throughout the world, and the accompanying struggle for liberation, a struggle that has helped dominant groups recognize that they too may be living in bondage to false goals (success, happiness, accumulation, power, privilege). This is a generalization from the more specific situations to which the liberation theologians characteristically refer. Some of them would question whether it is legitimate to speak of a global "situation" that characterizes the postmodern world. They would see the situation as too fragmented to generalize about. Perhaps so. For my part, however, it seems helpful to probe for common themes or paradigms that connect the various elements in the postmodern situation—elements such as epistemological relativity, a relational-energetic view of the cosmos, ecological and environmental concerns, the threat of nuclear destruction, black, feminist, and third-world liberation struggles, and interreligious dialogue (see chaps. 5–8). "Unitive pluralism" (Paul Knitter[14]) and "emancipatory praxis" (the liberation theologies) seem to be such integrative themes. They are not entirely adequate, but they come closer to characterizing our situation than Tillich's "existential estrangement."

It is to Tillich's credit that he called attention to the factor of "situation" in theological reflection; that factor has loomed even larger in post-Tillichian theology. His method of correlation—the correlation of "message" and "situation"—seems as relevant today as it was forty years ago. But we should recognize that we cannot simply attribute the "answers" to the message and the "questions" to the situation. The situation is also a source of answers, and the message poses questions to us as well as giving answers.

Religious Experience

Tillich also speaks of "experience" as an element in theological method.[15] By it he does not mean the root experience that gives rise to faith but the religious experience of the believer—as he expresses it, the experience of "ultimate concern" about the ground and meaning of our being. He says that experience in this sense is not a source but a medium of theology, the medium through which the answers contained in the sources are received. The medium does not contribute anything to the answers. But I have argued that all the "sources" are really "media" of a redemptive-revelatory reality with which they can never simply be identified. When examined, Tillich's distinction between sources and medium collapses, as well as his sharp polarization of questions and answers. Certainly religious experience can be considered a source of theology when we reflect upon its distinctive qualities and inquire into its meanings. The lives of mystics, the great religious autobiographies, and classic psychological studies such as those of William James, show how important a source experience is; and the liberation theologies point to the necessary role of spirituality, of personal religious experience, in a life of committed practice. Spirituality has become something of a fad today, but authentic spirituality—life in and through the power of the Spirit—is at the very heart of Christian faith.

Cone and Ruether identify experience as a source of their theologies—the African American experience on the one hand and women's experience on the other. Here "experience" is being used broadly to describe a complex set of factors, including historical, cultural, and religious practices, the distinctive sufferings of an ethnic or sexual group, the psychological and emotional experiences of blacks and women as they achieve a group identity and struggle for liberation. This sort of experience contributes directly to the substance of their theologies.

To sum up, I am proposing that we find five types of sources for the critical engagement that constitutes the work of theology: (1) scripture and tradition as vehicles of ecclesial process, (2) other religious traditions, (3) cultural history and theology, (4) cultural context (situation, social location), and (5) the religious experience of believers, both individual and corporate. The first three of these fall within the second element of our hermeneutical circle, while the last two fall within the third element. It is difficult to assign any hard and fast ranking to these sources. Obviously scripture and tradition have a primacy, but less so than we have been inclined to think. If theology were limited to them alone, it would be a very barren enterprise, not much more than a systematic arrangement of texts; unfortunately some systematic theologies have been just that. When we examine what are called "norms" and "authorities," we shall find that they too are closely related to this account of the "sources."

Norms (Criteria)

Norms are the *criteria* by which the content mediated through the sources is to be interpreted. It has been customary to distinguish between *formal* norms (that is, the bearers of the norms) and *material* norms (the content that norms). But formal norms have usually been identical with one or more of the sources—the tradition and teaching authority of the church for Catholicism, the biblical canon for Protestantism. And material norms have generally been a function of specific ways of construing the essential meaning of Christian faith in light of the situation. For traditional Catholicism the material norm was the Catholic Church itself as the sacred vessel of salvation; for Luther it was justification by faith; for Calvin, the divine decree of election; for Tillich, the New Being in Jesus as the Christ. These construals are a function of the situation and demands of a particular age, culture, community, or interpreter.

For us the situation is different and consequently our material norm will be different. The material norm I propose to employ can be put very briefly: a construal of the "gospel" as "liberation"—a simple proposal that will require a lot of unpacking. If "liberation" is privileged as theological norm in this way, then it must be extended to include not only the liberation movements but also ecological and interreligious concerns—as indeed happens when reference is made to the "liberation of life" and the "liberative core" of religions.

As for a formal norm, it is not in my view a matter of designating *one* of the sources as having a privileged authoritative status with respect to mediating the content of revelation/redemption. It is rather the complex interplay within the hermeneutical circle of the three elements of root experience, expression, and interpreter, or of message, sources, and situation. It is a matter of recognizing the inevitably hermeneutical character of all theology—the fact that *everything* is interpretation, that there is no escape from the conflict of interpretations, and that revelation occurs precisely in and through the conflict. This brings us to the question as to how the sources function as "authorities" for theology.

Authorities

My proposal is that the sources serve as authorities in a functional rather than a metaphysical and/or juridical fashion. They are authorities not because they have a special metaphysical status such that revelation is supernaturally deposited in sacred texts and then preserved from error through continuing divine interventions. Nor are they authorities because they are declared to have a canonical or legal status by the church. They are authorities because they function the way that they do in the actual life of a community of faith. David Kelsey has argued this point persuasively: Scripture has authority to the extent that it functions in the church to shape new human identities and transform individual and communal life.[16] It has authority because it is experienced to be authoritative and life-transforming—not just by individuals but by communities. No true classic has to claim authority or to defend its credentials; it simply is experienced to *be* authoritative by virtue of its intrinsic qualities and disclosive, life-giving power. In a sense it wins its authority ever anew; if it has to impose its authority, then it is a pseudo-classic.

Now if we want to ask theologically why it is the case that particular sources have authority, and what empowers them to function redemptively, then with Kelsey we could advance a theological proposal concerning God's "use" of these sources in the shaping of a new kind of corporate existence in which human beings are redemptively transformed. This does not imply any kind of special divine intervention or supernatural inspiration. God saves *through* the historical manifestation of redemption, not from history or in spite of it. God does not "cause" or "control" these manifestations, nor does any sort of direct identity exist between what God wills and specific worldly occurrences. Rather we may speak, with Kelsey, of God "shaping," "transforming," "occasioning," "making use of the uses" of scripture and tradition and the other sources. The model for understanding divine providence here is that of influence or persuasion rather than that of causality. Thus a certain construal of God-world relatedness, yet to be specified in detail, underlies the functional approach to authority: Metaphysics is not abandoned but revisioned.

Finally, the way in which theology makes use of the authorities will be understood differently today. Traditionally, the theologian has worked primarily in the genre of citation and translation rather than of critical inquiry and praxis.[17] The primary task was one of citing proof texts and then of translating their contents into appropriate modern forms. The question of truth was limited to formal operations such as working out the internal coherence of the system of doctrine by constructing a dogmatics, a house of dogma, out of the bricks and mortar of scripture texts and church doctrines. The foundations and walls of this house have been shaken, and the structure has been severely weakened if it has not already collapsed. In any event it will have to be torn down and the "house of authority" replaced by a new mode of dwelling. The theologian will use scripture and tradition and the other sources to the extent that they usefully mediate the root experiences of faith; but in the final analysis she or he will have to advance an imaginative construal or constructive interpretation of Christian faith that is informed by a variety of considerations—experiential, practical, critical, as well as traditional—and that will have to *win* a place in the ongoing process of theological reflection if it is to have any place at all. It will win it only by its persuasiveness in a community of free and open discourse; in this process, truth will come out. This is the way that all the great theologians have worked even when defending the traditional doctrine of authority. Attempts to legitimate theological claims solely on the basis of appeals to authority are not persuasive because they avoid the fundamentally hermeneutical character of all theology.

3

THE DIMENSIONS OF THEOLOGY

Recall the three distinct elements that together make up the circle of theological understanding: the root experiences or revelatory events that give rise to faith; the expressions of faith in language, texts, traditions; and the interpreters or believers who engage in both faith and practice in specific cultural contexts (chap. 1, pp. 10–12). On this basis a distinction can be established between three major dimensions within the discipline of Christian theological study. I prefer the term "dimensions" to that of "disciplines" since we really are talking about dimensions of a complex whole rather than autonomous disciplines. My primary concern is with the way these dimensions are related to each other rather than with their discrete domains and methods.

Theology, like other departments of academic study, has become preoccupied with disciplinary specialization, which is all too ready to sacrifice breadth of vision to highly compartmentalized technical competence. In fact, the word "theology" is rarely used any more to identify the encompassing subject matter of what is taught in theological schools or seminaries. What do Hebrew Bible, Christian Scripture, religious and church history, ecumenism, world religions, ethics, constructive theology, pastoral care, homiletics and liturgics, religious education, etc., have in common if not "theology" in the broad sense of a wisdom or habitus? I attempt to bring this out by naming the three main dimensions as all forms of "theology," that is, as having as their ultimate referent talk about or practice in relation to God (or the holy, sacred, divine). Not all religious traditions are theological in the way Christianity is, but Christian discourse should not shrink from its multidimensional *theological* character.

Historical Theology: Scripture, Tradition, Religions, Culture

The direct concern of "historical theology" is with the texts, traditions, and other cultural media by which the language of faith has been given expression in the past (up to and including the recent past): the Hebrew and Christian scriptures, the history of the church, the various streams of Christian tradition—and, we must now add, the history of other religions and the history of culture. It is only since Ernst Troeltsch[1] that the history of religions has been considered a part of historical theology, but the reasons for including it are now more urgent than ever before. History of religions provides a more adequate scientific context for understanding the distinctive development, contributions, and limitations of the Christian religion than an intramural history of Christianity, even if the latter includes the various ethnic, creedal, and geographical manifestations of Christianity and is not limited to the history of the West, as has been customary. What Tillich calls "history of culture" should also be included in historical theology although the more specific work of cultural analysis belongs to constructive theology.

Obviously, what I have named critical-interpretative thinking will prevail in the work of historical theology but not to the exclusion of practical-appropriative thinking. For the very purpose of the critical analysis and interpretation of past texts is to enable the experience to which those texts bore witness to become alive and meaningful for us today, and this is accomplished by constructing distinctive narrative accounts of what has happened. Thus historical theology, like all historical study, has an inherently practical and ethical dimension, which for the most part remains implicit in it. It is also based in one way or another on a worldview, a religious commitment, a theological construal of the meaning and purpose of reality. Recent discussions in the philosophy of history have made the case that every work of historical interpretation entails a narrative construction that has both ethical implications and metahistorical roots.[2] In the case of historical theology, the metahistorical aspect is a theology of history, whether explicitly acknowledged or not.

The umbrella term "historical" leaves something to be desired as a way of naming this first dimension of theology. The critical and analytical tools employed by theology to study past texts and contexts are by no means solely historical; sociology, linguistic and structural analysis, and literary criticism have grown in importance recently and in some respects are predominant today, especially in biblical studies. Perhaps what continues to make them "history" in a broad sense is their recognition of the narrative structure of texts and the temporality and relativity of contexts. These disciplines exhibit a historical mentality even when their analytic tools are not historical.

Practical Theology: Ecclesial Community and Emancipatory Praxis

In "practical theology" the direct concern is with the appropriation, enactment, and practice of the faith grounded in the revelatory/paradigmatic events to which the texts bear witness. As such, the practical-participatory mode of thinking will predominate but not to the exclusion of critical-interpretative thinking and the analytical use of reason. Here again we encounter the difficult question of the relation between theory and praxis. Theory without praxis is mere ideology; praxis without theory is mere technique. Praxis is not simply the "application" of theory but theory's own originating and self-correcting foundation. It provides the preunderstandings, values, and criteria in terms of which critical theories are constructed. At the same time, theological theory is not just a speculative flight of fancy but the foundation of praxis in the sense of offering an interpretation or construction of the events that point to the ultimate source of all praxis, namely God. Theory and praxis each ground the other, which means that there is no ultimate ground of theological knowledge apart from the spiral of interpretation, the interplay of theory and praxis, of critical analysis and practical engagement. It is at the point of practical theology that the method of "critical praxis correlation" and the character of theology as a *form* of praxis are most self-evident. For this reason practical theology is the culmination of all theology.

What constitutes practical theology? There is no general agreement on this, and I offer here my own ideas concerning two main aspects of it.

Ecclesial Community: The Church and Its Ministries

If the goal of all theology is the interpretation and enactment of redemptive, liberated community, then ecclesiology in the broad sense would seem to belong to practical theology. This would include an understanding of both the nature of the church and its ministries. One might say that the first of these matters, the question of the nature of the church, belongs to constructive theology. Yet "the church" was not one of the traditional doctrines of theology, such as God, Christ, Trinity, creation, sin, redemption, eschatology, etc. We do not believe *in* the church in the same sense that we believe in God or Christ; rather we *are* the church. Ecclesiology is an exercise in self-examination for the sake of self-transformation. It has a practical goal, that of actualizing the ecclesial community and of ministering to the world in and through it.

The church has need of leadership. This is where ministry comes in. Ministry as a whole serves the function of forming, preserving, and nurturing the faith and life of the ecclesial community.[3] Specialized ministries are called forth by the specific needs of community formation and preservation. These seem to fall into four groups: proclamation and teaching, worship and sacraments, care and service, governance and order. One responsibility of practical theology, then, is to develop the theory of the praxis of these specialized ministries. To understand the minister as "theologian" is to stress that education for ministry is concerned not so much with the acquisition of technical skills as with gaining a foundational understanding of what the church is and of what it needs to become and remain the church.[4]

Emancipatory Praxis: Ethics

Not only ecclesiology but also ethics is implied by the goal of theology to interpret and enact redemptive transformation in the world. Here we face another difficult question: whether Christian ethics should be considered a subdiscipline or component of systematic theology (Barth, Tillich) or an independent discipline under the general category of practical theology (Schleiermacher, Tracy). The latter seems to be the predominant view today. It has the advantage of allowing ethics to develop critical principles independently of constructive theology, drawing especially upon the social sciences, philosophical and religious ethics, etc.

Christian ethics must, of course, be closely related to constructive theology since ethics interprets the same symbolic, textual matrix by which faith is expressed and has reference to the same root revelatory events. In this sense ethics has a hermeneutical function. But it interprets these matrices and events not in the form of concepts, doctrines, theological systems, but in the form of principles of action or "policies" to guide the emancipatory praxis of faith in both social and individual dimensions. In doing so ethics must attend to the systemic distortions that are present in any social and psychological situation. For ethics, a hermeneutic of the symbols, while essential, is not enough; a *therapeutic* function is also necessary, on the basis of a critical social theory and a psychoanalytic theory. Conversely, of course, constructive theology also has a practical dimension, for the purpose of its conceptual formulations is to provide a foundation for the proclamatory, educative, and cultic acts that constitute the church, and for the emancipatory praxis by which Christians live in the world. And insofar as it has an effect upon the world, it is a form of praxis.[5]

Constructive Theology: The Revelatory Experience of God

This brings us finally to "constructive theology." My proposal is that it makes the direct object of its concern neither the practice of faith nor the texts of faith but the experience that gives rise to faith—a *revelatory* experience having as its source and referent *God*. The subject matter of constructive theology, as indeed the ultimate subject matter of all theology, is God. Of course, constructive theology has access to this subject matter not directly but only through the root experiences of faith as mediated by the texts of faith. And its purpose is to let the revelatory event come to expression anew, issuing in redemptive transformations of the world in which we live. Thus constructive theology mediates between historical and practical theology, drawing upon and contributing to both; and in it the critical-interpretative and practical-appropriative modes of thinking attain some kind of balance.

This mediating position between historical and practical theology might be viewed as advantageous, but it could also be considered hazardous. Perhaps the mediation is not really needed and can be dispensed with; perhaps all we need to have *is* the historical study of texts and traditions and their practical application in preaching and pastoral care. We can do without theological abstractions. The Bible and a preacher are all we need. Theology is either too difficult or too irrelevant. I have heard such ideas expressed a time or two!

If the temporal reference of historical theology is to the past, and if practical theology refers to the present, then constructive theology refers to the future. For the experience that gives rise to faith—the event of revelation—is not strictly speaking past in character; only its media of expression are. It is not simply "out there" as a tangible object or factual occurrence. We have seen that the meaning of a text does not reside behind it or in it but in front of it, ahead of it, and it is something that must be constructed ever anew in acts of interpretation. The definitive event of revelation for Christians, Jesus Christ, is an *ongoing* spiritual event, not merely past but present and future as well. The true referent of human experience is forward, toward the future; but the future by its very nature is something we can never have direct access to or experience of. Rather the future enters into the present through root experiences of the past; the root experiences are bearers of future possibility. The future approaches in this way but never arrives. This means that the ultimate subject matter of theology, God, can never come directly into view. God transcends us as future liberating power—a temporal rather than a spatial model of transcendence. God is not circumscribed by the hermeneutical circle.

I have suggested that we might think of this circle as a hermeneutical ship—not a self-powered ship but a sailing vessel. The ship has no foundation other than itself, and no permanent port. It sails on the open seas and is subject to the force of the elements. God is not on board this ship—but God propels it, draws it forward, is the wind blowing into its sails.[6] On most points of sail, the wind is ahead of the ship, pulling it forward through the vacuum—a negative force—generated on the leeward side of the sails. The ship was an early symbol of the church, which is itself a hermeneutical reality, an event of ongoing interpretation and appropriation. The ship can also serve as a metaphor for theology, and the relationship between wind and ship may help us to understand the relationship between God and theology. God is not an objectifiable, controllable object but blowing/living spiritual power, always ahead of theology, drawing and driving it. Yet without the ship of theology (and church), the wind would not be "caught," its redemptive power would blow for nature but not for humans. Wind or breath is the root metaphor present in the word "spirit," so to think of God as the wind blowing into the sails is to understand God as Spirit—the most unrestricted of the trinitarian symbols. Like the wind, the Spirit of God generates a mysterious, attracting-propelling power in the world. God's power is not predominantly that of a positive force. Rather, like a vacuum, it is the power of negation or emptiness, the power of powerlessness—which proves to be the greatest power of all.

Because the concern of constructive theology is with the interpretation of revelatory experience expressed in the symbols of faith, its tendency is to reduce the multiplicity of the symbols and textual forms to an intelligible unity. It is seeking to develop doctrines or teachings on the basis of symbols, and moreover to order these doctrines into a coherent whole on the basis of a thematic focus furnished by the cultural and religious situation of the time. Its quest is for unity and coherence, whereas the responsibility of the historian is to display variety and disparity. The tensions between the two directions are both inevitable and fruitful. Constructive theologians must remember that their unity has the character of a construct, and historians must remember that sheer diversity is unintelligible. Each in fact relies upon the other: Theological constructs must have some sort of reality referent anchored in determinate historical traditions, and historical analysis takes on the character of a narrative construction. In brief, the boundaries between the three dimensions of theology are really crossing points, not barriers.

4
REVISIONING THE CONSTRUCTIVE TASK OF THEOLOGY

"Construction" in a Deconstructive Age

"Constructive theology" has been called by other names (some not so complimentary!) in the theological tradition. At one time it was called "dogmatics" or "dogmatic theology." The Greek word *dogma* (plural *dogmata*) simply means "teaching," and it was first used in the New Testament (for example, Acts 16:4; Eph. 2:15) and early Christianity (for example, by Ignatius, Origen) to identify the distinctive teaching of Christianity in contrast to the Mosaic law. Already in Greek philosophy, however, *dogmata* referred to those teachings or opinions of the philosophers that must be accepted as unconditionally true and authoritative. The church borrowed this usage when it employed the word to identify those teachings or doctrines that were officially formulated and adopted by councils and bishops as containing absolute or revealed truth. A "doctrine" or "dogma" is a carefully formulated and authoritative teaching on an important subject.[1]

The term *theologia dogmatica* did not appear until the seventeenth century although the sort of works to which it referred had existed for a long time.[2] Through the abuse of the church's teaching authority, the term "dogmatics" became discredited and gained a pejorative connotation—meaning opinionated, authoritarian, inflexible. Moreover, the notion of revelation as containing propositional truths to be exactly formulated in theological dogmas seems highly questionable today. Nonetheless, Karl Barth attempted to retrieve an older and authentic meaning of "dogmatics" by naming his major work in Christian theology *Church Dogmatics*—a name that also expressed his critique of

Protestant liberalism. Despite the influence of Barth, the term "dogmatics" is no longer much used today except in some conservative and evangelical circles.

The primary alternative favored in modern times is that of "systematic theology," an expression that also goes back to the seventeenth century.[3] It has been popularized by Paul Tillich, who named his magnum opus *Systematic Theology*, perhaps in intentional contrast to Barth's work. A "system" is something that is "set up" or "arranged" from parts (Greek *syn*, together + *histanai*, to stand or set up) so as to form a unity or organic whole. But why have something like a theological "system" at all? Why attempt to think "systematically" in theology? We certainly have to admit that all systems have a heuristic, interpretative function. They serve as models or paradigms, not as descriptions of an objective, empirical, or metaphysical state of affairs. Every theological system is a *construct* that has the purpose of promoting coherence and consistency in thinking critically and practically about the language of faith and its foundational experience, the revelation of God. It is not an account of that revelation as such. Systems are the work of theologians, not of God (with all due respect to Charles Hodge).

But do we really need such systems? Is it not better just to let the various elements of faith present themselves in their fragmentary, partial character with unresolved differences and tensions? Tillich is helpful at this point. "It is easy," he says, "to discover gaps in the most balanced system, because life continuously breaks through the systematic shell. One could say that in each system an experienced fragment of life and vision is drawn out constructively even to cover areas where life and vision are missing. And conversely, one could say that in each fragment a system is implied which is not yet explicated. . . . A fragment is an implicit system; a system is an explicit fragment."[4] Tillich goes on to suggest that a system stands between a *summa* and an essay, treating not all problems or one problem but a group of interconnected problems relevant to a particular situation. "Today a need for systematic form has arisen in view of the chaos of our spiritual life and the impossibility of creating a *summa*."[5]

Just because of the chaos and fragmentation of modern life, we need to learn to think systematically. In fact, whenever humans engage in productive corporate activities, they do so by means of systems, constructed either unconsciously or deliberately, as modern systems-theory demonstrates. Systems define relations and enable parts to function together more or less smoothly; without them, we would continually have to reinvent and reorganize everything. In this we are simply imitating nature, for nature is constantly generating systems, resolving chaos into order and then eventually dissolving the order. System-building seems to be an intrinsic part of the universe in which we live. Everything is a system because everything is related.

Yet we can get carried away with intellectual systems, forgetting their limited, fragmentary, situation-dependent, heuristic character. This is where the word "constructive" has certain advantages over "systematic." Etymologically the words are similar: Whereas to "systematize" means to set up or arrange from parts, to "construct" means "to pile up," "build," or "put together" (Latin *com*, together + *struere*, to pile up, build). But the nuances are slightly different. The Latin verb *struere*, "to pile up," suggests a less orderly procedure than that of the verb *sistere* (the Latin equivalent of Greek *histanai*), which conveys the image of standing things in line, arranging them neatly. By a strange etymological quirk, *struere* comes from an Indo-European root that also means "to scatter," "to spread," or "to strew," and what is piled up may be more of a heap (cf. Latin *strues*) than a structure. To construe is to strew things together, to fashion a meaningful arrangement, to bring a semblance of order out of chaos, to make something out of straw. The words "strew" and "straw" are etymologically linked: Straw is what is strewn about and piled up. Thomas Aquinas, in December 1273, shortly before his death, is said to have remarked: "All that I have written seems like straw to me."[6] But Lucilius Vanini, a seventeenth-century Italian freethinker, just before he was burned at the stake, reputedly picked up a piece of straw and said, "A single straw suffices to prove the existence of God."[7] Straw is all that we have—everything worldly is like straw ("straw before the wind," Job 21:18)—but we *can* build things of it.[8]

The work of building construing, constructing is a basic human work; without it we could not dwell humanly in the world. But this work also always entails a kind of deconstruction—dismantling old structures, using up resources, strewing them differently. In order to build something new we must tear down or rearrange something that humans have already made or destroy something that nature has created (trees, stones, soil, minerals). Whenever we critically appropriate what has been thought before, we destroy (de-strue) it. This is part of the inescapable paradox and ambiguity of human activity. The word "construct" reminds us of this more forcibly than the word "systematize." It is not too farfetched to say that constructive theology is like grasping at straws.

In order to construct, we must deconstruct. But because of deconstruction, we must construct. Indeed, one of the challenges of a deconstructive age is to take up the constructive task afresh.[9] Because of the destruction, waste, fragmentation, and loss that are all around us, we *must* engage in constructive acts in order to exist as humans as well as to live as Christians and think theologically. Catherine Keller suggests that the action of "piling up together" (*com-struere*) involves "in community and solidarity gathering together resources for saving actions, refusing the ideologies of world-waste, woman-waste, people-waste, species-waste, by which we also waste whatever resources we may have as theologians."[10] "Gathering together resources for saving actions": That is as good a definition of "construction" as any I know. A constructive theology will attempt not to waste any of the resources available to it from the tradition; it will attempt to build these resources into new, wholesome wholes, oriented to the redemption of humanity. It is in this sense an eschatological activity. This too is a nuance not found in the word "system."

Finally, constructive activity is interpretative activity. To "construct" is to "construe," that is, to explain, deduce the meaning of, interpret. The task of constructive theology is to work out a construal of the meaning and truth of faith's language about God in light of a particular cultural situation. The result is not a finished, permanent, unchanging system but an interpretation and nothing but an interpretation. Every attempt to bring coherence into the rich matrix of religious images and experiences, every attempt to move from symbolic to conceptual language, is limited and incomplete. To speak of theology as "constructive" rather than "systematic" reminds us that it is a hermeneutical activity, that its construals are made on board a moving ship. It is rather like navigation. Navigation enables us to chart and sail the waters with some degree of safety and some sense of direction, but never to control the elemental forces that drive us.

Constructive theology can also be likened to a work of fiction. It is a product of human imagination whose subject matter is not an empirical object or a factual occurrence. Like good fiction, however, it is oriented to reality and is a construal of the real—a construal that highlights possibilities and perceptions, depths and dimensions hidden from ordinary experience but there nonetheless for those with eyes to see. The theologian "invents" but not simply out of his or her subjective fantasy. Rather the inventions are based on multiple resources ranging from ancient texts to communally shared experiences, and they elicit the root, radical dimension of these texts and experiences, namely a revelatory encounter with ultimate reality. Theological fiction has an experimental quality: One is invited to enter into its imaginative world, try out its construals, test and modify them in light of one's own experience. Good theology stands up against such tests; it proves its value, its veracity, in a community of discourse over space and time.

I believe that the time has come to take up the constructive challenge in theology once again. The deconstructive context in which we live today means that we are unlikely to see any dominant, all-comprehending systems; ours is not an age for another Barth, Tillich, or Rahner. Attempts to create such systems will prove pretentious and unpersuasive. Rather what is called for is a variety of constructive proposals and experiments, each limited and partial, each contributing to an unattainable and inexpressible whole from a particular angle of vision or insight.[11] It is precisely the urgency of our times that calls forth such efforts, which must be conceived more collegially and collectively than in the past. The present work is one modest contribution to this task. Alone it cannot accomplish much, but joined with others it may contribute something to building a new theological vessel.

Restructuring Constructive Theology

What gives structure to constructive theology? There are two ways of answering this question. One way is to attempt to identify a number of component subdisciplines or elements; another is to attempt to identify the actual themes or topics or symbols that together comprise the subject matter of Christian faith. These ways are not necessarily mutually exclusive; there could be both subdisciplines and themes or topics belonging to each subdiscipline.

Elements: Foundational, Symbolic, Philosophical Theology

It was typical of both Catholic and Protestant dogmatics to identify subdisciplines. Traditionally, four of these were named: (1) philosophy of religion or natural theology, (2) dogmatics in the strict sense (the doctrines or loci of Christian faith), (3) ethics, and (4) apologetics or polemical theology. If ethics is located elsewhere in the larger theological circle, for reasons indicated in chapter 3, then natural theology, dogmatics, and apologetics remain as component disciplines of constructive or systematic theology. However, I am no longer persuaded by such compartmentalizations. Rather than viewing these as independent blocks, Tillich is closer to the truth in regarding them as "omnipresent elements" within a single theological circle.[12] The element of natural theology asks whether there are foundations in the natural world and in our experience as human beings for the specific claims of Christian theology. The element of dogmatics examines these claims in a specific structure of relatedness. And the element of apologetics attempts to defend these claims against criticisms or alternatives, often by appealing to a more general philosophical construal of reality. All of these are important tasks, and they are interrelated in various ways.

On this basis it might be possible to rethink the disciplinary substructure of constructive theology in terms of three omnipresent elements:

1. Every theology must test its claims in relation to common human

experience in and of the world, experience that *may* provide a foundation for the experience of revelation and language about God. In accord with recent Catholic thought, this might be called *foundational theology*.[13] Such foundations do not *prove* anything in a deductive sense but rather *let us see* the natural and human structures of reality in terms of which revelation and faith may be *possibilities*.[14] The traditional "proofs" of the existence of God were instances of foundational theology although their probative power has always been questioned; they really represent approaches to God or ways of knowing God rather than proofs in the strict sense.[15] The cosmological and teleological proofs (or approaches) focused on features of the natural world such as causality, motion, and purposiveness, while the ontological proof was based on logical or mystical considerations and the moral proof on features of human religious and moral experience. Modern versions of foundational theology have been predominantly anthropological rather than cosmological in character.

2. Every theology must offer an interpretation of the primary symbols of faith, experimenting with new symbols as well as reformulating old ones; and every theology must fashion concepts or doctrines by which thought is brought to bear on the content of the symbols. This double task of interpreting symbols and raising them to thought is the work of constructive or systematic or dogmatic theology in the narrow sense. Since I am reserving the term "constructive" for the whole enterprise comprising these disciplinary elements, and since I am seeking alternatives for the terms "systematic" and "dogmatic," I propose to call this second element *symbolic theology*. "Symbolics" includes a hermeneutics of theological symbols, but it also constructs doctrines on the basis of symbols. In the history of theology, the word "symbols" was used to refer to creeds and confessions, which were authoritative summaries of faith. A symbol is something "thrown together" *(sym-ballein)*, a construction or comparison. In the post-Reformation era, "symbolics" designated the branch of theology that studied the creeds and confessions of the various churches (Catholic, Lutheran, Reformed), but it could also be used as a synonym for a confessionally based "dogmatics." I propose to take it out of the confessional framework and to use it ecumenically, oriented to the task of interpreting symbols in the sense not of creeds but of the central themes of faith, expressed in representational, imaginative, metaphorical language, and of raising these symbols to conceptual thought.[16] An example of such "raising" would be the interpretation of the symbol of the "fall" in terms of a transition from fallibility to fault, or the symbol of "worldly powers" as objectifications of idolatry in the form of ideologies and injustice (chap. 14, pp. 208–15, 225–30). This is the work of symbolics.

3. Every theology either implicitly or explicitly brings into play a worldview, a philosophical construal of reality, of the way things are as a whole. The philosophical construal may draw heavily on another discipline such as psychology, sociology, linguistics, or cosmology, but insofar as it constructs a worldview it has a philosophical character. The construction of worldviews can occur in many different philosophical modes: metaphysical, existential, phenomenological, analytic, even deconstructive. Such worldviews help to determine the truth-status or reality-status of the symbols and doctrines of a particular faith community. This is the task of *philosophical theology*, which derives its content from the doctrinal articulations of the faith community, but its criteria for determining truth from philosophical reflection that transcends the faith community. Thus philosophical theology occurs on the boundary between constructive theology and philosophy of religion.

Whether one or another of these disciplinary elements is stressed is as much a matter of theological style as anything else. The elements really ought to be understood as stylistically distinct dimensions of a single whole rather than as autonomous operations. Some theologians proceed in a more foundational-anthropological mode (Rahner, Tracy, Kaufman), others in a more symbolic-hermeneutic mode (Cone, Ruether, McFague), others in a more conceptual-doctrinal mode (Barth, Pannenberg), and still others in a more philosophical-reflective mode (Tillich, Farley). Each style must include as a submotif what for the other is a leitmotiv, a driving motif. If it does not, then the richness of constructive theology will be truncated. The symbolic-hermeneutic mode is in vogue today, especially among liberation theologians. There can be no objection to this so long as it is not accompanied by an imperialism that rules out the legitimacy of other theological styles that stress foundational, conceptual, and philosophical questions. Every theological style alone is limited and partial. My own work in constructive theology is primarily in the symbolic mode, focusing on the primary symbols of Christian faith while attempting to revision them conceptually. Into this task I shall draw foundational-anthropological and philosophical-reflective considerations as necessary.

Symbols: The Triune Figuration of God

The other approach to structure is to identify the key interrelated themes or topics or symbols that constitute the subject matter of Christian faith. This is the approach I shall follow in the present work although it is related to the first approach in the sense of providing a way of organizing the second of the elements, symbolic theology. My constructive theology, therefore, focuses on symbolics rather than foundations or philosophical theology; and it proposes to order symbolics in a particular way. Here there seem to be three questions:

where to start, how to identify the key symbols, and how to relate them. Fortunately, we are not the first to face these questions, and we can obtain some guidance from the theological tradition. In the absence of a compelling alternative, this seems the safest thing to do.

Anthropological versus Trinitarian Principles

The classical Christian creeds begin with the simple words "I believe . . . " (in Latin, *credo . . .*). Who is this "I" who believes? What is "belief"? It seems that these are the questions with which a constructive theology must start once it moves beyond questions of method and context and turns to the actual content of theological reflection, the language and symbols of faith.

The "I" who believes implies an anthropology, a theological understanding of human being. Even before we come to the word "God" in the creed, we say the word "I." There is never any knowledge of what comes later in the creed without the involvement of this "I," this irreducible self-conscious subject that does the knowing. But to focus on this "I" as a topic in its own right can be misleading, at least as a theological project. The "I" is already oriented to something other than itself in the act of belief.

In the first instance, it is oriented to the *community* of belief, as Langdon Gilkey points out.[17] When early Christians said "I believe," they said it as participants in a community and tradition, and by saying it they were committing themselves to the perspectives, norms, and life of the community. The *credo* they recited in unison with others was not a list of personal, idiosyncratic beliefs but an objective credo that regulated the believing community (the *regula fidei*). The "I believe" was really a "we believe"—and in fact a switch occurs from the first person singular of the Apostles' Creed to the first person plural in the Nicene Creed: *credo* becomes a *credimus*. More precisely, it is a matter of both an "I" and a "we." If I am serious, it is really *I* who subscribe to the values and commitments of the community, and that is why doing so is a significant act. I do not surrender my intellectual freedom and personal responsibility by so doing, but I modify them. I am not an isolated self but a dialogue of "I" and "we," of self and other, of individual and community. All this implies an anthropology—an understanding of who we ourselves are—and eventually it must be spelled out.

The "I" of belief is also oriented to God. *Credo in Deum patrem omnipotentum*. The ultimate subject matter of theology is God, not faith's language about God and certainly not faith itself or the believing subject. Without God, there is no theology (*theo-logos*). This is what distinguishes theology from all other disciplines and makes it so problematic. What gives structure to a discipline is its subject matter, the thing it is about. It follows, therefore, that the structure of the divine subject, the way that it shows, manifests, presents itself, is what ought to give structure to the discipline of theology. As is evident from the ancient creeds, this structure is a *trinitarian* one: It is a matter of believing (in the words of the Nicene Creed) in "one God the Father Almighty," in "one Lord Jesus Christ, the only-begotten Son of God," and in "the Holy Spirit, the Lord and Giver of Life."

Now this archaic and patriarchal language is likely to put us off immediately, and many people have concluded that the doctrine of the Trinity is no longer usable. In my view, that is a mistake. It is possible and in fact necessary to retrieve and reconstruct the doctrine of the Trinity in terms that attend precisely to the contextual issues of our time. One advantage of doing so is to clarify that God is not an isolated subject any more than human subjects are; the Trinity brings God into relationship to the world and ourselves, and it makes this relationship constitutive of God in a way that remains to be discussed. Sallie McFague observes that the primary thing our time lacks, "and hence a task that theology must address, is an imaginative construal of the God-world relationship that is credible to us."[18] Such a construal will structure the project of constructive theology.

The doctrine of the Trinity yields a distinctive structure for theology—a structure that is not simply theocentric or anthropocentric or cosmocentric. Rather it is all three of these; or better, as Raimundo Panikkar suggests, Christian theology engenders "a *theanthropocosmic* vision, a kind of trinitarian notion, not of the godhead alone, but of reality."[19] "The mystery of the Trinity," he writes, "is the ultimate foundation for pluralism"—a pluralism that embraces not simply other religions but the whole of reality, the key to which is simply complex networks of relationships. God is involved in this network, perhaps in some sense *is* this network. Within this network, correlations exist between the trinitarian structure of God and what appears to be a triadic structure of human being, perhaps also a triadic structure in nature. These correlations are central to all of theology. While God, humanity, and world are different, they are not utterly different, alien to each other.

The most difficult structural question facing constructive theology is where the discussion of human being should be brought into the theological project. I have struggled with this question and vacillated on it. One possibility is to start with anthropology as a form of foundational theology—a description of basic structures of human existence in the world, which may provide a foundation for the experience of revelation and language about God. This is the modern version of Catholic natural theology, refocused on human nature. The question, however, is whether such a foundation can really be provided for faith's language about God, or, if it can, whether it does much good. There is no secure Archimedean point outside the circle of interpretation on which theology might be founded, no secure port for our hermeneutical ship.

We assuredly know and can say a great deal about human being, but, as our postmodern culture makes abundantly clear, none of it necessarily entails any reference to God.

Another possibility, instead of putting anthropology at the beginning, is to make it an "omnipresent element" correlated with each of the major theological topics: revelation, God, Christ, the Spirit. This is a Protestant alternative to natural theology, the so-called method of correlation made famous by Tillich and his disciples. I have in the past found this option attractive too, but today it strikes me as less so. It gives anthropology too dominating a role in theological construction. It encourages the tendency to speak too globally and abstractly about "human existence" (its finitude, its estrangement, its sociality and historicality, etc.). As a consequence it tends to avoid concrete issues related to cultural and religious pluralism, political, social, and religious liberation struggles, the natural world and natural science—precisely the issues being thrust upon us by the postmodern world. Sallie McFague and others are urging us to seek an understanding in terms of a larger ecological, cosmological system,[20] of which we humans are, to be sure, a part but not the whole or the fundament.[21]

Thus it now seems to me better to say that anthropology has a place *within* a theological system structured by a principle that incorporates anthropology yet transcends it—a "theanthropocosmic" principle founded in the mystery of the Trinity. We can properly speak of human beings as created (finite yet free), fallen, and redeemed only *coram Deo,* in the presence of God. The distinctively theological things we want to say about human beings presuppose God. But how are we able to know and say anything about that which serves as the presupposition of theological knowledge, namely God? This is where the "believing" of the "I" comes into play. Even if we reserve anthropology to a later point in our theological construction, we cannot avoid addressing at the outset the distinctive sort of knowing called "faith" of which the "I" is subject and God the object.[22]

God in the World as Spirit

These considerations lead to the following outline for structuring constructive Christian theology:

A. God: The One
   Faith, Reason, and Revelation
   The Creative Being of God: The One Who Has Being Absolutely
   The Triune Figuration of God: The One Who Loves in Freedom

B. World: Love
   Creation of the World
   Nature: Energy, Dimensions, Process, Eros

Human Being: Finite Freedom, Fall, Sin and Evil
Christ Incarnate: The Shape of Redemptive Love

C. Spirit: Freedom
Christ Risen: The Shape of Reconciliatory Emancipation
The Spirit and Freedom
The Liberation of the World: Ecclesia, Religions, History
The Perfection of God: Eschatology

The structure is trinitarian, but it starts with a consideration of faith for the reasons just given. The assumption is that faith is a cognitive act but of a distinctive sort: It is a kind of thinking, knowing, or reasoning that is founded on and oriented to a revelatory experience that grasps and shapes it. Faith involves a correlation of reason and revelation; it is constituted by this correlation and in this sense is drawn into the trinitarian process, the process of God's self-giving, self-revealing, and self-knowing through faith's knowledge *of* God. In starting with faith, we are really starting with God, with God's self-revelation, if we assume that faith is not an autonomous act, an inherent human capacity, but rather is founded on something that transcends it, that draws it forth. In the mystery of faith, the divine and the human fuse into a kind of identity (a holistic identity in which difference is *not* reduced to the same). Somewhere within this mystery, theology finds its starting point.

The version of the Trinity that is proposed here must seem very strange although it has classical (Neoplatonic) and modern (Hegelian) antecedents. It is not so much "theanthropocosmic" as it is "theo-cosmo-pneumatic": *Anthropos* belongs to *cosmos,* and the third element is not *cosmos* but *pneuma,* Spirit. The latter figure (or "person") is the only one I retain unaltered from the classical Trinity; I am seeking alternatives for the patriarchal and masculine figures Father and Son. Underlying this approach is a definition of God that I have borrowed from Karl Barth: "the One Who Loves in Freedom."[23] God is a complex relational act or process or "figuration" involving identity (oneness or wholeness), difference (love), and mediation (freedom). Identity, difference, and mediation are Hegelian categories, and, as will become evident, the way that I develop the trinitarian model is influenced more by Hegel than by Barth. The identity of God apart from the difference and mediation remains abstract and ideal. God becomes a concrete, real God only in relation to that which is different from God, the world: This is Hegel's great insight.[24] God does not *find* this world but creates it, generates it out of the rich potential for relatedness that God is in and for godself. God's love requires an object of love; love posits and cherishes difference while at the same time bonding with what is different in the event of freedom. Thus the three figures or symbols that constitute the divine life as a whole are, on this model, "God" (identity), "World" (difference), and "Spirit" (mediation); and "triune figuration" names the interplay of these figures or modalities in the divine life, which encompasses worldly life. These figures become the organizing symbols for my constructive theology.

The world, as the realm of difference, is differentiated into an infinitely complex nexus of dimensions and entities, from which there has evolved what we call human being. Simply to distinguish between the natural and the human worlds is a gross oversimplification since we humans are only a tiny fraction of the whole, even though we are that part in which the whole becomes conscious of itself (an extraordinary development, to be sure). The long-standing neglect of the natural by theology is coming to an end, as the religious significance of the natural world has become increasingly clear to science and theology alike, and as the interconnectedness of all things has been heightened by ecological consciousness. I shall attempt to develop a holistic theology of nature oriented to themes borrowed from postmodern cosmology: energy (the relational potency that infuses all that is), dimensions (the interaction of the physical, organic, sentient, and mental in the constitution of a differentiated world), process (the evolution, both creative and destructive, that characterizes cosmic history), and eros (the alluring presence of God in nature).

Human beings image the freedom of God, and in that sense are one with God, yet they are different from God because their freedom is finite and fragile. By their free and tragic fall into sin they carry the differentiation and estrangement of the world from God to a higher level of intensity than anything found in the natural world: It becomes a conscious, deliberate, destructive opposition, reinforced in structures of alienation, death, ideology, injustice (evil). Humans are both nearer to and farther from God than any other creature.

Among humans Christian faith focuses upon one individual in particular in whom (along with the community of interactions in which he was involved) the shape of God's suffering, redemptive love for the other became incarnate: Jesus of Nazareth, the Wisdom and Word of God. His ministry imaged the basileia vision of freedom and inclusive wholeness that he proclaimed. The crucifixion of this one symbolized the uttermost negation of God: God is dead, God has died on the cross. Here God is at the farthest reach from godself. This is certainly not a sole pinnacle of negation; history is replete with many comparable and worse deaths; here one death stands for many.

But this pinnacle of negation is not the end of the story; the divine process goes on, and a reversal occurs. This reversal is symbolized by the resurrection of Jesus from the dead. Whatever else the resurrection entails, it means that the shape of divine love embodied in a particular historical figure does not die out but becomes a powerfully transformative, emancipatory factor in human history. The Christ gestalt fans and flames out from Jesus to the ecclesial community and thence to the world as a whole, to other communities both religious and nonreligious, where it interacts with other shapes of God's presence. Through interaction and mutual enrichment, world religions are undergoing change, and perhaps they are moving toward greater solidarity. What is desirable here is certainly not a single, monolithic world religion, which could only be totalitarian, but a plurality of mutually enriching and growing religions. But history as a whole remains open and ambiguous; every goal achieved in history is partial, and each has negative as well as positive consequences. History is a sequence of formations and deformations, victories and defeats, joys and sorrows. While we can and must work to create a more humane and a more ecologically wholesome future, our ultimate hope resides not in history but in God.

God does not remain unchanged in this process. Apart from the world God is purely self-related, ideal but not yet real, rich in potential but not actual. In and through relationship with the world, God becomes "Spirit." The images of spirit in the ancient languages—Hebrew, Greek, Latin—are those of a material vitality or power: breath, wind, air, light, fire, water. God as Spirit is engaged in, embodied by, the world; God is the power, energy, or love that enlivens and redeems the world; and when God returns to godself through worldly mediation, the freedom that God is in essence becomes existent. Freedom results from consummated relationships. The figure of the return and of freedom is God-as-Spirit. In the schema of this book it presides over the discussion of resurrection, spiritual presence, ecclesial community, the religions, history, and eschatology; just as the figure of God-in-the-world presides over the discussion of creation, nature, humanity, and incarnation/crucifixion; while the figure of God-as-God presides over the discussion of God's revelatoriness, creativity, and triune figuration.

Christology links the second and third figures, not being simply identifiable with either of them. This should not be viewed as diminishing the importance of Christ. Rather, as the turning point in the divine process, Christ is enhanced, indeed becomes the center of Christian theology. But as the shape of divine love-in-freedom, Christ is not contained within a single historical individual. This way of locating christology in the theological scheme means that redemption begins in the second moment, that of worldly difference and love, and becomes the predominant motif of the third moment, that of spiritual mediation and freedom. Redemption is something that happens in and to the world but as a spiritual process. It should be evident that these "moments" are not chronological epochs but interpenetrating dimensions of a divine life that transcends yet incorporates temporality.

For me, this is the structure that imposes itself on constructive Christian theology, a structure given by the subject matter of theology, *theos*. It is a structure of initial abstract identity, followed by a creative explosion of being, which first opens out into an incredible evolutionary richness, then comes to increasingly narrow focus in human beings and in a single human figure, and which then reverses, fanning out gradually to include once again the whole of creation as it returns, implodes, back into the Creator. This cycle, which has the shape of a double helix, or of an hourglass that opens out and then comes to a point at top and bottom, occurs not just once but many times on both micro and macro scales. It never simply repeats itself but spirals ahead into novelty. Perhaps there *is* a single macrocycle that encompasses and orders many smaller ones. If so, God is the macrocycle; but the microcycle appears in the daily life of each human individual (as Joseph Campbell has pointed out[25]).

This is my version of the Christian mythos or worldview. A mythos is a way of viewing God and the world as a whole; it tells in imaginative forms the story of the interaction of the divine and the human, the sacred and the profane, at constitutive moments along the way: creation, fall, salvation, consummation. This is an ancient mythos, which has been expressed in a variety of conceptualities, ranging from Hebraic salvation history and Christian Neoplatonism (Plotinus and Augustine) to medieval and Reformation dogmatics (Thomas Aquinas and Calvin). It reverberates in mysticism (Meister Eckhart), speculative idealism (Hegel), process philosophy (Whitehead), and dialectical and transcendental theology (Barth, Tillich, Rahner); and perhaps now it is confirmed by postmodern science.

This is the mythos I shall attempt to elaborate in the third part of this work. But we are getting ahead of the story. The context in which we find ourselves today demands a fairly radical revisioning of the classic versions of this mythos; indeed some people have argued that it demands the abandonment of the mythos entirely. I do not believe it does. Certain quests seem to be emerging out of the challenge of postmodernity—the challenge of how to speak meaningfully of God's presence and action in the world, if at all. I shall name these quests the emancipatory, the ecological, and the dialogical, and argue that in their own way they are pointing toward the same figures or symbols of the divine life that are given by the mythos: freedom, love, and unity (wholeness). In this way a correlation emerges between trinitarian tradition and postmodern context, a correlation that, if valid, reinforces the mythos and provides a basis for reconstructing it in a form and language that make sense and may even have saving power.

Part 2
CONTEXTUALIZING

5

THE CHALLENGE OF POSTMODERNITY: HOW TO SPEAK MEANINGFULLY OF GOD'S PRESENCE AND ACTION IN THE WORLD

A Paradigm Shift: From the Modern to the Postmodern[1]

What is it today that demands the revisioning of Christian theology? What is the new cultural situation that we face as North American Christians? It seems that it is not that of the "underside" of history,[2] as is the case with Latin American, African, and Asian theologies, but rather that of the "passage" of history—the passing of Western bourgeois culture, with its ideals of individuality, patriarchy, private rights, technical rationality, historical progress, capitalist economy, the absoluteness of Christianity, and so on. It *feels* as though we are reaching the end of a historical era since we find ourselves in the midst of cognitive, historical, political, socioeconomic, environmental, sexual/gender, and religious changes of vast importance, comparable perhaps to the great Enlightenment that inaugurated the modern age. Can we speak, then, of a second Enlightenment, a new watershed, a new paradigm in theology?[3]

A "paradigm" is an example, model, or pattern. As the Greek etymology of the word suggests, an example (*deigma*) is set up alongside (*para*) something to show what it is; it is a model on a microcosmic scale (a "scale model") of a large, complex, dispersed, difficult-to-grasp state of affairs. In his study of the history of science, Thomas Kuhn uses the term "paradigm" to refer to exemplary formulations of scientific theory, such as Copernicus's explanation of planetary motion and Newton's theory of mechanics. He describes major transitions in scientific theories as "paradigm shifts."[4] But we can also speak of a paradigm with reference to a culture or to an intellectual activity such as theology, meaning thereby a confluence of factors or elements that determines the predominant shape or pattern of the culture or theology in question. Major shifts in the cultural paradigm have generally elicited corresponding shifts in the theological paradigm.

As far as the Christian theological tradition is concerned, it is possible today to distinguish two great paradigms of the past and a third emergent paradigm that may or may not prove to be comparable in significance to the first two: the *classic* (from the patristic period through the Reformation, the theological "consensus" from Augustine to Calvin), the *modern* (from the seventeenth to the late twentieth century, the "Enlightenment age"), and the *postmodern*. Since we do not yet have a name for our emerging new paradigm and do not know how to characterize it fully, we simply call it "post-." Of course, the discernment of paradigms and of shifts between them is a matter of perspective. From *our* perspective, the important distinctions between the patristic, the medieval, and the Reformation periods of the church lessen in significance since these are now all seen as variations on the classic paradigm, which was prescientific and precritical. From the perspective of later centuries, our proposed distinction between the modern and postmodern paradigms will likely pale by comparison with even more far-reaching changes.

The Enlightenment was a period of revolutionary intellectual and cultural transformation that occurred throughout much of Europe and in parts of North America during the eighteenth and early nineteenth centuries, inaugurating the "modern era." It was precipitated initially by sweeping accomplishments in the natural sciences (beginning already in the seventeenth century) and by an emerging acceptance of the scientific worldview, which among other things called into question the possibility of special ("miraculous") divine actions in history and which demanded that claims be supported by reason and evidence rather than by appeal to authority. The impact of the Enlightenment spread to other cultural and intellectual domains, notably those of philosophy, politics, history, and theology. Philosophically there was the so-called "turn to the subject" initiated by Descartes and completed by Kant. Corresponding to this in the realm of politics was a new recognition of individual rights and personal freedoms. For history it was a matter of introducing scientific methods into the study of history and of recognizing the historical conditionedness and relativity of all human knowledge and experience. Theologically what was required was finding fundamentally new ways of understanding revelation, authority, and truth-claims.[5]

Is it appropriate to refer to the age that seems to be following upon the age of modernity or Enlightenment as "postmodern"? The term "postmodern" is bandied about frequently today with different meanings. I am using it, not to refer to recent shifts in literary, artistic, and architectural styles, or to a specific philosophical school, but rather as a way of indicating a broad historical passage. In the late twentieth century, there are abundant signs that the paradigm of modernity has run its course, even though it may in some respects remain "an incomplete project."[6] These signs are discernible in the various crises of our time that will be analyzed shortly. The recognition of and response to this situation is what I mean by "postmodernism," of which there are several forms or schools. Whether we are really entering upon a new cultural epoch is a much-debated question. Some interpreters argue that we are entering rather into a phase of "late modernity," in which the intellectual and cultural resources of the Enlightenment are being extended to quite new and unprecedented problems. My view is that the break is sharper than that: The foundations of modernity are too deeply shaken to allow for any simple continuity. But the labels finally are unimportant, and in any event we are too close to what is happening to know precisely how to characterize it.

There are several types of postmodernism. One interpreter distinguishes between the "postmodernism of reaction" and the "postmodernism of resistance."[7] The postmodernism of reaction is found among those who call themselves "neoconservatives" or "postliberals" and who denounce the secularity and liberalism of modern culture even as they affirm the economic and political status quo. Theological versions of this kind of postmodernism are represented by those who wish to renew confessional and narrative traditions while resisting the contextualization of theology or attempts to think pluralistically across cultural-linguistic boundaries. The postmodernism of resistance, by contrast, "arises as a counter-practice not only to the official culture of modernism but also to the 'false normativity' of a reactionary postmodernism." Theologically it can issue in either a deconstruction of all religious claims or a revisionist attempt to retrieve, rethink, and reconstruct the deconstructed tradition.

The options of renewal, deconstruction, and revisioning will be considered more fully below. In my view, renewal is not an adequate response to the challenges we face, while deconstruction presumes a more radical break with the tradition than I am willing to acknowledge; hence revisioning is the option I embrace. The postmodern does not cancel the essential gains of modernity—rationality, freedom, human rights, subjectivity, dialogue, etc.—but rather appropriates and reconfigures these modes of thought and action in new circumstances, often quite radically. It knows that the way forward is not via a return to the premodern or the classical. Access to the assets of classical culture are available only through the critique brought by modernity, just as the assets of modernity are available only through the critique brought by postmodernity.

This critique focuses attention on several interlocking crises of late modernity.[8]

The Cognitive Crisis

This appears in both technical and philosophical rationality. The use of reason since the Enlightenment has become increasingly technical and scientific, manipulative, and calculative. While such rationality underlies the tremendous productivity of our society, it is now being perceived as increasingly counterproductive. For example: Nuclear technology, while having beneficial uses, has produced the means of total human destruction, and the control of this technology is both costly and very risky. Medical technology, while making tremendous curative advances, has opened up ethical ambiguities that cannot be resolved by technical reason. Industrial technologies have reduced menial labor but also eliminated jobs, and they pose severe threats to the natural environment. As Langdon Gilkey says, "the human intellectual creativity represented by the Enlightenment has revealed itself not only as ambiguous but also as potentially lethal."[9] At the same time, the Enlightenment worldview (which was mechanistic, deterministic, self-enclosed) has collapsed, and scientists know that traditional rational categories can no longer provide a unified and coherent view of reality.

The crisis in philosophical rationality is epitomized by postmodernist literary and philosophical criticism, which claims to have deconstructed Western consciousness and its logocentrism. The first Enlightenment gave rise to a relativizing consciousness, but consciousness itself was not relativized. Now there appears no longer to be a universal logos, either religious or secular, and it is clear that thought and perception are more radically conditioned by perspective, circumstances, and interests than rationalism supposed. Some claim that language is nothing other than an arbitrary and self-referential interplay of signs embodied in an endless milieu of writing.[10] Much of what goes on in elite intellectual circles today is a kind of gamesmanship that serves the purposes of controlling domains of power and/or obfuscating reality.

The Historical Crisis

We have experienced in our time the collapse of "salvation history" as the empowering mythos of our culture, deeply rooted in the Jewish and Christian heritage: the belief that "divine activity, presence, and the gift of salvation have appeared in and through a special sequence of historical events and thus form a salvation history,"[11] issuing in the final victory of good over evil. This religious vision was secularized by the Enlightenment, reappearing as a "theory of progress" based on human accomplishment and control of our own destiny. A rival version emerged in the form of the Marxist-Leninist theory of class struggle and eventual triumph of the proletariat. All of these versions—the classical Judeo-Christian, the liberal-bourgeois, and the Marxist—have been severely challenged in our time. Natural science questions whether change of any sort is teleologically oriented toward a progressively better goal; and instead of a purposive teleology in nature, some scientists claim to find only chance and necessity. The deep experience of evil in the twentieth century has permanently shaken confidence in historical progress: two world wars, fascism, Stalinism, the Holocaust, the conflicts in Southeast Asia, Central America, and the Persian Gulf, resurgent ethnocentrisms in the Balkans and former Soviet republics, international terrorism, the potential for environmental catastrophe, the continuing threat of nuclear proliferation and conflict (especially among regional powers). Naive talk about the "end of history" with the triumph of democracy and capitalism (Francis Fukuyama) is an illusion.

The Political Crisis

John Cobb describes this as the ending of Western hegemony, meaning that Western Europe and North America are no longer the dominant centers of world power as they have been for the past four centuries. The balance is shifting to Asia and to the Southern Hemisphere. It is true that in one sense Western power and influence remain strong with the collapse of the former Soviet Union and its Eastern European satellites. However, the unification of Western Europe, which may not proceed as smoothly as hoped, is resulting partly because of competition from Asian economies. The military strength of the United States rests on a declining economic base. In fact, there are severe internal weaknesses of an economic, political, fiscal, educational, criminal, addictive, and cultural character in American society, and it is not yet clear whether the American people and their leaders have the resolve to face these realities and make painful decisions, especially in light of widespread cynicism about the political process. The age of the superpowers is coming to an end, and the United States is likely to find that the dominance it has enjoyed since the end of the Second World War is slipping away. Political power early in the twenty-first century will be much more dispersed, unpredictable, and unstable. On the one hand the world is increasingly bound together by economic and electronic interpenetrations, but on the other hand it is threatened by monomaniacal nationalisms and violent religious tribalisms. No integrative visions of a new world order have as yet proved persuasive.

The Socioeconomic Crisis

With the collapse of state socialism and the triumph of global capitalism, a new kind of crisis appears. It is no longer that of a destructive competition between rival systems. Rather on the one hand there are the severe traumas, dislocations, hardships, and even chaos brought on by the rapid transition from command to market economies. On the other hand there is the reinforcement of the injustices, inequities, and alienation endemic to capitalism when it is not balanced by an enlightened social policy. With the rise of multinational corporations, unrestricted international free trade, large military expenditures, the rationalization of controls and elimination of jobs through new technologies, the decline of labor unions, and the rescinding or underfinancing of welfare programs, capitalist economies such as the United States are experiencing an increasing concentration of power and wealth in corporate elites, a growing dichotomy between the core and the periphery, and massive public indebtedness. With the transfer of industrial and manufacturing activity to the two-thirds world, the choice in Europe, North America, and Japan will increasingly be between low-paying service jobs (or no employment at all) and high-paying professional and technical jobs. Real wages fell 6 percent in the United States during the 1980s despite a 42 percent increase in productivity, and this nation seems to be drifting toward a class society like those of Latin America. The effect of these changes on the two-thirds world is its continued marginalization and impoverishment. Whereas it was once used to provide raw materials, it will now be used to furnish cheap industrial labor for exported goods without owning or controlling the means of production. Global capitalism, if unchecked, tends to increase income disparity and financial instability, and it can have a profoundly despiritualizing effect on masses of people. Alternatives to both a failed socialism and a purely profit- and consumption-driven capitalism must be found for the sake of the future well-being of both humanity and the environment.[12]

The Ecological Crisis

The magnitude of the ecological crisis has become unmistakably evident during the past decade: atmospheric and water pollution, ozone depletion, global warming, nonsustainable development, depletion or destruction of resources, inappropriate and wasteful lifestyles, inability of people to see themselves in a symbiotic relationship with the earth and other species. The ecological crisis is also a crisis of the human spirit, as Vice-President Al Gore points out,[13] a matter really of spiritual survival, and until it is seen in these terms it is unlikely that the hard political decisions and necessary structural reforms will be made. Other priorities will crowd it off the agenda.

The Sexual and Gender Crises[14]

The sexual revolution has exposed the repression deeply ingrained in Western culture and Christianity, but it has also led to a great deal of freedom of sexual practice beginning in adolescence, much of it destructive, and it has rendered problematic all of the established sexual institutions, including the nuclear family and marriage. Intense debates over homosexuality, sexual abuse, abortion, and alternative lifestyles illustrate the emotional impact of this issue. There is also a gender crisis—the beginning of the ending of patriarchy as a way of organizing male-female relations and distributing social power. Cobb argues that this is the most fundamental change of our time, with unimaginably great consequences—deeply threatening to many, profoundly hopeful for others. The possibility of a truly liberated sexuality and of a true gender equality can be glimpsed on the horizon of these crises.

The Religious Crisis

Several quite different, even contradictory factors are at work here, some of which are deeply troubling while others are a cause for hope: (1) The decline of Christianity in the West, its rejuvenation in Latin America, Africa, and Asia, and the urgent need for Euro–North American Christianity to pass over into new and vital forms of faith and praxis. The decline in the West is closely associated with the secularization of culture, the turn away from the religious to the technical and the therapeutic as means of coping with crises and apprehending reality. (2) An alarming tendency to turn to violence in the name of religious fanaticism. Ironically, as the world becomes more secular, religion becomes more fundamentalist, and these fundamentalisms strike out at enemies in the name of God, seeking doctrinal, moral, ethnic purity. (3) A new kind of dialogue or encounter among the world religions, the very opposite of fanaticism. What is new about this encounter is that it is occurring mostly on the basis of the recognition of equality among the religions, equality of truth and grace, of illuminating and healing power. The former hierarchy of religions, with Christianity at the top, is no longer defensible. The religious, theological, and ethical categories of other religions now appear to many as potent thematizations of reality, yet for others the prospect of a plurality of valid religions, none of which can claim absolute truth, is deeply threatening.

Two unproductive responses are possible to the profound historical passage and cultural crises of our time. The first is essentially an effort to stop the process, to turn the clock back—indeed to turn it back to pre-Enlightenment times, to traditional bases of authority and conventional forms of religious belief. The resurgence of conservative and evangelical Christianity in recent years is symptomatic both of the magnitude of the experienced threat and of the deep desire to recover stable ethical and religious foundations in a topsy-turvy age. I do not intend to make light of evangelical religion as an authentic piety and vital conservative force. But its potential for idolatry and ideology must also be recognized, its tendency to over-belief in the face of the threats and insecurities of our time—a false security based on illusory absolutes. The predominant representations of religion in our culture have become anachronistic and anti-intellectual; what is offered too frequently is a fundamentalist embrace of traditional beliefs and values and an explicit refusal to enter into dialogue with modernity. Religion provides a convenient escape for those who lack the strength to cope with the threats of modernity; it does not often enough provide resources for those who wish to respond to its challenges.

The second and diametrically opposed response arises from those postmodernists who sense an "irrevocable loss and incurable fault,"[15] a perception that is likely to issue in a radical relativism for which nothing is known, believed, or acted upon. Again, I do not wish to make light of the honest, baffling intellectual questions raised by deconstructionist criticism. But the temptation here is to foster an apocalyptic mentality or to retreat into intellectual games and hedonistic play—a mask for despair, cynicism, nihilism. Ironically, such play assumes a stable order and has no staying power against demonic absolutes and political oppression. Others do in fact resist this temptation and seek instead to develop an ethical critique and a commitment to emancipation on the basis of poststructuralist and deconstructive readings of history.[16]

In contrast to the negative features of these responses, there are two potentially productive strategies for confronting the cultural challenges of our time. John Cobb calls these "renewal" and "transformation."[17] Renewal represents the approach of the more conservative forms of theological postmodernism referred to earlier, those associated with "postliberal" affirmations of biblical and confessional identity.[18] It warns against cultural accommodation and advances a prophetic critique of the negative features of modernity. It uses a sophisticated hermeneutic and does not attempt to turn the clock back to any sort of precritical authority. But it is suspicious of at least some of the potentially transformative resources of postmodernity that I shall discuss shortly, such as a holistic and organic worldview, religious pluralism and interreligious dialogue, embodiment and evolving sexual practices, liberation movements, nonhierarchical and nonpatriarchal forms of power. It is more concerned with the inner renewal of communities of faith and the preservation of Christian identity than it is to respond affirmatively to the ambiguous challenges of the wider culture.

This is principally what distinguishes renewal from transformation, or what I propose to call revisioning. The latter is convinced that, in order to preserve the heritage and identity of the Christian tradition, it must be allowed to pass over into new and often quite different forms, which will be shaped by resources and opportunities presently available to us.[19] Our task, says Cobb, "is to be transformed by the best of what we are now experiencing and learning and to share in the transformation of the world." This approach knows that there is no original, purely biblical expression of Christianity but only a series of contextualized expressions, each in its own way a more or less creative transformation of both the figure of Christ and the forms of culture. It is not convinced that the established confessional identities (Lutheran, Calvinist, Roman Catholic, Orthodox, Anglican, etc.) are very relevant to the cultural issues and theological choices we face today, and it believes that the future of theology is likely to be configured quite differently. Rather than engage in a wholesale critique of modernity, such as advocated by both deconstructionists and postliberals, the revisionist approach attempts to maintain a bridge between enlightenment and liberation, wagering that they are compatible and that in the end liberation is capable of subsuming and actualizing enlightenment. Enlightenment without liberation loses its emancipatory dynamic; liberation without enlightenment loses its critical rationality. Together they have the possibility of moving toward a communicative rationality, justice, and freedom. In this way the saving resources present in the classical Christian tradition can be reappropriated and reenacted.

The Absence of God in the Postmodern World

All of the crises of late modernity have contributed in one way or another to the experience of the absence of God: This is the primary theological signification of our cultural passage. Cognitively speaking, neither technical nor philosophical rationality seems capable of apprehending the transcendent, holy presence known as "God" in most religions; and the situation is made only worse if rationality itself is under attack, for then we are left with nihilism and indifference. From the point of view of history, we have lost confidence that a divine providence governs the course of events, directing them to some beneficial end. The experience of radical evil, as much as that of radical secularity, has undermined any sense of efficacious divine presence. The political, socioeconomic, and ecological crises reinforce this lack of confidence insofar as religious beliefs are intertwined with the whole fabric of our cultural and natural world, which seems to be unraveling. The sexual crisis unmasks the linkage of religious belief with sexual repression and calls into question the authority of scripture on issues vital to human sexuality, while the gender crisis is disrupting long-established ways of imaging divine power and presence, namely in androcentric and patriarchal terms. The religious crisis in its several aspects—secularism, fanaticism, pluralism—stirs deep doubts as to the validity of the monotheistic God-constructs with which we have long been familiar. Are atheism (no God) and fanaticism (one God with a vengeance) the only options? If there are many gods, can there be any true God?

The death-of-God theologies of the 1960s were a clear harbinger of the times. They tended to be faddish and were rather quickly dismissed, but the serious questions they raised remain with us. For the more radical of these theologians—notably William Hamilton and Thomas Altizer—God was experienced as absent because the God-concept and perhaps God had "died." Whether this was to be understood primarily as a cultural event or as an actual event in the life of God remained ambivalent in their thought. Hamilton saw it primarily as a cultural event, related to the inability to move beyond purely human experience in any sort of empirically verifiable way to a reality called "God," and related to the discovery by a humanity "come of age" that it no longer needs a God to solve its problems or satisfy its deepest longings.[20] Thus God is both unknowable and unnecessary.

Altizer saw it more as an event in the life of God. According to his "good news" of Christian atheism, the primordial God has put God to death, has renounced divinity, and enters into an absolutely immanent identity with the world. We thus have a basis for rejecting the terrifying, transcendent, repressive God of Christian tradition. Altizer's book *The Gospel of Christian Atheism*[21] is a remarkable instance of the pathos for immediacy that arises out of the experience of the absence of God. His solution is to identify God with a totally incarnate love, which is the principle of a new and transfigured humanity, present everywhere.

A striking continuity exists between the work of Altizer and that of Mark C. Taylor, whose *Erring: A Postmodern A/theology*[22] brings the radical theology of the sixties into the present context. While Taylor draws on the French deconstructionists (primarily Derrida and Bataille) along with Nietzsche, his theological insights are heavily indebted to Altizer. He shows quite brilliantly how the "Western theological network" woven of the concepts of God, self, history, and the book has progressively unraveled. The death of God, according to this scenario, leads to the disappearance of the self, the end of history, and the closure of the book (above all *the* Book, the Bible). As far as God is concerned, traditional "ontotheology" is said to be based on the definition of being as "presence." Since God is being itself, God is absolute, total eternal presence, and is present as such. But the dominant experience of postmodernism is that of the absence of such presence. Taylor repeatedly reminds us that "absolute plenitude and total presence are nowhere to be found." The God of ontotheology, therefore, has died and has been replaced, remarkably enough, by writing, which is the "divine milieu." Language in the form of writing is invested for Taylor, following Derrida, with a kind of sacrality since writing is understood to be a self-referential interplay of signs, an endless milieu of significations that refers to nothing other than itself, the condition of possibility for consciousness and the object of consciousness, an unending play of differences in which the "ever-never-changing-same" eternally recurs in a coincidence of opposites.

The deconstructionist critique of presence is well taken. As Sallie McFague remarks, in the real world in which we live, absence is more powerfully prevalent than presence. "The desire for full presence, whether in the form of nostalgia for the garden of Eden, or the quest for the historical Jesus, or the myth of God incarnate, is a denial of what we know as adults to be the case in human existence: such innocence, certainty, and absoluteness are not possible." Therefore she advises us to develop "negative capability"—"the ability to endure absence, uncertainty, partiality, relativity, and to hold at bay the desire for closure, coherence, identity, totality."[23]

Perhaps it should not surprise us that the theological tradition long ago developed such "negative capability." It never entertained the illusion that divine presence was totally, immediately available. It knew that God could be experienced and spoken of only indirectly, through signs and symbols, that God could only be "appresented" in what is historically and experientially available, that God would be "all in all" only at the eschaton. Paradigmatic events, disclosures, and texts make it possible to live in the absence of presence, between the times. Divine presence is a dialectical reality, never totally available, always mediated through symbols, metaphors, constructs, determinate events. To be sure, there may be a persistent tendency to forget that this is the case, but living in relation to such an absent presence is part of the meaning of faith. Ironically, those critics who cannot bring themselves to live by faith are those who at the same time speak most derisively of the metaphysics of presence. In Altizer and Taylor one senses a powerful eros for presence, and so the absent God is replaced by the signs and symbols themselves, the endless milieu of significations that is language. God becomes utterly immanent, totally incarnate in worldly inscription. It is odd that the postmodern sense of "irrevocable loss" and all-pervasive difference should here issue in the total having of divinity and an undialectical immediacy. In the process, however, divinity is de-divinized.

A Postmodern "Kairos," Practical Hermeneutics, and Intimations of Presence

The most effective response to the "Christian atheism" of Altizer and the "a/theology" of Taylor is not a theoretical discussion of the conditions of possibility for knowing and speaking of God, or a critique of the deconstructionist critique of presence. Such theoretical and epistemological debates will ultimately accomplish very little. Not many people are persuaded by intellectual arguments that God is present or absent, real or unreal, existent or nonexistent. Rather the truth and reality of God in people's lives is deeply based in experience, which has many facets. The atheism of Altizer and Taylor also has an experiential basis, namely their experience of the absence of God arising out of the eros or desire for an unavailable presence. Perhaps that presence is manifesting itself in the world in ways they have not noticed and in places they have not looked.

A *kairos* is a time of opportunity demanding a response—a right time or a special time when momentous things are happening or about to happen. "The *kairos* is fulfilled, and the kingdom of God has come near," proclaims Jesus in the Markan inauguration of his ministry (Mark 1:15). Paul Tillich introduced the term into theological discussion in this sense after the First World War, believing that Europe was on the edge of a kairos, a time of opportunity in which a new political order and a new religious sensibility might be born, responsive to the word of God and the deepest needs of humanity. The tragedy for Tillich and his generation is that the kairos did not come, and Europe plunged instead into an era of unprecedented violence. Many people today believe that we are on the threshold of a new kairos, presaged by emancipatory struggles throughout the world, the end of Western hegemony and the Cold War, awareness of the environmental crisis, new possibilities fermenting in cross-cultural contacts and interreligious dialogue, and the existence everywhere of vibrant communities of faith often under conditions of duress.[24]

Can we speak then of a "postmodern kairos"? John Cobb[25] identifies several "new beginnings" that correspond to the "endings" of modernity: (1) a wide dispersal of power, contrasted with Eurocentric hegemony, leading to the affirmation of a genuine pluralism of traditions, cultures, religions, and to dialogue among them; (2) earthism, contrasted with nationalism and economism, a refocusing of human activity on the healing of the earth; (3) holistic thinking, contrasted with Enlightenment rationalism and the fragmentation of academic disciplines, the quest for a new way of thinking that is more organic, ecological, relational, communal, nondualist, nonsubstantial, nonanthropocentric; (4) liberation from sexual repression combined with an awareness of new forms of sexual exploitation and the ambiguities of sexual practices; (5) new conceptions of power that are not patriarchal or hierarchical and that have the character not of control but of empowerment, reciprocity, and participation.

This is as good a list as any I know, but there are other ways of characterizing the opportunities present in our kairos-like time. Rebecca Chopp[26] identifies certain values that correspond to the themes of postmodernity: openness rather than closure in the face of the experienced ambiguities of life; solidarity through and across radical differences; embodiment as a basis for overcoming fragmentariness; and liberation in the face of systemic oppression. Another postmodern theme to which she draws attention is the connection between knowledge, power, and language. All forms of knowledge are power, and what grants knowledge is language. Language is constitutive, not representative, and Chopp argues that a shift is required from hermeneutics to rhetoric—the art and science of using language (speaking, writing) to persuade, empower, engender practices. This can also be described as a shift from theoretical to practical hermeneutics.

Many people question whether the time has really arrived culturally that will permit a transition from the fragmentation, hegemony, and alienation of late modernity to a holistic, organic vision, especially one that is theanthropocosmic in scope. The philosophical foundations for such a vision are lacking, they say. Perhaps so. But to retreat from the challenge to fashion such visions betrays a lack of courage and a failure to seize the kairos that is presently at hand. Without such visions humanity is unlikely to survive the passage into postmodernity. I say "visions" since no one is in a position to offer the definitive vision for our time. But from the ferment of multiple revisionings there may emerge a kind of global, multicultural, interreligious consensus on what is needed to enable human and cosmic flourishing. Such visions are fashioned not simply theoretically but out of concrete practices, out of what is actually going on in the world.

The challenge of postmodernity, I contend, is to "speak meaningfully" of God's presence and action in the world. The presence of God may indeed be a function of our ability to speak meaningfully of God. When language fails, so also presence fails since language is the means by which what is not empirically immediate is made present. Through language we call into being a whole world of near and distant things, events, ideas, values. In this sense the presence of God is a language-event since God is not an empirical, ostensible, worldly object. But language is always related to practices, and it may be that practices more than concepts are the clue to regaining meaningful discourse about God. Cognitive dilemmas may yield to practical resolutions. The presence of the transcendent God, who seems to be excluded from the modern one-dimensional, secular, closed world, may freshly appear in the liberation of the victims of history, or in the redemption of nature, or in the encounter of religions. The location of theology has shifted. Where is God? we ask. Look to the underside of history and the emancipatory struggles of oppressed peoples everywhere. Or look to the ecological quest for the wholeness and integrity of life. Or to the dialogical creation of common though shaky ground in the midst of cultural and religious differences.

What is called for is a hermeneutic of practices, of those practices that are most characteristic of postmodernity and that may provide a way beyond the very crises that produced them. In what follows I shall identify three such practices and, by interpreting them, attempt to draw out their theological significance. My thesis is that the answer to the challenge of postmodernity—how to speak meaningfully of God's presence and action in the world—is already implicit in these practices. They are not explicitly religious practices, but each has religious implications. The three practices are the *emancipatory,* the *ecological,* and the *dialogical.* Each of these practices is also a *quest,* a seeking to change present conditions in certain basic ways, and the discovery of resources to effect such change is a religious discovery, an apprehension of the sacred in a specific aspect.

Mark K. Taylor suggests that the task of a "cultural-political" hermeneutics is to reappropriate Christian tradition while celebrating plurality (the cultural aspect) and critiquing domination (the political aspect). Bringing these together constitutes a "postmodern trilemma."[27] But Taylor's analysis is incomplete. To the affirmation of plurality and the critique of domination there needs to be added another dimension, that of awareness of profound threats to the environment, thus producing a "cultural-political-ecological" hermeneutics and what might be called a "postmodern quadrilemma." The conversation with the tradition must take all three of these dimensions into account. The political motif of emancipation and the cultural motif of plurality do not fully account for what is going on late in the twentieth century; to these must be added the nature- and cosmos-oriented motif of ecology, the sense that we are an integral part of the natural world and are responsible for its liberation from life-destroying practices. When we consider all three of these quests, we may discover that they are profoundly connected, and that together they provide potent resources for retrieving the Christian tradition in such a way as to release its latent salvific potential.

6

THE EMANCIPATORY QUEST: OPPRESSION, LIBERATION, AND THE FREEDOM OF GOD

The crises of modernity identified in the last chapter point to the fact that the historical space in which we live today is the space of liberation. The reason for this is a heightened awareness of domination and suffering on the part of victims, an unwillingness to tolerate conditions of oppression any longer, and a recognition that changes *are* possible. An awakening of consciousness is as essential to a change in objective conditions as the political and social struggle itself; this has been recognized to be a decisive factor in all the liberation movements. Today, transformations of consciousness are sweeping throughout the world; historical forces are at work that can at most be hindered but not stopped or reversed. What began during the 1960s in the civil rights and black power movements in the United States and in the liberation theologies of Latin America following the Second Vatican Council, and which spread in the 1970s to the feminist movement and the formulation of feminist and African American theologies, now echoes around the world in Africa and South Africa, in Asia, in Eastern Europe, in Hispanic America and the Caribbean, among women of the two-thirds world, and among gays and lesbians, the physically challenged and the elderly. Its presence is felt as well among Jews and Muslims, Buddhists and Hindus—and with the latter in a sense it comes home since the spiritual legacy of Gandhi is present in all these movements. Liberation theology has become the ecumenical and global theology of our time.

It is impossible to do justice to this rich and growing diversity of voices within a single chapter and from the limited perspective of the author. I shall proceed very selectively, focusing on a few major figures who have had a deep impact on me personally and who have been among the most creative theological voices of our time. I want to engage their thought in more than a superficial way. Throughout this engagement I will be asking how it is that meaningful speech about God comes to expression in the emancipatory quests to which they bear witness. What clues do they provide for the task of revisioning that lies ahead?

The Experience of God in Latin American and Asian Theologies

The predominant reality of the two-thirds world is that of suffering and poverty, which are a product of classism on a global scale—the social, political, and economic stratification of cultures along the pattern of a core (the technological, post-industrial, capital-intensive nations of the so-called first world) and a periphery (the materials-producing, labor-intensive nations of the rest of the world). Thus the experience of God in the theologies of Central and Latin America, Africa, and Asia, and of marginalized groups in wealthy nations, arises directly out of the experience of poverty and injustice. The fundamental affirmation is that God is found with the poor, on the underside of history, in solidarity with the oppressed.

Latin American Theology

This is certainly the central theme of the first and still the greatest of the liberation theologians, Gustavo Gutiérrez. It sounded in his first work, *A Theology of Liberation* (1973), which launched the serious discussion of liberation as a theological theme, as well as in his most recent, *The Truth Shall Make You Free* (1990) and *The God of Life* (1991). Although Gutiérrez has become a world-famous author, he remains close to his primary vocation as a priest to the poor in the parishes and base communities of Peru.[1]

The theme is introduced into his earlier work in response to the question of how God is encountered in history. The answer is straightforward: God is encountered in the neighbor, in doing justice to the poor and oppressed, in acts of charity. To know God *is* to establish just relations among persons.[2] In face of the realities of poverty and oppression, it is impossible to maintain a stance of neutrality; hence Gutiérrez's formulation of the well-known and frequently misunderstood "preferential option for the poor," which is not incompatible with the universality of God's love for all persons, but which does demand recognition that one has enemies whose actions and policies must be opposed.[3]

The central theological question confronted by Gutiérrez in *A Theology of Liberation* is how God acts in history, specifically how God acts to liberate the poor and oppressed. He rejects any "distinction of planes" model, which juxtaposes two histories, one profane and one sacred. There is no special salvation history but only one human history: "The history of salvation is the very heart of human history."[4] But within this one history it is possible and necessary to distinguish between the liberation of humanity as a human, historical, political project, and the coming of the kingdom of God, which is a divine saving gift. The latter empowers the former but is not simply identical with it since it can never be fully realized within history.

> The growth of the Kingdom is a process which occurs historically *in* liberation, insofar as liberation means a greater human fulfillment. . . . But the process of liberation will not have conquered the very roots of human oppression and exploitation without the coming of the Kingdom, which is above all a gift. . . . The historical, political, liberating event *is* the growth of the Kingdom and *is* a salvific event; but it is not *the* coming of the Kingdom, not *all* of salvation.[5]

The mediation of these two factors prevents the human emancipatory project from becoming absolutized in a "political-religious messianism" on the one hand, and it prevents the divine gift of the kingdom from becoming an irrelevant theological abstraction on the other. Insofar as the kingdom comes, it comes through a human, historical process, but this process is both empowered and delimited by a reality that transcends it. Suggestive resources are available here for constructing a theology of the history of freedom (see below, chap. 18, pp. 315–23).

In *The Truth Shall Make You Free*, which contains several essays related to the award of a doctorate in theology from the Catholic Institute of Lyons in 1985 and to the Vatican "instructions" on liberation theology, which criticized aspects of his work as well as of other liberation theologians, Gutiérrez reminds us that "every theology is talk about God; in the final analysis, God is its only subject-matter."[6] In the modern, secular world the problem has been to find ways of speaking of God in relation to nonbelief. But the question for liberation theology is how to speak of God on behalf of and in relationship to those who are "nonpersons"—"that is, those whom the prevailing social order does not acknowledge as persons: the poor, the exploited, those systematically and lawfully stripped of their human status, those who hardly know what a human being is." "What is implied when we tell nonpersons that they are the sons and daughters of God?" Is such a claim even credible? There are no easy answers to these questions. Gutiérrez believes that there is a distinctive spirituality and joy found in the midst of poverty, a vitality in face of ever-present death, the expression of strong faith in songs, prayer, and thanksgiving, which enables people to endure terrible hardships and even to overcome them. The only theological explanation is that God is present with the poor. The poor have more spiritual resources at their disposal than we; they are not ministered unto but minister.[7]

The theme that God's self-revelation in history is accomplished through divine preference for the weak and powerless has become ever more insistent in Gutiérrez's work, confirmed by his own experience as a pastor in the barrios of Lima. So also has the theme of the preferential option for the poor, which is now closely associated with the presence of the God of the kingdom. "To the question asked by the psalmist, 'Where is your God?', the gospel of Jesus replied: 'In the kingdom.' But during the time when we await the Lord's parousia, God's presence in history makes itself known only in an unobtrusive way that necessitates a spiritual discernment." The kingdom is "hidden" in history, hidden among the poor; it is "inchoately present" in their midst for those who have eyes to see. "By identifying himself with the poor of the world, the Lord to some extent hides his face and activity behind them, thereby telling us that the casting out of the poor is a denial of the kingdom and causes his absence." Gutiérrez provides a remarkably clear and simple criterion: God is absent when justice is not done to the poor; God is present when they are recognized and supported, and more especially when they find resources to live joyously in the face of sorrow and death. "In the final analysis solidarity with the dispossessed and exploited—in their life and in their death—is anchored in our faith in God: the God of life who is not revealed among the dead, but among the living."[8]

Again, the preferential option does not detract from the universality of God's love for all people, rich as well as poor; rather it "gives universality a demanding concrete form in history."[9] The way of salvation for the rich leads *through* the poor, through a determination to address the vast structural and social problems that generate poverty, through a willingness to accept from the poor an authentic revelation of God. The fate of rich and poor in the world is intricately linked—in ways that we might not have suspected.

Asian Theology

The Jesuit theologian Aloysius Pieris occupies in Asian theology a position comparable to Gutiérrez in Latin American theology. Trained in both Buddhist and Christian studies, he is director of the Tulana Research Center in Kelaniya, Sri Lanka. Several of his key essays written over the past two decades have been collected in *An Asian Theology of Liberation* (1988), and he has contributed to interreligious dialogue through *Love Meets Wisdom: A Christian Experience of Buddhism* (1988). Asia, he points out, shares in common with Latin America and other parts of the two-thirds world its "overwhelming poverty," while what is special about Asia among the poor regions of the world is its "multifaceted religiousness."[10] In Latin America, Catholic Christianity predominates, while Asia has not only several forms of Hinduism, Buddhism, and Confucianism, but also large Islamic and mostly small Christian groups as well as numerous tribal or folk religions. Asia is the true meeting ground of religions today. The combination of these two factors—poverty and the multiplicity of religions—establishes the distinctive context and agenda of Asian theology.

Pieris addresses the first of these by arguing, in a fashion similar to Gutiérrez, that "God or the Liberative Agent is irreconcilably opposed to mammon or wealth-accumulation, the source of human enslavement." Furthermore, "this same God has made a defense pact—a covenant—with the poor against the agents of mammon, so that the struggle of the poor for their liberation coincides with God's own salvific action." Thus there are two axioms of biblical religion: antagonism between God and mammon and covenant between God and the poor. The first axiom is common to most Asian religions and is symbolized in the figure of the monk/nun and the monastic ideal of voluntary poverty. It forms a *via negativa,* by contrast with positive action toward reconstruction of a new order of love, which occurs only with the second axiom (God's partiality for the poor) and its concern for forced poverty. The distinction between voluntary and forced poverty is characteristic of Pieris, and is reminiscent of Gutiérrez's distinction between poverty as a scandalous condition (forced) and as spiritual childhood (voluntary). For Pieris as well as Gutiérrez, the two aspects of poverty come together in a commitment of solidarity and protest to overturn poverty, a commitment that is both religious and political. Holding together the religious and the political is important for Pieris. Liberation, he suggests, is a distinctively religious experience ("the God-encounter of the poor"), not simply a class struggle. He also holds together, as does Gutiérrez, human activity and divine initiative, which "merge into one liberating enterprise." Yet even the highest human achievement does not approach the immeasurable grace of God.[11]

In another context Pieris writes that the "double ascesis" of poverty forms the basis for "the one path of liberation on which Christians join Buddhists in their *gnostic detachment* (or the practice of voluntary poverty) and Buddhists join Christians in their *agapeic involvement* in the struggle against forced poverty."[12] Thus a connection is established between the first and the second contextual aspects of Asian theology. Pieris argues that what is common to religions, especially to Asian religions, is not divinity or *theos* as such but a "soteriological nucleus" or a "liberative core."[13] Thus the struggle for liberation provides a common meeting ground for many religions, both theistic and nontheistic or metatheistic. The salvific mystery or liberative core does have theological implications, according to Pieris, for religions that choose to develop them. In fact it is possible to detect a "trinal" form: the salvific "beyond," a revelatory mediation in history, and the inner human capacity for saving power. Whether this should be named Theos-Logos-Pneuma in explicitly Christian fashion is less important than the fact that "this 'triune' mystery constitutes the basic soteriological datum in many of our religious cultures." Speech about God leads to Christian love; silence about God leads to Buddhist wisdom. Both are appropriate and necessary attitudes in the presence of the mystery of salvation and the reality of human suffering.[14]

In conclusion, a common though multifaceted struggle against the conditions of poverty provides a basis for collaborative relationships among quite different religions. In this way the emancipatory and dialogical motifs with which we are concerned interact and are mutually enriched.

The Experience of God in African American Theology

James Cone has been the predominant African American religious thinker since the end of the civil rights movement and the death of Martin Luther King Jr. Certainly there have been other notable voices, but none has produced such an important and creative series of theological works over a span of twenty-five years. The primary development in African American theology in recent years has been its pluralization and globalization through the addition of womanist and African voices. It is no longer the exclusive prerogative of male theologians as it was during Cone's early days, and Cone himself has contributed to this development through extensive conversations, contacts, travels, and revisions to his own work. Today he is as much a global theologian as he is a black theologian, but the basic themes of his work have remained remarkably consistent. For my purposes his most important constructive theological statement remains that found in *God of the Oppressed* (1975), and I shall focus attention on this work, considering his ideas in light of the critique of William Jones, and comparing them with the recent constructive proposals of James Evans, who is at the forefront of the next generation of African American theologians.[15]

Two central themes are found in *God of the Oppressed,* namely the social location of theology and the image of God as liberator of the oppressed. While the first theme represents a departure from the main concern of this chapter, I want to devote some attention to it since it has implications for the methodological and interpretative questions discussed in the first two chapters.

The Social Location of Theology

Cone makes the telling point that, if there is a significant connection between thought and social existence, then the answer to the question, What is the connection between life and theology? "cannot be the same for blacks and whites, because blacks and whites do not share the same life. The lives of a black slave and white slaveholder were radically different. It follows that their thoughts about things divine would also be different. . . . When the master and slave spoke of God, they could not possibly be referring to the same reality."[16] The implication is that all of our thoughts about God are relative, shaped by our social location and class interests as well as our personal experiences and needs. It is naive of us to think that there is ever a direct, unmediated revelation of God or of infallible truths about God.

Cone provides a severe critique of the social location of white theology.[17] While emphasizing the relativity of faith in history, white theologians have rarely applied this insight to the color line. With rare exceptions, they have gone about their business as usual, ignoring the facts of slavery, racism, segregation, discrimination. Liberation of the oppressed simply has not been central to the agenda of mainstream academic theology in Europe and North America.

I am indebted to Cone for having opened my eyes on this matter. He speaks a hard truth that is difficult for whites to hear and accept. He says, for example, that "the values of white culture are antithetical to biblical revelation," and that "it is impossible to be white (culturally speaking) and also think biblically."[18] It is true, of course, that white culture (that is, the predominant culture of Europe, the U.S.A., Canada, Australia, the ruling minority of South Africa), like all cultures, is in fact an *ambiguous* reality, a mix of good and evil, of productive and destructive values. The Christian gospel demands of *all* cultures, not simply white culture, a radical transformation. But the racism that deeply pervades this culture blocks the good that is present in it as far as the victims of racism are concerned. It is entirely understandable how from a black perspective white culture should become the very embodiment of evil. This is the hard truth taught by Malcolm X. Nevertheless, Cone like Malcolm recognizes that whites as well as other peoples are able to transcend their cultural history,[19] and he himself has drawn upon positive resources in the mainstream theological tradition.

As for the social location of black theology, Cone believes that it is "closer to the axiological perspective of biblical revelation." He observes that "the social determination necessary for faith in God's liberating presence in Jesus Christ is present in the social existence of poor people in a way that it is not present among the rich."[20] He is correct in this so long as it is recognized that it is a matter of being *closer* rather than of being identical. But Cone does tend to convert this proximity into an identity, an identity between the black experience of oppression-liberation and the truth of the Bible. The divine will to liberate the oppressed is the a priori truth of revelation.[21]

But how should one respond when confronted by a rival claim regarding the a priori of revelation—for example, the claim that the truth of the Bible is the story, not of God's call of the people from slavery to freedom, but of Jesus' substitutionary atonement for personal sin? Most of us are familiar with this version of what is supposed to be an a priori truth. What do we do when confronted by these two a prioris? Simply assert that one's own view is *the* truth, with the help perhaps of proof texts? Or do we engage in a discursive process to see which side can more persuasively redeem its validity claims? If we do the latter, then there is no longer any a priori of revelation, only a process of interpretation. What the Bible "in fact centers upon"[22] is a hermeneutical question shaped by many different perspectives. Feminism has recognized that the Bible may very well *not* center on the liberation of women. I think we have to acknowledge that the Bible does not unambiguously and consistently construe the bondage from which we are liberated in racial, sexual, and sociopolitical terms. Scripture is more complex, more ambiguous, more polyvalent than Cone allows. To get at the heart of the Bible always requires a theological construal that highlights some things and deemphasizes others. Cone offers a construal of the Bible that is powerful and persuasive, but he cannot claim that this is simply what the Bible *is* or says. Throughout the ages the Bible has proven to be a "wax nose"[23] that can be twisted to many different agendas.

Cone himself acknowledges something like this.[24] In the final analysis, he says, there is no way of proving objectively that we are telling the truth about ourselves or about God. All we can do is tell our story. If our story concerns one who proclaimed liberation to the captives, who died on behalf of those who suffer, and who has been raised by God from the dead to empower the struggle for human freedom, we cannot prove the truth of this story but only bear witness to it. The proof is in the praxis, the witness, not in authoritative claims based on revelation.

Moreover, Cone observes that African Americans have been intuitively drawn to the distinction between biblical infallibility and biblical reliability. There is a mystery in scripture that is not exhausted by claims to infallibility, but the people have testified to its reliability. The authority of the Bible for christology does not lie in its objective status as the literal word of God; rather it is found in the power to point to the one whom the people have met in the historical struggle for freedom. Here Cone is moving in the direction of a functional interpretation of biblical authority—the function of scripture in the constitution and preservation of the black church.[25]

Divine Liberation and Black Suffering

The God of African American experience is not a metaphysical idea but the God of history, the liberator of the oppressed from bondage. Likewise, the God of Israel, Yahweh, was "the God of the oppressed, whose revelation is identical with their liberation from bondage." The oppressed of modern times as well as ancient are God's chosen people.[26]

But is this in fact the case? Doubts about this claim were raised within the circle of black theology itself by William Jones in a book that has not been sufficiently discussed, *Is God a White Racist? A Preamble to Black Theology* (1973). Jones argues that it is difficult, indeed finally impossible, to reconcile belief in a God who is both omnipotent and benevolent with the realities of black suffering and oppression. A God who could prevent or overcome such suffering but chooses not to do so would be an evil God, in effect a "white racist"; whereas a God who is opposed to such suffering but is unable to do anything really effective about it would be a weak God, an illusion, or perhaps a compensation for present suffering. This is the traditional question of theodicy, the question of divine justice. Jones thinks it becomes an unanswerably difficult question when applied to black suffering, which is an ethnic suffering (it appears that blacks have been singled out as a racial group to suffer, which could lead to the idea of divine disfavor toward blacks), as well as a suffering that has assumed an enormity well beyond ordinary historical evil. Jones himself is led to deny any sort of transcendent God—for if there is such a God he must be a white racist—and to embrace a "humanocentric theism" that places the emancipatory struggle solely on human shoulders.[27]

This is an honorable position, but it is fraught with ambiguities. It is similar to the situation of Judaism after the Holocaust. Emil Fackenheim has argued that the one thing commanded of Jews after Auschwitz is *not* to deny God, for that would be to hand Hitler a posthumous victory, the destruction of Jewish religion.[28] Jones is in effect handing white racism a victory, the destruction of black religion.

But how can it be avoided? Jones's book was effective because he demonstrated that the early black theologians had not dealt with this question very convincingly,[29] and following the publication of his book the issue has been too little discussed. In my view, the only way to refute Jones would be to argue that African Americans have experienced and continue to experience the liberating power of God *in and through* their historical emancipatory struggle. This argument is at the heart of Cone's theology, at least implicitly. But Jones contends that the argument fails because it is impossible to prove that the *decisive event* of liberation for blacks has in fact taken place. Jones seems to require a *Deus ex machina*, a miracle-working God, who will set blacks free all at once, in one "mighty act" such as the exodus of the Israelites from Egypt.

> How can blacks know that God disapproves of black suffering except by his elimination of it, except by his bringing it to an immediate halt? . . . Cone must identify what he regards as the definitive event of black liberation. . . . The scandal of the particularity of black suffering can be answered only by an appeal to the particularity of God's liberating activity—an Exodus-type event for blacks.[30]

Obviously, such a "definitive event of black liberation" has not occurred and will not occur. God does not intervene supernaturally in human affairs to bring about "definitive" or "immediate" or "total" liberation of any people or condition. The theological alternative demanded by Jones (either God intervenes supernaturally or God is not a liberating God) cannot tolerate the dialectical insight that redemption occurs and shapes of freedom appear in a not-yet-redeemed world, that liberation entails conflict, struggle, suffering, defeat, death-and-resurrection, that there are setbacks and advances in the history of freedom but never triumphal, unambiguous progress.

Cone rightly refuses the alternative posed by Jones. He and others have shown that freedom has in fact been experienced, affirmed, and sung about in the black community, not only after emancipation but also before it in the days of slavery, not only in the struggle for civil rights or the black power movement but also in the period of Reconstruction and segregation. This is not to downgrade the enormous importance of such events as the end of slavery, the dismantling of the legal structure of segregation, or the movement toward full human and civil rights. But it is to say that God's liberating action is not limited to such historical breakthroughs as these, and that God can set and hold a people free even in the midst of historical oppression and reversals. Indeed, the black spirituals make it clear that Christ was experienced as present precisely in the slave community, clearing a space of freedom in the midst of bondage and brutality, and the same has continued to be true for the black church as the central institution of a segregated, suffering people. The experience of the presence of the living Christ, rendered concrete by the Gospel stories of Jesus' life and death as well as by the accounts in Hebrew scripture of God's acts on behalf of the people Israel, took on the character of a powerfully transformative gestalt. This gestalt—the shape of the crucified and risen Christ, the Messiah of Israel who will set all oppressed peoples free—has been the definitive event of liberation for blacks, but it is a shape that appears in the world liminally, for those who have eyes to see, and it does not work miracles or provide supernatural rescues.[31]

James Evans acknowledges that the idea of God for black Christians is problematic. God, he suggests, is "ungiven" in African American experience, not because of the secularization that has infected much of the West, but because of the history of victimization and despoilment, and also because of a widespread notion in African religions that God, while once present, has withdrawn from humanity into the sky. Hence God is experienced as both present and absent, protective and remote. The otherness of the oppressed represents God's otherness. Materials are available here for a profound and partly tragic conception of God. Evans shows how this was developed in black religion by emphasizing both God's transcendence and immanence (or impartiality and partisanship, freedom and love) and by interpreting God's *work* in history. The latter was characteristically imaged in two ways for African Americans: God is one who patiently shapes resistant clay into worthwhile forms (Jer. 18:1–6), and God is one who gives birth, breathing the breath of life into the new-born cosmos, enabling it to live and breath on its own (Gen. 2:4–7).[32] I shall employ both images in this book. They provide an alternative to the logic of divine sovereignty and offer a way of understanding how God enters into a relationship with the world that is caring rather than controlling.

African American theology helps to teach us that there is no triumphal march of God in history, no special and privileged history of salvation, but only a plurality of partial, fragmentary, ambiguous histories of freedom. What is shaped in history are fragile syntheses of values and praxis that achieve momentary, relative victories over chaos and tyranny through a process of confrontation and compromise. Such syntheses endure for a while, but eventually they break down. Temporal passage involves not only a progressive, continuous evolution of practices but also disruptive, discontinuous revolutions and reversals. History is made up of such continuities and discontinuities, which cannot be patched into an overarching linear teleology. Not only are such teleologies indefensible from the point of view of historical reality as we know it, but also they captivate us by a totalitarian vision that diverts attention from the partial victories that are possible in the historical present and to which it is our responsibility to attend. These insights are reinforced by feminist theology.

The Experience of God in Feminist Theology

Rosemary Radford Ruether's voice was one of the first and still is one of the most important in feminist Christian theology. In terms of the range and creativity of her contribution—including works on ecclesiology, anti-Semitism, christology, the Israeli-Palestinian conflict, African American and Latin American theologies, ecology and ecofeminism, as well as feminist theology proper—she stands out among a distinguished group of scholars. Her major constructive work to date, *Sexism and God-Talk* (1983), effectively addresses the primary question with which we are concerned, the experience of God in the emancipatory quest. As Ruether points out in an introduction to the tenth anniversary edition of this book, there has not since been published another work of feminist theology that covers the whole range of topics of constructive theology, and she notes that she would not fundamentally revise it today.[33]

There have, however, been important works on specific themes in theology from a feminist perspective, for example, God, Christ, ecology.[34] There have also been significant works on theological method, language, and praxis, drawing upon resources in feminist theory that have been influenced by poststructuralism and deconstruction.[35] New approaches in feminist biblical hermeneutics have been of fundamental importance.[36] And, as Ruether mentions, "the multicontextualization of feminist theology across ethnic, cultural, and religious lines" has produced a chorus of diverse and creative voices.[37]

God/ess as Liberator and Primal Matrix

Ruether argues that the most ancient images of the divine were female, and that such images were widely diffused throughout the ancient Mediterranean world and India. The root image of the divine was that of the Primal Matrix, the great womb in which all things, gods and humans, sky and earth, are generated. Then, along with the emergence of urban and agricultural civilization and an aristocratic, sacerdotal ruling class, there appeared paired female-male deities. Ruether summarizes two central mythical versions (one Sumerian, the other Babylonian) of how these deities interrelate. She then recounts the emergence of male monotheism in nomadic herding societies, where women lacked a significant social role, and the consequent dualizing of gender metaphors (transcendent masculine spirit or soul versus inferior and dependent feminine physical nature). Into this monotheism, feminine goddess images were gradually appropriated, but in a subordinated status. Jewish, Islamic, and Christian monotheism became decidedly patriarchal religions.[38]

But within the biblical tradition, argues Ruether, a counterthrust to patriarchalism has also been present, a counterthrust in the direction of liberation. Yahweh was unique in that he was the God of a tribal confederation that identified itself as liberated slaves, and he was identified by his historical action as the divine power that liberated these slaves from bondage in Egypt and led them to a new land. This identification enabled the tribes of Israel to unite in a new egalitarian society. After the establishment of the Davidic monarchy, the prophets continued the tradition of protest against a newly emergent hierarchical, landowning class, which subverted the egalitarianism. Thus prophetic protest became established as something close to the heart of biblical religion, and it was this protest that was renewed and radicalized by the ministry of Jesus. Jesus universalized the protest, applying it to marginalized groups such as women who had been overlooked by the prophets. He transformed the patriarchal concept of divine fatherhood into a maternal or nurturing concept of God. He manifested, says Ruether, the kenosis (emptying) of patriarchy—revealing that the relationship to God is not that of a child to a father or of a servant to a master, but of fellow-sufferers (the crucified God and liberated humanity); and revealing too that no ultimate significance is to be attached to maleness (or for that matter to femaleness). What is important is a new humanity, a liberated community of sisters and brothers, Jews and Gentiles, friends among friends. Christic personhood continues in this community.[39]

There appears to be a tension between Ruether's two central images of God/ess, Liberator and Primal Matrix, in the sense that one is historical and future-oriented, while the other is natural and past-oriented. She struggles with this tension and attempts to resolve it as follows, if I understand her correctly. She insists that matter and spirit must not be split into a hierarchical dualism. "That which is most basic, matter (mother, matrix), is also most powerfully imbued with the powers of life and spirit."[40] She plays here on the etymological connection that may exist between *materia* (that of which any physical object is composed, "material") and *mater*, the word for "mother" in all the Indo-European languages. The word "matrix" (that from within which something originates, for example, a womb) comes from *mater*, so "Primal Matrix" means "Primal Mater," "Primal Materia."

Now is Ruether suggesting that God simply "is" the primordial physical matrix or womb out of which everything emerges? If so, then her theology would be grounded in a spiritless materialism. I do not think it is. She recognizes that this is metaphorical language for God. The matrix that images God is not simply an organic capsule like an egg but a living human being, a *wo-man*, and hence that which is most basic "is also most powerfully imbued with the powers of life and spirit." Thus God/ess "embraces both the roots of the material substratum of our existence (matter) and also the endlessly new creative potential (spirit)." God/ess does not lead us back to a stifling, dependent immanence (pure matter), nor does it lead us away from the earth into a rootless transcendence (pure spirit). Rather God/ess leads us to the "converted center, the harmonization of self and body, self and other, self and world. It is the *Shalom* of our being."[41] This "converted center" transcends the false, alienating dualism of spirit and matter. God/ess liberates us from this dualism in all of its forms (soul-body, reason-feeling, masculine-feminine). There is no such thing as "pure" matter or "pure" spirit. Spirit and matter are rather "the inside and the outside of the same thing."

What is this "one thing"? Ruether's response is at this point very much in accord with the new cosmology that is the topic of the next chapter. When we probe beneath the surface, into the depth of things, whether physical things or human consciousness, "the visible disappears. Matter itself dissolves into energy. Energy, organized in patterns and relationships, is the basis for what we experience as visible things. . . . Consciousness comes to be seen as the most intense and complex form of the inwardness of material energy itself." Following Teilhard de Chardin, Ruether suggests that "the radial energy of matter develops along the lines of increasing complexity and centralization . . . until the breakthrough to self-conscious intelligence."[42] At the center or core, then, is relational energy organized as intelligence. "Conversion to the center" is the turn to/into *this* center, which is what the symbol God/ess is pointing to.[43]

These ideas are further developed in Ruether's more recent book, *Gaia and God* (1992). Instead of settling for traditional oppositions, such as those between nature and spirit or female and male attributes of divinity, we should press for something like "Nicholas of Cusa's paradoxical 'coincidence of opposites,' in which the 'absolute maximum' and the 'absolute minimum' are the same." The absolute minimum appears at the subatomic level where matter dissolves into the "dancing void of energy," a "voidlike web of relationships." But here we also encounter an absolute maximum, the matrix of all interconnections of the universe, which has the characteristics of rationality, consciousness, mind, logos. Human beings as organic yet self-conscious selves represent the point of coincidence of these opposites. But human selfhood is ephemeral and transient. It sparks for a while, then dissolves into the environing matrix. We ask therefore: "Is there also a consciousness that remembers and envisions and reconciles all things? . . . Surely, if we are kin to all things and offspring of the universe, then what has flowered in us as consciousness must also be reflected in that universe as well, in the ongoing creative Matrix of the whole." If the value of the personal center of each being is to be affirmed and preserved even as individual selves pass away, then the center of the universal process must also be a Thou, a Great Self: This is Gaia *and* God, the earth Goddess and the cosmic Logos.[44]

Conversion to this center is liberation. Human beings experience this conversion not simply as a (re)turn into a cosmic womb, or better a cosmic communion—although there is a deep dimension of truth to this, which is expressed in terms of ecological sensitivity and the striving for a symbiotic harmony with nature. We also experience it as a historical project, the envisionment and actualization of an integrative human community. Nature and history form a single trajectory with critical breakthroughs.

Toward an Ecofeminist Theology of History

Ruether identifies three patterns of hope, or ways of relating human visions of the ideal to actual existence. The first of these, found in nature religion, thought of the projected ideal "as a sacred ambience surrounding ordinary human life that one imitates in ritual activity." This was the prevalent view in the ancient Mediterranean world. The second, historical religion, of which Israelite faith has been the primary example, projects this ideal "as a future, redeemed era of life on earth," to be brought about by God through a messianic figure. Only in modern times, says Ruether, has this concept of a redeemed future been imagined "as something achievable through secular processes of historical change." The limitation to this view is that it has no immediate answer to "the untimely sufferings and deaths of present and past generations." The Hebraic idea of the resurrection of the dead evolved to bridge this painful gap, but it is an idea on which modern, secular revolutionary hope cannot rely; the latter can only promise that someday our descendants will see a better day. Finally, eschatological religion, exemplified mainly by Christianity, evolved out of Judaism. Here the emphasis falls on the drama of the personal soul, reborn to eschatological life in Christ. Eschatology has been severed from historical hope, or, expressed otherwise, the eschatology of space (the eternal, timeless kingdom of heaven) has triumphed over the eschatology of time. The latter has survived only among heretical Christian sects. In mainstream Christianity, eschatology developed a thoroughly ambiguous attitude toward women, who are, on the one hand, the expression of corruptible bodiliness, and on the other hand (in the figure of Mary), the pure, virginal body of the eschatological church. The female body is negated in physical form, yet appropriated in spiritualized form.[45]

Ruether wants to draw on all three of these patterns, reconnecting eschatology with history and history with nature. She does not intend to return to "a linear view of history as a single universal project leading to a final salvific end point." This is the old salvation history mythos, secularized in modern revolutionary movements. Such a view tends eventually either to become purely eschatological, relying on a suprahistorical divine intervention, or to absolutize a particular social revolution. Moreover, it is increasingly evident that it is anti-ecological, disregarding finite limits and exploiting the nonhuman environment.[46]

Against this linear view, Ruether introduces the image of *metanoia*, "conversion to the center." "Conversion suggests that, while there is no one utopian state of humanity lying back in an original paradise of the 'beginning,' there are basic ingredients of a just and livable society. These ingredients have roots in nature and involve acceptance of finitude, human scale, and balanced relationships between persons and between human and nonhuman beings." A "humane acceptance of our historicity demands that we liberate ourselves from 'once-and-for-all' thinking," and attend rather to the needs and possibilities at hand. Ruether notes that Hebraic thought combined both linear and cyclical patterns, and she suggests that this conversion to the center, a "return to harmony within the covenant of creation," is not a cyclical return to what existed before, but rather involves ever new achievements of "livable, humane balances" under new and different historical circumstances. "It is a historical project that has to be undertaken again and again in changing circumstances."[47]

Thus we are brought, by a somewhat different route, to the same conclusion at which we arrived from our study of the view of history implicit in African American theology, namely, that there is no triumphal march of God in history, no special history of salvation, but only a plurality of partial, fragmentary, ambiguous histories of freedom, which appear in the form of "livable, humane balances" or fragile syntheses of values and praxis that achieve a momentary liberation from the chaos and tyranny of human affairs without falling into the illusion of "once-and-for-all" thinking.

That Ruether is in fact concerned about the history of freedom, although she does not use the term, is evident from her feminist vision of an integrative society. It is a society that would affirm the values of democratic participation, the equal value of all persons, and equal access to educational and work opportunities. It would be "a democratic socialist society that dismantles sexist and class hierarchies, that restores ownership and management of work to the base communities of workers themselves, who then create networks of economic and political relationships." Still more, she says, it would be an organic community in which activities are shared and integrated, and an ecological community in which human and nonhuman systems have been harmonized. Such an alternative society can be built up, she thinks, either through small utopian experiments or by working on pieces of the vision separately. But she is quite clear that "the alternative nonsexist, nonclassist and nonexploitative world eludes us as a global system" because "the powers and principalities are still very much in control of most of the world."[48] The most we can hope to achieve are fragmentary pieces of the vision, which do, however, when realized have the effect of making this world a tolerable place in which to dwell humanly and of interrupting the sway of the worldly powers, constraining their sphere of influence, and occasionally leading to structural reforms.

But is this enough? What of massive, silent, unredeemed human suffering, and the tragic drama of history as a whole? What of the good and worthy accomplishments of which we are justly proud and which deserve to be preserved? The only appropriate response to this question, says Ruether, can be an agnosticism. We do not know what happens in death other than that our individuated existence ceases and dissolves back into the great matrix of being. But we have reason to believe that this matrix is not only the ground of all personhood but is personal itself—it is "the Holy Being in which our achievements and failures are gathered up, assimilated into the fabric of being, and carried forward into new possibilities." We do not know what this really means, and we do not need to. "Our responsibility is to use our temporal life span to create a just and good community for our generation and for our children."[49]

The God of Emancipatory Freedom: The Basileia Vision

The questions with which Ruether leaves us cannot be immediately answered. They are similar to the questions raised by Latin American, Asian, and African American theologies. They have to do with the fundamental nature of God and with how this divine nature relates to the human emancipatory struggle, if at all. To speak of God in the face of massive poverty and suffering, systemic racism, deeply rooted sexism, blind homophobia, pervasive ethnocentrism, is not easy. In the face of such destructive practices, many have grown silent, and silence is preferable to glib and confident talk about the "mighty acts" of God.

If God is to be spoken of in the context of the emancipatory struggles that have given rise to the liberation theologies, it can only be as the One who *is* free and *gives* freedom. First, God is the One who *is* free: Freedom becomes the defining quality of divinity. This should not be taken to refer to the sovereignty of God in line with the dominant tradition, meaning that the transcendent God is free from worldly influence and limitation. Freedom does not mean the cutting off of relationships but just the opposite, the most intense sort of relationality, forged in a community of equality, reciprocity, solidarity. To be free means to belong to a community of friends; our words "freedom" and "friend" derive from the same Indo-European root, which contains the sense of belonging to a community that confers rights and responsibilities. The God of freedom constitutes such a community and participates in it, empowering it by the divine friendship. Freedom means a presence to self, a being with self, mediated in and through a presence to others. God is the primordial event of mediation by which freedom is constituted as a self-and-other-relatedness.

Second, God *gives* freedom: This means that the divine freedom is an emancipatory freedom. It is a freedom oriented not to divine self-maintenance but to giving freedom to creatures—first by calling them into being out of nothingness, then by preserving and liberating the gift of freedom from destructive human encroachments upon it. For those who suffer and are heavy laden (and at one time or another all humans are), the name of God is "Redeemer" or "Liberator." These ideas are developed more fully in chapter 11 and subsequent chapters.

The God whose freedom is emancipatory is the God of the basileia vision of Jesus. Jesus spoke of God not in abstractions but in terms of an empowering personal presence that establishes a new kind of human/cosmic community as God's "project" or "realm"—the *basileia tou theou*. Its quality can best be named "freedom": The realm of God is a "realm of freedom." This can only mean that in the basileia-event something happens that radically restructures human relationships, reversing all the privileges based on class, race, sex, wealth, ethnic identity, religious piety, social acceptability. In the basileia it is the last who shall be first, the poor who are blessed, the social outcasts who are invited to the banquet, unnamed women who exhibit true piety, sinners who are forgiven, lepers who are cleansed. It is as if a tremendous wind has swept away the whole tangled web of constricting human relationships, bringing about a clearing of freedom in which everything becomes open, direct, and whole. This wind is the Spirit of God, the Spirit of freedom—and of the Spirit we shall have much to say in chapters 17–18, just as we shall attend to the freedom proclaimed by Jesus in chapter 15. All the great liberation movements have been motivated by the basileia vision of Jesus and empowered by the Spirit of freedom; they are, in the profoundest sense, spiritual movements.

The basileia vision reminds us that the theme of freedom cannot be isolated from the other primary themes that will be seen to emerge from the ecological and dialogical quests, namely love and wholeness. For the basileia in question is a communion of reconciling love and inclusive wholeness; in it these three themes are in fact inseparably interwoven. There can be no emancipation without reconciliation, a healing of the terrible enmity that exists among humans and between humans and the natural world, a healing that extracts the hatred from differences but affirms and glories in the differences themselves: That is the profoundest meaning of love. Nor can there be any emancipation without creating a realm of inclusive wholeness in which unity is fashioned out of an incredible diversity.

In each of the quests a different aspect of the divine is highlighted, but in the final analysis these are only aspects of the impenetrable mystery of God. Whether the mystery of God is in fact encountered by the quests is always a matter of personal risk and objective uncertainty. We can only listen to the testimony of those who find themselves on one or another of these ways. If we do not find ourselves among these postmodern pilgrims, perhaps it is because we are not prepared to take the necessary risks and lack the requisite courage. To become free, we must stop clinging to all that constrains and kills us. We must open ourselves to an emptiness that is an utter fullness: That is freedom.

7
THE ECOLOGICAL QUEST: COSMOS, LIFE, AND THE LOVE OF GOD

Postmodern Science and the New Cosmology

The ecological sensibility with which we are concerned is closely related to a fundamentally new view of the cosmos that has been emerging in the natural sciences, especially physics and biology, during the past forty years. This view opens up the possibility of a more unified, nondualistic interpretation of the universe, one that sees the material and the spiritual as different aspects of the same reality ("one world," as John Polkinghorne expresses it). As over against the older, objectifying mechanics, this one reality is being described in terms that are increasingly "spiritual" and "subjective." Instead of being made up of tiny material particles, the universe is an open, indeterminate, evolving process that is essentially relational and energetic. The dominant paradigm today is that of *relations of energy* rather than bits of matter; reality has more the character of subjectivity than of substance. In other words, the new physics lends itself more readily to a religious interpretation of reality than the old Newtonian mechanics. So does the new biology if we are able to view chance and randomness, not as destructive of all meaning but as creative instruments by which the potentialities of a universe are being "run through" or "explored" (in Arthur Peacocke's terms).[1] It is ironic, therefore, that many conservative Christians should find the new science so threatening, and that they should turn back to an older mechanistic model to give their "creationist" account of the origin of the world. Their anachronistic theology with its interventionist God requires an anachronistic science that is much closer to a seventeenth-century worldview than it is to the Bible.

John Polkinghorne captures the holistic vision emerging from the religion-science dialogue with his thesis that we live in one world and that science and theology are exploring different aspects of it. They are capable of interacting because theology attempts to explain the source of the rational order and structure that science both assumes and confirms in its investigations, and because science establishes "conditions of consonance" that must be satisfied by any account of God's activity in the world. He notes that both science and theology are ultimately concerned with "unpicturable entities" (quarks, gluons, divine presence, grace) whose reality is more subtle than that of naive objectivity. This means that they both make use of language imaginatively and metaphorically, and that a "sophisticated web of interpretation and judgment" is involved in any scientific results of interest as well as in all religious claims. Scientific seeing, like religious seeing, is always "seeing as"—through "the spectacles behind the eyes," that is, through the categories, tacit judgments, hints, and intuitions of our minds. Polkinghorne is seeking a broader rationality, a recognition that reason has a "broader base" than that which corresponds to empirical verification or the application of mathematical rules. "The mind has reasons that computers know not of." Scientific thinking has a kindred character to aesthetic, ethical, and religious thinking. Even mathematical systems, we now know, contain undecidable propositions.[2]

I shall briefly examine three aspects of the new cosmology that seem to be especially pertinent to theology: the shift from a substance to a relational-energetic view of the world, the multidimensional character of reality, and the creative process by which order is brought out of chaos. These will be further developed in chapter 13.

The Shift from a Substance to a Relational View of the World: The Metaphor of Energy

Arthur Peacocke helpfully compares the modern (Newtonian) and contemporary (post-Einsteinian) scientific worldviews under four themes, all of which are aspects of a basic shift from a substance to a relational view of reality—a shift that has occurred within the past seventy-five years or so and is one of the most impressive intellectual achievements of all time.[3]

1. Nature is no longer a relatively simple, stable structure made up of a few basic entities; rather it is enormously complex and various, relational rather than substantive in character, consisting of many levels of organization, ranging from the microworld of the subatomic through the macroworld of the biosphere to the megaworld of intergalactic space-time. Matter does not consist of tiny little substances called atoms but of relations of energy. According to quantum theory, which represents a refinement of Einstein's general theory of relativity,

energy is radiated discontinuously in subatomic units called quanta. These quanta (composed of "quarks" and "gluons") have a dual character, sometimes behaving as waves and sometimes as particles. Part of the difficulty of even thinking about this unstable, fitful structure is that we cannot measure both the position and the momentum of a quantum at one and the same time—Heisenberg's principle of indeterminacy or uncertainty. Reality at the subatomic level has become essentially unpicturable and indeterminate.[4] "Energy" is the prime metaphor by which to name this reality, but in fact we do not know what it is. The metaphor simply points to something that is active, at work—*energeia* (from *ergon*, work). It moves mysteriously like the wind.

2. The natural world is no longer mechanically determined and predictable but is rather the scene of the interplay of chance and necessity, in which there is indeterminacy at the microlevel (microbiology) and unpredictability at the macrolevel (evolutionary biology). Without chance there would be no change and development; without necessity there would be no preservation and selection.

3. The natural world is no longer static, unchanging, and closed, but is dynamic, always in process, a nexus of evolving forms, inexhaustible in its potential for change and novelty. The key to world-process is the interplay of randomness and regularity.

4. There no longer seems to be a ground level of simplicity, an accessible bedrock of subatomic particles on which to build the structure of the universe, but rather an "infinite complexity that can be fitted into a finite domain"—the domain of matter-energy in space-time that makes up the universe.

Reality as a Complex, Multidimensional Unity

Modern and even contemporary science has tended to operate with a reductionistic hierarchy of explanatory relations: the mental (consciousness, thought) is explained in terms of the physiological (the brain), the organic (biology) is explained in terms of the inorganic (chemistry), the atomic is explained in terms of the subatomic (physics). But we now know that this is not possible. Genuine novelty emerges in each of these dimensions, a novelty that is not reducible to that out of which it has emerged or evolved. The higher and more complex dimensions of reality are qualitatively distinct; they incorporate the lower dimensions but cannot be explained in the terms appropriate to those lower dimensions. Reality as a whole is a complex interplay of dimensions, which can neither be reduced to the single one-dimensional picture of modern science, nor be divided into the two-dimensional worldview of classical theology—the supernatural and the natural, the eternal and the temporal, the sacred and the profane.[5]

Dimensional analysis can be extended in the direction of greater or lesser degrees of complexity. Beyond the physical dimension we should want to recognize the mental or psychological, the cultural-historical, the ethical, the aesthetic, and the religious—all of which interpenetrate in various complex ways. Within the physical dimension we can identify subdimensions, between which there occur what Polkinghorne calls "level shifts," which are often quite puzzling. The most perplexing level shift of all is that between the physical and the mental, or between brain and mind.[6]

Reality, then, is a complex, multidimensional unity. What this unity consists in, how it is to be described, can never be completely grasped since we encounter it only as mediated, never in raw form; and, because it is not directly observable, we can describe it only metaphorically, not empirically. The favored metaphor at the moment is that of "energy" or "potency" (Heisenberg): At the heart of the universe is a highly organized and intense energy, which arranges itself fluidly and cannot in principle be exhaustively measured, known, and predicted because every attempt to do so interacts with it and thus alters it. What is this "energy"? Is it intrinsically physical or mental, material or spiritual? It should be evident that a reverse reduction is also unacceptable, namely of the material dimensions of reality to the mental or ideal. Neither abstract idealism nor undialectical materialism can do justice to the actual complexity and diversity of the world in which we live. We are seeking to find a way beyond monism and dualism, a way of understanding the whole as both one and many. If the unitary principle is in some sense energy, then this principle must itself be understood as multidimensional, manifesting itself as both spiritual love and material potency, reducible to neither alone. The fundamental theological question is how to understand God in relation to this all-pervasive cosmic *energeia* (see chap. 10, pp. 139–45).

Creativity: Order out of Chaos

Most of us are familiar with the Big Bang theory of origins now favored by astrophysics. Our universe seems to be expanding from a common origin about fifteen billion years ago. At the beginning instant, referred to as the "infinite singularity" because it escapes all scientific analysis, the whole universe was the size of an incredibly dense atom. This atom exploded, and within the first fraction of a second the basic gravitational, electromagnetic, and nuclear forces of our universe appeared. While the process of change slowed down considerably after the first three minutes, the universe continued to expand and to develop increasingly rich, diverse, and complex forms, and it is still doing so. At some remotely future time, the whole cosmos may crunch back in upon itself or disappear into black holes.[7]

Perhaps there are some similarities between the Big Bang and the biblical story of creation, which also depicts an absolute beginning. But it would be a mistake to draw conclusions too quickly. The Big Bang is after all only one of several astrophysical theories (even though the prevailing one); there might instead be an oscillating or cyclic cosmos in infinite time, with successive eras of expansions and contractions and hence no single beginning. More importantly, however, the creation story in Genesis does not contain scientific information; it is rather an intuitive picture based on the religious experience of dependence, wonder, order, contingency, etc. As Ian Barbour suggests, between creation and cosmology what should be sought is not direct implication but rather "coherence" and "consonance."[8] The most interesting coherence is not the notion of an absolute beginning but rather the idea that creation involves bringing order out of chaos. This is the central motif of the Genesis story. When God began to create, the earth was a formless void, a dark swirling watery chaos. The act of creation consisted in imposing distinctions and hence order on this raw material: light and darkness, stars and planets, dry land and water, plants and animals, animals and humans, finally man and woman (Gen. 1:1–2:4). Creation did not occur all at once; it is an ongoing process in which at every moment the world owes its existence and refinement to God.[9]

The image of bringing "order out of chaos" is from the title of an influential book by Ilya Prigogine and Isabelle Stengers.[10] It points to a second phase of the new scientific paradigm. The first phase was that initiated by relativity theory and quantum physics toward the beginning of the twentieth century through the work of Planck, Einstein, and their followers. The second phase has opened up only in the last third of the century, stemming from the pioneering work of Edward Lorenz on weather systems. It is the science of the computer age. Ironically, given the linearity of computers, this is the science of "chaos" or of nonlinear systems, and today it is being widely discussed.[11] It promises to modify the quantum paradigm as radically as the latter modified the mechanical paradigm of Newton. It does not negate quantum relativity but pushes it further in the direction of large-scale flexibility, extending indeterminacy from the subatomic to the macrocosmic level. A nonlinear system is one in which a response is not proportional to a stimulus and also feeds back into the system with ramifying effects. Most of the systems in which we live are nonlinear in this sense; and in such systems chaotic, that is, unpredictable and random, behavior is readily observable. But it took the large-scale computational capability of computers to make these observations possible in a scientifically verifiable way.

The sort of chaos to which chaos science points is not sheer confusion, disorder, and irrationality, not the unstructured mass or the formless void that preceded the infinite singularity. Chaotic events are not lacking in causal explanation and do not violate natural processes; rather they compose what are called "complex dynamical systems." We are familiar with such systems in the everyday world: heart beats, swinging pendulums, dripping water taps, fluid flows, weather systems, traffic patterns. The order that is present in such systems is exceedingly complex and even incalculable because their motion is extremely sensitive to initial conditions (for example, the effect of a butterfly on a weather pattern), changing influences (external "noise" or interference), and an almost infinitely ramifying variety of possible behaviors—so much so that even the most powerful computers are unable to predict the course they will take although computers are able to display the intricate and beautiful patterns they often trace.[12] As they progress, nonlinear systems become more and more highly individualized so that they can only be understood holistically rather than atomistically. Ultimately the whole cosmos is a very large and a very complex dynamical system.[13]

Now it is the randomness, indeterminacy, flexibility present in such systems that is the source of cosmic creativity, that is, of the freedom to explore a vast range of behavior patterns; and it is the regularity present in the laws of nature that preserves the novel patterns. We can speak of the first of these elements as "chance" if it is understood that what is involved is not something that lacks natural causes. It is rather that natural causality operates in both a highly fluid and a very repetitive fashion. Creativity occurs through the interplay of these factors.[14] In dynamical systems small fluctuations are amplified rather than damped down, which is what happens in a closed mechanical system. This provides the needed variability if the cosmos is to grow toward novel, more complex forms. The variability itself may be either life-enhancing or destructive, cancerous. Through natural selection, the life-enhancing variations prevail.

Thus an intrinsic flexibility or openness seems to be present in the material world. It is reasonable to assume that analogies or connections may exist between this flexibility and what we human beings experience as "consciousness" and "freedom." Perhaps there is a continuum of matter and mind of which we are still only dimly aware, a continuum based not on panpsychism but on differentiated levels of "structured openness" or "freedom within regularity." At some indefinable point on the continuum, consciousness emerges, which is the ultimate flexible system.[15]

We should not assume that there is scientific evidence for divine purposiveness in cosmic process, despite the apparent similarities between the cosmic and biblical creation stories. The creativity to which science points is at best ethically neutral, and the second law of thermodynamics continues to operate in nonlinear as well as linear systems. This means that the reserve of usable energy is gradually dissipating and eventually will run out. Forces of life and death coexist in a precarious balance; the cosmic story is both comic and tragic. We can argue theologically that God acts purposively in natural and human history, but we cannot claim that God simply *is* cosmic energy or that God has endowed the world as a whole with a "cosmic blueprint."[16] Just how God does act in the world is a matter to be discussed in later chapters. For the moment it is enough to note that there is a creativity, dynamism, and contingency in world-process that allows for a coherent theology of divine activity but does not require or prove it.

Ecological Sensibility and the Interrelatedness of Life

What is the connection between the new cosmology and an ecological sensibility? They are very closely related and in part identical. On the one hand, ecology is simply one aspect of the sort of holistic, relational cosmology sketched above; it draws out its ethical and religious implications for an understanding of that dimension of cosmos known as "life." On the other hand, ecology is the clue to the new cosmology because the model of the latter is not mechanical but organic, not atomistic but interconnected, not substance-based but relational and processual. The new cosmology is precisely and only an "ecological cosmology." Ecology spells this out more explicitly and with a specific orientation to living systems.

We can arrive at a rough-and-ready definition of ecology by starting with the meaning of the Greek term from which it derives, namely *oikos* or "house." Ecology has something to do with the study (*logos*) of how a house works. The house in question is our natural home, the earth, as well as *its* home, the whole cosmic system in which planet earth is a tiny speck. Sallie McFague, who approaches the topic along this line, goes on to suggest, in a phrase borrowed from Stephen Toulmin, that ecology involves treating the earth as a home rather than a hotel: One takes care of a home but uses the conveniences of a hotel. For too long the human race has treated the earth as a hotel.[17]

According to the more traditional definition, ecology is the study of the relations between living organisms and their environments; but in much of the recent literature it is also used in a broader, less technical sense to indicate "the interdependence of all the living and nonliving systems of the earth"[18]—and indeed, not just of the earth but of the whole cosmos because the earth-systems are themselves integrally related to cosmic dynamics. The point of ecology is that everything is internally interconnected in a very delicate web of living and nonliving systems. An ecological sensibility involves returning to a more comprehensive vision of the entire universe and the sense of being sustained by a "cosmic presence" such as was found in many of the ancient religions.[19] Ecology has been expanded beyond the arena of the biological sciences and has become a religio-ethico-philosophical model for a way of being in the world. It is a systemic way of thinking, but the system is ecological rather than mechanical. As such it is an excellent model for systematic thinking in theology as well.

The ecological model, according to Charles Birch and John Cobb,[20] is a model of internal relations, which means that relations are constitutive of entities rather than being something incidental or accidental to them. It is not as though entities first exist as self-contained substances, and then are subsequently connected with each other. Rather entities exist only as constituted by relations to other entities in complex and interlocking systems. There is no way of going below systematic interconnections to another level at which there are self-contained entities; rather the system is primary. Birch and Cobb describe this as the transition from substance to event thinking and from the mechanical to the ecological model. They suggest that the Indo-European languages and Western metaphysics are biased toward substance thinking: Substances are primary realities and events are the result of the interaction of substances. The ecological model reverses this priority: Events are primary and substantial objects are enduring patterns among changing events. Events are the complex interacting of entities, and the latter are simply relations. An entity *is* a mode of relating. The ecological model applies to the inorganic as well as the organic, the nonliving as well as the living, but in truth there are no sharp boundaries between living and nonliving components of the cosmic system.

It is evident, then, how the ecological model requires, indeed is the clue to, a new cosmology. Field theory, relativity physics, quantum mechanics, evolutionary biology, have all contributed to the articulation of this model, as has the process philosophy of Alfred North Whitehead, which is central to the work of Birch and Cobb. There are also striking similarities with Eastern, especially Buddhist, ways of thinking, and these have been explored especially by Jay McDaniel.[21]

The primary ethical challenge of ecology is to "liberate life," that is, to liberate it from various forces of death and destructiveness that threaten the viability of life on this planet. These include the pollution of air, water, and soil, alteration of the chemistry of the planet, the rapid depletion of natural resources, the destruction of rain forests, the elimination of living species through the loss of habitats, ecoterrorism, the uncontrolled growth in human population, the biological manipulation of human life, the ideology of unlimited economic development—on the whole the breakdown of ecological balance and an increasingly dysfunctional relationship between nature and the human spirit. World Watch estimates that only some forty years remain to reverse the destructive practices before irreversible damage is done. The odds seem to be against decisive action being taken in time unless there is a massive change of consciousness.[22]

Thomas Berry observes that violence and conflict are a necessary part of the cosmic system but that it takes on a new destructiveness in human hands. Ecological damage is caused by human interference in the life systems of the planet. His "dream of the earth" is to bring about a kind of cosmic peace, not by an impossible escape from conflict but through a creative resolution of antagonisms.[23]

The change in sensibility with which we are concerned involves a shift not only from a mechanical/substantial to an ecological/relational model but also from an anthropocentric to a biocentric/cosmocentric perspective. This involves a broadening of horizons, not an elimination of concerns for human flourishing; rather it requires seeing the connection between political justice and ecojustice. It also involves recognizing that the relationship of power and dependency between the human and the natural has reversed with the impact of modern technology. Humans once struggled to survive against the often destructive forces of nature, but these forces have been largely harnessed, and now it is nature that struggles to survive. The fate of the earth is in human hands—and this requires that we enlarge our perspective beyond human needs and desires. Is it the case that through humans the earth is now taking its fate into its own hands, for better or for worse? If so, we humans have a crucially important role to play but in a much larger frame of reference. As we contemplate the cosmic horizon and the mystery of our place in it, we find that we are drawn beyond ourselves to the ultimate mystery.

The God of Life and Love: Primal Eros

At this point ecological sensibility issues in religious sensibility. Similarly, many of the intuitions of the new scientific cosmology point in the direction of religious mystery, affirmation, and experience. The days of warfare between science and religion are past; instead we find ourselves drawn together and relying upon each other in the quest for a better understanding of the mystery at the heart of the universe. Principally two metaphors have emerged out of the ecological movement to name this mystery: life and love. The two are closely related and mutually define each other: Love is the interrelatedness of life, and life is the dynamism of love. The two aspects are perhaps best captured by the Greek word *eros,* which unites spiritual love and material potency. *Eros* is a love that is at once natural and supernatural.

God as Life

It is not surprising that "life" should be the primary metaphor applied to God by ecologically oriented theologians. After all, the central theme of ecology is life, and in some dialectical sense God is life itself, "the vast interdependent and interwoven matrix of all evolving nature."[24] Birch and Cobb develop this way of thinking about God: "In some ways a religion of life must distinguish the central part of life, the principle of life, the ground of life, or life itself from every particular form and manifestation of life and also from the sum total of individual living things." The distinction is analogous to the one drawn by Henry Nelson Wieman between "creative good" and "created goods."[25]

Life, according to Birch and Cobb, "is that in nature which actualises creative novelty whenever it can." It is the dynamism that counters the law of entropy in the physical world. Entropy, which is based on the second law of thermodynamics, means that, while the quantity of energy in the universe remains the same, the quality and versatility of energy declines as it is converted from one form to another. It moves into less differentiated and usable forms (primarily as heat), along with a move toward disorder (the breakdown of differentiations). But life is a counterentropic force since it accomplishes creative transformations and cumulative integrations of experience. Thus we find a conflict between two powerful and opposed cosmic forces, the forces of death and life. "Life as the cosmic principle that works for higher order in the midst of entropy is enormously powerful." Its power is not limited to clearly living things; rather "we may think of life as exerting its gentle pressure everywhere."[26] It should be clear here and in what follows that these are philosophical and theological assertions about life, not biological ones. A theology of nature cannot be derived from science. It seeks to be congruent with science but is not scientific cosmology.

Birch and Cobb contend that life "is not the fundamental energy of the universe as such. It is instead an aim at the realisation of novel forms and richness of experience."[27] Unfortunately this distinction is not elaborated. Does it suggest that there is a more fundamental cosmic principle ("ultimate reality") of which life or God is a determinate though supreme manifestation ("ultimate actuality")? But what might this more fundamental cosmic principle be other than the creativity that is life itself? Presumably the fundamental energy of the universe is not entropic but creative; entropy would rather be the diffusion of this creativity under the conditions of finitude, limitation, competition, and struggle. Perhaps this is simply a way of asserting that life is not identical with the world as such, the whole created order with all its conflicting forces. But the "fundamental energy" within this created order would seem to be precisely life itself, the principle of creativity.

In any event, "Life as the central religious symbol is God." Cobb seems to go further here than in other works toward identifying God with creativity. To name life as God is to "trust life to achieve some end other than extinction"; it is to trust in a power of redemption to overcome evil, and to speak of redemption is to speak of God. The idea of God as life itself is elaborated in the categories familiar to process theology. God "is the supreme and perfect exemplification of the ecological model of life" because God is internally related to the world and the world is internally related to God. The first of these relations is what Whitehead called the "primordial nature" of God, which is the inclusion within God of the entire sphere of cosmic possibilities, both realized and unrealized, and the envisagement of these possibilities in their relevance for each situation, thus lending ordered novelty to cosmic process. The second of these relations, the "consequent nature," is that aspect of God which is perfectly responsive to the joys and sufferings of the world and which preserves all that perishes in the world. Thus God and the world are internally related but not identical; each needs the other to be what it is: no world apart from God, no God apart from some world.[28]

Is God as life itself a purposive, loving being? In answering this question, Birch and Cobb move toward the second of the metaphors with which we are concerned, namely God as love. Life is purposive, they claim, because it aims at the realization of value. This is not a specific value or goal, such as the creation of human beings, but value as such, which is "the realisation of richer experience" and "the attractive vision of unrealised possibility." Life is also the supreme instance of love in a twofold sense. On the one hand love provides a specific purpose for each entity in each moment, aiming to achieve some optimum value for it, and in this sense is very personal; on the other hand it is awesomely disinterested, favoring all things, and in that sense is impersonal. Thus love seems to specify the distinctive character and purpose of that life which is named God. Life as a symbol of God by itself alone does not, as Birch and Cobb acknowledge, "highlight the fullness of God's personal being or redemptive action."[29] Perhaps it is better, therefore, to focus on the attribute of love in developing the concept of God implicit in an ecological sensibility.

God as Love

My intention is to incorporate the symbol of life, not leave it aside, by establishing love as one of three central symbols for depicting God's being-in-process (the others are freedom and oneness/wholeness). Not only is this symbol deeply rooted in the biblical and theological tradition, but also it is prominent in the ecological literature. To incorporate life, let us employ the Greek term *eros*, which names a kind of love that unites the material energy of life with the distinctive spiritual quality of entering into relationship with an other—a relationship in which the other is intended for the sake of the other and in which one finds one's own fulfillment in and through the other. Such loving relationship is at the heart of the ecological model.

The expression "primal eros" is intended to suggest that God is present and active in all dimensions of the cosmos as the *ultimate* creating, shaping, alluring energy, potency, or wind. This energy is profoundly alive and in the deepest sense personal although it manifests itself in both impersonal and personal forms, and its fundamental quality is that of allurement, of drawing all things to itself, and of sustaining and cherishing all things in relationship to it. Arthur Peacocke suggests that what is experienced at the personal-spiritual level as God's "love" and "fulfilling presence" can be described more broadly at the cosmic level as "energy." "God as creator, redeemer, and sanctifier is a living energy who never ceases to create, redeem, and sanctify us and none of these activities can, for long, be considered in isolation from the others."[30] But this living energy has precisely the quality of eros. The personal-spiritual experience of it as love is the basic clue to its meaning.

Let us think of eros as "allurement." In his "cosmic creation story"—a cosmological fantasy that does not purport to be scientific—Brian Swimme suggests that love begins as allurement or attraction, an "attracting activity" that is the fundamental mystery of the cosmos. It is everywhere present, but we cannot penetrate into its operation. It is primal: "This alluring activity is *the* basic reality of the macrocosmic universe." What humans experience as love is in fact "the basic binding energy found everywhere in reality." It "permeates the cosmos on *all* levels of being." Without this mysterious drawing of things together, the universe would fly apart. Galaxies, human families, atoms, ecosystems—all would disintegrate immediately if the allurement pervading the universe would shut off. Thus we can say that allurement is the "evocation of being, the creation of community." Love "ignites" and "evokes" being; it calls things into being by pulling them together into ordered relationships. In human beings "this supreme dynamic of love, of allurement and evocation, in action since the beginning of the universe, after billions of years, becomes aware of itself." What this supreme dynamic is in and of itself, whether it is what religions call "God," remains unasked and unanswered by Swimme. He shies away from drawing any explicitly religious conclusions from his cosmic fantasy. He only describes the ways in which the "ultimate mystery" appears and is at work through various natural forces or "cosmic dynamics," which cohere into self-awareness in human form.[31]

Jay McDaniel makes explicit the connection between God and love. The divine nature is unlimited love, by which McDaniel means a love "that is universal in scope, inclusive of all creatures with sentience and needs," and "that is infinitely tender, desirous of the well-being of each sentient being for its own sake and cognizant of each being as an end in itself."[32] Feminine imagery is especially appropriate for understanding this aspect of God, who may be thought of as a universal Matrix or divine Mother who creates the world within herself out of a reservoir of immanent potentiality. In accord with process theology, we must recognize, however, that while God is all-loving God is not all-powerful. God's power is persuasive or invitational rather than coercive; the natural world has a creativity independent of God, and patterns of behavior emerge that God cannot prevent if there is to be life at all. God created the world out of a chaos of energy events, availing the flux of possibilities for order and novelty. The divinely offered possibilities for order are goals for a creature's creativity. God has the power of persuasion to harmonize the whole but not the power of coercion to manipulate the whole. In sum, God is the inwardly felt lure or attractant toward self-actualization of each entity in communion with the whole of the cosmos. This lure is the Holy Spirit, "the eros toward life by which biological (including sexual) eros is itself elicited, and to which it is responsive."[33]

Two questions in particular remain to be discussed more fully in later chapters. (1) Is God simply identical with cosmic energy, the life-process, or universal eros? I shall argue for a twofold distinction. On the one hand, God is not simply a process, power, or energy but a person or subject, the One who "has" this power "absolutely." On the other hand, the power that God has absolutely is not cosmic process per se but the ideality or pure possibility that *creates* this process and *lures* it in the direction of love, freedom, goodness, beauty, enhancement of life. Hence I call God's power *primal* eros. It is a wind *of the Spirit,* not a physical force. God transcends the cosmos, is not identical with its energy-system: We cannot say with Spinoza, *Deus sive natura.* Nature remains what is not-God within the divine life; it is the body of God, not God. Elaboration of these distinctions will require a theory of the being and act of God such as that provided in chapters 10 and 11. (2) How and toward what ends does God act in the world? I shall argue that God acts continuously within natural and historical processes rather than sporadically from outside them, and that what God provides is not a macroplan or "cosmic blueprint" but ideals, lures, resources for the realization of specific values in specific biohistorical trajectories. This requires the articulation of a theology of nature and history such as that offered in chapters 13 and 18.

8

THE DIALOGICAL QUEST: DIVERSITY, PLURALITY, AND THE WHOLENESS OF GOD

Dialogue and Difference

The third of the terms by which we are attempting to mark the post-modern temper and the quests associated with it is "dialogue." It specifies the rational and discursive dimension that is characteristic of our times, just as "emancipation" specifies the practical dimension and "ecology" the relational dimension. Certainly these dimensions are interwoven and inseparable even if distinguishable. Dialogical discourse is oriented to emancipatory practices and ecological wholeness. Dialogue, while arising out of respect for differences, is always pressing toward wholeness and mutual transformation; thus the dialogical and the ecological are very closely related. Likewise dialogue, while related to conceptual or logical rationality, is always pressing toward discursive or communicative practices that have freedom as their telos; thus the dialogical and the emancipatory are very closely related.

The latter connection is especially evident in the thought of Jürgen Habermas, whose work on critical social theory lays the foundation for a theory of discursive or dialogical rationality.[1] Habermas's central concern has been for a "theory of the pathology of modernism" from the viewpoint of "the deformed realization of reason in history."[2] There is indeed a realization of reason in history, as Hegel claimed, but it is always "deformed" by conflicting ideologies and interests—psychological, social, political, religious—and is never able to attain its final ends. Thus Habermas set himself the task of elaborating a new comprehensive theory of rationality as the ground for a critical theory of society, a theory that would provide "a way of redeeming, reconstructing, and rationally defending the emancipatory aspirations of the Enlightenment."[3]

The centerpiece of this theory is what Habermas calls "communicative action," which is a type of social interaction mediated by discourse and oriented toward reaching understanding through and across differences. For the sake of the "argumentative redemption of validity claims," communicative action must presuppose the possibility of an unconstrained, undistorted dialogue, a dialogical rationality, and this possibility, Habermas believes, is grounded in the very character of linguistic intersubjectivity. It is "always already" there despite its empirical deformations. Despite the claim of some critics that Habermas exhibits "totalizing" tendencies with his notion of unconstrained dialogue and an alleged a priori status of reason, he guards against this in a number of ways that cannot be elaborated here. The key point is that differences are never dissolved by dialogue and that every holism remains "decentered," every communication incomplete, every project unfinished. This is why for Habermas rationality is essentially dialogical rather than logical, communicative rather than conceptual.

It is true that I am privileging the dialogical rather than the deconstructive moment of postmodern rationality. The dialogical, properly understood, includes a deconstructive moment since it rejects totality and is generated out of difference. Dialogue is a way of speaking (*logos*) through and between (*dia*) difference. Thoroughgoing deconstruction does not recognize a way through difference but *only* difference: Things and signs are radically particular, irresolvably fragmentary. The dialogical provides a way toward meaningful speech about God's presence and action in the world, whereas deconstruction excludes all positive possibilities of such speech, arguing instead for a purely apophatic or negative theology, if any at all.[4] This in itself does not establish the validity of dialogue. My reason for privileging the dialogical is the intuitive conviction that we basically experience the world and function in it dialogically rather than deconstructively. Deconstruction does not provide a way of being in the world for most people, but it does provide a critique of the excesses of dialogue, a reminder that the dynamic of dialogue remains precisely the irreducible differences of cultures, practices, persons, values.

The particular application of dialogue with which we are concerned in this chapter is to *religious* differences, that is, to the rich diversity of religious practices across cultures, history, and geography. The expression "interreligious dialogue" has become one of the shibboleths of our time. Dialogue is *the* method for a productive encounter among the religions. John Cobb suggests that dialogue provides the only alternative to an essentialist view of religion, on the one hand, and conceptual relativism, on the other. The first claims that there is a common essence shared by all religions, the second that each tradition is best by its own norm and that there is no normative critique of norms. Dialogue, by contrast, proceeds on the assumption that

> while one's own tradition has grasped important aspects of reality, reality in its entirety is always more. This means also that the ultimately true norm for life, and therefore also for religious traditions, lies beyond any extant formulation. As dialogue proceeds, glimpses of aspects of reality heretofore unnoticed are vouchsafed for the participants. This is not felt as a threat to the religious traditions from which the participants come but as an opportunity for enrichment and even positive transformation.[5]

Dialogue does not deny that a circularity exists between beliefs and the norms by which they are judged. Rather it prevents this circularity from becoming a static, self-enclosed system by insisting that it is possible to bring alternative traditions into productive encounter with each other, thus keeping them dynamic, growing, open to transformation. Dialogue involves a spiraling toward new and always open possibilities, as opposed to the circularity of relativism or deconstruction and the linearity of essentialist views.

Religious Pluralism and Interreligious Dialogue

The Transition to a Pluralist Perspective

The discussion of the relationship of Christianity to other religions and the theological significance of religious pluralism has mushroomed in recent years. A watershed event occurred in 1986 with the gathering of leading theologians for a conference at Claremont Graduate School. Their papers were published in a book entitled *The Myth of Christian Uniqueness*.[6] The participants adopted the image of crossing a "theological Rubicon" with the move beyond both an *exclusivist* attitude toward other religions, "which finds salvation only in Christ and little, if any, value elsewhere," and an *inclusivist* attitude, "which recognizes the salvific richness of other faiths but then views this richness as the result of Christ's redemptive work and as having to be fulfilled in Christ"—a move beyond both of these to a *pluralist* position, "a move away from insistence on the superiority or finality of Christ and Christianity toward a recognition of the independent validity of other ways." One of the conference participants, Langdon Gilkey, described this as "a monstrous shift indeed, . . . a position quite new to the churches, even to the liberal churches."[7] Just as the step Caesar took when he crossed the River Rubicon to march on Rome was a final and irrevocable one, so also is the step to religious pluralism: It is like entering new territory from which the whole terrain of Christian truth looks different, and there is no turning back.

While this is indeed a paradigm shift of great significance, reflection on the history of the discussion of the relationship of Christianity to other religions makes it seem in retrospect almost inevitable. Once the exclusivist dogma—rooted in the medieval Catholic doctrine that outside the church there is no salvation but expressed equally emphatically by the Protestant conviction that salvation is to be found only in Christ—is surrendered, the logic of the discussion sweeps through and beyond the inclusivist option, which proves finally to be a halfway house, to religious pluralism.

Exclusivism

John Hick shows why the trajectory that results from the abandonment of exclusivism leads ultimately to a pluralist posture.[8] Conservatives recognize this too, which explains why they cling so tenaciously to an exclusivist position with its insistence on scriptural inerrancy, christocentrism, and Christian absolutism. Hick has a very interesting criticism of this absolutism. He points out that, human nature being what it is, Christian absolutism has lent itself to the validation and encouragement of human exploitation on a gigantic scale. "The picture would be very different," he says, "if Christianity, commensurate with its claim to absolute truth and unique validity, had shown a unique capacity to transform human nature for the better." Unfortunately it has not. Christians individually have proven to be about as acquisitive, self-centered, prideful, and intolerant as adherents of other faiths, and the civilization they produced in the West proves this to be the case. Christian anti-Semitism is a direct by-product of Christian absoluteness. This absolutism has also sanctioned the Western imperialistic exploitation of the two-thirds world. The British Empire is a prime example: It was driven primarily by acquisitiveness and aggrandizement, but it was morally validated as a great civilizing and uplifting mission, one of whose tasks was to draw the heathen up to the highest religion. Exactly the same arguments were used to justify the slave trade, which was part of a larger colonial system.

Hick goes on to point out that a similar indictment can be brought against the religious absolutism found in other religions. Each of the great religious traditions has its own unique mixture of good and evil. Each contains great redemptive potential, and each has sanctified vicious human evils. When measured by ethical criteria, the religions seem to be more or less on a par with each other; none, Hick concludes, can be singled out as manifestly superior.

Inclusivism

Revulsion against the destructive effects of this absolutism together with the increase of knowledge about other religious traditions led to a gradual shift in attitude on the part of mainstream Catholicism and Protestantism toward the inclusivist view that all of humanity without exception is redeemed in Christ, even if humanity is unaware of it. Karl Rahner was the most theologically astute proponent of this view, which he called "anonymous Christianity." But the fact is that the old sense of Christian superiority has not died out but has moved into the background; revelation, truth, and salvation are present in other religions, but all of them are viewed as "preparatory" for the final revelation and salvation in Christ.[9] One sees this view clearly in the documents of the Second Vatican Council and the World Council of Churches, and there are still articulate advocates of it.

Pluralism

While "benevolent inclusivism" is certainly preferable as an attitude, especially one that drives policy, to "intolerant exclusivism," it does not hold up very well to rational scrutiny. Once it is granted that salvation is mediated by a diversity of religious traditions, it seems arbitrary to insist nevertheless that one of these ways somehow includes the others or is the goal toward which they are pointing. Hick observes that "this would be like the anomaly of accepting the Copernican revolution in astronomy . . . but still insisting that the sun's life-giving rays can reach the other planets only by first being reflected from the earth."[10] Another way of making the point is simply to reflect on the fact that whatever is included in something else is necessarily subordinated to that which includes it. Therefore "inclusion" cannot provide a satisfactory basis for religious dialogue. Most Christians, for example, would not be satisfied with the "inclusion" of Christianity by Buddhism or Hinduism.

The first major Christian theologian to make the transition to genuine religious pluralism was Ernst Troeltsch, who revised his views on the "absoluteness" of Christianity just before his death in 1923. Troeltsch was a pioneer, and for many years his views were held in contempt, dismissed as "relativism" and "historicism." As part of the Barthian reaction against theological liberalism, exclusivism was back in vogue, and Hendrik Kraemer became a forceful exponent of it. But the science of history of religions as well as the force of world events were steadily undermining this posture. In the 1960s, Wilfred Cantwell Smith, a distinguished comparative religionist, began advocating a pluralist theology of world faiths (as he called it), and he was joined by two Indian Christian scholars, Raimundo Panikkar and Stanley Samartha. Also in the 1960s, shortly before his death, Paul Tillich revised his earlier Christian inclusivism and indicated that the whole of systematic theology needed to be rethought in relation to a genuine encounter among the religions. In the early 1970s, John Hick underwent a conversion from evangelical Christianity to a pluralist paradigm, and in the 1980s the floodgates opened.[11]

Hick and Knitter, in their editing of the papers from the Claremont conference, identified three principal ways in which the participants were making the pluralist move or, retaining the image of the Rubicon, three "bridges" by which they were crossing over from the shores of exclusivism or inclusivism to pluralism.[12]

The Historico-Cultural Bridge: Relativity

Those who take this bridge argue that forces of modernity rather than Christian ideals have for the most part occasioned the transition to pluralism. Historical consciousness makes us aware that all religions are constructions of worldviews, not simply descriptions of the way things are. These thinkers assume that the criteria of truth are practical more than theoretical. On ethical grounds there exists a "rough parity" among religions in terms of truth, beauty, goodness, mediation of saving power; and there may be some broad consensus among them, not about doctrinal truth, but about what is ethically *in*tolerable. Pluralism does not entail neutrality but collaboration in areas where humanity and the earth face common threats. Pluralism requires Christian theology not only to acknowledge the relativity of all faith claims but also to think about its ultimate object, God, as in some sense a relative reality, a relative absolute.[13]

The Theologico-Mystical Bridge: Mystery

On this bridge, the content of authentic religious experience is seen to be infinite, a mystery beyond all forms, exceeding every grasp of it. Mystery is the ontological basis for tolerance, for at its heart it is diverse, plural, neither monistic nor dualistic but advaitic, not-two. The mystery is a "concrete universal": Its universality, its plural wholeness, is available only in and through concrete forms, which mirror it in a variety of ways. This view acknowledges a certain incommensurability among religions, for they are different and irreducible expressions of the unattainable mystery. Any religious claim to have the sole or final revelation of the mystery is idolatrous. This requires among other things a reconstruction of christology.[14]

The Ethico-Practical Bridge: Justice

Here the main motivation to cross over to a pluralist approach arises from a confrontation with the sufferings of humanity and a determination to work collaboratively in the promotion of justice. Thus arises a "liberation theology of religions" and the beginnings of an interface between emancipatory and dialogical motifs. Traditional claims of Christian superiority have led to "an outrageous and absurd religious chauvinism." A global liberation movement needs a global interreligious dialogue and vice versa. Something like a preferential option for those most in need might serve as the context for a new meeting of religions. Persons of different religious traditions could enter into a shared liberative praxis for those who are poor and suffer, as well as a shared reflection on how that praxis relates to their religious beliefs.[15]

Critiques of Pluralism

The argument for religious pluralism has not gone unchallenged. In a review article, Schubert Ogden poses a number of important questions to the authors of *The Myth of Christian Uniqueness.*[16] Part of Ogden's critique is that the case for pluralism thus far has been made primarily on external and practical grounds. That is, Christians have found themselves being confronted more forcefully and directly by rival religious worldviews of undeniable salvific power. They have become increasingly aware of their own complicity in Western cultural imperialism and of the cultural relativity of all their categories of explanation. They have recognized a need for global collaboration in order to struggle collectively for justice and to counter threats to the very survival of humanity and the natural environment. These may all be valid and persuasive considerations, but they are not *theological* arguments. They do not establish the appropriateness, indeed necessity of a pluralist position from the inner dynamic and self-understanding of Christian faith itself. Is there something intrinsic to the Christian understanding of God and of God's redemptive presence in Christ and the ecclesial community that drives Christian theology to a posture of religious pluralism when such a posture opens up as a historical possibility?

This is a fair question to put to the pluralist camp. The answer really requires rethinking the central Christian themes in light of interreligious dialogue. It requires working out a pluralist understanding of God, Christ, the church, and history. This is an immense task, to which I can make only a small contribution. I explore the possibility of rethinking the doctrine of the Trinity in light of the pluralist challenge in the last section of this chapter, and I turn to other doctrinal themes in later chapters.

Various critiques of religious pluralism are offered by the contributors to the volume prepared in response to *The Myth of Christian Uniqueness*, namely *Christian Uniqueness Reconsidered*. Some defend Christian inclusivism in one form or another, arguing that the central Christian doctrines, since they derive from an authoritative revelation, provide the only adequate basis for assessing and relating the diverse claims of world religions. Others argue that religions are unique cultural-linguistic systems with distinctive truth claims that must be debated rather than reconciled. Still others suggest that the whole project of global dialogue is a subtle form of Western hegemony that imposes Western values and homogenizes differences. I will consider some of these criticisms in chapter 18.

John Cobb offers yet another perspective.[17] He believes that the chief defect of the pluralist approach is the assumption that there exists a common essence of religion, expressed more or less equally in all the great religions. This view is held most clearly by John Hick, and Cobb's remarks seem to be aimed primarily at Hick. I suspect that several of the authors of *The Myth of Christian Uniqueness* would agree with Cobb's claim that what is called for is an even more "fundamental pluralism," namely the view that there is no self-identical element within and behind the diversity of religions; rather each religious tradition must be allowed to define its own nature and purpose.

As we have seen, Cobb attempts to avoid the traps of essentialism and conceptual relativism by turning to the strategy of dialogue, which opens all religious traditions to the possibility of learning from and being enriched by other apprehensions of truth. From this he derives "one relatively objective norm" by which religions can be evaluated, namely their capacity to be transformed by openness to other traditions, to expand and enrich their own understanding of reality while remaining faithful to their own heritage. In this respect, Christianity *may* be relatively better equipped than other religions, if its central symbol "Christ" is understood as creative transformation, calling us to listen to the truth and wisdom of others, to integrate that with truth from our own tradition. In other words, there is within Christianity itself a self-critical, de-absolutizing impulse, a willingness to be open to the universal relevance of wisdom from all traditions—although this impulse is frequently trampled upon and forgotten by Christians themselves.

The Goal of Interreligious Dialogue

The goal of interreligious dialogue can best be understood as that of exposing idolatries and drawing out convergent truths.[18] The encounter of the religions provides a way of exposing the idolatries, falsehoods, and destructive practices present in any religion from different angles of vision. The tendency of all religions is to universalize their cultural particularities rather than their disclosures of truth. Thus Christianity has tended to absolutize its scriptures, its institutional forms, its dogmatic claims about God, Christ, sin, and salvation, rather than what is truly distinctive about Christian ecclesial existence, which is its radical gratuity, its deep relationality, its intrinsic nonprovinciality. By absolutizing its Western cultural provincialisms, whether expressed institutionally or dogmatically, the Christian church weakens its own distinctive essence. Other religions have their own cultural provincialisms and ethically ambiguous practices. The provincialisms are exposed when different cultures and traditions are brought into conversation with each other. Through mutual questioning and exploration from a multiplicity of perspectives, a religion may find itself reduced to its core truths and stripped of its pretensions and petty accretions. Dialogue can function as a refining fire that burns away what is false, evil, and idolatrous. Through dialogue we see ourselves as others see us, and what they see of us is often what we are blind to ourselves. We do not truly know ourselves until we know ourselves through the eyes of others. This is surely one of the greatest benefits of interreligious dialogue.

The encounter of the religions also provides a way of drawing out and reinforcing the capacities for self-transcendence and truth that are present in the great religious traditions. The dialogue between Buddhism and Christianity has gone farthest in this regard, with Buddhism providing deepened insight into the Christian understanding of grace as a radical detachment or letting-go, and Christianity providing deepened insight into the Buddhist understanding of selfhood and freedom. Jews and Christians have much that they still need to learn from each other, as do Hindus and Buddhists, and Muslims and Westerners. So it is a matter not simply of exposing idolatries but also of drawing out convergent truths and practices. The convergence is likely to occur more along practical than theoretical lines, at least initially—a common quest for liberation, justice, peace, love.

We must be cautious at this point. Cobb reminds us that what we will encounter is not a common essence of religions but a diversity of truths and practices. Yet this diversity need not be contradictory; our task is to convert what is contradictory into what is different. These differences are, in Cobb's words, "diverse modes of apprehending diverse aspects of the totality of reality. They are true, and their truth can become more apparent and better formulated as they are positively related to one another."[19] Even if there is not a common essence, there is a totality of reality, which is apprehended in a diversity of ways, and each of these ways is more likely to be true in what it affirms than in what it denies. By focusing on the affirmations rather than the denials, we will discover how these diverse truths are positively related to each other, and similar insights into what is true might even emerge beneath surface differences. This is what I mean by drawing out convergent truths and practices. We should not assume that a unitary "world faith" will someday appear, but we may see a coalescing around some fundamental values, principles, and practices of benefit to all peoples—not something that exists in advance but only something that emerges, if at all, through a process of dialogue, encounter, debate, and conflict. This coalescing structure of religious truths and practices will emerge as something not fully present in any extant religion but as something to which each tradition will contribute the best that it has to offer and from which it will have much to learn. Such a structure would in all likelihood not be unitary but pluralistic, reflecting the fact that reality itself is plural, not monolithic. The center toward which the religions are converging, the divine center or liberative core, is concentric and multidimensional, not a simple point.

Such a convergent vision, even if always multidimensional and pluriform, will undoubtedly appear to be a utopian idea—but if some such vision does not begin to emerge, humanity may destroy itself through global conflict. If it should begin to appear, it would undoubtedly represent a kairos, a new disclosure of God's truth more powerful than anything we have known for centuries. Should we Christians fear it? Would it spell the end of the Christian faith and church as we know it? In my view, there is nothing to fear in this. The church "as we know it" is in any event only a veiled, fragmentary, ambiguous image of God's kingdom, the basileia vision of Jesus. What we call God's kingdom other religions call by other names. The names, finally, are unimportant. What is important is the transformative power of God's redemptive presence in the world. This presence will continue to take shape in a plurality of religious forms, of which the Christian will remain one of the most important. Insofar as there occurs a convergence of such forms, we should only rejoice, for it would be a sign of the coming of the basileia. In addition to convergent truths, there will undoubtedly also remain divergent truths, unresolved contradictions; and even though our hope is that they will not prevail, there is much to be learned from them as well.[20]

The God of Unity in Diversity: Toward a Refigured Trinity

Paul Knitter argues that the shift in attitude from exclusivism to inclusivism to pluralism can be viewed as a shift in Christian theology from ecclesiocentrism to christocentrism to theocentrism, and he describes the pluralist option as the "theocentric model"—many ways to the center, God.[21] God alone must be understood as the center of religion, displacing all finite human centers: Only on this basis can authentic dialogue take place among the religions, yet it must be acknowledged that God has many names, that God appears in a diversity of forms. This is not a new idea. Ernst Troeltsch observed more than seventy years ago that "in our earthly experience the Divine Life is not one, but many." The center itself is experienced not as singular but plural. Yet, Troeltsch added, "to apprehend the one in the many constitutes the special character of love."[22] Apprehending the one in the many seems to be the task of what Knitter calls a *unitive pluralism* of religions.[23]

There are problems with the term "theocentrism." First, not all religions are theistic (Buddhism being the most notable exception), hence theocentrism cannot provide a common meeting ground for all religions. At best we might claim that Christian self-understanding is more likely to be open to interreligious dialogue if it is theocentric rather than christocentric or ecclesiocentric, and that claims about Christ and the church need to be rethought on a theocentric basis. Second, the *theos* with which we are rightly concerned in Christian faith is not necessarily a centered, unitary, monistic reality; thus the "centric" aspect of theocentrism is problematic as well. Knitter is aware of this, but he does not explore alternative formulations since his primary concern is with a "theocentric christology."

Not only are the *ways* to God many, but also there is a sense in which the *one God* is many, multiform. Raimundo Panikkar explores this theme in a very suggestive manner.[24] The exploration starts by stressing that the ways to God are in fact many. Panikkar expresses this in a powerful metaphor: The rivers of the world that symbolize the religions—the Jordan, the Tiber, the Ganges—do not actually meet each other on earth or flow into each other; but they do meet, in the skies or "heaven," in the form of vapor or clouds, whence rain pours down upon all mortals and rivers. Likewise, "religions do not coalesce, certainly not as organized religions. They meet once transformed into vapor, once metamorphosized into Spirit, which then is poured down in innumerable tongues." Thus the religions of the world remain distinct, perhaps even to some degree incommensurable, but they do meet in and are metamorphosized by a transcendent and ultimately mysterious universal reality that can best be named "Spirit." Only this universal knows itself as universal; we know it only as incarnated in a multiplicity of concrete forms, each of which reflects the whole in quite discrete and nonsynthesizable ways.[25]

More than this, the universal or whole is itself plural or multiform. Panikkar expresses this as "a theanthropocosmic vision, a kind of trinitarian notion, not of the godhead alone, but of reality." The center is neither God alone, nor humanity alone, nor cosmos alone. Rather than having a single, absolute center, reality is concentric; and pluralism affirms that truth is neither one nor many but "advaitic," nondual yet plural.[26] There is neither a singular, monolithic truth nor a plurality of truths but rather a truth that is itself inherently pluralistic, reflecting the pluralism of universal reality.

This ontological pluralism is best described in trinitarian terms: "The mystery of the Trinity is the ultimate foundation for pluralism." Panikkar elaborates this in terms of the dialectic of Being (source), Logos (form), and Spirit (life). Being mirrors itself or becomes transparent to itself in Logos. But Being is not exhausted in its image: It retains its opaqueness and freedom in the Spirit. The intelligibility of Logos is restrained by the vitality of Spirit; the tension and difference between Logos and Spirit in Being remains unresolved (that is, no subordination of Spirit to Logos), and in that sense ultimate reality remains pluralistic, irreducible to a universal system. This view is "incompatible with the monotheistic assumption of a totally intelligible Being"; intelligibility is not shunned, but it stands in a tensive relationship with freedom and vitality in a pluralistic whole.[27]

These suggestive ideas are sketched very briefly by Panikkar, and a number of questions remain. For example, if a correlation is intended between Being-Logos-Spirit and *theos-anthropos-cosmos*, it is difficult to grasp precisely what it is. The correlation would be more successful if, instead of a theanthropocosmic vision, we thought in terms of a "theocosmic-pneumatic" vision, with *anthropos* (humanity) understood to belong to *cosmos*, and the whole of *cosmos* being understood as that moment of difference in which *theos* (God) mirrors and knows godself; then the third trinitarian moment would be that of spiritual mediation in which the freedom, mystery, and wholeness of God are consummated. This is in fact the model of the Trinity I shall propose in chapter 11. The three moments of the divine life are God (Being), World (Logos), and Spirit; or the divine wholeness, the divine love, and the divine freedom.

It is noteworthy that others who have thought about God in relation to the challenge of religious pluralism have been drawn to a trinitarian model. For example, Aloysius Pieris postulates a trinitarian mystery of salvation: the source of salvation (*theos*), the medium of salvation (*logos*), and the force of salvation (*pneuma*). He believes that this tridimensional mystery and process of salvation is found in most of the major religions although for Buddhism the first dimension is not a source but a goal, nirvana, and there is no *theos* in the strict sense. But the pluralism of the soteriological process, and by implication of ultimate reality, is widely confirmed by the religions, even when explicit trinitarian formulations are lacking.[28]

This pluralism remains, however, a "unitive pluralism" in Knitter's term. The question about God that arises from the challenge of religious pluralism and from the postmodern project of dialogue, which seeks a kind of communicative engagement in the midst of diversity and difference, is whether God is in some sense *one* and *whole.* It would be easy enough to conclude from the fact of pluralism that there are simply many diverse and irreconcilable images of God, or that truth is totally relative to context, or that ultimate reality itself is an inexhaustible multiplicity of conflicting forces. But there is something deeply unsatisfying about such a conclusion. The fundamental quest of dialogue is precisely for communication, enlargement of horizons, newly configured wholeness in the midst of irreducible difference and recalcitrant diversity. A quest for human unity is present in all the great religions, and interreligious dialogue allows these culturally determinate quests to begin to fructify and modify each other. Paradoxically, perhaps, out of pluralism emerges the eros for unity. But the unity cannot be a simple, undialectical, static, empty oneness, a null-point. Rather it is a unity constituted out of a pregnant, seething diversity, and it continually takes shape in novel, protean forms. To name this dynamic of unity-in-diversity, I am proposing the term "wholeness." God is the whole but an open, dynamic, relational whole, not a closed totality.

For the Christian tradition, the doctrine of the Trinity has attempted to express this truth about God. Whether trinitarian or tridimensional patterns are present elsewhere is not of crucial importance; other religions may have their own quite different ways of articulating a similar insight. For Christians to think about God in the context of religious pluralism, it makes sense to utilize the resources already present in our tradition rather than to invent totally new concepts. But for trinitarian dogma to be utilized in this context, it must be revisioned or refigured in a fairly radical way. My own refiguration identifies the moments of God, World, and Spirit; or of identity, difference, mediation; or of oneness (wholeness), love, and freedom. The traditional trinitarian figures of Father, Son, and Spirit are not sacrosanct. In this respect I disagree with those postliberal theologians who are attempting to use a patriarchal and/or christocentric trinitarianism as the basis of an inclusivist theology of religions. For them the orthodox doctrine and categories set the parameters within which plurality can be legitimately discussed, and no enlargement of trinitarian vision is achieved.[29] By contrast, other theologians are attempting to retrieve a more radical Christian tradition in response to the dialogical challenge.[30] Process theology points in another direction, which is not so much trinitarian as binitarian since it identifies the primordial (Logos) and consequent (Spirit) natures of God but seems to have no place for the oneness or wholeness or being of God, perhaps because of its intent to distinguish God as "ultimate actuality" from "ultimate reality" (dynamic emptiness, creativity, being-as-nothingness).[31] I believe the more fruitful approach is to hold these three aspects together within the concept of God.

The Interplay of the Quests and the Revisioning of Theology

We come to the conclusion of Part 2. An attempt has been made to identify three quests characteristic of the postmodern temper: the emancipatory, the ecological, and the dialogical. The first articulates the heightened awareness of suffering and oppression out of which are being generated historical struggles for the liberation of human beings from classism, ethnocentrism, racism, sexism, homophobia, and other destructive practices. The second articulates the sense of the interrelatedness of life and the quest for a harmonious dwelling of the human in the whole of the natural world. The third articulates the cultural and religious diversity of human experience and the quest for a dialogical wholeness that challenges all epistemological provincialisms. The first is oriented to practices, the second to relations, the third to knowledge.

It should be evident that these quests do not exist in isolated compartments. Rather they are mutually reinforcing. They participate in each other and are incomplete without each other. The emancipatory struggles in history must not be cut off from ecological sensitivity to nature or from dialogical openness to a plurality of soteriological projects. "Liberation" is a term that applies to all of the quests: We have found references to "the liberation of life" and "a liberation theology of religions." Similarly the ecological awareness of the unity and interrelatedness of nature must be especially sensitive to the ecology of the human in a world of tragic conflicts, and its relational understanding of reality not only recognizes the pluralism of human experience but also promotes the dialogical method. Finally, the fact of religious pluralism requires sensitivity to a multiplicity of emancipatory struggles, and it generates a quest for wholeness similar to that found in the new science and "the dream of the earth."

Postmodernity presents a complex picture that has numerous interacting aspects and that cannot be simply named. What is interesting is that a certain coherence seems to emerge from the analysis. Perhaps on the brink of the twenty-first century humanity finds itself moving toward a common though elusive goal, which has something to do with the fundamental survival and flourishing of life on this planet. We know that if we do not move toward this goal—along sociopolitical, multicultural, and environmental paths—we will destroy ourselves and much else.

This quest beneath the quests has a religious significance. It is in some way a quest for God, for the power that creates and sustains life and enables it to flourish. I have attempted to identify certain theological motifs in relation to the quests, namely the freedom, love, and unity (or wholeness) of God. These motifs also interact. All three are present in each of the quests; none can be named without the other two. The wholeness of God is constituted precisely by the interplay of love and freedom in the life of God; the love of God is nothing if not a liberating love; and the freedom of God is precisely what cherishes differences, favors those who suffer, and integrates the whole in a more comprehensive unity. God is the One who loves in freedom. I wish to stress that these theological motifs are not simply "answers" given by revelation or the tradition to existential and cultural "questions." Rather the motifs emerge from within the quests themselves. There is a sense in which the questions already contain the answers, the quests contain the treasure. It needs only to be discovered as already there.

To discover it does involve making explicit a correspondence between the three quests and the trinitarian structure of a revisioned theology. The triune figuration is at work in the matrices of postmodern culture. To name it as such involves a certain kind of "theology of correlation." This is not a correlation based on anthropological or epistemological structures; rather it is based on the way the cultural context presents itself to a theological reflection rooted in the tradition. It is a correlation of context and content rather than of humanity and divinity or of natural knowledge and revealed knowledge. To see the triune figuration at work in the matrices of postmodern culture, we must have some idea of what that figuration is. Conversely, our idea of what it is will be profoundly enriched, modified, and confirmed by the correlation. Without the correlation the Trinity would be a theologoumenon, a theological abstraction; but without a theological preunderstanding, the cultural situation would remain religiously ambiguous. Here is further evidence of the circle (or spiral) of understanding.

What is involved is a correlation, a pairing of relations, not an identity. It would be false to identify the emancipatory quest solely with the emancipatory freedom of God (or "Spirit"), the ecological quest with the differentiating love of God (or "World"), and the dialogical quest with the unity-in-diversity of God (or "God"). Each quest is seeking and finding the whole of God in different ways. What is important is not the precise correlations but rather that these three moments in the triune life of God seem to find confirmation in the various dimensions of our cultural quest—and not just ours. Perhaps the reality of God has always been connected in some fashion with a threefold human search: for wholeness (some would say wisdom or knowledge), for love (some would say life), and for freedom (some would say liberation). God engenders the search, corresponds to the search, *is* the search, fulfills the search.

If the Trinity is the truth about God, then this truth manifests itself in different ways in other cultural contexts, historical and geographical. The triune figuration was at work in the matrices of ancient, medieval, and modern Christian cultures as well, and perhaps it is at work in the other great religio-cultural trajectories. I believe this to be true, but the attempt to comprehend our own time and place is more than enough to occupy us.

Part 3
REVISIONING

God: The One
World: Love
Spirit: Freedom

God: The One

9

FAITH, REASON, AND REVELATION

Three themes are to be addressed in the first unit of "Revisioning": the *knowledge* of God, the *being* of God, and the *activity* of God. The knowledge of God arises out of the interplay of faith, reason, and revelation (chap. 9); the being of God is oriented to the primary motif of divine creativity (chap. 10); and the activity of God assumes the form of a triune figuration (chap. 11). These distinctions between knowledge, being, and activity are, of course, abstractions. The knowledge of God is grounded in what God *is* as an intrinsically revelatory, creative being; the being of God is not a static sameness but a dynamic act of self-distinguishing and self-relating; and the triune figuration of God is not a separate activity but simply the explication of the being of God. Thus the knowledge of God implies the being of God, and the being of God implies the act of God; and vice versa. We encounter the indivisibly one and whole God no matter where we start or finish our analytic distinctions.

The primary concern in the first unit is with what might be described as the *divinity* of God. But there can be no discussion of the knowledge, being, and act of God apart from the *world-relatedness* of God, which is the primary concern of the second unit. So this distinction too, between God's divinity and world-relatedness, is posited only to be overcome. Yet another distinction is found between the abstract divinity or *oneness* of God (first unit) and the concrete, mediated divinity or *wholeness* of God (third unit). But the wholeness is already implicit in the oneness, and the symbol "the One" can be used to name both the first moment of the divine life and the whole triune figuration of God. We must posit distinctions and think through them because we cannot think the whole all at once—a whole that is incredibly rich and multidimensional.

Faith: A Distinctive Form of Knowing

The knowledge of God is already a part of the doctrine of God; it is not simply an anthropological prologue. The "I" who "believes," "we" human beings who "believe" (the opening *credo/credimus* of the ancient creeds), cannot be properly discussed *theologically* apart from our relationship to God, in terms of which we are known as finite, fallen, redeemed creatures, made in the image of God, as well as free and responsible subjects. Yet how can we humans know anything at all about God apart from the cognitive act by which God is known, namely faith? The hermeneutical circle in theology is no more apparent than at the beginning. We cannot start with God alone, or with humanity alone, but only with God and humanity together in some sort of correlation. This correlation is what is meant by "faith."[1]

Faith is a cognitive act but of a distinctive sort. *It is a kind of thinking, knowing, or reasoning that is founded on and oriented to a revelatory experience that grasps and shapes it.* Two things need to be stressed about this definition. The first is that faith *is* a kind of thinking, knowing, or reasoning. It is not an antirational activity but precisely a form of knowledge, a form of practical reason. I have distinguished between two ways of reasoning or thinking, both of which are essential to the work of theology: critical-interpretative thinking and practical-appropriative thinking (chap. 1, pp. 10–16). The first of these involves a critical, questioning movement from interpreters through textual media to the root or revelatory experiences at the heart of Christian faith. In the second, a reversal in the flow of meaning occurs, so that now the root experiences disclose themselves on their own terms and by their own power, through their own basic symbols, rather than simply having a constructed meaning imposed upon them by our critical theories. In this second way of thinking, we are appropriated *by* the disclosure, are caught up in it; yet at the same time, we appropriate *it,* make it our own in a participatory, practical knowing called "faith." "Faith" is another name for this second movement in the dialectic of theological thinking—a movement that generally precedes the critical-theoretical movement in an existential sense. A quest for understanding is already implicit in this faith: *Fides quaerens intellectum,* Anselm called it. Theology is the explicit development of the quest for understanding implicit to faith, of the reasoning that permeates faith.

Another way to specify the distinctive sort of cognitivity characteristic of faith is to follow the lead of H. Richard Niebuhr in his posthumously published lectures on faith.[2] According to Niebuhr, if "knowledge" in the strict sense is a direct and immediate apprehension of truth, "belief" is an indirect relation to truth mediated by a person or community we trust. Belief is holding something to be true on the ground of trust in another. Belief in this sense "constitutes by far the major part of our intellectual furniture and of the basis of our daily actions." Our understanding of nature is largely a matter of belief, dependent on the authority of the community of scientists and physicians. Our understanding of history involves believing statements about events to which we have little direct relationship. Historical inquiry is largely a matter of discovering how trustworthy our various mediators of knowledge are. This sort of trusting knowledge is intrinsically social in character. Knowing begins with such social believing and is constantly accompanied by it. Just as there is a believing present in all our knowing, so there is a knowing in all our believing—an acknowledging of the person, group, or authority that we trust and a recognizing of what it is they bear witness to.

Faith in God is not an immediate knowledge of God but a knowledge mediated by trustworthy persons, texts, testimonies, communities. What renders these mediators trustworthy? Ultimately it is the trustworthiness of the truth to which they witness. What elicits trust is trustworthiness. Perhaps then we can say that revelation is the self-manifestation of the trustworthiness of ultimate reality—of its being, truth, value.

This brings us to the other matter to be stressed. Faith is a kind of knowing founded on and oriented to a revelatory experience that grasps and shapes it. It is a knowing that finds itself at the disposal of what is known; it encounters a disclosure that it cannot manipulate or control but that it can trust. The "I" is cognitively active, but what it knows is a "gratuity" that shapes, empowers, and defines *it* rather than vice versa. This experience of encountering something ultimate in being, truth, and value *that discloses itself in and through our very act of knowing and trusting it* lies at the heart of all authentic religious experience. Thus faith is a theme not only for theological anthropology but also for the doctrine of God. It is a moment in the triune figuration of God, that moment in which God knows, reveals, and is related to *godself* in and through faith's knowledge *of* God.[3]

Faith, then, mediates between and engages both (human) reason and (divine) revelation. The central problem in understanding faith is that of determining just how reason and revelation interact. It will be helpful to look at this problem first as it unfolds in the history of the doctrine of revelation.

Revelation: Classical Models and Enlightenment Critiques

Two models for understanding revelation are found in classical theology, the *illuminationist* and the *encounter* models.[4] The first, which is characteristically Catholic in substance, understands revelation as illumination of the intellect (see Augustine, Aquinas). The human intellect is capable of grasping God, but it is weak (finite) and darkened by sin. What occurs is a kind of empowerment or enlightenment of the intellect by a supernatural light, the divine light. What results is a kind of synthesis or integration of human reason and divine truth.

The second model, which is the characteristically Protestant form, assumes for one reason or another the breakdown of this synthesis (see Luther, Calvin). Revelation is not so much the empowerment or enlightenment of a human potentiality as it is an encounter with something that radically transcends the human, the word and will of God incarnate in Christ and written in scripture. To be sure, this objectively mediated word must somehow make contact with our intellect and conviction, so Protestantism adds the idea of an inward testimony of the Holy Spirit—a testimony that for many Protestants affects the emotions and feelings more than it does the intellect.

Despite their differences, the two models have some important similarities. Both describe the content of revelation as truths about God given directly *by* God. Both reflect a common metaphysical view of God as standing outside the created order and being only externally related to it (God as an extraworldly supreme being). Yet for both, statements about God seem to have a cognitive status similar to statements about empirical realities (although the classical theologians knew very well that God is not an empirical object).[5]

It was precisely these common assumptions of the classical model that were called into question by the Enlightenment and that remain problematic for us today. In the critiques of "revealed religion" that appeared in the eighteenth century, reason and revelation were pitted against each other, and reason (or "natural religion") was given the primacy. All that is beneficial for human happiness can be known rationally, and Christianity as essentially a "reasonable" religion should be freed of its supernatural dogmas. Revelation, said the deists and rationalists, is superfluous, indeed harmful.

The alternatives facing post-Enlightenment theology were whether it might really be possible to do without revelation in religion, or whether there might be a substitute for it, or whether it might be possible to retrieve something like revelation. Basically three strategies evolved: (1) a turn to moral experience, (2) a turn to religious feeling, (3) a postcritical retrieval of the category of revelation and cognitive knowledge of God.

Over against the optimism of the Enlightenment, *Kant* stressed the limitations of reason and argued that in theoretical terms we can know nothing of God. He proposed rather a turn to practical or moral reason as the basis for an understanding of "religion within the limits of reason alone." But with the Enlightenment, he rejected any notion of revelation.[6]

Schleiermacher, by contrast, reinterpreted revelation in terms of religious feeling, arguing that what we mean by "revelation" is not the apprehension of propositions about God but rather the "originality of the fact" at the foundation of religious communities and religious piety, an originality that involves a kind of divine causality. "Feeling" is a distinctive mode of apprehension that is presupposed by both knowing and doing, namely a prereflective awareness of the whole of reality (the universe or world) and especially of that upon which we are utterly dependent—God or the infinite. By locating religion in the realm of feeling, Schleiermacher avoided not only the categories but also the problematic of reason and revelation.[7]

Hegel attempted to overcome the Enlightenment dichotomy between reason and revelation by arguing that Christianity is both the "revelatory" and the "revealed" religion. On the one hand, it is precisely reason and truth that are made open and manifest in this religion. God is what is rational, ultimately rational, rational mystery, but it is the characteristic of this God to be open, manifest, revelatory (*offenbar*), not hidden, withdrawn, locked up within godself. What is ultimately rational is intrinsically revelatory. But on the other hand, this truth is mediated or made available through empirical historical events, above all for Christians through the event of Christ. Everything that is true *for* consciousness must also be *objective to* consciousness, must come to us from the outside because of our finitude and sinful blindness. What is *revealed (geoffenbart)* by and through Christianity in historical, "positive" fashion is precisely the *revelatoriness (Offenbarkeit)*, the openness, the manifestness, the rationality of God. Thus in his own way Hegel was attempting to rebuild the Augustinian-Thomistic synthesis of reason and revelation. But he avoided the classical metaphysical assumption that God is a supernatural being externally related to the world. What is revealed according to Hegel is not "truths about God" but the truth, the rational openness, that *is* God. God is not the object of revelation but the subject, the *event* of revelation; and this event takes on a complex historical configuration of which Christ is the center but in which we too share as participants in the community of faith.[8]

Most of the contemporary theological efforts to rehabilitate the idea of revelation are indebted to Kant, Schleiermacher, or Hegel in one way or another. Rather than discuss these, I am going to explore the possibility of a correlation of reason and revelation that stands in continuity with the older illuminationist model of Augustine and Aquinas, that is indebted to Hegel and especially to Tillich, and that attends to some of the issues raised in recent communications theory.

Reason and the Quest for Revelation

A relationship to something like revelation is not unique to religious knowledge. Tillich argues that all nontechnical, noninstrumental rationality points to and participates in a reality that transcends it and yet has itself a logos-character or a rational structure—a structure that in some sense manifests or discloses itself to the knowing mind. In all genuine knowledge or cognition there is an element of *ac*-knowledgment, of *re*-cognition. We find ourselves related to something we did not invent but in which we participate. Yet we also find ourselves separated from it; it is *other* than we, and we cannot fully grasp or comprehend it no matter how rigorously we think. There is distance as well as union between mind and reality, knower and known. In a phrase reminiscent of Hegel, Tillich describes knowledge as "the unity of distance and union."

> Knowing is a form of union. In every act of knowledge the knower and that which is known are united; the gap between subject and object is overcome. . . . But the union of knowledge is a peculiar one; it is a union through separation. Detachment is the condition of cognitive union. In order to know, one must "look" at a thing, and, in order to look at a thing, one must be "at a distance." Cognitive distance is the presupposition of cognitive union.[9]

Recent deconstructive philosophy has stressed the aspect of distance much more sharply than Tillich and Hegel did, perhaps to the point where union is no longer possible. If so, this is a loss of the dialectical insight that union in fact occurs in knowledge although always only fragmentarily and ambiguously.

Because of the distance that is present in every act of cognitive union, reason remains unfulfilled and unstable. It seeks for something that can fulfill and secure it; or, expressed in religious terms, something that can "redeem" or "heal" it. Redeem it from what? Tillich suggests that there are three basic conditions of reason: It is finite; it experiences conflicts among its structural elements; and it falls into the ambiguities characteristic of all life. These conditions generate a "quest for revelation," that is, for a self-manifestation of the rational mystery that is the goal of all knowing. Intrinsic to the very structure of reason is an incompleteness and an openness to what theology calls revelation.[10]

These quests can be described in terms somewhat different than those Tillich himself used. I shall describe them as: (1) The fragmentariness of reason and the quest for wholeness. (2) The ambiguities of reason and the quest for truth. (3) The systematic distortions of reason and the quest for authentic communication.

The Fragmentariness of Reason and the Quest for Wholeness

The fragmentariness of reason is an aspect of its finitude. We know only by means of categories drawn from finite experience (time, space, causality, substance, etc.), yet in every act of knowledge there is a quest for wholeness.[11] I say "wholeness" rather than "infinitude" or "totality" since the quest for infinitude can readily fall into illusion ("transcendental illusion," Kant called it) and the quest for totality can suppress the otherness of the other,[12] but the quest for wholeness seems to me an authentic quest. There can be such a thing as "open wholeness," an openness to the whole that can never be grasped and comprehended, only anticipated or prefigured. The perfection of a single work of art is an instance of "open wholeness." So also is the perfection of a work of love. Such works cannot be improved upon; within their own parameters they have a kind of wholeness, a wholeness that does not enframe but models. When such wholeness occurs, we experience something like revelation. The quest for wholeness is a quest for the ultimate wholeness or oneness or unity-in-diversity that is God—a unity that is intrinsically open, encompassing all that is precisely in its diversity, not reducing it to a dead identity.[13]

The Ambiguities of Reason and the Quest for Truth

The ambiguities of reason are another aspect of its finitude. All of life is ambiguous. Everything we do or think has negative as well as positive implications. When one thing or course of action is chosen, another thing or action is excluded. Every affirmation entails a negation. Choosing one life partner excludes others with whom an equally good, or worse, or better relationship might have been possible; or choosing not to have a life partner excludes a certain kind of intimacy from one's life although it may open up other kinds of relationships. We say that there are trade-offs in such choices, and that is a fair way of putting it. These choices often have a fateful quality, shaping our lives in fundamental ways, while at the same time we know that things might have been different. Such ambiguities drive us to a quest for truth, but in this quest, as Tillich points out, we encounter another ambiguity, that of certainty versus ultimacy. The only things we can really be certain about are not of ultimate concern, while the ultimate always eludes certainty. Recognition of this ambiguity can lead reason either to a resignation of truth or to the quest for revelation, a revelation that gives a truth that is both certain and of ultimate concern.[14] This truth is the truth of God, but whether such a revelation actually occurs is another question. Its occurrence is a matter not of logical but of existential certainty. There must be a sense of "rightness" for me personally and for us as a community, and this is where the confession of faith—the *credo* and the *credimus*—plays an essential role.

The Systematic Distortions of Reason and the Quest for Authentic Communication

Tillich refers to the "existential conflicts" of reason.[15] I propose to supplement his existentialist analysis by one informed by recent philosophies of action, communication, and sociality (Habermas, Bernstein, Peukert, among others[16]). The purpose or telos of human rationality is to communicate, to speak the truth, to reach mutual understanding, to engage in an unconstrained, undistorted dialogue, in solidarity and respect, and by the use of arguments that are persuasive rather than coercive, clarifying rather than deceptive. This telos represents a utopian possibility in human affairs since much if not most of the time our communication is broken, distorted, calculated to deceive, to coerce, to advance our own interests at the expense of others. Knowledge is a matter of power: Whoever controls knowledge controls power, and vice versa.[17] The question then is what (if anything) enables reason, in the state of systematically distorted communication, to achieve such a telos even partially. Theologically the claim is that it is divine revelation that empowers authentic communication, that the latter is not simply a human potentiality that can be tapped therapeutically or accomplished politically. Reason needs to be *redeemed,* set free from its distortions and power conflicts, released from enervating ambiguities, stirred by a vision of the whole.

Tillich rightly points out that a description such as this of the fragmentariness, ambiguities, and distortions of reason should replace the popular religious attacks on the weakness or blindness of reason.[18] The enemy is not reason as such but the distortions of reason. Evil is not sheer irrationality or chaos but reason put to destructive ends. Just because reason is the highest human achievement, when it falls into self-deceiving illusion, estranging conflicts, and enervating ambiguities, it can become the most powerful and malicious instrument of evil imaginable. Reason run amok, put to violent, distorted, and deceptive uses, is what gives evil its terrible power. The rationality of the death camp operations was impeccable, as is that of nuclear war-games. The only weapon powerful enough to fight reason is reason itself. Rather than being viewed as antirational, revelation needs to be understood as what empowers reason to fight its own distortions and as what enlists reason, in the form of "communicative rationality," to be an instrument of emancipatory praxis. Revelation does not destroy or replace reason but redeems it. When this occurs, reason becomes "faithful."

The Reality of Revelation

The Meaning of Revelation

The Concept of "Revelation"

Our word "revelation" derives from the Latin *revelatum*, which means to remove or take back (*re*) a veil (*velum*). The Greek word *apokalypsis* has a similar root meaning, to remove or take back (*apo*) a covering (*kalumma*). The last book of the New Testament canon is known as the Apocalypse or Revelation of John. It is a "revelation" in the sense of removing the seals or covers from the scroll that contains the secrets of the living God (Revelation 5—7). Hence "revelation" in its root sense means an "unveiling," an "unconcealment," a "disclosure of what is hidden." It is not without significance that the Greek word for "truth," *alētheia*, has a very similar derivation, meaning to "unconceal" or "unforget" (*a-lēthos*). The Johannine literature closely associates the concepts of revelation and truth (which is the highest rationality). Precisely as the revealer, Jesus is the way, the truth, and the life (John 14:6). This truth, brought by the revealing word, has a liberating effect: "If you continue in my word, you are truly my disciples; and you will know the truth, and the truth will make you free" (John 8:31–32). For the fourth Gospel, freedom means above all a liberation from false knowledge, from the deception that is sin; the devil is "the father of lies" (8:44). This linkage of revelation and freedom, via truth (reason), is significant for our analysis. Revelation is a form of liberation; liberation is a revelation.

Following these etymological hints, let us define revelation as an event or manifestation that removes the veil from something that is hidden but without destroying its hiddenness and mystery.[19] If we are talking about *divine* revelation, then the "something that is hidden" is the object of ultimate concern, God. For this reason, the last clause of the definition—"without destroying its hiddenness and mystery"—is essential. For the object of ultimate concern (being-itself, God, the sacred or holy) retains its ultimacy only insofar as it remains hidden and mysterious. Thus "divine revelation" has a paradoxical character: It entails a veiling as well as an unveiling, a concealing as well as an unconcealing. Luther and Barth referred to this as the *terminus a quo* and *ad quem*, the beginning and the end, of God's revelation: *Deus absconditus et revelatus*, God hidden and revealed.[20]

What is "mysterious" is not irrational or inscrutable or absurd. "Mystery," rather, for the ancient Greeks described the attitude that should be assumed when one is being initiated into a cult (*mystērion*, a secret rite); namely, one should keep one's eyes and mouth closed (*myein*). One is "mute" in the presence of mystery. The reason is that an extraordinary sort of knowledge is being conveyed by the cultic ritual and oracles, the sort that cannot be seen or talked about but that requires a very intense sort of listening. A mystery contains a higher rationality, a higher truth, which cannot be described in ordinary subject-object terms and can be referred to only indirectly. For the Neoplatonists, after the time of the mystery cults, *mystērion* came to mean "speculative philosophy," which deals with such higher truths; the same is true of the "mystical theology" of the Neoplatonic theologians.[21] It is evident, then, that silence before God does not demand perpetual silence; rather it empowers us to speak by opening up the possibility of a new kind of discourse.

A mystery does not cease to be a mystery when it is revealed. Rather, what is revealed is precisely its mysteriousness, its inexhaustible, inconceivable, impenetrable rationality. It drives ordinary reason beyond itself to its ground and abyss, to that which precedes reason, to the original fact that there is something and not nothing. This, says Tillich, is the negative side of mystery. Its positive side is that it becomes manifest in actual revelation. Here the mystery appears as ground or logos and not only as abyss. It appears as the power of being, conquering nonbeing. The manifestation of the ground of being does not destroy the structure of finite being and reason. It causes this structure to transcend itself or point beyond itself.[22] God is a mystery but a rational mystery.

Revelation as Event of Worldly Unconcealment

Because the hiddenness and mystery of God cannot be abolished (without destroying God's divinity), it would be a mistake to think of revelation as laying bare the divine essence, perhaps in the form of truths or propositions that tell us what God is. Unfortunately, most of us tend to think of revelation this way. It is difficult to escape the notion of revelation as the transmission of information about divine things in supernatural form by God.[23] But revelation is not a body of truths from another world. It is an event of unconcealment—of opening, healing, communication, liberation—in this world, in the process of which God is disclosed indirectly. The "unveiling" that occurs in re-velation refers directly to the world and only indirectly to God. God is not the object of disclosure, at least in a direct sense; rather God makes godself known or communicates godself in and through the event by which the *world* is unconcealed (opened, healed, emancipated) as the One who speaks (and therefore *is*) the primordial word that opens beings, redeems reason, liberates persons and structures.

God is revealed as liberating power by the way in which God's word works in the world. The wind that blows, the light that lightens, the word that opens, remain the *means* of revelation rather than becoming its object. We cannot see the divine wind, look into the divine light, or speak the divine word; we must close our eyes and shut our mouths. To see God we must look at the world and what is going on in it; to speak about God we must engage in worldly words and deeds. We do not see wind but rather what it moves; we do not listen to breath but to the words it forms; we do not look *at* light but see *by* it. If we attempt to fix our gaze upon the burning/glowing source of light, we will be blinded; light itself we see only as reflected by illumined objects. The association of God, God's Spirit, with wind, breath, and light in the Hebrew Bible is of great significance. These are fluid, intangible media of divine power and presence.[24]

The indirectness of God's self-disclosure can perhaps be illustrated from our own experience of personal relationships. Persons are accessible to each other only if they disclose themselves. There is an irreducible transcendence of each person: My freedom, identity, and body are not at another's disposal without my personal integrity being violated. Even in the face-to-face encounter, the other remains other; indeed precisely the face is the sign of the inviolateness and otherness of the other.[25] We must *open* ourselves to each other, but we do so *not* by a direct, objective account of who and what we are, but rather by the style and configuration of our actions in the world, which must be "read" or deciphered by others. This is true because we have access to ourselves only by means of our relationships with others in the world; we do not have direct, unmediated knowledge about ourselves to be dispensed at will. This is not to say that immediacy is lacking in human experience; rather it is a *mediated* immediacy. We find ourselves only insofar as we find ourselves in others, and others find us disclosed in the shapes of our worldly relationships.

The indirectness of personal relationships is doubly appropriate when we speak of God's self-revelation. For God clearly is not one whom we meet face to face and speak to as another human being; the immediacy that is possible in human relationships is not possible here. We may meet God *in* the face of another human being, but this is still a mediated encounter. We may speak to God directly, but we do not *see* God, and our speaking is mediated by human language. God tells Moses, "You cannot see my face; for no one shall see me and live." But God continues: "While my glory passes by I will put you in a cleft of the rock, and I will cover you with my hand until I have passed by; then I will take away my hand, and you shall see my back; but my face shall not be seen" (Ex. 33:20, 22–23). This means that we cannot gaze directly into the divine glory, but we *can* see God's "back," that is, God's embodiment in a multitude of worldly shapes.[26] Thus God's revelation is doubly mediated: first, by the worldly word and deed that characterize personal disclosure in general; second, by the fact that we cannot point to a direct divine word and deed but only to the words and deeds of human beings distinct from God, as well as to the sounds and sights of the natural world. It is the whole world, natural as well as human, that is God's "back" or "body," and that discloses God's glory even as it shelters us from it. The indirectness of God's self-disclosure means that knowledge of God always occurs, as Niebuhr points out, in the trusting mode of faith.

Revelation, then, directly refers to (discloses) the world, not God. It is an event of worldly unconcealment by which new meaning and new possibilities of being are created. I propose to understand the new meaning in terms of a redemption of *reason*, and the new possibilities of being in terms of a new birth of *freedom*.

The Redemption of Reason: Communicative Rationality

The expression "communicative rationality" is suggested by the work of the philosopher and sociologist Jürgen Habermas and his followers (notably Richard Bernstein).[27] I cannot go into Habermas's complex theories here. Rather I am appropriating his basic insight and applying it to the analysis I have sketched of the quest for revelation intrinsic in the fragmentariness, the ambiguities, and the distortions of reason. What we are looking for is a rationality that approaches a kind of open wholeness without denying the fragmentary and limited character of all human knowing; that experiences a degree of certainty with respect to the truth about matters of ultimate concern, thus enabling us to endure the ambiguities inherent in every cognitive and practical act; and that achieves a level of dialogue in which communication actually occurs despite the distortions that pervade all our social contacts. When this actually happens in our human speech and thought, we experience a redemption of reason (not a redemption from reason but of and within reason itself).

Perhaps "communicative rationality" can be taken as a cipher for reason under the condition of redemption. Communicative rationality at its highest involves a discursive or dialogical rationality in which literally everything is open to question, in which reasons must be given for every claim, in which consent is sought only through agreement rather than by the imposition of authority. Such communication levels all hierarchies, dissolves all privileges, transcends all provincialisms, overcomes all distortions and concealments. What we are describing is a religious condition, and a utopian one at that, for which the word "salvation" or "redemption" is appropriate. Expressed in a Pauline metaphor, such communication is the "wisdom of God," which destroys all human "boasting" (1 Cor. 1:18–31). What is involved here is not the work of humanity but the work of God—it is the Wisdom of God, God's Sophia. But notice what happens: a transformation of human reason, not its cancellation. We experience an epiphany of Sophia—God's Wisdom—in the redemption of worldly wisdom. One possibility for understanding the redemptive significance of the figure of Jesus is as the incarnation of divine Sophia. We shall explore that.

Revelation as Liberation:
Communicative Freedom

The telos of communicative rationality is free and liberated human community, based on unrestrained dialogue, mutuality, solidarity, and equality. For this utopian ideal I propose the term "communicative freedom," which is a revisioning of the image of the kingdom of God as a "realm of freedom." This too is the work of revelation. The wisdom of God is a cognitive image, the kingdom of God a practical one.

Recall the linkage of revelation and liberation in the Gospel of John. It is no accident that in this Gospel the revealer gives no information about God. Rather what we are continually referred to are the words and deeds of Jesus the revealer—words and deeds by which he discloses the truth, brings light into darkness, heals the diseased, sets human beings free from the bondage of sin, manifests the glory of the Father, overcomes the old world and creates a new world. Thus "revelation" focuses our attention on human speech and action in the world, not on God per se. The same is true of the Synoptic Gospels, where direct talk about God is quite rare. Jesus speaks about God parabolically, which is an indirect mode of discourse; and the subject of the parables is typically the *kingdom* or "project" of God, not God directly. The kingdom of God is about what God does in the world, and what God does is to shape a new way of being communally human in the world in which old relations, values, and consequences are set aside and a radically new logic prevails—the logic of grace, freedom, unrequited love. God is revealed indirectly through the "coming," the "drawing near," of God's project.[28]

Such indirection is essential to any talk about God. I do not mean to suggest that as a consequence nothing is known of God; rather all that needs to be known is known. What God is, is reflected in the worldly transformations brought about by God's revelatory, transformative, illuminating power. We see God reflected in the world. On the basis of this reflection, we can indeed make statements about God, not just about our relations to God, but these statements are our own, the products of our trusting faith and bold imagination, not direct revelations of God. What reflects God in the world are precisely the redeemed rationality and communicative freedom we have been talking about. Thus we can say that God simply *is* the perfection of communicative freedom, the One who loves in freedom. God *is* the light that illumines, the word that discloses, the reason that communicates, the love that cherishes, the freedom that liberates, the revelatoriness that reveals, the being by which beings are. God *is* the event of worldly unconcealment by which new meaning and new possibilities of being are created. As such God is radically immanent in the world but also radically transcendent. God is neither an entity in the world nor an entity outside it but the revelatory-communicative-emancipatory event-process-power by which the world is. "God" is a verb more than a noun—a verbal noun, not a substantive noun.

The Occurrence of Revelation

How does revelation, thus understood, happen? How is it to be understood as an occurrence in and for the world but not of and from the world? How is God to be understood to "act" in the world in a way that is both revelatory and redemptive? This is one of the most difficult questions facing a revisionist theology. I propose to distinguish between a focus, a ground, and a process, or God as revealed, revelatory, and revealing.

Christological Focus (God as Revealed)

First, it is clear that for Christians the focus is Jesus as the Christ. It is appropriate that there should be such a focus. By "revelation in history," writes H. Richard Niebuhr, we mean "that special occasion which provides us with an image by means of which all the occasions of personal and common life become intelligible." The revelatory moment or center not only shines by its own light but "illuminates other events and enables us to understand them." Revelation means "an event in our history which brings rationality and wholeness into the confused joys and sorrows of personal existence and allows us to discern order in the brawl of communal histories." Through it "a pattern of dramatic unity becomes apparent."[29]

Not the whole of history is revelatory; most of it is confused, chaotic, ambiguous. But we do experience luminous centers, focal events from the perspective of which not necessarily everything but at least much else is cast into the light or takes on a meaningful pattern. "Sometimes," says Niebuhr, "when we read a difficult book, seeking to follow a complicated argument, we come across a luminous sentence from which we can go forward and backward and so attain some understanding of the whole."[30] For Christians, Jesus Christ is such a luminous sentence in the book of history. From him we can go forward and backward. As revelatory moment, he enables us to "understand what we remember, remember what we have forgotten, and appropriate as our own past much that seemed alien to us."[31] He also enables us to go forward, to live toward the future, with a sense of what our historical responsibility is and a clue to the purpose of history. Just why and in what sense Jesus Christ should be the central revelatory moment for Christians—the person-event in whom God was definitively revealed—remains to be seen. The Christ is not the *only* revelatory moment, but for us he is the one who illumines and activates the others.

The christological focus is in some sense unique and definitive for Christians, but need it be understood as exclusive and final? The question of the "finality" of Christ has become more pressing in the context of religious pluralism. A revelation is final, says Tillich, if it has the power of negating itself without losing itself. Every revelation is conditioned by its medium, which is finite and fragmentary. Those who are bearers of the final revelation must surrender their finitude—their life, finite power, knowledge, perfection. By so doing, they become completely transparent to the mystery they reveal. Jesus became the Christ by conquering the demonic forces tempting him to claim ultimacy for his finite nature, and above all by his death, through which he surrendered his own purposes and became transparent to the divine purpose. Hence the cross is the symbol of the finality of Christ. In the crucified Christ, revelation occurs in unambiguous although still fragmentary form.[32] What characterizes this finality is, paradoxically, the sacrifice of any claim to finality; and, were *we* to advance such a claim to finality on behalf of Christ, then, paradoxically, we would destroy the very finality that is distinctively his. So let us give up talk about the finality of Christ.

A different way of making the same point is to reflect on one of Niebuhr's insights, namely, that a truly revelatory moment enables us to appropriate as our own past much that seemed alien to us. It does so by giving us a common, shared history and common memories. The memory of Christ is something that all Christians share, be they Jews or Greeks, rich or poor, male or female, Europeans or Africans, Americans or Asians, Catholics or Protestants, medieval persons or modern. In this common revelatory center, our provincial histories break down. But more than this, says Niebuhr, the Christ-event becomes an occasion for Christians' "appropriating as their own the past of all human groups." As the Jew who suffered for the sins of Jews and non-Jews, he is the one "through whom the whole of human history becomes our history. Now there is nothing that is alien to us. . . . Through Christ we become immigrants into the empire of God which extends over all the world and learn to remember the history of that empire, that is of humanity in all times and places, as our history."[33] The particularity of this center of revelation by its very nature is not exclusive but opens out into the totality of human history. It requires that we learn to make the histories of others our own history—and this means for us today Buddhists and Hindus and Muslims, as well as Russians, Asians, Africans, South Americans. Only then will the dividing wall of hostility be broken down. Christ is for Christians the path of entry into this common history; other peoples have other paths, other ways. Paul Knitter makes precisely this point when he describes the uniqueness of Jesus Christ as a relational uniqueness, namely, "his ability to relate to—that is, to include and be included by—other unique religious figures."[34]

Trinitarian Ground (God as Revelatory)

The ground or source of revelation is not human rationality but the divine life. I agree with Tillich's statement that "the doctrine of revelation is based on a trinitarian interpretation of the divine life and its self-manifestation." Tillich understands the divine life as the structural unity of Abyss, Logos, and Spirit. The abysmal character of the divine life makes revelation mysterious; its logical character makes revelation of the mystery possible; and its spiritual character creates the correlation of miracle and ecstasy in which revelation can be received.[35] I will develop this idea in different terms in chapter 11. God simply *is* the event of revelatoriness, and God is so as an inexhaustible process of communicative freedom both within God and in the world. God is the One who loves in freedom.

Historical Shapes (God as Revealing)

Assuming that the revelatory being of God is the ground of revelation, and that revelation occurs in history in the form of certain luminous events that provide an image or paradigm by means of which other occasions in our personal and communal histories become intelligible and attain a purpose—assuming this, the question remains concerning the nature of such events and how they occur. The Protestant tradition, in line with one of the major themes of the Hebrew and Christian scriptures, has understood them as essentially *verbal* events, words, human words that serve as the bearers of the Word of God. God acts revelatorily in history by "speaking," speaking through the media of the words of Jesus, the words of scripture, and the words of prophets and preachers.

This is a great and powerful insight. Language is at the heart of what is distinctively human, and the imaging of God as the revealing, redemptive Word has much to commend it. But this is not the only biblical metaphor for representing God's revelatory presence in the world, and it is subject to a peculiar sort of misinterpretation and distortion. We tend to have a literalized picture of a divine calling or speaking, with which the words of Christ or of scripture are simply identified. We believe that God "tells" us who God is and what God requires of us, and that this information is contained in the texts of scripture and the sayings of Jesus, which assume a superhuman status. Or we hypostatize the Word of God into a divine Person, the Logos, who is incarnate in the human flesh of Jesus as his active, personal, divine nature. Both of these are mythological and highly misleading notions.

I want, therefore, to propose another metaphor, which is intended to help us both avoid idolatrous illusions about words and understand how God's revelatory word may work in the world to effect redemptive transformation. What God's word does is not so much to *inform* as to *shape*—to shape specific patterns of praxis that have a transformative power within historical process, moving the process in a specific direction, that of the unification of multiplicities of elements into new wholes, into creative syntheses that build human solidarity, enhance freedom, break systemic oppression, heal the injured and broken, and care for the natural world.

The metaphor of God as shaper is found in the prophet Jeremiah—the metaphor of the potter who shapes and reshapes the clay into a new vessel every time it becomes disfigured or broken (Jer. 18:1–11). The image of molding or kneading clay is present in the Indo-European root of our word "figure"; and our word "shape" (a synonym for "figure") derives from another root meaning to cut with a sharp tool or to carve. Both images have an earthy, physical basis, but what is involved is shaping something natural to spiritual ends in which the original form of the substance is transformed, such as clay into pottery or wood into a carving.[36]

The metaphor of shaping, of creating figures or shapes, is a very rich one. It lies at the heart of human cultural activity. It has the advantage of shifting the focus away from the more purely intellectual or theoretical realm—the realm of words and ideas—to that of concrete historical praxis, which presupposes and incorporates words, ideas, intellectual activity. The distinctively human way of shaping is by means of words. And the shapes reveal more accurately than the words who we are and what we intend. It is not the verbal formulae of religion that are revelatory but the ways in which such words are put to practice, shaping and reshaping the world. The image of shaping also has the advantage of shifting attention away from individual personal agency to something more fundamental and pervasive, namely the structuring patterns and paradigms that underlie everything that we think and say and do.

These two shifts are helpful as we seek to understand the form that God's revelatory presence in history might assume. God appears in history not as an individual person performing observable acts, nor as a supernatural voice dictating sacred scriptures and doctrines or calling individuals to repentance, nor as a supernatural force disrupting the normal forces of nature and history, nor as a generalized inspiration or lure, nor as an abstract moral ideal. Rather God appears as the shaper of patterns of praxis that constitute and redeem human persons and give history its orientation and meaning. God shapes a multifaceted transfigurative praxis by giving, disclosing, in some sense *being*, the normative shape, the paradigm of such a praxis.[37] I shall return to this idea and develop it more fully as we consider the "triune figuration" of God (chap. 11) and the "shape" of God in Christ (chap. 15, pp. 249–64).

10

THE CREATIVE BEING OF GOD: THE ONE WHO HAS BEING ABSOLUTELY

The whole of constructive Christian theology is about God: the divinity of God (God as God), the world-relatedness of God (God as/in the world), the consummation of God (God as Spirit). These are interrelated modalities of the divine life; thus world-relatedness and spiritual consummation are already implicitly present within the divinity of God and become explicit in God's creation and redemption of the world. The various other topics taken up in theology—creation, nature, humanity, sin and evil, Christ, church and ministry, history, texts, religions, culture, eschatology, etc.—are distinctly *theo*logical to the extent that they too are about God. God is the one and the whole, beginning and end, alpha and omega, and is involved with everything in between. God is *the* subject behind and within every theological subject. But God is also the most difficult subject for theology and the most avoided subject. Divinity students and professors avoid it, sensing that no talk about God is better than cheap talk.

Students have wondered what "cash value" the idea of God has. Why not attend to all the other interesting and more accessible topics but declare a moratorium on discourse about this alleged subject within the subjects? Does it make any concrete difference in how we live whether we affirm the reality of God or try to understand the connection between "God" and "being"? Is it not enough just to live *as if* God is real without engaging in metaphysical speculation about God's reality status? After all, one can be a devout Christian without being a theologian or philosopher.

I contend that the idea of God has value for both worldview and ethics, for both how we *dwell* in the world and how we *act*. If we cannot reach some understanding of reality that permits us to dwell, we will go mad. The idea of God has ethical implications, but it is more than an ethical postulate. We face fundamental questions of meaning as well as of practice, of truth as well as of value. To claim that God's creative power of being works in the world to engender fuller and richer possibilities of being, to enhance love, freedom, and wholeness, has deep metaphysical as well as ethical implications. It provides the ontological conditions of possibility for historical liberation and cosmic redemption. Liberation, feminist, ecological, and pluralist theologies *need* a doctrine of God. So let us turn to the question of the being of God.

God as "Being-Itself" or "the Power of Being"

Tillich is of help in our approach to this question. He says that the question about God is present as both a possibility and a necessity in the finite structure of human being. The question is *possible* because of the awareness of infinitude implicit in our awareness of finitude, and the question is *necessary* because of the ever-present threat of nonbeing of which we are also aware. To know that we are finite is to know that we are not infinite and thus to be *aware* of the infinite. It is also to know that we *could* not be at all and someday *will* not be, at least as we now are. *If* there is an answer to the question raised by our finite being, it would seem to be "being-itself" or "infinite being," or the "power of being" conquering nonbeing. In this way, Tillich arrives at his most formal, abstract, nonsymbolic statement about God: God is simply being-itself or the power of being.[1]

What does this mean? It means that God cannot be *a* being—either a finite being or the highest, supreme being. Rather God is the *power* of *being* by which all *beings* are. "Being" (or "being-itself") is not to be understood as a universal essence or substance in which everything participates. If this were the case, and if God were being-itself, then God would be identical with the unity and totality of finite potentialities—and that is pantheism. Rather, "being" is the *power* by which all finite beings or entities are; it is the *ground* of finite beings. The term "power" is preferable to "ground," for it makes clear that being is an event or process rather than a substance or a cause; it is dynamic rather than static. In Elizabeth Johnson's terms, the being of God is "sheer liveliness."[2] Since we are attempting to create a nonfoundationalist theology, it is best to avoid the metaphor of ground. The ground, as Tillich himself well knew, is not stable but shaky. The God of the Hebrews thunders out of a thick cloud, descends like fire, rises up like smoke, and shakes violently (Ex. 19:16–18); this is the God of storm, volcano, and earthquake, not of terra firma. Tillich himself expressed this in his famous sermon, "The Shaking of the Foundations."[3]

The expression "power of being" is somewhat misleading or ambiguous. I take the preposition "of" to be a subjective rather than an objective genitive: Being is the subject of power (power belongs to or is a quality of being, it is "being's power") rather than an object of power, something resulting from power. That which is the object of power is not being but *beings*—the finite entities of the world, including human beings. Thus it might be less confusing to say that God is the *being* of *beings*, with the word "being" (in the singular) understood as a verbal noun or gerund referring to a process or power, and the word "beings" (in the plural) understood as a substantive noun referring to things or entities. God is the *power of being* by which all *beings* are. This is clearly what Tillich intends.[4]

This statement provides the basis for affirming both the transcendence and the immanence of God. As being-itself or the power of being, God qualitatively transcends every finite being and the totality of finite beings, the world. There is no proportion or gradation between God and the world, for that would suggest that they participate in a common substance, to which they are both subordinate. At the same time, every finite being participates in or is dependent upon being-itself, for otherwise it would have no *power* of being and would be swallowed up in nonbeing. Being-itself is not a common substance in all beings, nor an independent substance apart from beings. Rather it is pure power—pure creative and liberating power—which is qualitatively distinct from all *things* as the power upon which they are radically dependent for their being, yet which is available only in and through finite things.

The precise sense in which God "is" the power of being remains to be seen; first we shall examine the metaphor "power of being."

The Power of Being and Divine Creativity

The power of being is the divine *creativity*. The most central of God's activities is that of being creator, "maker of heaven and earth." Among contemporary theologians, Langdon Gilkey has consistently emphasized this point. The tradition identified two symbols of God's worldly power, creation and providence, but Gilkey argues that the latter is really an extension of the former. "Creation" symbolizes God as the sole ground of all that is, and "providence" symbolizes God's ongoing preservation and ordering as it unfolds through temporal process—a continuous divine creativity.[5] Gilkey develops a dynamic conception of God—stressing such divine attributes as potentiality, relatedness, changeability, temporality—and indeed this seems to be the only viable concept of God today.

Not only does our conception of God need to be dynamic; we must also attempt to balance the cosmological and anthropological aspects of divine creativity. Sallie McFague points out in *Models of God* that the monarchical model not only distances God from the world but also leaves out "nine-tenths" of reality by focusing on God's governance of human beings. A word-of-God theology is an extension of anthropocentrism since only human beings can hear and respond to God verbally.[6] I take this admonition to heart since my own work has been in the past and still is to some extent oriented to the word of God. Finding alternative, cosmological metaphors and developing them conceptually is a difficult task, which theology is only beginning to address.[7] The suggestions offered below are based on the discussion in chapter 7 of the new cosmology and anticipate the discussion in chapters 12–13 of creation and nature.

The Power of Being as Primal Energy

My proposal is that God's creative power of being manifests itself in different modalities in different dimensions of the created world. These are winds of the Spirit. In the dimension of physical-organic life, the power of being appears as a primal and all-pervasive *energy*. In the dimension of consciousness, spirit, and history, it appears as the creative and liberating power of *language*. These dimensions interpenetrate rather than being externally related. The dimension of history subsists within the larger dimension of life, and language is a refinement or inwardizing concentration of the radial power of energy. In the modalities of both energy and language, God's creative power is a shaping, forming, *ideal* power, the primordial power of *pure possibility*. It is present in, yet distinct from, natural and human powers; it empowers these powers.

Some features of the natural world as interpreted by contemporary science should be recalled at this point.[8] (1) Nature is not a relatively simple, stable structure made up of bits of matter called atoms; rather it is an enormously complex relational process. The relations consist of energy, radiated discontinuously in subatomic units called quanta, which behave sometimes as waves and sometimes as particles. (2) The natural world is not mechanically determined and predictable but is rather the scene of the interplay of chance and necessity. Without chance or randomness there would be no change and development; without necessity there would be no preservation and selection. (3) The natural world is not static, unchanging, closed, but dynamic, always in process, a nexus of evolving forms. (4) The natural world is a complex, multidimensional unity—an interplay of dimensions, which can neither be reduced to the single one-dimensional picture of pre-twentieth-century science (a lowest-common-denominator approach), nor be divided into the two-dimensional worldview of classical theology (supernatural and natural, sacred and profane). It is one world, but the oneness is vast and complex. (5) The energy units of the universe seem to have built in the potentiality of becoming organized into those complex systems that give rise to what we call "life" and "consciousness." The universe has evolved so as to produce beings who are capable of observing and knowing it; it is both cognizable and (in and through human beings) self-cognizing. Therefore the energy that drives the universe must in some sense be rational; that is, it occurs in accord with the processes of human thought.

Let us try imagining God's creative power of being as a *primal* energy or potency working at all levels of the evolutionary scale, including the human, granting the world being and drawing it toward certain ends and values. This is in fact one of the oldest religious insights. According to Rosemary Radford Ruether, in many of the ancient religions the root image of the divine was that of the primal matrix, the great womb in which all things are generated.[9] This matrix, however, is essentially energy. When we probe beneath the surface, into the depth of things, "matter itself dissolves into energy. Energy, organized in patterns and relationships, is the basis for what we experience as visible things. . . . Consciousness comes to be seen as the most intense and complex form of the inwardness of material energy itself." Following Teilhard de Chardin, Ruether suggests that "the radial energy of matter develops along the lines of increasing complexity and centralization . . . until the breakthrough to self-conscious intelligence."[10]

Here we might follow a hint from Hegel and suggest that at the point of breakthrough a reversal occurs. Whereas material energy gravitates or radiates outwardly toward a central point, and thus is essentially composite, composed of discrete parts pulled toward a cosmic core (ultimately the sun for our solar system), spiritual energy, divine and human, radiates inwardly toward a center and unity within itself, this being what we call consciousness, freedom, presence-to-self.[11] The instrument of this inward integration is thought and language, which exist in a profound continuity with the outward integration of material energy.

Thus the primal matrix of goddess religion can, for a postmodern sensibility, be named primal energy, and this is the metaphor I propose for the manifestation of God's power of being in the dimension of physical-organic life. In chapter 7, God was named primal eros, but eros is simply another metaphor for energy (which is itself a metaphor for the mysterious dynamism at the heart of the cosmos). Primal energy or eros works through the energy system of the cosmos, but in virtue of its *primordial* and *ideal* (possibility-giving) status, it is not identical with natural processes; rather it is the spiritual ground of such processes.[12] In the organic dimension, we can imagine it as affording an infinite number of possibilities for novelty, for the enhancement of value and life, perhaps in a graded relevance for specific situations. Some of these possibilities are actualized in nature through accidental and random mutations in the chemical structure (the DNA code) of genes. When a combination of such mutations creates a more viable organism, then by means of natural selection that organism will prevail over others and have a better chance of surviving. According to molecular biology, this is the secret of the process of evolution, an interplay of chance and necessity, random variation and lawlike uniformity.

Must we understand this process as one utterly devoid of purpose? The French biologist Jacques Monod argues that it is, in his well-known philosophical biology, *Chance and Necessity*,[13] and he speaks for many scientists. Evolution cannot be understood as the unfolding of an initial purposive principle inherent at the core of matter but rather as the product of a pure and purposeless creativity. Monod goes on to note that while evolution is "explained" by the theory of random and unpredictable mutations in the DNA code, "it does not strike us as any less miraculous."[14] This is partly true because of the extraordinary improbability that precisely Homo sapiens should have evolved from the biosphere, or indeed that life itself should have emerged out of inorganic matter. Both of these developments are based on totally unpredictable unique events. *Why* evolution should have taken the course it did, Monod insists is unanswerable, for the whole process is without purpose, devoid of design.

But it is possible to interpret the process differently—and it should be clear that all such interpretations are philosophical or religious, not scientific. Unless we are to believe that the universe was rigidly programmed from the first moment of creation, then the most potentially fruitful source of innovation is random variation. Computers simulate creativity by generating a large number of possibilities of response, enabling the most appropriate ones to be selected. Thus randomness is the essential precondition of creativity; and *if* we wish to affirm that God acts creatively in the universe, then chance and random variation, far from being antithetical to this purpose, would be essential instruments of it.[15] It is misleading to suggest that chance and randomness are themselves creative agents by means of which the potentialities of universes are being "run through" or explored.[16] Chance rather is the space or instrument of creativity. Creativity is the work of God, of God's power of being. Any reference to "creativity," whether viewed as purposeless or purposive, entails a metascientific perspective.

The Power of Being as Liberating Language

The twin metaphors by which Ruether describes God are "primal matrix" and "historical liberator." We turn now from cosmos to history, from energy to language, and language is centrally connected with human liberation. Cosmic creativity and historical liberation are opposite sides of the same coin, parallel manifestations of the same primordial power of being. Process philosophy helps us to understand the linkage between these two themes.

According to Alfred North Whitehead, the infinite possibilities for novelty in the world, which are possibilities for the fuller and richer actualization of being, are contained in (indeed, constitute) the primordial nature of God. Hence Whitehead called them "ideals" (pure possibilities for being and value), and proposed that a "relevant" ideal is offered to each occasion of experience (a unit of energy in the natural world, ranging from subatomic particles to moments of human consciousness), by which its potentialities can be maximalized although this ideal is only occasionally seized upon and enacted.[17] John Cobb describes this process as follows:

> Each moment of experience in its entirety is the self-determining outcome of the meeting of the energies and forms derived from the past with new possibilities for present achievement. The past requires of each experience that it be somehow reenacted or conformed to. Here is the power of conformity that determines the vast repetitiveness of things. But the ideal exercises also its power upon the becoming experience, *calling* it to be something more than merely repetitive, and offering it the possibility of achieving some novel synthesis out of all that it receives from the past. . . . We are thus offered a vision of something beyond ourselves and our past that *calls us forward* in each moment into a yet unsettled future, luring us with new and richer possibilities for our being. That something is an ever-changing possibility which impinges upon us as the relevant ideal for each new moment. It is the power that makes for novelty, creativity, and life. Its power is that of an ideal, a power which is not coercive, but not, for that reason, ineffectual.[18]

What is described here is not a creation out of the past, which is usually the way creation is thought of (although it locks us into the determinism of a mechanistic world and the traditional cause-effect model), but rather a creation out of the future—that is, an offering of appropriate possibilities for the actualization of finite beings by the power of being, which accordingly has the character of the power of the future, which "calls forward." If God *is* this power of being, then God can be defined, in Cobb's words, as "the One Who Calls us forward"—forward both into being and into ever new possibilities of being, above all the possibility of freedom in the case of human being. God exercises a causality, but it is that of a final cause (exercised as "real influence") rather than a first cause (necessitation of the effect from the cause). This avoids a host of problems with respect to the traditional problem of free will versus determinism. God does not determine us from the past but lures us, calls us, shapes us from the future.

The metaphor of "calling" introduced by Cobb suggests that for human beings the power of being manifests itself not just as energy but as language (which is a higher, inwardly concentrated form of energy). Used as a metaphor of the power of being, "calling" should not be construed as something auditory, a literal cry or voice, but as an invitation, summons, vocation. It is in the broad sense a language-event, a word-event. Language is the symbolic transformation of experience by which a distinctively human world is shaped and reshaped. It is the unique and self-constituting capacity of human beings, based on the ability to use sound and signs symbolically to create and communicate meaning. It distinguishes humans from all other living beings although there are analogues to language in the higher primates.

Human language as such is deeply ambiguous. It can be used both creatively and destructively, liberatingly and oppressively, truthfully and deceitfully. It is a self-constituting human capacity, but it is also rooted in a power that is not simply at our disposal—a power that has the character of a gift or calling, a creative gift, a liberating call, which indwells and comes to speech in our speaking. While language is often just routine and repetitive, we do sometimes experience it as a *creative* power that shapes our very being as self-related and other-related, the means by which we have and dwell in a world. While language is often binding and oppressive, we sometimes also experience it as a *liberating* power, the means by which we transcend the world. It "calls us forward" into new possibilities out of the bondage of the past, or the constraints of our physical and social environment, or set ways of thinking. By means of language, we can engage in free fanciful variation, which is at the heart of all creativity. In short, we do sometimes experience language as the power of a creative, liberating transcendence—not as something remote or distant from us but rather as the dimension of depth, of power, of futurity within our very human being.

When language is used and experienced in this way, as opposed to being an autonomous human instrument of control and deception, we encounter something very similar to what theology means by the word of God. According to Christian faith, it is precisely *God's* word that calls us forward into being and freedom; it is the power of God's word that can constitute this world as a realm of freedom. The word *of God* is a word that impinges upon human beings as the power of the future mediated through certain normative events of the historical past; a word that comes to expression in human speech and activity when such speech and activity are liberated from systemic distortions and oppressions and restored to faithfulness; a word that can only be understood as a gift, for it lies beyond our capacity to produce it and our worthiness to have it (we remain always at its disposal rather than disposing it); a word that functions as the inmost, abiding power of human nature. Without such a word, whether it is acknowledged as God's word or not, human beings would not be, or at least would not flourish. The word of God is a higher, more complex and articulated manifestation of the power of God, which is the power of being.[19]

In concluding this section, I want to stress again that God's creative power of being is not simply identical with cosmic energy and human language. God works *within* energy to render it creative and upbuilding, resisting its destructive and wayward tendencies. God works *within* language to lure it toward freedom, truth, and love, resisting its oppressive, deceitful, and alienating tendencies. Thus I have spoken of the divine power of being as *primal* energy and *liberating* language. These are metaphorical ways of talking about God's being-in-the-world. The adjective "primal" means that God's being exercises an ideal, life-enhancing, goal-directed primordial power within cosmic energy; and the adjective "liberating" means that God's word evokes, measures, and transforms human words. By creating it, God sets the world free to move by its own inner dynamisms, which have both creative and tragic potentials. God does not control these dynamisms but works through them toward ends that can be properly discussed only in relation to specific religious traditions. God's power of being has the quality of *ideality*, of pure possibility, by contrast with the materiality of cosmic energy and human speech; it is an ideal that works *within* the material, a spiritual power that indwells the natural world. It is a wind *of the Spirit*.

God as "the One Who Has the Power of Being Absolutely"

We still face a puzzling question. How are we to understand the relationship of God to this power of being? Is God simply identical with being or in some way different from it? I will explore three possibilities that follow from an ambiguity present in the participle "being": It can be used as either a substantive noun (*a* being or entity, an "actual being") or as a verbal noun or gerund (be-ing as an event or process, the pure possibility of being, letting-be).[20]

God as a "Supreme Being"

Is God an extraworldly "supreme being" who exists, as it were, on the other side of or beyond worldly beings? This is not an acceptable theological option any more although it is the standard theistic view and probably the one that most people hold. To think of God as *a* being is to reduce God to the status of a worldly entity, even if God is regarded as the supreme being, the metaphysical first cause. To think of God as a supreme being is still to think of God in finite terms: God is the biggest, the oldest, the most powerful, the wisest being that we can imagine. This is what Hegel called a "spurious infinite," which is merely an indefinitely extended finite. Theism is the doctrine that God is a (supreme) being, but the true God, as Tillich says, is the God "beyond the God of theism."[21]

God as "Being-Itself" or "the Power of Being"

If God is not a being behind or beyond being, then it seems logical to identify the power of being with God. Using the metaphor for this power favored by much of the biblical tradition, namely logos or word, and appealing to the authority of the Johannine prologue, we could state that "the word *is* God" (or "was God"). This is clearly Tillich's position—God *is* being-itself, the power of being—and I find myself closer to this alternative than to the first. But there is something dangerous and misleading about it. Biblical language ordinarily does not reverse the relation between subject and predicate and make the divine attributes the subjects of statements about God. The word order in the last clause of John 1:1 is actually *kai theos ēn ho logos*, "and God was the word," but the lack of definite article preceding *theos* makes it clear that *logos* is the subject of this clause. In 1 John 4:7–8, however, we read that "God is love" (*ho theos agapē estin*) and that "love is *of* God" (*ek tou theou*) but not that "love is God."

There are two dangers here. First, a reversal of the predicates can lead to the hypostatizing or personifying of the divine attributes; that is, "word," "being," "wisdom," "love," "energy," etc., can be regarded as gods, as supernatural, quasi-personal powers or agents. There was a tendency toward this in late Judaism, a tendency reflected in the Johannine prologue. But it must be resisted because word or being as such is not a personal agent although it is the event or shaping power that *constitutes* personhood. Tillich does not intend to hypostatize being-itself, but he avoids this first danger only by falling prey to the second.

If the hypostatizing of being is avoided by insisting always that it is the power or event by which beings are, then the danger is that God will simply be identified with this power or event without remainder. God *is* the power or primordial energy at work in the world that creates, sustains, and redeems natural and human life. But in this case the biblical language about God as person, as personal agency or subject who enters into relationship with human persons is at best imprecise and at worst wrong. Such language characterizes Christian (and not just Christian!) religious experience and language of all ages. Yet such language would have to be dismissed as inappropriate or regarded as merely symbolic of a reality that in itself is not personal but rather the power of (finite human) personhood. This is in fact Tillich's position.

God as "the One Who Has the Power of Being Absolutely"

If God is not a being, and if the power of being is not to be hypostatized into a god or simply identified with God, then we seem to have a problem when it comes to understanding the relationship of God and being. Perhaps it is not only impossible to understand this relationship but also inappropriate since it represents an attempt to think ontologically or philosophically about God, whereas the God of the Bible is not a philosophical concept. The biblical God is known on the basis of revelation and can be represented only in concrete images or existential metaphors: Such is the view of Barth, Bultmann, Ebeling, and many others.[22] To give up on the question or to ignore it will not cause it to go away, however. If we are concerned to *think* about God, and indeed about the reality status of God, this question is unavoidable. We can employ concepts other than being, such as event, power, energy, becoming, nonbeing, or emptiness, but the question remains.

I am helped by an ingenious proposal of Karl Rahner: God is "the being that has being absolutely" (*das Seiende absoluter Seinshabe*).[23] Of course the being that has being *absolutely* is no longer simply "a (supreme) being" but *is* being, that is, the event or power of being. Thus Rahner can speak of God as "pure being," "absolute being," etc., just as Tillich speaks of God as "being-itself." But Rahner insists that this be understood as shorthand for "the being that has being absolutely." For being (*Sein*) is always the being of some actual being (*Seiendes*) or society of beings; the power of being is the pure *possibility* of being and cannot be thought of apart from that which it enables to be, even as it must not be confused with what it enables to be, namely beings. It is a *potency*, not an entity. For this reason, it is "nonbeing" as much as "being," emptiness as much as fullness.

Moreover, Rahner's formula discourages a reversal of predicates so as to state that "being is God." The power of being is at the *disposal* of God, who has it absolutely, whereas all finite beings are at *its* disposal. To have the power of being *absolutely* means to be able to release it, to let it go into the world, to "absolve" it. This is suggested by a play on the root sense of the word "absolute" (from the Latin verb *absolvere*), which means to absolve, loosen, release, let go. As absolute, God is not something independent or isolated, cut off from everything finite, as we tend to think, but rather God is relational, releasing the divine power, giving rise to what is other than God, namely the world. God has and gives being absolvingly.[24]

It would be helpful to modify Rahner's formula to read: God is "the One who has the power of being absolutely." And a simpler version of the latter would read, "the One who lets be," for the power of being is precisely what lets beings be. The simpler version approximates a translation of the divine name given in Exodus 3:14, *'ehyeh 'asher 'ehyeh,* safeguarded in the sacred tetragrammaton YHWH, which is here connected with the verb *hayah,* "to be." YHWH means "I am who I am" or "I am the One who lets be." As such, YHWH is "the One who has being absolutely."[25]

This modification makes the difference between the two senses of being clearer—an actual, personal subject on the one hand, and a process, event, or power of letting-be on the other. Of course, in the case of God and God alone, these two senses absolutely cohere. In a way that we cannot clearly grasp, God is *both*—both a noun and a verb, both actuality and potentiality, both personal subject and creative/redemptive power—not any personal subject but that personal subject who has, disposes, releases the power of being absolutely, and who therefore, in a way we cannot adequately express, *is* this very power. From the coherence or identity of actual being and the power of being in God, there follows the irrevocable difference between the power of being and all finite beings.

In agreement with Gilkey and McFague, I do want to affirm that God is in some sense personal. The difficult question is in what sense since there are a number of senses in which God is not a person.[26] My proposal is that God is the one true and perfect person—not *a* person but *the* person, person*hood,* since the power that God has absolutely is the constitutive power of personhood. Because God has this power absolutely, God is distinguished qualitatively from all finite persons. God is not a finite subject but infinite subjectivity—which is really intersubjectivity, a communicative interplay of subjects. God is social being, not an isolated, albeit supreme, being. Elaboration of this idea requires turning to the third main part of our discussion of God, namely the Trinity.

Before doing so, it may be helpful to attempt a further clarification in terms of the category of relationships. Is God simply the nexus of relationships and differences that exist among worldly things? This seems to be implied if God is exhaustively identified with the power of being. If so, God becomes a function or element in world-process—a crucially important element to be sure, but one that is not ultimate; "world" or "process" remains the more encompassing category. This is not what most people experience as or mean by the word God, either intuitively or reflectively.

If God is not simply relationship but has relations, then God is in some sense the *term* of a relationship, something or someone who enters into relationships. And the condition of possibility of entering into a relationship, of being related to an other than oneself, is to be self-related. At least so it seems if we think in terms of our own experience as selves, and we really have no other basis for thinking about this matter. Our self-relatedness is not a distinctionless identity, nor is it something cut off from relationships with others, but it is distinguishable from other-relatedness. We are inwardly self-related primarily by means of memory, and this forms a kind of self-identity that is able to enter into relationships with other selves and things, with what is different, without being utterly dissipated or dissolved in such relationships and differences.

Considerations such as this lead me to hold on to the distinction implied in the statement "the One who has (the power of) being absolutely." They are also what is at stake in the distinction between the "immanent" and the "economic" or "worldly" Trinity. The danger in the distinction is that it can lead us to think of God as a supreme being cut off from the world and only externally related to it. Perhaps that danger can be avoided by thinking of the immanent Trinity as a moment *within* the economic. God *is* inwardly and reciprocally related to the world, and this world-relatedness is of the very essence of God, but the being of God is not exhausted by world-relatedness. The condition of possibility of God being *God* in relation to the world, and of letting the world go as something radically different from God, is that God is also God in relation to godself. A moment in God's infinite intersubjectivity is God's purely inward subjectivity.

Undoubtedly this is a thoroughly Western way of thinking about the matter. In Eastern philosophy and religion, there is a much more radical understanding of selflessness and emptiness. Perhaps there are irreducible cultural differences that lead to different God-concepts (or non-God concepts). All we can do is express as best we can what seems to be truth for us. We can attempt to appropriate insights from other cultures, but when we do so they are likely to be modified in the process. The eminent Buddhist thinker Masao Abe has attempted to bring the idea of "dynamic sunyata" (emptiness) into relation with the Western idea of the self-emptying or "kenotic" God. In doing so, he utilizes terms, relationships, and paradoxes similar to ours, yet different. "The kenotic God who totally empties Godself and totally sacrifices Godself is, in my view, the true God," writes Abe. "And it is precisely this kenotic God who thoroughly saves everything . . . through self-sacrificial, abnegating love." This is not nihilism, claims Abe, because "the kenotic God sacrifices Godself not for relative nothingness but for *absolute* nothingness, which is at one and the same time absolute Being."[27] Perhaps we can understand this paradox through an analogy drawn from nature: That which is most empty, a vacuum, is also one of the most powerful of natural forces. It is truly a *dynamic* emptiness; it is the dynamism of wind, of Spirit.

God is the One who has absolute being/nothingness absolutely. By having it absolutely, God overreaches the difference between "the One" and "the power of being"—which as pure possibility is also the power of nonbeing. God is both ultimate actuality (the One) and ultimate reality (being/nonbeing, sunyata). The temptation is to allow this tensive unity to dissolve into identity or slip apart into duality so that God's selfhood or actual being is sacrificed to dynamic emptiness (a totally self-emptying God: Abe), or God's actuality is restricted to something less than ultimate reality (creativity) and regarded as a factor in it (a supreme nontemporal actual entity: Whitehead).[28] Whether this ontological identity-in-difference between the divine selfhood and creative power can hold is perhaps the central question facing philosophical theology today.

11
THE TRIUNE FIGURATION OF GOD: THE ONE WHO LOVES IN FREEDOM

The Model as a Whole[1]

What more can be said about the One in whom "actual being" and "power of being" absolutely cohere? The being of this One is an activity or event, a relational process that is triadic in structure. God is not a simple, static thing but a complex network of relations by which God's own being is constituted as well as the being of the world and the relationship between God and the world. I name this network of interrelations the "triune figuration" of God, meaning by this expression the interplay of three primary figures or modalities of the divine life.

The divine activity *is* one of configuring or shaping. God is an ongoing configuring activity, which in terms of essence is eternally complete and self-constituting, but in terms of existence is eternally unfinished and open to otherness, difference. What is shaped or configured is in the first instance the matrix of ideal self-relations that comprise the abstract subjectivity of God; and in the second instance, the matrix of real spatiotemporal relations that make up the world in which we live and through which God becomes a concrete, spiritual, existent God. With respect to the latter, God is augmented or diminished by what actually happens in the world. God's real existence is at stake in the world but not God's ideal or essential being as the One who has the power of being absolutely. The configuring process as a whole is what the theological tradition has called the "economic" or worldly Trinity; on the model proposed here, it *includes* as its first moment the "immanent" or preworldly Trinity.[2]

The three figures in which God appears were understood by the tradition as the "persons" of the Trinity: Father, Son, and Holy Spirit. There are two essential problems with this language. First, it is patriarchal and hierarchical. It encourages us to think of God as three male beings who are arranged in a definite rank, going from the Father (the supreme authority) to the Son, and thence to the Spirit, whose standing in the Trinity was never clearly explained by the tradition and who remained thoroughly subordinated to the other persons. Such a way of thinking about God totally excludes women and ignores the female imagery for deity that is present in scripture and human experience. As a consequence many feminist theologians have concluded that the doctrine is useless, in fact dangerous, and should be discarded.[3] It also reflects a society organized around the principle of monarchy and aristocratic/patriarchal privilege as opposed to democracy and civil equality.[4]

The second problem is that the language is mythological. It encourages us to think of God as three persons or personal agencies who interact with each other in a divine society and make supernatural appearances in history. To be sure, the Latin term *persona,* and its Greek equivalents, *prosopon* and *hypostasis,* did not mean "person" in the modern sense of a self-conscious ego but referred rather to the role played by an actor (symbolized by his or her mask, *persona*), or to a functioning entity, an individuating principle. Yet, despite this fact, the introduction of *persona* terminology into trinitarian theology had the inevitable effect of literalizing talk about God along personifying and familial lines. It is so obviously misleading to think of God as a fraternity of male deities who are begetting, spirating, and proceeding from each other that it is just best to drop this language entirely.

We should not abandon the conviction that God is both personal and communal, but we need to rethink the sense in which this is true. My view is that the triune God is *the one* true and perfect person, whose personhood is constituted by relational acts of love and freedom, and who subsists in three modes of being or existence, but who *is not* three supernatural persons or agents. The *personae* of God should be construed as figures that represent "moments" of relating, "modes" of being, or "shapes" of acting. This position might be said to approximate "modalism," which is often criticized for excluding real relations from the Godhead and for understanding God as a monarch instead of a community.[5] There is some validity to this criticism, and I want to propose an approach that draws upon the insights of both modalist and social models of the Trinity.

God is not a community of three persons, nor is God a solitary ego or a windowless monad. Rather God is the ultimate and inclusive event of communication—communicative action or communicative freedom par excellence. God simply *is* the community of relations that creates all things and holds all things together. Within this community there are terms of relations. A plurality of such terms comprises the *world* as God's alterity, and they can be gathered under the figure of Christ. There is also a *divine* term, God's own self-othering and self-relating without the mediation of the world, the figure of the One. And there is a *theo-cosmic* term, God's self-relatedness enriched by mediation with the world, and the world's alterity reconciled in God, the figure of the Spirit that emerges out of the interaction between God and world. The figures are terms or subjects *constituted* by relations, not simply unfocused relationality or antecedently existing subjects. We confront a paradox: Persons dissolve into relations, yet relations crystallize in distinctive shapes, figures, practices, identities. The divine life has a structure that derives from patterned relationships. The *personae* or figures of the Trinity name the patterns, the gestalts, by which God is God.

There are several ways by which these patterns can be named and described. The ways are complementary, not contradictory.

(1) The three figures of the Trinity can be expressed in terms of the dialectical pattern of thought that replicates the movement of life itself: identity-difference-mediation, or unity-separation-reunification.[6] Understood *cognitively* and *existentially*, the triune God *is* the relational process of identity, difference, and mediation that constitutes spiritual personal being as such and is intrinsic to the life process. Life repeatedly goes through these phases of an initial unity, a separation, and a reunification or synthesis in which the moment of difference is preserved and something new emerges. This is a spiraling triad that never simply returns to its starting point but moves ahead into novelty. A triad is nonlinear, unstable, generative.

(2) In order to balance the predominant intellectualism of the Western theological tradition rooted in the Augustinian and Thomistic models of memory, knowledge, and will (of which the first approach is a modern variant), a more *personal* and *praxis*-oriented model may be introduced, whose three terms are "the One," "love," and "freedom." God is "the One who loves in freedom,"[7] the One who is constituted as the true and perfect subject by relational acts of love and freedom.

(3) Finally, we may think of the three modes of divine being in *symbolic* and *figural* terms as "God," "World," and "Spirit." For reasons to be indicated, the figure "God" is intended to substitute for that of "Father"; the figure "World" is intended to include the traditional figures of the Second Person (Son, Logos, Christ, etc.); and the figure "Spirit" will be rethought as the true and consummate name of God. I combine these three ways of naming the trinitarian relations—the cognitive/existential, the personal/practical, and the symbolic/figural—in the following model.

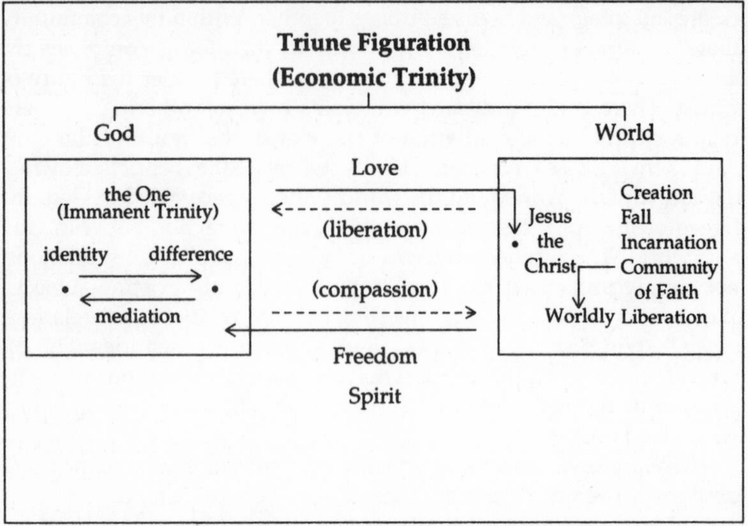

Reflection on this scheme suggests the following points about the model, some of which will require further explication as we consider the three figural moments more closely.

(1) The immanent Trinity comprises an inward dialectic of identity (unity), difference (separation), and mediation (reunification) by which God's ideal selfhood or subjectivity is constituted, and which is outwardly reenacted (not repeated) in the realm of real difference and historical events. This dialectic is underived and self-constituting. As the tradition claimed, God is "unbegotten," from godself (*a se*). Models of the dialectic will be considered more fully in the next section.

(2) The economic Trinity embraces the immanent Trinity as its first moment—a trinity within a trinity—and it encompasses both God and world as distinguishable moments of the total event of triune figuration. These two Trinities are not identical, as is sometimes implied.[8] The difference between them is that between two kinds of otherness: a logical other (the other as merely a self-othering of the self) and an empirical other (the other broken free into real otherness or other-being). The immanent Trinity must not be allowed to subsume or replace the economic, which has been the tendency of the theological tradition. In this case, history becomes a sideshow to what is already complete within God. As Hegel claimed, the divine "play of love" falls into "mere edification, and even insipidity, if it lacks the seriousness, the suffering, the patience, and the labor of the negative." Nor must the economic Trinity be allowed to subsume or replace the immanent, as implied by those modern theologians who believe that nothing can be said about God in and for godself. Rather the economic

Trinity must be understood to *include* the immanent as a necessary moment and to result from a mediation between a self-constituting God and a created world. An internal complexity *is* a necessary and irreducible condition of external relations, but the latter are not contained within and controlled by the former. The two Trinities are related dialectically, the economic Trinity overreaching but not annihilating the immanent.[9]

(3) The relation of love *from* God *into* the world shows that God is immanent in the world; for Christians this world-immanence or "incarnation" has its focal point in the figure of Jesus as the Christ, but its telos is to become a communal and world-transforming embodiment. God is present in and to all things, but the autonomy of the creature is not diminished. God's presence is not a "suffocating, overwhelming shadow but . . . the ground of freedom."[10] God is incarnate within that which remains not-God. In the classical models of the Trinity, love is the third, mediating figure, representing the Spirit. Following Karl Barth, I have moved it to the second moment, replacing knowledge as the figure of difference, and allowing space for freedom.[11] Thus in place of the Augustinian-Thomistic processions of knowledge and love (or will) there stand love and freedom. In this way the predominantly epistemological model of Western theology is moderated into a trinity of praxis. Knowledge is not lost but becomes insight into the oneness of God, a oneness that is dia-logical.

(4) The relation of freedom *from* the world *into* God shows that the world is immanent in God, returning God to godself, establishing God's now-doubly-dialectical identity as Spirit, the generic name "God" now yielding to the concrete name "Spirit." The question whether such a view eventuates in pantheism or panentheism will be considered shortly. At the moment it should be noted that feminine metaphors are especially helpful in thinking about how the world dwells in God. "To be so structured that you have room inside yourself for another to dwell is quintessentially a female experience. To have another actually living and moving and having being in yourself is likewise the province of women." After birth and maturation, the relationship between mother and child changes and is replaced by another sort of mutual indwelling, that of friendship, which has also been highlighted in feminist discourse. Friendship is a form of freedom, of being present to oneself in and through another.[12]

(5) Spirit encompasses the whole, God and world together. Within this whole, God and world are related *asymmetrically*. God is inwardly self-constituted in a way that the world is not; the world as created depends on God for its very being, whereas God as creator does not depend on the world to be "the One," the One who simply is—although God becomes truly and fully God, God as Spirit, only through the

world. *God* is the beginning and the end of all things, not the world; the final consummation is in God, not in some future state of the world. Thus the way God transcends and is immanent in the world is different from the way the world is immanent in and transcends God. The transcendence of God means that God is not simply a factor within a categorical scheme or a cosmological process; rather God is the whole.[13]

(6) Each of the two basic economic relations, love and freedom, generates a secondary reciprocal relation, indicated by the reverse broken lines. God's love for the world, which posits separation and difference and entails suffering, is at the same time a *liberating*, redemptive love, a love that does not simply die in the agony of the cross. God's freedom in and through the world, by which the divine life is perfected, is at the same time a *compassionate* freedom, a freedom that is not sheer divine indeterminacy or transcendence but rather is bound to and determined by love for the world. We may think of these as four relations corresponding to the two processions of classical trinitarian thought. The relations of love and freedom represent the "appropriation" of operations and attributes to the second and third trinitarian figures, while liberation and compassion represent the "perichoresis," the passing into one another of the two figures, and their union with the first. The term *perichōrēsis* signifies a cyclical, revolving movement, and suggests the encircling of each of the divine persons around the others, an "eternal divine round dance," a dynamic koinonia of the divine life. Johnson envisions this perichoretic dance as a triple helix, a dance of separation and recombination that "twirls around in a never-ending series of moves," and which "includes human partners and their decisions for good or ill, toward the fullness of shalom for all creatures."[14] A theory of divine attributes could be generated out of the perichoretic interplay of love and freedom, as Barth proposes.[15] In addition to attributes of divine love and freedom would be attributes of divine oneness/wholeness. The attributes (or "perfections," as Barth calls them) of God are not as basic as the figures or gestalts, which identify the constitutive relations of the divine being; the attributes are qualities that characterize these relations. I have not developed a theory of divine attributes in a systematic way.

(7) If we appropriate the word "God" to name the abstract identity of the One, what name shall we use to designate the event of triune figuration as a whole? Augustine faced this question and answered it by suggesting that the name of the Christian God is "Trinity," "the one and only and true God," and he addressed this God as "Holy Trinity," "Blessed Trinity."[16] If we find this too jarring, then, keeping in mind Augustine's further statement that the Trinity may be called

the Holy Spirit, but not the Father or the Son, we could name the whole God "Spirit," perhaps using Hegel's expression "Absolute Spirit"—the Spirit that absolves, lets the world go forth from itself freely and sets it free from every constraining factor. Or if this is too unconventional, then the word "God" will do since these gestalts or figures do not connote separable entities but distinct moments or patterns in an indivisible divine process. Each includes all and can stand for all. The love of the divine One is a liberating love, oriented to redemption; the freedom of the divine One is a compassionate freedom, riveted to the world; the divine One is the One who loves in freedom. What more can be said? Only that in truth God cannot be named; all our words are but metaphors and figures.

(8) The model of the Trinity presented here can be characterized as a triadic, social holism. It is neither a monism nor a dualism, nor is panentheism the best designation of it. The fundamental conviction driving the model is that God's absoluteness does not exclude but includes relation, and that the world to which God is related remains irreducibly other to God even as it is encompassed within the diversity and plurality of the divine life. God as absolute "absolves" or "releases" the other to be a free and independent being, thus bringing into being a world that is and remains not-God within a larger whole that is Spirit. As opposed to the absolute ego of idealism (I=I), for which the other is merely the self-othering of the ego, in a holistic system there is a triadic social structure with a threefold mediation (I–You–We). There is not only an I but also a You that is equivalent to the I, and the final identity is not I but We. This We is Spirit, an intersubjective, social matrix formed by the reciprocal recognition of subjects, in which there is no reduction of the other to the same. God as Spirit is an infinite intersubjectivity. The "otherness" or alienation of the other is overcome in Spirit but not the other itself. Domination is abandoned in favor of releasement, reciprocity, and holism. The whole that is Spirit has a multiplicity of centers; the multiplicity is symbolized as "three" in trinitarian thought, three being the mediating number, intrinsically generative of new shapes. Thus "Spirit" is the most adequate name for the truly infinite and whole God.[17]

In principle, the doctrine of panentheism (all things *in* God) holds a similar view since it preserves both identity and difference; but the *en* can too easily slip into the notion that the *pan* (the all) is merely the self-othering of *theos* and ultimately the same as *theos* (pantheism). Holism offers a trans-theistic vision of a whole that is theanthropocosmic, or, as I prefer to express it, theo-cosmo-pneumatic. A unitive or holistic pluralism can help prevent the delicate "in" of panentheism from being interpreted or used in a monistic direction.

Identity: The One (God)

The One

God is in the first instance "the One," the One who is primordially self-identical. This One is not, however, a windowless monad; the identity in question is not sheer undifferentiated substance. God is already, in the first moment, a subject-event or person-event, an act or process of self-distinguishing and self-relating that cannot be derived from or traced to anything other than itself. In this respect God is "unbegotten," *a se*, from godself. If God is not in this sense self-generating, then it is difficult to avoid the conclusion that God is generated from something other than God, namely, world-process, which may, as a matter of fact, generate many deities. The function of the moment of identity in the triune figuration is to establish the ontological priority of the One vis-à-vis the world. Thus the immanent Trinity should not be displaced by the economic but rather encompassed within it as a necessary generative moment. The One already anticipates and allows for the world's otherness. Hence the "oneness" of God is also potentially a "wholeness," an identity that encompasses real difference, a unity that encompasses diversity.

Obviously we have no direct knowledge of the oneness of God, which remains an inexhaustible mystery for us. We encounter God revealed in the world in a threefold pattern, and from this we reflect on the being of God. We are able to think of the immanent Trinity analogically and imaginatively on the basis of our own limited experience of personal identity and self-relatedness, but what we produce are *models* of the Trinity, not literal descriptions.

Models of Trinitarian Relations

According to Hegel, the truth of the Trinity is most adequately grasped in logical categories as the dialectic of identity, difference, and mediation, or of unity, separation, and reunification—categories that reflect the movement of consciousness and ultimately of life itself (see the first model below).[18] Barth expresses this in terms of the dialectic of subject, object, and predicate, or of revealer, revealed, and act of revelation.[19] This pattern is in fact the basic structure of subjectivity or selfhood, which was first articulated by Augustine in a series of analogies of the Trinity, drawn from sense perception, external relations, knowledge, and mind or consciousness (the second model).[20] The model describes a subject that constitutes itself as subject by a twofold act: an act of self-distinction, through which the subject becomes objective to itself or enters into relation with a real object, and an act of self-relation or return to self. Thus the three constitutive elements of the model are a subject, an object, and the relationship between them.

Yet this is misleading since in fact all three elements of the model are *relations* that constitute *terms* or moments or figures, as a more detailed analysis would show. Both subject and object are inwardly constituted by relations as well as having a double relationship between them, as is evident when the analogy is based on knowledge or mind (the third model). In the case of God, in the moment of identity God is constituted as "God" through the relation of aseity or self-generation (the inner divine "play" of self and other). In the moment of difference, God constitutes the "world" as object, as other-than-God with its own internal complexity, through the relation of creative/redemptive love. In the moment of mediation, God and world are co-constituted and consummated as "Spirit" through the relation of freedom (the fourth model).

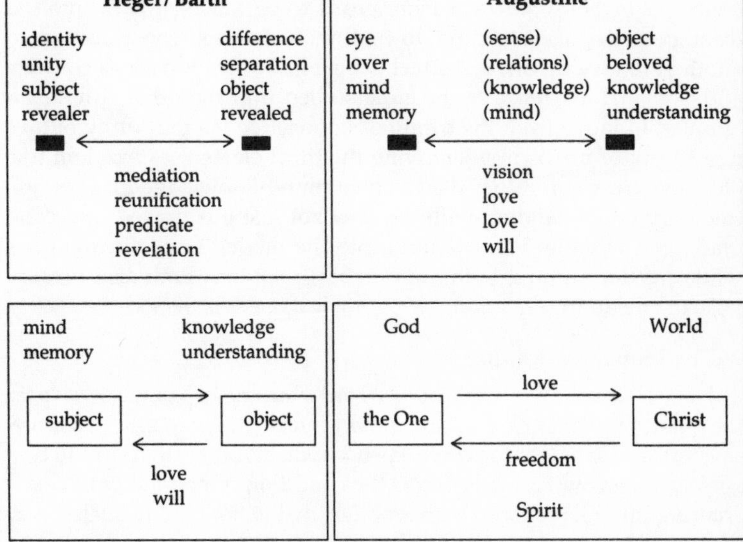

"Exploded" and slightly modified the fourth model would look like this:

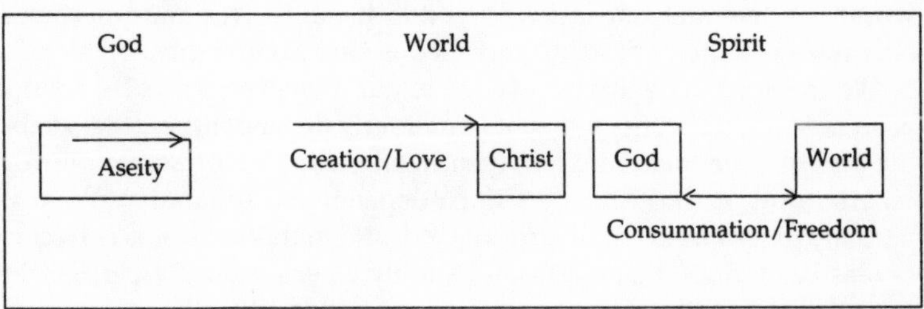

The final model shows that each of the trinitarian figures or "persons" is a term (in the case of Spirit a double term) constituted by relations. The terms are represented by boxes, the relations by lines with arrows. In the case of God, the relation of aseity is represented as being generated from *within* the divine subject, whereas in the case of the world and Spirit, the relations *enter* into the terms from without. The divine term is also represented as being open rather than self-enclosed. The exploded model shows how the three figures differ in their constitution and are increasingly complex, each presupposing the previous figure. God is self-generating; world/Christ is generated by God in the relation of love; Spirit is co-generated by God and world in the relation of freedom.

The truth of the Trinity can also be grasped in the figurative, metaphorical language of love and personality, as both Augustine and Hegel recognized. Love entails a union mediated by relationship and hence distinction; to be a person means to be reflected back into self through an act of distinction, to find one's own self-consciousness in another, to give up one's abstract being and to win it back as concrete and personal existence by being absorbed into the other. I have attempted to move from the trinity of knowledge via the trinity of love to a trinity of praxis by identifying the third element as freedom (the One-love-freedom) rather than as love (mind-knowledge-love) or will (memory-understanding-will). Love is not lost but moved to second place, and freedom is introduced into the model. Love distinguishes while freedom unites; both are practical relations. Both also presuppose the theoretical relation, the dia-logical oneness of God.

The Immanent Trinity

Now God is in the first instance God's *own other*. As Barth says, in the event by which God is God, God is subject, object, and predicate. This means that God does not depend upon an other than God to be a subject, a person. Precisely this is the condition of possibility of God's entering into relationship with an other that is not God in such a way that the autonomy and independence of the other are allowed to stand, are not utterly absorbed into God's own being. It is *for the sake of the world*, for the sake of the world's freedom, that God's love for the world is a free and unexacted love, and it can be free and unexacted only insofar as in the first instance God is God's own other.

We can appreciate this by analogy to our own experience. If I am not in some sense self-constituting, if I am utterly dependent on others to be the personal identity that I am, then I will either lose myself or destroy others in my relationships (as in co-dependency situations). What is partially true of us is wholly true of God, and in this sense it is correct to say, as Barth does, that God is not simply *a* person but *the* person, the one true and perfect person, not merely the ideal but the real person, "not the personified but the personifying person." The divine person is both utterly absolute and utterly related, and the assumption of a conflict between the "absoluteness" and the "personality" of God is false.[21] In fact the distinction between absoluteness and relativity loses its significance if absoluteness means to be both utterly self-related and utterly other-related; to be both is to be utterly personal. Of course *our* self-constituting is always preceded by something else, namely the nexus of world relations; we cannot be utterly independent of the world. But God's self-constituting act is not preceded by anything other than itself: God is *a se*, unbegotten, eternally self-generating.

The relationality of God must be understood as something that is not hierarchical and linear but rather equal and reciprocal. The "persons" have a relationship not of super- and subordination but of mutuality and friendship, in which each serves and is served by the others. God is a dynamic, dancing, perichoretic community of partners in which the first is last and the last first.[22] Moltmann refers to this as the "trinitarian doxology" or the eternal glory of God, a circular, spiraling movement, which is "God's own stream of life."[23] The latter is a nice metaphor for the triune figuration since it emphasizes the streaming, fluid character of the God who is consummated as Spirit.

God as "Father"

The tradition spoke of this first gestalt of the divine life, which specifies God's self-identical, self-constituting, unbegotten quality, or aseity, as God's "fatherhood," the one who makes all things but is not made. For us the symbol "father" has become problematic. How then shall we speak of God if we want to continue using personal metaphors? One possibility, suggested by Paul Ricoeur, would be to destroy the idolatrous elements of this figure so that "the image of the father can be recovered as a symbol. . . . An idol must die so that a symbol of being may begin to speak." Ricoeur proposes to do this by subjecting the father-figure to a critique that displaces and destroys it but also allows it to return after the dispossession, reinterpreted by other figures and relations that are nonbiological and nonparental. What must be dispossessed, of course, is the patriarchal father-figure who both threatens and consoles, evoking the most archaic forms of religious feeling: the fear of punishment and the desire for protection. Ricoeur thinks this destruction and retrieval is accomplished in Israelite and Christian faith first through the figure of the king or ruler who enters into covenant relations with his people, then through the spouselike father of the prophets (whose "love, solicitude, and pity carry him beyond domination and severity"), and finally through the conversion of the father from the figure of origin to the figure of new creation by its association with the inbreaking *basileia* in the proclamation of Jesus.[24]

God as "Mother"

It is important to recognize that a process of depatriarchalization is already at work in biblical faith. But it does not go far enough, and Ricoeur is insensitive to this since he is primarily concerned with the atheistic critique of religious belief as advanced by Nietzsche and Freud, not with the feminist critique. From the point of view of the latter, the reappropriation of the forgotten, suppressed, and concealed feminine images of God present in the biblical tradition despite its patriarchal bias is essential: God as mother, midwife, nurse, lover, friend, sophia. Moreover, the figure of the mother was by far the dominant image for divinity in most of the ancient religions throughout the world, from India to Iceland, as Joseph Campbell has shown.[25] The father may be the begetter, but it is the mother who gives birth and nurtures, and there is no more powerful an image of creation than this.

Two basic strategies are available at this point. We need not choose one of them exclusively since both make a valid contribution, but most of us will probably prefer one or the other. The first strategy is to retain and multiply the personal models of God. Since the masculine images have been overwhelmingly dominant in our tradition, and since there has been a long-standing repression of female sexuality, a good case can be made for privileging the feminine images at this time, perhaps even declaring a moratorium on the use of masculine images, but without contending that the latter are inappropriate in principle; rather in time they will be retrieved and revisioned. This is Sallie McFague's strategy, and she makes a very good case for it, opening up many rich insights into the love, activity, and ethic of "God as Mother." She does recognize the limitations that are present in this strategy. Maternal imagery for God—in fact, parental imagery in general—"can tend toward infantilism; it can suffocate and 'swallow.'"[26] McFague's way of dealing with this "restriction" is to introduce other, "balancing" metaphors for God's relationship to the world, namely "lover" and "friend."

God as "God"—the One

The problem with this strategy is that all personal metaphors for God ultimately remain inadequate. One could agree with this but add that they are the best we have. Without judging whether they are the best we have, I observe that they are not all we have. An attempt can be made to move from personal metaphors to what might be called "metapersonal" concepts, recognizing that metaphorical elements remain present in all concepts, and that no concept is adequate to grasp the being of God. Concepts have a heuristic function ("serving to find out") just as metaphors do.[27] They too involve thinking in as-if fashion, and the conceptual task is to experiment with ever new, yet always fragmentary, constructions. Concepts differ from metaphors principally in their attempt to assemble images into more holistic patterns, and they attend especially to the connections between concepts and the coherence of the constructions they produce. The impulse of conceptual thought is toward universality and necessity rather than particularity and contingency. Both impulses are valuable. I believe that a way of thinking and speaking about God needs to be found that goes beyond the distinctions that mark the personal but without losing the personal—distinctions of sex and family as well as those of class, position, nation, and race. God does transcend all these distinctions even as God is mediated through them.

What name then shall we give to the first divine figure, the figure of identity, of "the One"? Perhaps there is no appropriate name. My own simple proposal is to employ the generic symbol "God." Ruether's neologism "God/ess" is better in that it transcends the masculine gender of the word "God," but she acknowledges it does not work well liturgically and its constant repetition is awkward in theological discourse.[28] The etymology of this name probably is not of much significance, but it is worth noting that it derives from an Indo-European base, *ĝhau-*, meaning "to call out," "to invoke." "God" is a cry of anguish and joy. A child cries out to its parents; thus the parental names of God, mother and father, may be rather close to the root sense of the word "God," and it can be used along with them or in their stead. "God" is not exactly personal, but it is a metapersonal image, and in this respect is preferable to the abstract term "divinity" (even though the Latin root of the latter is feminine in gender). It is possible to pray to God but not to divinity.

The word "God" designates the oneness, the unity, the wholeness, the holiness, the sublimity, the aseity of God, the One upon whom all things are utterly dependent and in whom they find their final fulfillment. If we are unable to say this of God, then nothing else can be said. The great accomplishment of Israelite faith is that it was the first to attain the true meaning of the word God—the One.[29] Using "God" in this sense is rather like the usage of the Hebrew word *Elohim*, which is simply translated as *theos* in Greek, *deus* in Latin, and *Gott* or *God* in the Germanic languages. "God" is not strictly a name but the circumlocution for a name, in the case of Israel the unpronounced tetragrammaton YHWH. As God becomes more sharply configured through the dialectic of differentiation and return, love and freedom, other names are introduced: Sophia, Logos, Christos, Kyrios, Pneuma. All of these, however, presuppose the word "God."

Difference: Love (World)

By the act of love, God posits externally the moment of distinction and difference that is already implicit within God. God goes out from godself, creates a world seemingly infinite in extension but strictly nondivine in its perishability and contingency, yet enters into relationship with that world, makes it God's own "body," becomes embodied or incarnate in it, suffers its estrangement, conflict, death, but also works toward its reconciliation, renewal, salvation. Thereby the nonserious "play of love with itself," by which Hegel characterized the immanent Trinity, becomes deadly serious. The absolute is "released" into "the seriousness of other-being, of separation and rupture." In the world it is interrupted, broken, "dismembered."[30] God becomes a tragic God but also sublates tragedy, overcomes tragic conflict.[31]

Love and Freedom

God's love is a *free* love since it is not necessitated by the creature and is purely gratuitous. The freedom of God indicates that the relation between God and world is in the first instance strictly a divine action, the ever-original divine act of self-distinction, self-othering, self-giving. But it is also the case that God *needs* the world to become fully the God that God is capable of becoming—not locked into a self-enclosed unity as the abstract isolated One but opening the divine self up to encompass genuine otherness, becoming thereby concrete and spiritual, being no longer simply the One but the "All in all" (1 Cor. 15:28), "the All that remains utterly one."[32] Ernst Troeltsch referred to this as God's capacity to grow and characterized it as "the self-augmentation of God."[33] This growth is intrinsic to the very being of God, not an outwardly imposed necessity; the necessity is internal and thus identical with God's freedom to be God.

The divine love is also a love that *liberates,* for it sets the world and human beings free from their self-imposed bondage and reestablishes the rightful relationship between creatures and Creator. This is the reciprocal of the outward divine relation of love, the return already contained within the diremption, the reconciliation already anticipated in the moment of estrangement. Speaking from the point of view of Christian faith, Jesus of Nazareth, as the focus of God's act of love for the world, not only suffers from and dies for our sin but also is our historical and risen redeemer—from his "infinite anguish" arises an infinite and liberating love.[34] There are not only scenes of violence in this world but also acts of self-giving love and clearings of freedom, which indeed sometimes are embedded in the very scenes of violence.

That God's love for the world is a free and liberating love provides a context for thinking about a vexing problem: If the world is created merely in order for God to have an object to love, an "other" that augments the divine life, then the world seems to be contained within God and reduced to a function lacking intrinsic value of its own. A student of mine once complained that according to Hegel we seem to be nothing but thoughts in the mind of God. I replied facetiously that I could think of much worse fates. There is truth in both the complaint and the response. The freedom of God's love must mean that God creates for the sake of the creature as well as the creator and that God really does grant the world its own otherness and independence. The world is an end in itself as well as having an end in God. Tragically, insofar as it cuts itself off from God, the world converts its divinely given otherness into a structure of domination and oppression, of "us" versus "them," of forced otherness. But God will not abandon the world to its otherness; indeed God is present in a special way to those who become "the others" of history—the sick and impoverished, the scorned and rejected. God's love not only frees the world to be other but liberates from the alienating otherness the world imposes on itself.

God, Death, and Nothingness

The death of God on the cross of Christ means that we must think "God's unity with perishability" or "mortality." Perishing, says Eberhard Jüngel,[35] is necessary to the process of becoming. Over against what he calls the ontological discrediting of perishing, which multiplies its negation into annihilation and allows the shadow of nothingness to fall on all that is perishable, Jüngel contends that perishing also contains a positive possibility, the possibility of becoming something new, even for something that is past. In this sense, "the essence of perishability is disclosed as *history*, which does not permit what has been to remain nothing." History, the telling of a story, means precisely not to lose the possibility of past reality but to preserve it, to re-collect it, to re-construct it in narrative form. The history of perishability is "the struggle between possibility and nothingness."

The death of God in anguished love means that God *is* in the midst of this history, this struggle. God's essence is not outside and above it but is precisely in it. "God shares in the struggle between the ontological undertow toward nothingness and the capacity of the possible." Although God creates *ex nihilo* and is the condition of possibility for the struggle in the first place, God is not superior to the struggle. Rather the being of God is revealed "as creative being in the struggle with the annihilating nothingness of nothing." The God who died on the cross of Christ and arose from the dead draws this nothingness into God's own history, defining and determining it, contradicting and resisting its annihilating power. God is the one who can bear and suffer the annihilating power of nothingness without being annihilated by it, converting it rather into a positive possibility. In God "nothingness becomes concrete negation which gives to concrete affirmation its critical edge. . . . It becomes the differentiating power in the identity of being."[36] This is Jüngel's suggestive interpretation of the words of Paul: "When this perishable body puts on imperishability, and this mortal body puts on immortality, then the saying that is written will be fulfilled: 'Death has been swallowed up in victory'" (1 Cor. 15:54).

World and God

Now the world as such is what is perishable. To say that the perishable puts on imperishability, and that God takes the nothingness of perishability into the divine life, can only mean that the world as such is an element within the divine life. The world is by no means divinized in this process; on the contrary, just the opposite is the case because it is precisely the perishability of the world, its nondivine character, that is taken into the divine life. When the perishable "puts on" the imperishable, it does not cease to be perishable. Rather (following Jüngel) its annihilating nothingness is converted into possibility for the new. It becomes "the differentiating power in the identity of being." By taking on the perishable, God's own being is historicized, becomes a being-in-process. The world remains precisely the moment of difference, concrete negation, otherness, finitude, perishability—the realm of ongoing struggle between creativity and destructiveness, good and evil—within the triune figuration of God.

When I say "world," I mean the whole world—the cosmos as we know it, the stars and planets, biological life, human consciousness, culture and history (see chaps. 12–14). This whole world is the figure, shape, or gestalt of God in the moment of difference; metaphorically, it is "God's body." "God's got the whole world in God's hands."

Undoubtedly many will dismiss this as a heretical notion, not only because it seems to border on pantheism, but also because it displaces the second person of the Trinity, the Son of God, from his rightful place. I insist, however, that it is not pantheism, certainly not crude pantheism, the sort of pantheism that confuses all things with God and divinizes physical and human nature. The world is precisely *not*-God, and *because* it is not-God it is a moment within the divine life. The extraordinary thing about God is that God overreaches and incorporates what is not-God within God. God is the identity of God and not-God, the event that takes place between God and world. Thereby God is a God whose being is in process, and what is not-God has the possibility of being saved from its annihilating nothingness. The world fulfills its role within the divine life only by remaining other than God. If it were reduced to the same, all real difference would evaporate, and God would be a "bloodless abstraction—solitary, lifeless, and alone like Aristotle's unmoved mover or the Neo-Platonic One."[37] If a label is required for such a view, it is panentheism, or better, holism, not pantheism.

World and Christ

But does not such a view substitute "world" for "Christ," thus renouncing any claim to being distinctively Christian? I do indeed affirm that one of the challenges of postmodernism to Christian theology is to give up its christocentrism, its potentially idolatrous fixation on Jesus Christ, the only-begotten Son of God, the incarnate Logos, the God-man. There are a number of reasons for this, including not only the well-known conceptual difficulties of classical christology and the sad history of Christian persecution of the Jews as Christ-killers but also the much more recent challenges of religious pluralism and feminist consciousness. It is unnecessary to go into all of this here. I will simply observe that giving up christocentrism or "christism" (as H. R. Niebuhr called it[38]) by no means entails giving up Christ, but it does require thinking about Christ differently (see chap. 15).

God's loving, suffering, transformative embrace of the world is an inclusive embrace, but like everything else in the world it does not appear everywhere all at once but in distinctive shapes, patterns, configurations. It appears in the world liminally, at the margins of the dominant world-formations, requiring for its discernment hard labor. It also appears in a plurality of forms, none of which can legitimately claim finality or exclusive validity. All such claims are parochial and arbitrary because all are tinged by the contingency and relativity of history. But distinctive religious traditions and communities *have* experienced God's redemptive, suffering presence in the world in distinctive ways, and they have a right, indeed an obligation, to make it known, to proclaim it.

For Christians, the paradigmatic shapes by which God's love of the world is discerned emerge from the life, death, and presence of Jesus Christ—the shapes of basileia and of cross, which, when superimposed and fused in resurrection, constitute what I shall call the "divine gestalt" by which human history is redemptively reshaped. This gestalt is normative for, and perceived as such only by, the Christian community of faith, the ecclesial community; but at the same time it is a construal of the whole of history. It is both particular and universal. The same is true of God's presence in history. Those figures in whom God is most luminously, revealingly present point beyond their own particularity to the world as a whole.

The particular figure Jesus of Nazareth disappears into his ministry, takes the misery of the world literally into himself, suffers in its place in such a way that his own identity merges with that of the world.[39] He points beyond himself not only to God and God's kingdom but also to the community of brothers and sisters, the little community of table fellowship and the great community of disciples through all ages. His personal, ethnic, sexual, cultural, historical, and religious specificities are taken up into a new corporate, intersubjective embodiment that cuts across all provincial modes of existence and whose telos is simply the world as such.

Thus Christ and world are figures of God's love at opposite ends of a continuum, each presupposing and completing the other: Christ is (for Christians) the revelatory clue to world as an ambiguous process; and world is the telos of the emancipatory praxis that arises from Christ's life and death. When I speak of "world" as the second figure of the triune figuration, I speak of it in these terms. It means "God-in-the-world-in-Christ" and "God-in-Christ-in-the-world." God is in Christ as the representative human being (the *huios tou anthrōpou*, "son of humanity"). Precisely his not-Godness, his common identity with the world, is the bearer of divinity. What makes him Christ is not a privileged, superhuman divine nature but utter identification with the anguish and joy of human nature. It is the intensity of his humanity that radiates divinity; it is as "son of humanity" that he is "son of God."

Because "world" is the more encompassing way of naming the second moment of the divine life, and because anthropocentrism and christocentrism are yielding to a more cosmological and pneumatological perspective, "world" is favored as a trinitarian symbol in this project in a way that may seem unorthodox but in fact is not without precedent. The cosmic christologies of the New Testament (Colossians, Ephesians) point in this direction, as do Stoic and Neoplatonic theologies, certain forms of mysticism, Hegelianism, process thought, and now feminist, pluralist, and ecological theologies. One advantage of this strategy is that it allows the symbol Christ to retain its determinate connection with the historical figure of Jesus and his community. Another is that it allows Christ to serve as the hinge or turning point between the second and third trinitarian moments, between love and freedom, between worldly differentiation and spiritual mediation. In my view, this is the proper place of Christ in theology (see chaps. 15, 16). On the one hand Christ is only a moment in world-process, that moment in which the anguish of love reaches its greatest intensity; and Christ is only one in whom the Spirit dwells, albeit with a fullness that continues to reverberate in history. In this sense Christ is subordinate to both world and Spirit. But on the other hand this very Christ is at the heart of each: The world has a cruciform shape, and the Spirit is the Spirit of Jesus Christ. In this sense Christ is at the center of Christian theology.

Mediation: Freedom (Spirit)

Freedom and Love

If love is the figure of difference, freedom is the figure of mediation. But differentiation and reunification are inseparable. Difference occurs for the sake of a richer unity, and mediation preserves and cherishes differences. If, as we have seen, freedom qualifies the divine love, so love qualifies the divine freedom. The latter is not simply the capacity to choose options or actions voluntarily, without external constraint. It is far more than that; it is a concrete presence-to-self mediated in and through presence-to-others. Thus it presupposes love's positing of distinction and completes love's act of reunion. Love without freedom is an impossibility, and freedom without love is merely capricious choice.

Just as the outward relation of love has its reciprocal in liberation, so also the inward relation of freedom has its reciprocal in compassion. The divine freedom is not sheer indeterminacy but a freedom determined by and bound to compassion for the world. Because this compassion is an aspect of the *divine* freedom, it is not left hanging in the anguish of death and separation but is completed by overcoming estrangement, negating the annihilating power of death, reestablishing communion by the "subjection" and return of all things, "that God may be all in all" (1 Cor. 15:28). In this sense, just as love signifies the immanence of God in the world, so freedom signifies the immanence of the world in God.

The Perfection of God

Freedom thus means both the perfection of God and the liberation of the world. Freedom as a perfection of God is eloquently articulated by Barth in his discussion of "the being of God in freedom."[40] God lives, loves, and has being uniquely, this uniqueness being God's freedom, the depth in which God is. God's freedom may be construed as both negative and positive, transcendent and immanent, absolute and related. Indeed, it is just God's unqualified world-transcendence that is the condition of possibility of an equally unqualified world-immanence. "God has the freedom to be present with that which is not God . . . in a way which utterly surpasses all that can be effected in regard to reciprocal presence, communion and fellowship between other beings." God's absoluteness signifies "not only [God's] freedom to transcend all that is other than [godself], but also [God's] freedom to be immanent within it." God is present to another "as the being of its being with the eternal faithfulness of which no creature is capable towards another."[41]

This insight is compromised, in my view, by Barth's unwillingness to acknowledge that that which is "not God" can and must be a moment within the divine life. If God is so immanent in the world as to be "the being of its being," then the world must be immanent in God as the nonbeing of God's being-in-becoming—for there is no becoming without nonbeing as well as being. In the final analysis, Barth draws back from the economic Trinity into the innertrinitarian relations between the Father and the Son. "The existence of the world is not needed in order that there should be otherness for [God]," because "God himself is the Son who is the basic truth of that which is other than God." "There are strictly speaking no Christian themes independent of Christology."[42] Nothing could make it clearer that Barth's christocentrism finally overwhelms and subverts an authentic trinitarianism. The Spirit remains an appendage to, a function of, the inwardly complete relations between the Father and the Son. The Spirit is not really, for Barth, the perfection of God in and through the mediation of God and world.

I will develop the theme of perfection in the form of an eschatology, the consummation of freedom in God, who simply *is* freedom and whose being as God is completed by the return of all things to God (chap. 19). Freedom means the mediation and thus the completion of relationships; perfect freedom means the consummation of all relationships in God, whose being is one of inclusive and absolute relationality. This is God as Spirit. In God's being there is no difference between absoluteness and relativity, transcendence and immanence: In the Spirit they become one and the same.

The Liberation of the World

Freedom signifies not only the perfection of God but also the liberation of the world. This liberation of the world is, as we have seen, the reciprocal of God's love for the world. God loves the world toward an end, which is that of shaping scenes of freedom out of the repeated scenes of domination that make up world history. Within history, these configurations of freedom are fragmentary, ambiguous, incomplete, and the configuring process is as endless as the disfiguring one. But precisely within this endless process the world has an end, a telos, in the sense not of a chronologically future consummation but of a goal or purpose, which infuses and transfigures the process. This end is the liberation of the world in God, which occurs by means of "subduing" or "subjecting" the world's endless, restless, creative-destructive, annihilating difference in the eternal peace and unity of God. This process is going on all the time; it is not reserved just to some future end. It is rather what gives the world future, new possibility, enabling the fragmentary shapes of freedom to survive and sometimes to prevail against the much more massive scenes of violence and domination. The ground of emancipatory praxis within the world is the liberation of the world in God, and this in turn is the perfection of God's freedom. The return of all things to God is a transhistorical consummation that infuses the historical process in every moment, not just at the "end" of history.

I will develop this theme in the form of a theology of the ecclesial community, the religions, and world history, tracing the liberative work of the Spirit through enlarging concentric circles (chap. 18). Spirit is *generated* in the process of world-liberation.

God as "Spirit"

What name shall be used to designate the final figure of the triune figuration? The tradition named it Spirit, which, unlike Father and Son, is a retrievable symbol for the postmodern context. At first this seems implausible. "Spirit" is to say the least a difficult concept that has long been criticized for being both vague and dualistic, implying a separation of and a hierarchy between the mental and the physical, the soul and the body, the human and the natural, the male and the female, the holy and the profane. What is being rightly criticized here is a lingering Neoplatonism, which has reinforced dualistic, anticorporeal, and misogynist attitudes on the part of Christianity for far too long.

By contrast with this dualistic attitude, in all Indo-European languages the word "spirit" has etymological associations with natural forces—breath, wind, air, light, fire, water—forces that themselves are vital and that give life, "the breath of life." Spirit is what is alive, active, vital, moving, fluid. But spirit is also what is rational and conscious. In the Hebraic and Christian traditions, the Spirit is closely associated with the figures of Wisdom (Sophia) and Word (Logos). Spirit is in fact the unity of nature and reason, body and soul, vitality and mentality (chap. 17, pp. 276–82). It assumes the form of both primal energy and liberating language. We are now able to name the power of being by which God creates and redeems the world as "Spirit." This power, which God has absolutely (absolvingly, releasingly), is intrinsically spiritual power. God is Spirit insofar as God is present to, active in, embodied by that which is other than God, namely the natural and human worlds. Thus in scripture Spirit refers to that modality of divine activity whereby God indwells and empowers the forces of nature, the people of Israel, the ecclesial community, and individual persons (above all, Jesus of Nazareth). The Spirit is the indwelling power of God that brings the natural and human worlds to consummation by bringing estranged and fallen beings back into everlasting, liberating communion with the one God, whose true and proper name is now Spirit. Thus the Spirit is already present in the second moment, the moment of creation and differentiation, but it is fully recognized only in the third moment, the moment of liberation and consummation. This is because the Spirit is an *emergent* figure; it emerges out of the interaction of God and the world (chap. 17, pp. 282–84).

If this is correct, then the Spirit both precedes Christ and follows Christ, and we shall have to address the question of the relation between Christ and the Spirit, avoiding any subordination of the latter to the former as well as any supercession of the former by the latter (chap. 17, pp. 287–91). The theological tradition does not provide much help at this point since it never found a proper place for the Spirit. Its logic tended to be binary rather than triadic, and it viewed the Spirit as a vague sort of relationship between the Father and the Son. By contrast, it can be argued that Spirit is the richest, most encompassing, and unrestricted of the trinitarian symbols.[43] In his last lectures on religion, Hegel said: "The abstractness of the Father is given up in the Son—this then is death. But the negation of this negation is the unity of Father and Son—love, or the Spirit."[44] In other words, the abstract God, the supreme being, the Father, dies in the death of the Son, a particular male human being; and both Father and Son are reborn as concrete, world-encompassing Spirit. The abstract oneness of God and the specific incarnation of God are not lost but preserved in a richer, more inclusive unity.

Thus the Spirit is not a masculine figure. Nor is it a feminine figure, a "feminine principle" in the godhead, even though feminine images are often rightly associated with it, just as they are associated with the first two figures as well. All three figures transcend the categories of male and female, just as all three may be spoken of in both masculine and feminine metaphors.[45] Among the traditional trinitarian symbols, Spirit has the advantage of giving us a way of naming God that is not patriarchal and gender-specific. I have used the neuter singular pronoun, but perhaps plural forms would be more appropriate because the Spirit is essentially a communal, intersubjective figure, a personal power emerging out of many persons. Spirit is plural, fluid, emergent, and whole. Spirit is "we"—the wholeness toward which the oneness of God is pointing.

World: Love

12
CREATION OF THE WORLD

Creation ex Nihilo

The power of being that God "has" absolutely is essentially *creative* being. How does this power work in relation to the world? I have suggested in chapter 10 that the power of being not only calls into being everything that is but also creates a more complex and differentiated world by offering novel possibilities for advancement, thereby luring finite beings forward into new and richer possibilities of being, perhaps moving the world toward humanization and ecological order. This power is the *divine eros* or *love* at work in the world—the power of differentiation and relationship. Through reflection on the Trinity, I have named it the power of the *Spirit,* which echoes a profound biblical insight: Spirit is the "wind from God" that is sweeping across the cosmos, creating and calling. In the dimension of physical-organic life, this spiritual erotic power operates as a primal and ideal energy; for higher forms of consciousness, its allurement is experienced as in some sense a "call," that is, as a word-event or language-event, an event of pure creative possibility.

How well does this theological vision cohere with the biblical story of creation on the one hand and modern scientific cosmology on the other? The biblical story begins with familiar yet majestic images: "In the beginning God created the heavens and the earth. The earth was without form and void, and darkness was upon the face of the deep; and the Spirit of God was moving over the face of the waters" (Gen. 1:1–2, RSV). Or: "In the beginning when God created the heavens and the earth, the earth was a formless void and darkness covered the face of the deep, while a wind from God swept over the face of the waters" (NRSV). "In the beginning—God." God is the event of beginning, is the beginning, just as God is the end, Alpha and Omega. Human beings are located in the middle between beginning and end; they appear in the middle of the story, in the middle of the garden. They have beginnings and endings, but they are not beginning and end. Only God is. Hence God's creative act is one of pure freedom; it is unconditioned, uncaused, unpreceded, unlocatable in time and space.[1]

In this sense it is a creation "in the beginning," out of nothing, *ex nihilo*. This is not the void or darkness that "covered the face of the deep," for that void was already an aspect of the created earth, prior to God's word that separated light from darkness. The text does not say, "In the beginning was the void" but rather "In the beginning—God." If we can move away from the notion of a temporal beginning, then perhaps we can understand that "in the beginning" characterizes every divine creative act. It symbolizes the quality of the divine creativity—in the beginning, out of nothing, that is, in God and out of God.[2]

The doctrine of creation *ex nihilo* does not appear as such in the creation story of Genesis, which focuses instead on the theme of bringing order out of chaos (a theme to which I shall turn below). Rather it was elaborated by the early church in order to affirm that God is the source of matter as well as form. Thus it guarded against ontological dualism, which posited matter as an antidivine substance or force and predicated an eternal struggle between matter and spirit, the demonic and the divine. The doctrine also guarded against the notion that the world was an emanation of God and thus against philosophical monism, which blurred the difference between Creator and creation and reduced everything to a common substance.[3] While the world comes *from* God, it is not *of* God but rather *of* nothing. This nothing is the condition of possibility for the *difference* of the world from God; it is what makes the world not-God. Of course this nothing is not alien to God; it is included within the divine life as the moment of negation or difference that makes the divine being a becoming.[4] Thus *ex nihilo* also means that God creates out of nothing other than God, that is, out of the sheer creative potency that God is. The world images this potency in the mode of difference and finitude. It does not emanate from the divine substance because, strictly speaking, there is no divine substance.[5]

If God creates out of nothing other than God, that is, from godself, then perhaps the more appropriate metaphor for creation is that of procreation (a mother who encloses new reality in her womb and bodies it forth) rather than production (a primarily masculine image of making something outside oneself).[6] That which is bodied forth from God does not share a common substance, as in classical emanationist doctrine; rather it is the genuine other of God, which God lets go forth on its own at the moment of birth. A child does not emanate from its mother or extend her substance; in the moment of conception a genuinely other being begins to develop, and birth marks the transition of this other being into a life of its own. The divine mother, by contrast with human mothers, generates new being *ex nihilo,* that is, solely out of herself.

The Process of Creation: Biblical and Scientific Perspectives

Obviously, the biblical story of creation does not offer scientific information. It is based rather on human religious experience of the cosmos and expresses important aspects of that experience: a sense of dependence, finitude, and contingency; a response of gratitude for life; a recognition of interdependence, order, and beauty in the world. Nonetheless, there are some striking consonances between the biblical story and the emerging common creation story of the new scientific cosmologies. Our objective is not to derive a theology of creation from science but to reflect on these consonances.[7]

The Initial Void

Might the void or darkness or chaos (the face of the deep) that was God's first work of creation be understood as a mythic representation of the incredibly dense mass that exploded, according to the Big Bang theory, in the first instant of cosmic process? To be sure, the biblical story represents what physicists call the "infinite singularity" as infinite emptiness, whereas for science it is more like an infinite density,[8] but symbolically these have the same meaning: There is not yet any recognizable form or measure. This unstructured and therefore chaotic mass is not God but the stuff God posits in order to have material with which to create, that is, to separate and define. It is the common origin of all that is in the cosmos, but it itself is *not,* it has no determinate features.[9] What precedes the beginning is beyond the reach of all science; it is the sheer no-thingness of God. There is a first, wordless act of creation, impossible for us to grasp, which precedes the word that shapes the formless cosmic matter into a world.

The Emergence of Order and Diversity

The story continues: "Then God said, 'Let there be light'; and there was light. . . . And God said, 'Let there be a dome in the midst of the waters, and let it separate the waters from the waters.' . . . And God said . . ." (Gen. 1:3ff.). God speaks, and it happens; the divine imperative is an indicative. The link between God and the world is solely the creative word, not a common substance in which they share or a material causality on God's part. The word establishes the power and freedom of God, who is able to call into being merely by speaking, by using this most fragile and intangible and seemingly powerless of instruments. At the same time the word signifies that God is radically immanent in the world as the very power of being upon which everything in the world is directly dependent: If God did not speak, it would not be.[10] Of course, this is a metaphorical, not a literal speaking. The word (articulated breath) here represents the fluid, invisible, immense, and pervasive power of the Spirit of God, which sweeps like wind across the formless waters and sculpts them into a patterned cosmos. Language is an element and instrument of this power, and metaphorically can stand for the whole, but in fact it is only a tiny portion of the whole.

The word creates by wresting form out of the formless, order out of chaos. Word is what forms, shapes, configures. God's word shapes the formless cosmic matter into a *world*—a world of light and darkness, of heaven and earth, of waters and dry land, of vegetation and living creatures, of animals and humans, of man and woman. Forming or shaping is a matter of distinguishing, separating, refining, reuniting.

Here again there seems to be a striking consonance between the biblical myth and the scientific picture. According to the latter, following the instant of the beginning, the universe expanded into increasingly rich, diverse, and complex forms, and it continues to do so. What is this if not a process of separating, distinguishing, multiplying into ever more refined forms? Out of the initial chaos, order emerges through an ongoing creative process. Bringing order out of chaos is a central theme of both biblical and scientific cosmogonies.[11]

Both also depict creation as a process that occurs through time; the world does not spring fully formed from the head of Zeus. The time frames are, of course, dramatically different: seven "days" and "finished" (God rested and saw that it was good) versus fifteen billion years and counting. But according to modern astrophysics, in the initial phases the process was astonishingly rapid. Within a trillionth of a second from the Big Bang ($T+10^{-10}$ sec.), the four basic physical forces had separated. At $T+10^{-4}$ sec., subatomic quarks had changed to protons and neutrons, and at T+3 mins., nuclei were formed (hydrogen, helium). With the basic building blocks in place, the process slowed down: It took half a million years for atoms to form, a billion years for galaxies, and ten billion years for planets. But then, with the emergence of life on planet earth after twelve billion years, the pace quickened and in just three billion years life has evolved into its present incredible diversity and complexity.[12]

Which is primary in this process, the increase in order or the increase in diversity? It is possible to stress one to the detriment of the other, but this is a false alternative. The new science of "chaos" has shown that the most diverse, flexible, and unpredictable dynamic systems at the same time reveal the most intricate and beautiful patterns of order.[13] Those who wish to affirm the often wild, wondrous, fecund diversification found in nature and to resist imposing a premature purpose on an essentially open process are surely right, but at the same time they recognize that things are interconnected in the most radical way; and some believe that the creative process has a strangely serendipitous, even quasi-teleological, quality.[14] At the heart of creation is a mystery that evokes awe from scientist and theologian alike. It is from such awe that faith in God as Creator has arisen.

The Creation of Human Beings

Formed of Dust . . . in the Image of God

The story goes on:

> Then God said, "Let us make humankind ['*adham*] in our image, according to our likeness; and let them have dominion over the fish of the sea, and over the birds of the air, and over the cattle, and over all the wild animals of the earth, and over every creeping thing that creeps upon the earth."
>
> So God created humankind in his image,
> in the image of God he created them;
> male and female he created them (Gen. 1:26–27).

In contrast to this rather grandiose Priestly account, the Yahwist provides a more modest version: "Then the LORD God formed human being ['*adham*] from the dust of the ground, and breathed into his nostrils the breath of life; and human being became a living being" (Gen. 2:7, author's translation).

These two texts taken together epitomize the central themes of a theological anthropology, discussed in more detail below (chap. 14, pp. 199–208). The Yahwist's account underscores the continuity of human beings with the rest of the natural world. '*Adham* was formed of dust from the ground, '*adhamah,* and became a living being, a *nephesh,* through the inbreathing of the breath of life, *ruach.* The very name of human being, '*adham,* means "ground," but this ground is brought to life by the breath or Spirit of God. As a living being, '*adham* is essentially a *free* being. This is the central theme of the Priestly text. Freedom is defined in terms of certain constitutive relationships: the relationship to God, in whose image (as the utterly Free One) human beings are created; the relationship to the earth and its living creatures, over which '*adham* is to have "dominion"; and the relationship between man and woman as the primordial community in which human beings can be free for the other. Freedom is not an individualistic but a communal, relational concept for the Hebrew Bible. To be sure, these relationships are defined hierarchically and patriarchally, at least in the Priestly text. God has dominion over humans (yet they are God's truest image), humans over nature (although dominion carries with it stewardship), and man over woman (even though they are created as equals and partners). Today we must develop a concept of freedom that affirms the repressed intuitions of the ancient text, replacing hierarchy by equality and dominion by reciprocity and mutual responsibility.

Human beings are free primarily by virtue of their capacity to speak: Language is the road to freedom. This is already reflected in the biblical story of origins: God creates by calling into being; God communicates with *'adham* by means of spoken commands; *'adham* is given the capacity of naming the animals; the man and the woman speak to each other; and the subtle speech of the serpent is the instrument of deception (a point to be discussed further, chap. 14, pp. 212–15). This ancient insight is confirmed by modern anthropological and linguistic studies. That which decisively distinguishes human beings from all other living beings is not simply intelligence but language, thought, and freedom. The higher animals possess greater or lesser degrees of intelligence, but they lack the capacity to speak and thus to think and to be free in relation to the natural environment. To be sure, certain prototypes of human language, thought, and freedom are discernible in their signlike communication and playfulness; and sometimes animals and humans are able to communicate in extraordinary ways. But a fundamental threshold crossing remains, nonetheless; human being is "created" when language emerges and the determinacy of nature gives way to the freedom of spirit (a process that took place over thousands of years). Human freedom remains determinate, of course, and within the determinacy of nature there are to be found ciphers of freedom: All distinctions here are thoroughly dialectical. Yet we can agree with the philosopher Herder that human being is the first liberated being in creation. It is appropriate, therefore, to designate human being, not only as *Homo sapiens* (wise) but also as *Homo liber* (free). And it is as *Homo liber* that human being is the *imago Dei*.

The Anthropic Principle and Human Evolution

Is there a consonance between the biblical account of the creation of human beings and the so-called "anthropic principle" of postmodern science as well as the theory of human evolution? Humans exist in profound continuity with nature, having evolved from more primitive forms of life, yet they also understand themselves to be the telos or goal of the whole creative process. Is that blind hubris or a recognition of the glory of the process, which eventuates in free and intelligent beings?

The anthropic principle has been formulated by present-day physicists in a number of versions. In its strongest form it holds that the very nature of the physical universe makes the emergence of life and the evolution of intelligent observers within it not only possible but inevitable, and according to one philosophical interpretation it implies that such a process reaches its culmination not in finite human intelligence but in infinite and all-comprehending mind or spirit.[15] Is not this simply a return to a discredited anthropocentrism? Those who espouse the principle hold that it does not have an anthropocentric but a holistic evolutionary basis, the principle of which is the continuity of mind with matter in a unified world: More properly speaking, it is the anthropic *cosmological* principle.

If the tendency of the cosmos is to produce complexity, then by far the greatest complexity we know is precisely we ourselves. Ian Barbour puts it this way: "There are a hundred trillion synapses in a human brain; the number of possible ways of connecting them is greater than the number of atoms in the universe. A higher level of organization and a greater richness of experience occurs in a human being than in a thousand lifeless galaxies."[16] We should not, however, confuse this complexity with the goal or the center of cosmic process. Barbour goes on to point out: "The chemical elements in your hand and in your brain were forged in the furnaces of stars. The cosmos is all of a piece. It is multileveled; each new higher level was built on lower levels from the past. Humanity is the most advanced form of life we know, but it is fully a part of a wider process in space and time."[17] We know little about this wider process, and the process itself is unfinished. There could well be intelligent beings living in more advanced civilizations on other planets, and there is no reason to think that the evolutionary process will come to a halt with the human brain. Mentality set loose in the world has a tendency to ramify into ever more complex structures, some of which may exceed human capacity, as the science of cybernetics suggests.

While avoiding anthropocentrism, we must recognize that through a curious reversal human beings are becoming increasingly important for the rest of the natural world. We have attained the power to destroy or to sustain the environment, and we cannot avoid our responsibility as guardians and caretakers. We must acquire a sense of belonging, of being at home in the world as mature adults rather than as children who are at the mercy of nature or adolescents who carelessly play with it.[18]

The theory of evolution certainly underscores the sense of belonging. We are formed of cosmic dust—almost literally, through random variations in the genetic code combined with a process of natural selection (both competitive and cooperative) by which higher species emerge. Humans and apes are descended from common ancestors going back four to five million years. The first form of the human species, *Homo habilis,* was present about two-and-a-half million years ago in Africa. Archaic forms of *Homo sapiens* appeared 300,000 to 500,000 years ago. The Neanderthals were in Europe 100,000 years ago, followed by the first modern *Homo sapiens,* the Cromagnons, some 12,000 to 40,000 years ago. They made significant advances in arts, crafts, tools, and other skills of primitive civilization, as evidenced by their wall paintings, artifacts, and burial rituals. During the Neolithic period (10,000–3,000 B.C.E.) the pace of change quickened, with the taming of animals, the development of agriculture, the invention of writing (Sumerian inscriptions, about 4,000 B.C.E.), and the beginning of the great civilizations in Mesopotamia, Egypt, and India.[19]

Sometime prior to 30,000 years ago language must have begun to appear. Only humans are fully capable of language, which requires not only sufficient brain capacity but also vocal organs for articulated speech. When the physical conditions were ripe, a threshold crossing to language and mentality occurred (language being the precondition of mind) and with that the appearance of human being in the strict sense, *Homo liber,* liberated by language and thought from bondage to nature and to qualitatively new possibilities of being. With the invention of writing, these possibilities ramified in an astonishingly rapid and ever accelerating process. But we must not forget that linguisticality and mentality are higher-level emergent properties of the brain, unique and irreducible yet rooted in physiological processes. What is called for is a multidimensional understanding of the relationship of human being to nature.[20]

As we look back, we are filled with awe. An extreme fine-tuning was required for the process to have turned out the way it did. Minute changes in the physical constants would have resulted in an uninhabitable universe.[21] Some interpreters have argued that chance mutation and natural selection alone are not enough to account for the evolution of highly adapted organisms, and they point out that the odds against human evolution are extremely low, especially in the limited time span within which it in fact occurred.[22] Is this proof of a divine Creator? No, there is no such scientific proof. But the belief that God really did form human beings "of dust" and "in the image of God"—not instantly but through an amazing evolutionary process—is not incompatible with what we know today from scientific observation. The postmodern scientific paradigm is far more congruent with a religious interpretation of creation and nature than was the Newtonian paradigm.

13

NATURE: ENERGY, DIMENSIONS, PROCESS, EROS

A Holistic Theology of Nature[1]

Only recently have theologians begun to address the tasks of a theology of nature. The experimental theses of the present work are (1) nature is a differentiated yet unitary interplay of material energy in space (dimensions) and time (process); (2) God is present in this interplay as the propelling-attracting power of life/love (eros) that creates all things in distinction from itself and draws all things to itself; (3) human beings as embodied natural beings share the exteriority of space and succession of time, but as conscious spiritual beings achieve an internal integration of space-time in the form of freedom.[2] These theses are elaborated as a holistic theology of nature. The first task is to explain in what sense this is a "theology of nature" and in what sense it is "holistic."

Natural Theology and Theology of Nature

"Natural theology" can be construed as an attempt either to found theological claims about nature at least partly on natural science and thus to marshall scientific evidence in support of religious belief, especially belief in God, or to extend theological claims about nature into the arena of science, offering, for example, "creationist" versions of how the world originated and evolved. In either case the result is confusion since religious apprehensions of the world and theological interpretations of these apprehensions are not scientific in an empirical-experimental sense. What should be aimed at instead are connections of coherence and consonance between the knowledge of science and the knowledge of theology, which has its own distinctive sources and character. This is the approach of what Ian Barbour calls "theology of nature."[3]

Theology of nature can be described as a theological interpretation of nature, which affirms that God is the giver and redeemer of all life.[4] Theology of nature draws upon a variety of resources, including scripture and theological tradition, personal experience and intuition, philosophical interpretations of nature such as those of Whitehead and Collingwood, as well as the cosmologies that emerge from natural science and that do represent interpretations of empirical evidence. The theological picture of nature and of the God-world relationship does not rest solely on faith and revelation; it also has an empirical referent with which it must be congruent. The same is true of theological claims about other subjects with an empirical or historical referent such as human nature, evil, Jesus of Nazareth, church, the history of religions.

This approach of coherence and consonance between science and theology, as opposed to direct dependence or confusion, was anticipated by Ernst Troeltsch in his lectures on Christian faith in 1912–13. Troeltsch argued that faith cannot establish scientific or historical facts, but it can and must interpret them if it is to maintain contact with the real world. It must accept the facts as established by historians and scientists. But it works out its distinctive interpretations on the basis of a concept of "world" and "history" that is not a scientific theory but a religious idea. "The concept of the world can emerge as a self-contained and real unity only in connection with the concept of an ordering world-reason, or a creative divine will." Troeltsch also insisted that revelation does not offer a "sacred cosmology" or a "sacred physics" but rather "religious strength and a religious approach to the world as a whole."[5]

In other words the task of a theology of nature is not to make empirical claims based on revelation but to interpret the empirical evidence in the light of revelation, religious experience, and theological reflection. Natural theology, by contrast, encroaches on the legitimate boundary between religion and science, either appropriating science in support of religion or overextending religion in the form of quasi-scientific claims.

A Holistic Model of Nature

We cannot know the whole of the world as it is in and for itself. Rather we construct models or paradigms, which are limited ways of imagining what is not observable. But models are not simply fictions, and we can make tentative reality claims based on them.[6] There is widespread consensus that in the twentieth century we have experienced a profound paradigm shift from medieval and Newtonian cosmologies to postmodern (post-Einsteinian) views. The medieval paradigm represented a synthesis of classical (Greek) and biblical ideas about nature, which remained essentially unchanged for more than fifteen hundred years. The Newtonian view, which emerged in the seventeenth and eighteenth centuries, is often described as "early modern," while the postmodern or twentieth-century paradigm is sometimes termed "late modern." The nineteenth century represents a middle ground: The Newtonian paradigm was beginning to fragment with the emergence of organic and evolutionary theories, but a scientific basis for its replacement was not provided prior to Einstein's theory of relativity. Assuming that the seventeenth through nineteenth centuries represent the age of "modernity," and in light of the profound shift of consciousness occasioned by twentieth-century physics, it is better to speak of a transition to a genuinely "postmodern" perspective.[7]

Barbour lays out the contrasts as follows:[8] (1) Whereas in the medieval view nature was a fixed order, and for Newtonian science the only change consisted in rearrangement of unchanging components, for twentieth-century science nature is understood to be evolutionary, dynamic, historical, and emergent. (2) While the medieval view was teleological (purposive) and the Newtonian deterministic, postmodern science sees nature as a complex interplay of law and chance, of structure and openness. (3) In terms of what constitutes nature, the medieval view was substantive (independent and externally related entities), the Newtonian was atomistic (tiny separate particles), while the new view is relational, ecological, and interdependent (reality is constituted by events and relationships rather than separate substances or particles). (4) Classical and medieval society viewed the cosmos as hierarchical, with human beings on top (just under God and angels); Newtonian science was reductionistic and mechanistic (physical mechanisms at the lowest level determine all events); and twentieth-century science is organismic and holistic (parts can be understood only in relation to systems or wholes). (5) Over against the dualism of both medieval and Newtonian worldviews (spirit versus matter in the first instance, mind versus body in the second), postmodern cosmology is multidimensional and holistic (spirit and matter are distinctive dimensions of a larger whole, human being is a psychosomatic unity).

If a single term were selected to characterize the postmodern paradigm, it might be "holistic." Errol Harris offers a philosophical theory of holism that is well-informed by recent science and systems theory as well as by Hegel and Whitehead.[9] He argues that a whole is a concrescent system, united by a universal principle of organization that expresses itself in the mutual adjustment of diverse parts, which overlap in their reciprocal definition and interdependent relationships. Parts are themselves wholes or systems on a smaller scale, so a system is actually a system of systems, and as it develops it achieves both greater complexity and greater integration. Because wholes are complexes of relations, and relations exist only as recognized, systems are most fully realized at the stage of consciousness. The goal of a system is to achieve full self-awareness, which at the same time is its unitary principle. This principle is not static but dynamic, a form-shaping form (Plato, Whitehead), a self-realizing *nisus*, an *energeia*, an active self-knowing reason (Aristotle, Hegel). Holism need not issue in the theistic conclusions toward which Harris is pointing, but his description of how natural systems work, his recognition that they develop toward greater complexity, his hunch that a unitary principle underlies the complexity, and his observation that relations exist qua relations only for states of consciousness or awareness are of considerable value.

The ecological holistic model claims that relations are internal rather than external, that is, they are constitutive of entities rather than being incidental to them, as though entities first existed and then came into relationship. Consciousness represents a further intensification of the internality of relations rather than a sharp break with nature.[10] But the spatio-temporal realm in which relations transpire has an aspect of externality to it. Space and time enable difference, the condition of possibility for relations, the opening out from the Big Bang. In this sense there is exteriority in nature, as Hegel claimed.[11] But within the space-time continuum entities are related both externally and internally. There is both spatio-temporal separation and organic interpenetration: I am different from everything else yet part of everything else. Consciousness attains inner fluidity in relation to space-time even as it remains bound to it.

Energy: A Relational-Organic View of Matter

Nature, Matter, and Energy

"Nature" is linked to the idea of being born (*natus*); "matter" to the mother (*mater*) that is the source or womb (*matrix*) of all that is. It is not surprising that in Latin *natura* and *materia* are feminine in gender and that they are closely linked concepts.[12] Nature *is* matter, that which comes into being from the maternal source, the sum total of what exists physically. The etymology of the terms already suggests a dynamic reality: "Nature" refers to the inborn character of a thing, its vital powers, its impulse to act; "matter" to the potency that infuses things.

The dynamic understanding of nature and matter characteristic of ancient religion and philosophy was lost in the Newtonian mechanical paradigm ("the death of nature," Carolyn Merchant calls it[13]), but it has been regained by postmodern physics and given for the first time an adequate scientific basis. Matter, we now know, does not consist of tiny substances called atoms but of relations of energy. Einstein's theory of special relativity held that energy is equivalent to mass (a quantity of matter) multiplied by the square of the velocity of light ($E=MC^2$). Quantum theory (a refinement of Einstein's general theory of relativity) tells us that energy is absorbed and radiated in subatomic units called quanta, behaving sometimes as waves (vibrations), sometimes as particles (points). Particles seem to be temporary manifestations of shifting patterns of waves that combine at one point, dissolve again, and recombine elsewhere. A particle is not a solid thing but a local outcropping of a continuous substratum of vibratory energy, which is essentially fluid. Everything is fluid, moving, unstable, indeterminate.[14] Thales was close to the truth when he said that everything is made of water; Anaximenes, when he said that air is the basic form of matter; and Heraclitus, when he said that everything is an everlasting fire.[15] These are ancient metaphors of matter. "Energy" itself is a metaphor, pointing to something that is active, at work (*energei, ergon*); "potency" (Heisenberg) is perhaps a better term. Energy, this fluid potency organized in patterns and relationships, is the basis for what we experience as visible things and also as mental activity.[16]

Unified Field Theory

The energy that generates matter in a space-time continuum consists of four basic forces: the electromagnetic force responsible for light and the behavior of charged particles; the weak nuclear force responsible for radioactive decay; the strong nuclear force that binds protons and neutrons into nuclei; and the gravitational force evident in the attraction between masses. At the instant of the Big Bang these forces were unified, but they separated out between $T+10^{-43}$ and 10^{-10} sec. (the latter is a trillionth of a second), and by T+3 mins. nuclei had formed. Physicists are now seeking a unified field theory that would unite these four forces under one theory and become in effect a fundamental law of everything[17]—Harris's universal principle of organization. Harris points out that the physicist David Bohm spoke of the world as a dynamic totality, a "holomovement" in which the whole is implicit in every part. The world is a unitary field, an orderly energy system describable by linear equations although the fundamental equation cannot yet be precisely formulated. Even the study of nonlinear dynamical systems shows that chaos is a "mask of the most intricate and entrancing forms of order and pattern."[18]

Might we say that the initial dispersion of the four forces in the Big

Bang laid the foundation for the exteriority of the physical universe as a continuum of space and time? Are these forces in some sense reunited in consciousness even if they have not yet been unified mathematically? We can think or imagine their unity and in that sense transcend their dispersion.

If energy is the unity of the cosmos, space and time are the difference. I shall now look more closely at the latter two.

Dimensions: Radical Unity and Radical Diversity

Space, Time, and Difference

Space and time were generated out of the Big Bang (at T=0 there was no space and time, only an immeasurably dense, tiny, and timeless mass). As Einstein showed, they form an interactive continuum rather than being separate and absolute containers. Movement in one affects measurement of the other. Our understanding of space has been "temporalized": Spatial bodies are dynamic, changing events rather than static substances.[19] Perhaps also our understanding of time has or ought to be "spatialized": Evolution in time results in an incredible spatial diversification. Sallie McFague argues that space ought to be given a new primacy in ecological thinking, counteracting our Western tendency to subordinate space to time. This is partly because the ecological crisis is basically one of space (rain forests, atmosphere, habitat, population, etc.) rather than of time (although time is running out for effective countermeasures). It is also, she says, because we should celebrate the wild, fecund diversification of evolutionary process and not seek a premature unity.[20]

I shall first address this spatial diversity under the theme of "dimensions." But dimensions that are distinguished spatially evolve temporally, so it is impossible to talk about dimensions without process (and vice versa). The fact that dimensions interact and are overlaid means that spatial relations within nature are not just external but also internal. Space involves both an "outside" and an "inside." Perhaps this is part of the meaning of the temporalization of space: What we find are dynamic interpenetrating events rather than unchanging monadic substances.

A Multiplicity of Interacting Dimensions: Physical, Organic, Sentient, Mental, Cultural

"Dimensions" are elements, coordinates, or measures constitutive of a whole. This is a more appropriate term to describe the spatial constitution of nature than that of "levels," which suggests a discrete and often hierarchically arranged set of planes. Alternatively, we might speak of "spheres" or "realms" if these are not thought to exist simply outside each other.

Nature as a whole is a complex interplay of dimensions, which can be neither reduced to the single one-dimensional picture of Newtonian science, nor divided into the two-dimensional worldview of classical theology—the supernatural and the natural. Rather what we find is a multiplicity of dimensions and subdimensions: the physical-chemical (which can be further divided into the subatomic and atomic), the organic (composed of plant life and animal life), the sentient (animal and human), the mental (humans as self-conscious, thinking, speaking beings), and the cultural (the products of human spirit: aesthetic, ethical, political, scientific, religious). The "higher" or more complex dimensions are qualitatively distinct; they incorporate the lower dimensions but cannot be explained in terms appropriate to the latter, hence reductionism is ruled out. Dimensions reflect the almost infinite ramification of differences in the universe. But dimensions do not exist outside of each other in hierarchical layers; rather they intermesh and participate in a mysterious unity that again can best be described in terms of the metaphor of energy.[21]

In a fascinating analysis—in effect an updated rewriting of Hegel's philosophy of nature with help from Teilhard de Chardin and evolutionary science—Errol Harris tries to show how these dimensions are necessarily generated out of each other.

(1) The *physical world* is in contradiction with itself because it is spread out in space and time, its contents are externally related, yet it is an integral whole, governed by a single principle of order. As physical, its unity is merely implicit, its ordering principle immanent; its wholeness is incomplete. So physical-chemical processes tend to become more complex and self-enfolded and to drive toward greater self-determination, bringing the whole into more concentrated centreity: the organism.

(2) *Organism* is the imposition of a new and more plastic form on more complex substrate processes. Its essential capacity is for self-maintenance, metabolism, hence it is the first form of freedom in nature. Organisms are open, self-maintaining systems in dynamic equilibrium with feedback from the environment. They represent a new kind of wholeness, entailing radial as opposed to tangential energy (Teilhard).

(3) But mere organism as such is self-contradictory since it too does not find the integration it seeks, hence the transition to *sentience* (the ability to experience, feel, respond, or what has been called "soul," which is common to all animals) and ultimately to *mentality* (speech, thought, "mind," found just in humans). These involve no additional entity or process, just new forms of coordination and integration.

There is no supernatural or immortal soul inserted into a natural body: Human being is not two things (body and soul/mind) but one thing, the body-as-sentient/conscious. What appears is a new shape or life-form, not a new supramaterial entity. Mind is due to the same activity that has been operative throughout, with a higher degree of unified complexity and self-determination. It is anticipated by what comes before but is a distinct shape of life, which rules out panpsychism (the theory that psyche, mind, is found in primitive forms throughout all the dimensions of nature).

(4) Finally there is what Teilhard called the *noosphere* (the sphere of mind, *nous,* a subset of the biosphere), the realm of human culture, politics, morality, art, religion. Between these successive spheres there are no breaks, none is independent of the others, and those prior are incorporated by those that supervene and grow out of them. In the noosphere the cosmos comes to consciousness of itself and explicitly realizes its essential nature. This, claims Harris, is the basis and justification of the anthropic principle.[22]

Process: An Evolving Cosmos

Temporality and Historicity

Here the stress falls on the temporalization of space rather than the spatialization of time. Everything in the world is fluid, dynamic, changing, evolving. "History" is a category that applies to nature as well as to human culture. In fact R. G. Collingwood argued that history and historical consciousness provided the basis for the revolution in the interpretation of nature that has emerged in the twentieth century.[23] The cosmos as a whole, not just terrestrial life, is now understood in processive and evolutionary terms. Evolution is a "story" that is unique and directional rather than repetitive and cyclical.[24] History is a process that extends beyond the realm of the human to encompass the whole of life although it can be argued that "historicity"—the act of living self-consciously as free and purposive historical beings—is fully accomplished in the human sphere, and indeed that "historicity" is what the "ultimate nature of things" is pressing toward.[25]

Creativity: Order out of Chaos

Bringing order out of chaos is the central theme of the Genesis story. The act of creation consisted in imposing distinctions and hence order on the raw material of the primordial chaos or void: light and darkness, stars and planets, dry land and water, plants and animals, animals and humans, man and woman. It is also a central theme of postmodern science. Paul Davies refers to "the new paradigm of the creative universe" as opposed to the Newtonian and thermodynamic paradigms. The universe is not a dead, sterile machine, or in a state of degeneration and decay, but rather is full of creative power, able to produce "a progressively richer variety of complex forms and structures." Even though the amount of usable energy is gradually dissipating through the operation of thermodynamic laws, the universe is at the same time "progressing—through the steady growth of structure, organization, and complexity—to ever more developed and elaborate states of matter and energy." The fact of entropy means that the universe is finite, but the power of negentropy means that it is evolving toward greater richness, wholeness, and complexity of life.[26]

It appears that the creativity present in the universe results from the interplay of chance and regularity. Chance consists in random variations and interactions, and in the indeterminacy present in complex dynamical systems. It allows for the flexibility needed to explore all the potential forms of organization of matter. Chance alone, however, would produce sheer chaos, so the regularity and determinacy of the causal nexus are also needed to preserve those novel patterns that represent a creative advance.[27]

Perhaps it is necessary to distinguish between disordered and ordered chaos, or between "sheer chaos" and "patterned chaos." Sheer chaos would be the initial formless void prior to the formation of the cosmos, or destructive and uncontrolled change such as occurs with the breakdown of systems or the clash between them. It hints at a tragic or evil dimension in nature to which I shall return. Patterned chaos is what characterizes complex dynamical systems (weather systems, fluid flows, swinging pendulums, traffic patterns), and it in fact embodies more complex forms of order, which are often of remarkable and varied beauty. The order is difficult to comprehend because such systems are exceedingly sensitive to initial conditions and to environmental feedback. The order they exhibit is one of fractals—infinitely repeating variations on a theme. This kind of chaos, then, is part of the emergent order of the cosmos, whose complexity exceeds the grasp of both our imagination and our instruments of measure.[28]

Characteristics of Evolutionary Process

Gordon Kaufman characterizes the cosmic evolutionary process in a suggestive way.[29] Movement through time seems to be irreversible and unidirectional, always toward new forms and unprecedented developments, not simply repetitive patterns. There seems to be momentum for development in certain directions, not others; evolution does not run backward and extinct forms do not reemerge. Cosmic time is creative of the new, continually branching out. Cosmic process has produced more than one would have expected, more than seemed possible, moving toward complex and higher forms, toward "history" and "historicity." Historicity emerges only gradually through a long, complex, and diverse development.

Where is it all going? If it is too much to speak of a goal-directed causative power, we can at least, says Kaufman, point to "creative trajectories." What we find are trajectories of various durations rather than a single overarching unilinear teleology. Retrospectively viewed, these "directional movements" are "quasi-teleological," and on this basis we can say that there is a tendency in the ultimate nature of things toward the production of ever higher and richer, centered forms of being. This cannot be a matter of chance alone but of what seems to be a "serendipitous creativity" at work in the world. Thus the appearance of humans is not a metaphysical surd but grounded in the ultimate nature of things, the ultimate mystery. To be sure, it is an act of faith to understand the evolutionary process this way, but it is not inconsistent with what we know on the basis of natural science.

Kaufman believes that the symbol "God" does not name a particular existent being but the "ultimate mystery" that expresses itself in the cosmic-historical trajectory working toward humanization and ecological order. God is not a particular being but a particular form of order or ordering going on within the world, which has a humane, person-enhancing quality. While I do not accept the concept of God that Kaufman elaborates here, I do find his characterization of evolutionary process helpful. In my view God is not simply the cosmic ordering process itself but a personal spiritual eros that empowers the process and makes creativity serendipitous rather than destructive.

The Future of the Universe

Despite its evolutionary trajectories, the universe remains finite and eventually will die out—either through an endless expansion with decreasing energy ("freezing death") or by collapsing in a Big Crunch ("heat death"), possibly followed by another cosmic cycle. The current expanding phase will last at least a hundred billion years, but our sun will run out of energy well before then, in another five to ten billion years, and human civilization may be wiped out in the next ice age if not earlier through ecological or nuclear catastrophe. The universe is a strange mix of entropy (the dissipation of usable forms of energy) and creativity (or negentropy, the emergence of complex, rich, and intelligent forms). It is an illusion to think that intelligence can be preserved on a technological basis after this planet is no longer habitable although there may well be intelligent life on other planets. In the end, entropy will win out and the universe will die, but this does not imply that the process is meaningless or that divine eros is exhausted. Genuine value is created, the challenges and opportunities are enormous, and the adventure of life is full of joy as well as anguish. But the ultimate preserver of the values, challenges, opportunities, and adventures cannot be the universe itself but God, who is the beginning and end of all that is.[30]

Eros: The Presence of God in Nature

Does World-Process Require a God?

Natural theology has attempted in a variety of ways to demonstrate the existence of God from features of the natural world. Errol Harris offers a modern version of such an argument. He believes it can be shown that the cosmos must culminate in an end or totality that far exceeds what humans are able to accomplish and that this totality is what religions call God. God is the absolute universal principle of order manifesting itself in and as the universe, transcending all finite phases. All natural activity is the process of God's creation; all nature is God's self-revelation. The argument for God arises from the inevitable implication of the unity of the universe as a self-differentiating and self-explicating whole that cannot be complete as such and requires a consummation in a totally self-sufficient, self-conscious mind. The resort to God is not a cloak to cover our ignorance but the logical consequence of the nature of our knowledge and of the structure of the universe as discovered by empirical science.[31]

Many theologians are suspicious of this sort of cosmological or teleological argument for God. I share the suspicion even as I find much of Harris's cosmotheological speculation suggestive; it is just that it lacks the probative power he claims for it. A theistic interpretation is *consistent* with what we know of cosmic process, but it is not *required* by it. It could be that there simply is no culmination to the cosmological dialectic but an endless and forever incomplete expansion or contraction. It could be that what appears to us to be "serendipitous" is really nothing but chance, and that what we perceive as value is merely a human projection on a meaningless process. Rather than having a direction or purpose, evolution may simply open out into an incredible diversity—more like a bush with many branches than a ladder of progressive forms or a cone funneling toward a central point.[32] Theological claims depend on additional and different sorts of evidence than that provided by science, namely on personal religious experience, on the witness of communities of faith, on paradigmatic revelatory figures such as Jesus of Nazareth. We can, however, construct models of God's presence in nature that are informed by science and congruent with it.

Models of God's Presence in Nature

Basically such models understand God as interacting in cosmic process continuously rather than intervening sporadically from outside it.[33] This has been worked out most carefully by process theology. God acts in the mode of persuasion and influence rather than of compulsion and coercion. God is effective not as a first cause or efficient cause but as a final cause, evoking responses, calling or luring toward new and richer possibilities of being. God works patiently, gently, unobtrusively, as a creative participant, a wise teacher, a procreating and nurturing mother. God's power is the evocative power of love and inspiration, an empowering power. As such God's power must be understood as *spiritual*. As Spirit, God is present, influences, and in-spires from within. How God does this ultimately remains a mystery, but we can testify to the reality of it in our own lives. Can we think of something analogous to inspiration working at physical and biological levels? Can we say that God shapes cosmic energy to life-giving, love-enhancing, liberative ends by spiritually indwelling all creatures in a mode appropriate to each creature? Spirit is precisely what evokes response: the witness of the Spirit to spirits (human and non-human, organic and inorganic—the very stones cry out).[34]

God is present in the world both generically *as* world (the body of God, the material world that constitutes the moment of difference within the divine life, the other of God that is not-God) and determinately as personal spiritual eros that shapes and lures the world toward love and freedom. As spiritual, this eros works inwardly, evoking response, empowering power.

God's Spirit as Creative and Alluring Cosmic Eros[35]

Eros names a kind of love that unites the material energy of life with the distinctive spiritual quality of entering into relationship with an other for the sake of the other, which is what we mean by love as *agapē*, *philia*, and *caritas*. Love is the interrelatedness of life, and life is the dynamism of love. These two aspects are captured by the Greek word *eros*, which unites spiritual love with material potency and sensual desire. Erotic love lures, attracts, connects, empowers. God's love for the world is erotic in the sense that God creates, desires, and allures the world in its vitality and materiality, while at the same time transfiguring that materiality into relationships of spirituality, that is, of inwardness, recognition, mutuality, self-giving. These are the relationships characteristic of persons.

My proposal is that God's Spirit is present and active in all dimensions of the cosmos as creative, shaping, alluring, energizing *eros*. It is what I referred to earlier as the power of being that takes the form of *primal* energy and *liberating* language. I now characterize this power as that of spiritual/erotic love. This eros is profoundly alive and in the deepest sense personal although it manifests itself in both personal and impersonal forms, and its fundamental quality is that of allurement, of drawing all things to itself and of sustaining and cherishing all things in relationship to it. Brian Swimme speaks of "cosmic allurement": an "attracting activity" that is the fundamental mystery of the universe. What humans experience as love is "the basic binding energy found everywhere in reality." It permeates the cosmos on all levels of being. Without this mysterious drawing of things together, the universe would fly apart. It manifests itself on a range from the primary physical forces (electromagnetic, nuclear, gravitational) to spiritual love.[36]

Borrowing an image from chaos theory,[37] perhaps we could say that God is the ultimate "strange attractor" of the cosmos—an attractor that is not directly visible but appears in and through the turbulence and fluidity of countless dynamic events in natural and human history. Naming this attractor God, attributing cosmic allurement to God, identifying the eros toward life with the Spirit of God—this is of course an act of faith that takes us beyond all science, but it is congruent both with science (at least postmodern science) and with biblical images of God's spiritual presence and empowerment. One of the most striking biblical images is that of the wind that draws things into itself through that most powerful of natural forces, a vacuum. God, the strange attractor, is like a mighty whirlwind (Job 38:1).

While the divine eros is everywhere present and available, it creates and attracts toward specific ends, ends that may be defined, in light of the Christ-event, as life-giving, love-enhancing, and liberative. The christic paradigm determines the shape and telos of God's worldly embodiment; God's erotic Spirit is the Spirit of Christ. God is not simply cosmic spiritual eros but the One who "has" this eros "absolutely" and releases it to work in the world in determinate ways. God is more than a force or power; God is a personal subject, *the* personal subject who relates to each and every thing by spiritually indwelling that thing.[38] Whether the creative and alluring possibilities that God offers are actualized depends on the contingency of each situation and the free play of conflicting forces. God is a factor in the way the world goes, but precisely where and how it goes is not controlled by God. God is at risk and suffers in the world but also rejoices in the emergence of everything that is good.

A similar conclusion can be arrived at by using Kaufman's notion of "serendipitous creativity." The divine eros is what makes creativity serendipitous, restraining its potential for destructiveness. There is a tendency in nature for the necessary thrust toward difference and differentiation to overreach itself, to disintegrate into rivalry and violence, to engender chaos and disorder, to move toward death rather than life. Difference under the conditions of finitude tends to become rupture, separation, estrangement, self-centeredness. The struggle for life tends to be excessive, to go beyond what is actually necessary for survival; this manifests itself among other things in cancerous growth and gratuitous violence among animals. Natural systems sometimes interact destructively, such as volcanic eruptions, floods, and hurricanes that destroy existing forms of life. Nature sometimes seems to be more of a butcher than a mother.[39]

This is the presence of *evil,* or more properly of *tragedy,* in nature—what might be called the "waywardness" of nature.[40] Such a view is commonly regarded as anthropomorphic: It is only from a human perspective and in light of human interests that nature has tragic consequences. Of course it is true that everything is seen from a human perspective and in light of human interests. But what we see in nature may actually be there, a kind of ontological undertow toward disintegration and destructiveness—an undertow in which we too participate as natural beings. This may belong to the condition of possibility of there being a created world at all, but that does not render it less tragic. In this case, God's presence in the form of creative and alluring eros is essential for the redemption of nature, for moving it toward the ends that God envisions. God lets the world go, but God also loves the world and does not abandon it to its own devices. God draws things toward godself and out of their isolation. This is another way of answering the question, "Does world-process require a God?"

14

HUMAN BEING: FINITE FREEDOM, FALL, SIN, AND EVIL

Anthropological Challenges

Anthropology is properly treated in the middle of theology, in the context of an interpretation of world as radically different from God yet profoundly related to God. In this way I wish to emphasize that humans are finite, natural, material beings, but at the same time spiritual beings created in the image of God. We are a tiny part of a cosmic whole, yet that place where cosmos becomes aware of itself and of the greater whole of which it too is a part—a whole that is cosmotheandric, and as such pneumatic, of the Spirit.

At the same time, all of theology is grounded in experience—in human experience, which is experience not just of ourselves as self-conscious subjects but of our being-in-the-world. In this sense, anthropology belongs at the beginning of theology. I discussed earlier the dilemma of determining where to locate anthropology in the theological project (chap. 4, pp. 44–46), and from the desire to avoid anthropological foundationalism I opted for a trinitarian structure, which places humans in the middle. Yet I prefaced the treatment of God with a discussion of faith (chap. 9, pp. 120–21), and the entire "triune figuration" is preceded by several chapters of "contextualizing" (chapters 5–8). The postmodern quests described in these chapters are in fact human quests, and I have argued for a correlation between these quests (emancipatory, ecological, dialogical) and the gestalts of the triune figuration (freedom, love, oneness/wholeness). In this sense anthropology appears at the beginning of this project as well as in the middle.

From the postmodern quests emerge a number of anthropological challenges that demand a revisioning of theological anthropology. From the emancipatory quest comes the expectation that the material and social condition of humans be highlighted theologically. The inequitable distribution of power and resources, resulting in extremes of poverty and wealth, is a violation of human dignity, argue theologians of Asia and Latin America: This is an evil that must be resisted by converting forced (material) poverty into voluntary (spiritual) poverty. African American theology reminds us that racism is one of the most destructive and illusory forms of human idolatry. Feminist theology articulates an anthropology that emphasizes psychic and sociological integration, the rejection of gender dualisms and phobias, the recovery of holistic psychic capacities and egalitarian access to social roles.

The ecological quest calls for the rejection of the anticorporeal bias that has long been central to the Christian tradition, and the overcoming of all forms of nature-spirit and body-mind dualism. Spirit emerges out of nature and presupposes embodiment; mind or soul is not a separate, supramaterial substance but a more complex and unified life-form. We are part of a multidimensional matrix in which reality *is* relations. Because of the interrelatedness of life, human activity, when enlarged by technology and driven by consumption, can have profoundly devastating consequences for the environment. The violation of the earth can be described as "naturism," and it too is a primary form of idolatry.

The dialogical quest reminds us that there is a common humanity despite the amazing diversity of forms and expressions in which the human appears on this planet. Every attempt to describe the human condition arises out of a particular cultural trajectory, and we must be wary of naively universalizing our descriptive categories. Anthropology is driven to the concrete, but out of multiple particularities (sexual, ethnic, cultural, religious) may emerge a new and richer sense of the human whole. Intercultural and interreligious dialogue heightens our sensitivity to ethnocentrism and xenophobia as terrible manifestations of human fear and aggressiveness.

These postmodern anthropological challenges lie more in the background than at the forefront of the chapter that follows. My primary objective has been to identify the underlying structure of human being as finite freedom, and the underlying structure of sin as a syndrome of idolatry-flight-alienation, rooted in a pervasive illusion about the human condition. The objectification of sin in what I call structures of evil—which is where the postmodern quests focus attention today—should not be regarded as merely an application or illustration but as integral to an interlocking dynamic that demonically reinforces and generates sin as well as being produced by it. The picture that emerges of the human condition is primarily tragic—but redemption is a possibility, both because human beings remain open in the midst of their bondage and because God remains faithful in the midst of broken relationships.

Human Being as Finite Freedom[1]

Freedom, Nature, and the Spheres of the Human

Human being, created in the image of God, is not merely *Homo sapiens* but *Homo liber*, "the first liberated being in creation" (chap. 12, pp. 179–80). Freedom is the image of God in humanity, and thus freedom must be the central theme of a theological anthropology. Yet this same being was formed "from the dust of the ground" and thus is essentially a natural, material being, at one with the whole of creation, made of cosmic dust, merely one of countless living species within a complex evolutionary history.

Expressed more abstractly, human beings exist on a continuum between freedom and nature, the voluntary and the involuntary. This is the fundamental mystery of their existence. Human freedom is an *embodied freedom*—a freedom limited by and reciprocal with the body, both our individual bodies and the body politic, both an organic and a social body. Ours is an incarnate, contingent, finite freedom, yet still a freedom. With respect to our individual responsibility and action, we are determined, limited, sometimes controlled by our interests and motives, and by our physical needs, desires, and capabilities. With respect to interpersonal and social relations, we are dependent upon a structure of intersubjectivity and a social world that are always already given. And with respect to relating to the transcendent horizon that encompasses both ourselves and the world, we are determined and strictly limited by the fundamental necessities of the human condition: the contingency of birth, genetic and psychic endowment, the role of the unconscious, processes of growth, maturation and adaptation, and the finality of death. Despite all of this, our freedom is not obliterated but constrained, rendered fragile yet tenacious, vulnerable to destruction but capable of being restored.

Above all it is *language* that serves as the matrix of this continuum. Language itself is a synthesis of nature and freedom; it is rooted in a physical act, whether that be speech or writing or signing, articulated sounds and signifying shapes, yet it transcends the physical. Language grants freedom yet rivets it to the finitude of bodily existence in the world. It enables persons to have access to themselves, to establish communication and culture, and to transcend environments while at the same time remaining bound to them. *Homo liber* is the "speaking animal."

Human beings are not simple entities but complex networks of relationships. Assuming that they are created in the image of God, it is plausible to suggest that they image in their own way the triune figuration of God, and therefore that the same dialectic of identity, difference, and mediation that shapes the divine life also shapes human life. Thus are established three spheres of the human: (1) the sphere of identity, selfhood, or self-relatedness; (2) the sphere of difference, otherness, or world-relatedness; and (3) the sphere of mediation, wholeness, or God-relatedness.[2] In the case of the exemplification of this structure by *God*, the third sphere is the mediation of God with the world through the Spirit and hence God's return to godself. But in the case of human beings, the element of mediation or reunification is not with self but with that which transcends and is the ground of both self and world, namely God. Precisely this is the difference between God and humanity, Creator and creature, infinite and finite. A relationship to God is intrinsic to our very being as free but finite, embodied beings. The disruptions that infect the interactions between self and world can be healed only through the power of God, not by human autonomy or social engineering. This is the unique contribution of theology to anthropology, but it is also the most problematic. Establishing that a relationship to God is constitutive of human being, and the only possible ground of redemption, is the most difficult task ahead of us.[3]

The spheres of the human can also be described in terms of structures or dimensions of freedom, and this is the path I shall primarily follow, in accord with the approach of understanding human being as finite freedom. At this point we discover that the three spheres yield four structures. The reason for this is that human beings encounter difference or otherness in two distinct but related forms: both as a network of interpersonal relationships with other selves, and as an institutionalized social and cultural world. Thus, as Edward Farley insists, we must distinguish between the interhuman (or interpersonal) and the social.[4] In addition to interpersonal and social freedom, the schema proposed here posits personal freedom (based on selfhood, subjectivity, individual identity) and transpersonal freedom (an openness to and capacity for relating to God's spiritual presence, a presence that manifests itself in relation to all the other structures and is the basis of their reconciliation). The four structures of freedom can also be described as the spheres of agency, community, society, and openness. Within each of them occurs an interplay of voluntary and involuntary components.

Drawing these considerations together produces the following schematic representation:

		Embodied Freedom	
Spheres of the Human	**Structures of Freedom**	**Freedom (Voluntary)**	**Nature (Involuntary)**
Self (identity)	Personal (agency)	presence to self	temporality
		responsible action	bodily motivation and capabilities
World (difference)	Interpersonal (community)	relations/ communion	intersubjectivity
	Social (society)	just practices/ values	social world/ systems
God/Spirit (mediation)	Transpersonal (openness)	limit experience, courage, faith/ hope	necessity: birth, genetics, the unconscious, growth, maturation, death

An objection that could be raised against this whole approach is that it represents another so-called universal analysis of the human condition, a foisting of Western Eurocentric categories on a diversity of ways of being human. Clearly the ontological categories that inform the present analysis derive from a specific cultural, theological, and philosophical trajectory. The logic of discourse is such that we make universalizing statements and reality-claims on the basis of concrete situations and experience. There is nothing wrong with this. We cannot avoid moving from concrete history to historicity, but we must not forget to return to history. Let other proposals about the constitution of human being come forth from other cultural and religious trajectories, and then let there be a conflict and interplay of interpretations. When the Buddhist says that there is "no self," this statement is not meant to apply just to Buddhists. When Christians say that selfhood or individuality or personhood is an essential sphere of the human, this is not meant to apply just to Christians. Each of these universalizing statements is "true" since each represents an authentic interpretation of human experience, but each is also relative to concrete domains of experience. Through dialogue we enlarge our domains of experience and learn to modulate our categories. Thus the Buddhist doctrine of the no self warns me to avoid the notion of human "autonomy" and to stress the interconnections among the personal, the communal, the social, and the open. Human beings are indeed, as Buddhists claim, networks of relationships. The sphere of openness offers a point of contact with the Buddhist notion of emptiness, despite clear differences over what is encountered in the open.[5]

Personal, Interpersonal, and Social Freedom

The order in which the spheres or structures of freedom are addressed is not in itself important since each is necessary to a holistic understanding of human being. Each in turn has a certain primacy, and each is irreducible to the others. There is no proper starting point; rather what is important is to grasp the interconnections, what Farley calls the "interspherical dynamics."[6] From a theological perspective, the first three structures are all contingent upon the fourth, that of transpersonal freedom or openness to transcendence, which will be treated separately.

1. Our *personal being* is elusive since it is so immediate to us. It has the quality of self-presencing or self-knowing since we intuitively know ourselves to be subjects or persons engaged in decisions and actions for which we are able to assume responsibility. This is perhaps the most elemental form of freedom: self-knowing presence-to-self. We catch sight of ourselves in the process of choosing and acting. We avail ourselves of resources provided by the past and by our environment, and we have the capacity to project or intend new possibilities for the future through decisions and actions taken in the present. In this way we achieve an integration of time and are not captive to its mere succession any more than we are to our physical environment. We have an identity that is not simply given by something other than ourselves; we become agents.

At the same time we know ourselves to be embodied, biological beings who are an integral part of the natural world. We know that we are motivated by powerful biological drives and instincts, and that we are limited by our bodily capabilities. We are unable to return literally to the past or leap ahead into the future. We are subject to the fundamental necessities of finite physical existence. Yet we sense that we need not be trapped by these things. Motives become causal factors in the freedom of decision, and they can "incline without compelling," as Paul Ricoeur says. Bodily capabilities and limits challenge us to new heights of achievement, and we are able to extend these capabilities almost indefinitely through tools and instruments. We do not simply live and die but transfuse this simple facticity with a complex network of meanings and purposes. Yet it is tempting to surrender to the involuntary, to give up on the human project; we often lack courage and give in to debilitating fears.

In addition we know that we hunger or desire something. This "something" appears in the form of three elemental passions, according to Farley: the passion of the agent for its survival and well-being;

the passion for other human beings, that is, the need for relations and sociality; and the passion for reality, for being in touch with the world and rightly interpreting what is going on in it. Ultimately these are passions for a whole, a totality, a meaning, a fulfillment, and a security that we can never find in this world. Such passions or desires are not simply physical instincts or drives or motives. They have been transfused by language and converted into quests for the infinite; hence they occur at the intersection of freedom and nature, of spirit and body: They are spiritual desires.[7]

2. We know that we are not alone in the world and that we exist in *interpersonal relations*. There are others like ourselves, others in whom we see ourselves reflected, others whom we must *recognize* to be other, and whose experience we can never immediately experience ourselves. This "strange elusiveness" of the other constitutes the fact of "alterity," which is the precondition of all genuine relationships. Emmanuel Levinas refers to it as the "face," "the infinitely strange and mysterious presence of something which contests my projected meanings of it." The face of the other makes claims upon us, claims of both compassion (suffering with the other) and obligation (suffering for the other). When persons provide compassion and sympathy for each other in a relationship of mutuality and inclusion, then freedom is experienced in the realm of the interpersonal. Freedom means not only presence to oneself but also presence with and for others; it means to exist as "spirit" as well as "self." There is in human being the possibility for an authentic communion of free and equal persons, in which is found a full mutuality of recognition and an intending of the other for the sake of the other. But there is also the possibility for intense conflict, suffering, and alienation. And there is, finally, an involuntary dimension to the interpersonal, which can be described as "intersubjectivity." What we find are not private and isolated egos calling out to each other across an empty abyss but a preformed set of postures, meanings, languages, roles, values—the "always already thereness" of the interpersonal.[8]

3. Intersubjectivity is based on the *social*—"the sphere of specific human interactions plus all of the structures and processes through which they take place."[9] These structures and processes consist of a past legacy of customs, laws, values, and roles, which are borne by such vehicles as language, belief systems, institutions, and rituals. If such things did not already exist, there could be no interpersonal relations and not even any personal agency. Thus the social possesses at least a chronological primacy vis-à-vis the other spheres of the human. In this respect it functions as the involuntary substratum of social freedom. The social involuntary is made up of a social world, constructed by human agents primarily through the use of language, and a social

system, consisting of face-to-face communities (the realm of the interpersonal), functioning subsystems (political, judicial, economic, familial), and culture (which creates and preserves the values of a society through religion, education, the arts).

Social freedom might be described as just systems, practices, and values. The goal of society is to create a space or realm of freedom in which human beings can dwell humanly, a liberating sociopolitical structure. Hegel envisioned "the system of right" (the social-political-economic system) to be "the kingdom of freedom actualized, the world of spirit brought forth out of itself like a second nature"—an expression that is reminiscent not only of Jesus' proclamation of the kingdom of God but also of Aristotle's definition of the *polis* as the "community of the free."[10] Of course this is accomplished only very partially and fragmentarily under the conditions of historical existence. Nowhere is the fragility of human freedom more tragically evident than in the realm of the social.

If the world of spirit, the social world, is humanity's "second nature," then our "first nature" is precisely the natural world. Nature is the ultimate alterity of human being, a difference that can never be reduced to the same, the identity of the self. Yet we dwell in the natural world and are dependent on it for the actualization of our humanity. Nature enters into the constitution of human being not only through the social world, which simply represents the construction of the system of nature into a human dwelling place, but also through our individual embodiment and through the fundamental necessities of life on this planet. World appears as the element of difference in the dialectic of the human through the totality of the involuntary, not just in the second of the spheres.

Transpersonal Freedom: Openness to Transcendence

The fallibility and tragic vulnerability of the human condition, to which I shall refer shortly, are such that this condition cannot be self-rescuing or self-redemptive. Thus the third moment in the dialectic of being, that of the mediation or reconciliation of difference, cannot, in the case of human being, entail merely a return to self. Rather it must, if there is to be such a mediation at all, involve a relationship to that which transcends the polarities of self and world, freedom and nature, as their ground and goal, a relationship to the eternal horizon of being, which discloses itself as God, as sacred presence and Holy Spirit, in and through specific communities of redemption. *Only God* is able both to create genuine difference and to overcome its alienation without reducing the other to the same. Human beings do not create difference but find it, and their attempts to overcome its tragic features on their own only deepen the tragedy, converting it into sin and evil. Thus, if humans are to be saved along with the world, they must be related to that which is other than both themselves and the world, the sacred other.

I refer to this relationship as *transpersonal freedom* and contend that it is a structural component of human being as such. In fact it is the ground and goal of all other forms of human freedom, personal, interpersonal, and social. This relationship does not come into existence only in concrete experiences of redemption.[11] Rather it is already there as a structural possibility for all human beings: It is the *imago Dei* in humanity. If humans are *fallible,* as a consequence of their fragility and vulnerability, then they must also be *redeemable;* otherwise the human condition would be purely and solely tragic. This is a theological claim, but evidence for it is found in the way human beings actually exist in the world, namely as *free* in fact despite their finitude, fragility, vulnerabilities, and fallenness.

How are the evidences of freedom that we do experience in the world to be accounted for? What prevents interpersonal relations from simply being absorbed into an all-consuming narcissism? What draws us out of ourselves into communion with others? What prevents the voluntary from simply being absorbed into the involuntary? How is it possible to have determination and control—through motives, physical needs, the social system—without compulsion and coercion? What enables human beings to survive in the midst of an alienated and oppressive social environment? What enables persons to go on in the face of tragic choices, defeats, suffering, and death? What grants us courage in the midst of debilitating fear? In short, if human freedom is finite, embodied, contingent, fallible, by what power can it be sustained against the seemingly crushing force of physical and social environment, and be rescued from its own narcissism, alienation, weakness, and aggressiveness? The quest for an answer drives us beyond both personal and interpersonal freedom to look for the possibility of a transpersonal freedom.

My thesis is that finite, embodied human freedom remains a viable possibility in the context of the organic and social necessities of life and its own intrinsic instability only if persons are *open* to a liberating power that transcends all their physical and social environments and redeems them from a self-imposed bondage. It is a peculiarity of human beings that they remain open into the beyond, the infinite, the eternal horizon.[12] No other living creature demonstrates this characteristic. Human needs and instincts, like those of animals, are not in themselves infinite; it is only when they are traversed by language that they become desires, quests, passions, intrinsically unfulfillable. No matter how frequently we are positively reinforced, we remain unsatisfied, unfulfilled, unable to attain a final happiness. Augustine perceived the infinitude of human openness: "The heart is restless until its finds its rest in thee." *Openness* is the key structure in a theological anthropology. It is the foundation of the responsible action that makes up personal freedom, of the communion that creates interpersonal freedom, and of the just practices and values that characterize social freedom, for it alone provides the context in which freedom can not only survive but flourish.

Openness comes into view in several forms:

1. *Limit Experience* or existence on the boundary. As finite yet conscious beings, we are constantly aware of limits. Yet the very awareness of a limit implies that we are already beyond the limit, that we are capable of transcending it. Animals experience limits as barriers that stop them; humans experience limits as boundaries that can be crossed, and we are always crossing them even as we encounter them in ever new forms. It is at the boundaries that disclosures occur, that truth is opened, that religion emerges. Religion is a type of limit experience.[13]

2. *Courage.* Courage is a way of existing as fragile and vulnerable in the midst of sufferings and tragic incompatibilities, and in the face of the absolute necessities of the human condition (birth, genetic and psychic endowment, the unconscious, growth and maturation, death). According to Farley, three attitudes converge in the posture of courage: a relativizing of finite goods (recognizing that in themselves they can never satisfy the longing of our hearts), an attitude of consent to goods at hand including the world itself, and a willingness to risk our being in the perils and adventures of existence.[14] Ricoeur elaborates on the attitude of consent by suggesting that, when confronted by the involuntary necessities and vulnerabilities of life, human beings can comport themselves in several possible ways. Refusal of the involuntary gives rise to freedom but leads to a denial of finitude and an apotheosis of the autonomous self (atheistic humanism). Surrender to the involuntary leads to a repudiation of freedom and an acquiescence to merely natural or bodily existence (romanticism). Consent to our condition preserves both finitude and freedom. Consent implies that, in spite of appearances, the world is a possible home of freedom. It is not merely a network of tragic incompatibilities and contingencies of survival but the cipher of a liberating transcendence more perfectly revealed at critical points in nature and history. It *is* possible to live in this world, to affirm its goodness and accept its limits, but we can do so only if we have courage, faith, and hope.[15]

3. *Faith/Hope.* Faith is the posture of courage in relation to God, and hope is an orientation to the future in radical openness. That to which we are open beyond all limits and beyond all forms of the involuntary is the final home of freedom—or to use an image associated with

Jesus, a "kingdom of freedom," which will reconcile the splits between self and world and nature and freedom, furnish a utopian image of a liberating communion of free persons, and set humans free from the self-imposed bondage into which they have fallen and from which they cannot rescue themselves. Such openness implies faith in God as the One who fills the transcendent horizon, for it is God's power and project alone that engender the true home of freedom. The opposite of hope is despair, which before God is sin. The opposite of faith is unbelief or broken faith, which is at the heart of idolatry. The opposite of courage is fear, which is at the heart of flight. Without courage, faith, and hope, we fall into a debilitating alienation from self, other selves, and world.[16]

If human beings are open to transcendence, then they are open to the possibility of redemption; they are *redeemable*. But are redemption and liberating power *realities* as opposed to mere possibilities? Are human beings not simply redeemable but in fact redeemed? These are questions that cannot be answered by analysis of essential human possibilities. They require turning to a determinate community of faith with its symbols of bondage and liberation. But in the final analysis even redeem*ability* in some sense presupposes the actuality of redemption: If redemption were not in fact available, then redeemability would be a tragic deception, and it would be senseless even to speak of it. If the vision of a home of freedom is simply an illusion, then all such religious visions, indeed religion as such, would have to be rejected as a false form of consciousness, an illusion, a wish-fulfillment—as is claimed by the great critics of religion: Marx, Nietzsche, Freud. We could perhaps speak of fallibility without fault since it would not be a cruel hoax should fallibility not issue in fault. Yet the fact of fault is empirically certain in ways that redemption is not.

Thus the relation between redeemability and redemption is a thoroughly dialectical one. This does not mean, however, that redeemability is simply reduced to redemption. For the fact that human beings really do have courage and hope, really do play and love—and that they do so quite soberly and without illusions—suggests that the event of liberation has already inscribed itself upon the very structural possibilities of human existence and is discernible there *prior to and apart from* a theology of redemption, a christology and a pneumatology. But the inscription remains ambiguous and obscure, subject to varying interpretations. To construe it as a structure of openness is a theological act. Theological anthropology already presupposes a relationship to a redemptive God; thus it cannot be a "foundational" anthropology from which everything is launched but rather is part of a circle of interpretation in which each moment both presupposes and founds every other moment.

I prefer to think of the human relationship to God as a form of radical "openness" rather than of radical "dependence," as theologians have done in the tradition of Schleiermacher.[17] Dependence casts the discussion in terms of human submission, passivity, obedience; and it suggests that God is a sovereign lord and master. Openness casts it in terms of human liberation, activity, and responsibility, and suggests that God is the One who loves in freedom. The most fundamental of all human relationships must be one of freedom rather than of dependence.

In this work I develop the theme of "openness to transcendence" primarily in the form of a cultural anthropology oriented to the postmodern quests for freedom, love, and wholeness (chaps. 6–8). What is presupposed by and manifested in these quests is precisely the radical openness of human beings. Thus the whole of Part 2 serves as an anthropological prolegomenon to an emergent trinitarian structure. Precisely in terms of the trinitarian structure, anthropology belongs in the middle of theology. But because openness to transcendence is a constitutive structure of the human, a structure that appears even in the midst of postmodern fragmentation, anthropology belongs also at the beginning of theology, not as a foundation but as a correlation.

Fall: The Transition from Fallibility to Fault[18]

This schema provides an overview of the analysis to follow:

Preconditions (Fallibility)	Anxiety (internal: finite freedom)
	↓
	Temptation (external: destiny)
	↓
Origin	Deceit (Fall)
	↓
Structures of Sin	Idolatry (broken faith, aggression)
	↓
	Flight (fear, submission)
	↓
	Alienation (violation, resentment, guilt)
	↓
Results	Bondage of the Will
	↓
Objectifications: Evil	Law: Objectification of Alienation
	↓
	Death: Objectification of Flight
	↓
	Worldly Powers: Objectification of Idolatry Ideologies: –isms and phobias Injustice: oppressions

Fallibility: The Tragic

The structures of human being are fragile and fallible, subject to distortion, fall, fault. This can be attributed to a peculiar instability inherent in the fragile synthesis of finitude and freedom that characterizes human existence.[19] Or it can be attributed to a tragic vulnerability inherent in the human condition. These are slightly different ways of describing essentially the same human reality. The tragic, writes Farley, "refers to a situation in which the conditions of well-being require and are interdependent with situations of limitation, frustration, challenge, and suffering."[20] The tragic shows itself in the form of distinctive vulnerabilities that adhere to the various spheres of human being, personal, interpersonal, social, transpersonal. With respect to *personal* being, we are vulnerable temporally, socially, and biologically. For example, we transcend time yet are subject to it, so that we suffer disappointments, frustrations, boredom, depression, worry. Because of limited resources and conditions, we face tragic choices (for example, selecting a small number of qualified applicants to an academic program, retaining workers in a lay-off on the basis of seniority). Biologically, we struggle to survive under conditions of limitation, a striving that takes the form of seeking and opposing. Both lead to benign aggression, "a biologically adaptive capacity for self-assertiveness which can result in attacks on others." Benign aggression is one of the tragic preconditions of malignant aggression, the concrete destructiveness wrought by human idolatry.[21]

There is also a distinctive vulnerability of the *interpersonal,* which may be described as interpersonal suffering and benign alienation. Just because interpersonal relationships can become so intense, intimate, and fulfilling, they are also subject to intense suffering when they are wounded or cease to exist; death ultimately terminates every such enduring relationship. Benign alienation arises from the fact that "at the heart of the interhuman is a vast set of incompatibilities that originate in the irreducible otherness of the participants." It is simply impossible to harmonize all the desires and agendas of self-initiating agents, and thus there are hurt feelings, accusations, competition, etc. When such alienation issues in specific violations, it becomes malignant and thus a form of sin.[22]

Vulnerability in the realm of the *social* appears as incompatibility and social suffering. Incompatibility occurs not only interpersonally but also socially, in the form of conflicts between social groups, competition for resources or living space, and cultural strategies of repression for the sake of order. Out of this emerge impulses toward social, ethnic, and gender stratification, which eventuate in concrete ideologies of evil (classism, racism, sexism). Social suffering is the result of these incompatibilities and the precondition of social evil, which produces the most intense and destructive suffering known to humanity, namely subjugation, oppression, victimization.[23]

If the *transpersonal* is a distinctive sphere of the human, then it too is subject to tragic vulnerability, which appears above all in the fact that the most inescapable condition of our finitude is death. We perceive death as the enemy because it cuts off life-sustaining relationships. We become preoccupied with death, both fearing and venerating it; it becomes our god, corroding courage and faith, shutting us off from the true and holy God. The anxiety that drives to sin has its root here.

Persistent questions arise. Why did God create us as fallible beings with these tragic vulnerabilities? Is it because we were created out of faulty material in the first place—chaotic matter that God could only partially subdue? This is the answer of the theogonic myth of origin (found in ancient Near Eastern religion), which posits a primordial evil principle as co-equal with God. Or is it because there is an evil or demonic or destructive dimension within divinity itself? This is the answer of the tragic myth (Greek religion), according to which an ultimate, inscrutable, and terrible fate governs the affairs of gods and humans alike. The Jewish and Christian traditions, rooted as they both are in the Adamic myth of origin, which locates the primary responsibility for evil in humanity rather than in God or primal matter, rejects these two answers although elements of tragedy and theogony are present in the Hebrew and Christian scriptures: Job, Ecclesiastes, and the cross suggest that God too is somehow implicated in the human condition.[24]

The logical answer to our questions is that if God intended to create free beings distinct from godself, that is, finite beings, then the disproportion between freedom and finitude and the tragic vulnerabilities were endemic to that very project, the human project. This answer may be logically correct, but, like all theodicies, all attempts to justify the ways of God, it is religiously unsatisfying, as Job eloquently testifies. In the final analysis, we cannot explain evil, cannot explain why God "allows" it, either by creating a world in which it could occur, or by not stopping it when it does occur, or by using it as an instrument toward redemption. The only religiously satisfying answer would be that of a God who takes the human tragedy upon and into godself, thereby both completing and overcoming tragedy. This is the meaning of the redemptive suffering of the cross, a suffering undergone by God in Christ; thus the Christic myth is required to complete the Adamic myth. We cannot finally make sense of the fall, sin, and evil apart from Christ and redemption.

The Preconditions of Sin: Anxiety and Temptation

The theme of fallibility, of vulnerability to failure or fault, has generally been taken up by theologians in terms of two sorts of preconditions of sin, one of which is said to be internal to the self and the other external. The theological tradition from Augustine through Søren Kierkegaard to Paul Tillich and Reinhold Niebuhr has identified the internal precondition as the condition of *anxiety*. Tillich traces anxiety to an inherent tension that occurs in finite being when its polar elements begin to pull against and compete with each other. Tension occurs the moment that finite freedom becomes *aware* of itself, aware, that is, of both its finitude (which means that it is noncoincident with its destiny) and its openness to the infinite. Self-aware freedom is anxious freedom.[25] Reinhold Niebuhr's formulation is well-known: "Anxiety is the inevitable concomitant of the paradox of freedom and finiteness in which humanity is involved. Anxiety is the internal precondition of sin. It is the inevitable spiritual state of humans, standing in the paradoxical situation of freedom and finiteness."[26]

This situation of tension, conflict, instability, ontological anxiety becomes the actual occasion for sin only when it is falsely interpreted, which is not purely the product of human imagination but is suggested by a principle or force of evil antecedent to any individual human action. The tradition has called this *temptation* and viewed it as the external precondition of sin. As we shall see, in the story of the fall, temptation is the function of the serpent who falsely interprets the human condition of finite, anxious freedom. But this false interpretation is already the product of sin; hence we catch sight of this precondition only in motion, in the telling of a story. This is what Kierkegaard meant by saying that "sin presupposes itself."[27] There is always something sinful antecedent to each act of sin.

Tillich attempts to demythologize the element of temptation by locating it in what he terms "destiny," understood as the totality of the biological, psychological, sociological, and historical forces by which individual selves are determined.[28] Destiny, as a form of the involuntary, becomes the seat of the objectifications of sin in structures of evil, which in turn tempt to more sin. The dilemma is that we cannot begin to understand sin without understanding what the end of sin is, what it results in. Here too we are involved in a circle of understanding.

According to Niebuhr, the internal and external preconditions provide the occasion for sin but do not cause it. Sin remains a free act for which individuals must assume a measure of responsibility. Hence the Niebuhrian paradox: Sin is "inevitable though not necessary." "Inevitable" means "always in fact happens" or "universal," and it points to the tragic dimension.[29] "Not necessary" means that sin does not belong to the essential nature of human being; indeed it involves a flawing of that nature for which each individual is responsible although there is already a powerful bias toward sin in the linguistic and social environment ("temptation").[30]

In sum, one of the preconditions of sin, anxiety, simply describes the tragic, fallible condition of human beings as finite yet free; while the other precondition, temptation, points to the dynamics of the passage from fallibility to fault, namely deception or false interpretation, which becomes sedimented in destiny. The discussion of preconditions mediates between and connects these two themes.

The Fall into Sin: Deceit

The transition from fallibility to fault cannot be directly captured by thought any more than the transition from essence to existence or from sin to redemption. We face a series of logical paradoxes: Sin is inevitable but not necessary; human beings freely render themselves captive; human freedom is a bound freedom. "Why is this so?" we ask. Ultimately the only answer to this question is, "Because it happened this way." Thus our strategy is to tell a story, the story of the fall, just as we must also tell the story of creation in answer to the question, "Why did God create the kind of world we know?" and the story of redemption in answer to the question, "How are we saved?" The transitions and connections involved here are those characteristic of narrative, not formal logic, although another sort of logic may attempt to reduplicate, to grasp conceptually, the narrative connections. The logic of life has a historical structure.[31]

The story that we tell should not be understood as a historical account of origins or an etiological explanation of sin. Rather it has the character of disclosure, of insight into this mysterious transition that each of us makes individually and that the human species has made collectively.

> Now the serpent was more crafty than any other wild animal that the LORD God had made. He said to the woman, "Did God say, 'You shall not eat from any tree in the garden'?" The woman said to the serpent, "We may eat of the fruit of the trees in the garden; but God said, 'You shall not eat of the fruit of the tree that is in the middle of the garden, nor shall you touch it, or you shall die.'" But the serpent said to the woman, "You will not die; for God knows that when you eat of it your eyes will be opened, and you will be like God, knowing good and evil." So when the woman saw that the tree was good for food, and that it was a delight to the eyes, and that the tree was to be desired to make one wise, she took of its fruit and ate; and she also gave some to her husband, who was with her, and he ate. Then the eyes of both were opened, and they knew that they were naked; and they sewed fig leaves together and made loincloths for themselves.
>
> They heard the sound of the LORD God walking in the garden at the time of the evening breeze, and the man and his wife hid themselves from the presence of the LORD God among the trees of the garden. But the LORD God called to the man, and said to him, "Where are you?" He

> said, "I heard the sound of you in the garden, and I was afraid, because I was naked; and I hid myself. [God] said, "Who told you that you were naked? Have you eaten from the tree of which I commanded you not to eat?" The man said, "The woman whom you gave to be with me, she gave me fruit from the tree, and I ate." Then the LORD God said to the woman, "What is this that you have done?" The woman said, "The serpent tricked me, and I ate." (Gen. 3:1–13)

The plot of this story is woven around the theme of *deception*. It was interpreted this way by the Apostle Paul, who focused attention on it in a way that had not been characteristic of Judaism. "I am afraid," says Paul, "that as the serpent deceived Eve by its cunning, your thoughts will be led astray from a sincere and pure devotion to Christ" (2 Cor. 11:3). The theme of sin as deceit or falsehood echoes elsewhere in the Pauline and Johannine literature.

The serpent is a symbol of humanity's fundamental self-deception: "The serpent was more crafty than any other wild animal that the LORD God had made" (Gen. 3:1). The deceit—*spoken* by the serpent in the form of an insinuating question—consisted in the falsehood that the creature, without penalty to itself, could become its own creator, its own God. "You will be like God [Vulgate, *sicut Deus*], knowing good and evil": This is a distortion of the truth that human being is created in the image of God (*imago Dei*) and that knowledge and freedom are what constitute the image of God in humanity. Hence this is not an outright falsehood but one that conceals the truth. An out-and-out lie would be easier to detect and resist. Knowledge and freedom *are* what make us "like" God, but they are a finite knowledge and freedom. The ensuing "punishments" (Gen. 3:14–19) are reminders of our finitude, our earthy nature (pain in childbearing, the toil and sweat of labor, death as return to the ground from which we were taken).[32] The prohibition against eating from the trees of immortality (whether of life or of knowledge) is what constitutes the *difference* between divinity and humanity. The question about the prohibition, which the serpent cunningly exaggerates ("Did God say, 'You shall not eat from *any* tree in the garden'?"), arouses the human desire for infinity—the "evil infinite"—which perverts the finitude of freedom, tempting us to transgress the limits of our bodily nature.[33]

Human self-deceit is symbolized by the serpent (the only monster to survive from the theogonic myths) because it is experienced as a seduction from without. "The serpent," writes Ricoeur, "would be a part of ourselves which we do not recognize; he would be the seduction of ourselves by ourselves, projected into the seductive object."[34] Such a view is reflected in a passage in the letter of James: "No one, when tempted, should say, 'I am being tempted by God'; for God cannot be tempted by evil and he himself tempts no one. But one is tempted by one's own desire, being lured and enticed by it; then, when that desire has conceived, it gives birth to sin, and that sin, when it is fully grown, gives birth to death. Do not be deceived, my beloved" (1:13–16). Our inclination, however, is to deny this, to blame the object of desire or seduction or contempt rather than accepting responsibility ourselves: Men accuse women, victimizers accuse victims, humans accuse the serpent. We conceal our acts of deceit from ourselves: Just as sin presupposes itself, deceit deceives itself, and we lose the capacity of recognizing it when it occurs.

But, continues Ricoeur, "the serpent is also 'outside' in a more radical fashion. . . . In the historical experience of humanity, every individual finds evil *already there;* nobody begins it absolutely. . . . Evil is part of the interhuman relationship, like language, tools, institutions. . . . There is thus an anteriority of evil to itself." The serpent "represents the aspect of evil that could not be absorbed into the responsible freedom of human beings."[35] Pursued too consistently, this theme would lead to a version of the theogonic myth, namely a belief in Satan as a supernatural, demonic power rivaling that of God. Within the context of the Adamic-Christic myth, the figure of Satan is already implicitly demythologized. The Johannine Jesus says of the devil, "When he lies, he speaks according to his own nature, for he is a liar and the father of lies" (John 8:44). The devil is a personification of the power of the lie. But in fact the evil that precedes us is the objectification of our own acts of sin, which take on a binding power over against us. I shall return to this theme.

As we know all too well, the role played by the woman in the story of the fall, and the subsequent interpretation of sin as deceit by the Apostle Paul and his successors, became the occasion for a theological justification of the subordination of women. The most notorious instance of this is found in the first letter to Timothy (which is not, of course, written by Paul): "Let a woman learn in silence with full submission. I permit no woman to teach or to have authority over a man; she is to keep silent. For Adam was formed first, then Eve; and Adam was not deceived, but the woman was deceived and became a transgressor" (1 Tim. 2:11–14). This interpretation reflects a hardening of prejudices against women in the early Catholic church, and the prejudices have scarcely receded in two thousand years.

To be sure this interpretation seems to misrepresent the Genesis text. Far from being weaker and more gullible than the man, the woman is clearly the more intelligent and venturesome member of the primordial pair. The serpent approaches her rather than the man because he surmises that she will appreciate a theological discussion and will perceive the possibilities afforded by the fruit. The man merely passively eats what is handed to him. Deception occurs at the point of human strength—intelligence, linguisticality, imagination—rather than of weakness. If Adam was formed first, then Eve was formed last and is the crowning achievement of creation, the completion of the work of God. The woman becomes the representative human being in this story.[36] But yet this observation does not avoid the difficulty that the story places the burden of responsibility on the woman. She may indeed represent the whole of humanity in the act of sin, but she is *blamed* for the act and a stereotyping of sexual roles is perpetuated. *Fear* of the woman, of female power, may underlie the exalted place she occupies in the story. Thus the role of the woman remains thoroughly ambiguous in the Adamic myth (why don't we call it the myth of Eve—too threatening, perhaps?), and it is rightly argued that new, corrective myths need to be created. But the old myth will undoubtedly continue to echo in the new ones.

Personal and Interpersonal Structures of Sin

Sin entails a disruption of the personal and interpersonal structures of human being. These disruptions—to be identified as idolatry, flight, and alienation—correspond to specific features of the vulnerability that attends finite freedom. They are rooted in a primordial brokenness of faith; they are driven by debilitating fears that arise out of ontological anxiety; and they issue in a bondage of the will (personal and interpersonal) that stifles the freedom at the heart of human being. This bondage, in turn, assumes certain cosmic and social objectifications that demonically intensify sin, converting it into structures of evil, which correspond to the structures of sin. Pauline categories are helpful at this point: "Law" as a symbol of the constraints of civilization entails an objectification of alienation; "death" regarded as a suprahuman force represents an objectification of flight; and "worldly powers" objectify idolatry in the form of both ideologies and injustice.

Such at least is my thesis, and it has three immediate implications for viewing the connection between sin and evil: (1) No genuine liberation or salvation is attained simply by removing the objective conditions of alienation, death, ideologies, and oppression. For the powers that enthrall humanity are not simply external to the psyche (individual and corporate) but internal to it. (2) The cosmic and social objectifications of bondage *do* reinforce and demonically intensify personal and interpersonal acts of sin. Hence there is no genuine liberation or salvation that leaves these objectifications untouched. Psyche is not reducible to society, nor society to psyche. (3) Because deception deceives and forgets itself, and because freedom binds itself, liberation is not possible by knowledge alone or self-emancipation alone. Rather what is required is *saving* knowledge, a revelation, a redemptive deliverance, a divine reshaping of broken and distorted relationships. This reshaping might be thought of as the divine wisdom, which counters human deception ("foolishness").

Idolatry (Broken Faith)

Sin entails a rupture of relationships and a loss of wholeness. Perhaps rupture is the fate of the world, the outcome of having real difference in the divine life. We have observed a cosmic thrust toward separation and alienation: In nature it issues in destruction and disorder, in humans in idolatry and flight.

Why call it "idolatry"? Because in the first instance it is a relationship to God that is broken or distorted or rejected in some way. The Hebrew Bible identified sin as the rupturing of a covenant relationship with God and the setting up of ourselves as gods. Several words for sin expressed this rupture of a relationship: *chattat* (missing the target), *'awon* (a tortuous road), *pesha'* (revolt, stiff-neckedness), *shagah* (going astray, being lost, alienation, dereliction, abandonment). The Apostle Paul used different terms to express the idea of sin as rebellion, pride, disobedience: *epithumia* (self-reliant pursuit of one's own ends), *merimnan* (concern or anxiety about worldly affairs), and *kauchasthai* (boasting, which is characteristic both of the Jew, who boasts of God and Torah, and of the Greek, who boasts of wisdom). The Greek term *hubris* (pride), while occurring only rarely in the New Testament, was established by the Greek tragedies as the basic flaw of humanity, involving a wanton insolence and arrogance vis-à-vis the gods, an overextension of human capacities and desires.[37]

The biblical terminology lent credence to a classical theological version of sin as prideful rebellion against a dominant monarch. This interpretation is unfortunate since it suggests, in Farley's words, that "the primary relation between human beings and God is the relation of inferior and relatively powerless subjects to a superior and commanding will. Submissive responses of honor and obedience are what this relation properly requires. The very essence of sin, then, is to fail to acknowledge the sovereign as sovereign and to repudiate the subject to master relation." Such a view led to a juridical understanding of sin and redemption, for which the central metaphors are rule, punishment, and acquittal.[38]

This interpretation distorts the divine-human relationship and misses the essential character of sin as idolatry. Driven by fear of nonbeing (or chaos) and the desire to be founded, human beings strive to secure their condition through attachment to false foundations and mundane goods—in the form of material possessions, economic security, social status, erotic attachments, political ideologies, religious belief-systems, and so on. As Farley puts it, sin arises from "a skewed passion for the eternal"; it represents a "mundanizing of the eternal horizon."[39] It is a substitution of finite gods or idols for the true and holy God. It is a refusal to believe that God alone is the source of our strength and salvation. It is, in other words, a primordial act of unbelief, which according to Tillich lies at the root of all particular forms of sin.[40] It is, in H. Richard Niebuhr's eloquent expression, "broken faith," a pervasive distrust that appears in the form of hostility, fear, and isolation.[41] Personal and interpersonal sin, as well as cosmic and social evil, have their root in the violation of the third fundamental sphere of human relationship, that of openness to and trust in God.

For most of us, idolatrous unbelief assumes the form not of a Promethean defiance of the divinities but of domination over our fellow human beings. If we set ourselves, our goods and interests, up as gods in place of God, our tendency is to draw everything into our domain and make it subservient to our desires. Thus idolatry issues above all in the distortion and destruction of *interhuman* relationships.[42] The benign aggression inherent in our biological self-assertiveness becomes malignant and destructive aggression. Aggression is released and legitimated by idolatry, the ideology of self-securing and self-absolutizing, the denial of finitude and limit. Thus the brokenness of our relationship with God manifests itself in the brokenness of interhuman relationships, and the reconstruction of each of these relationships depends upon the reconstruction of the other.

God appears in the picture not primarily as the object of sin and certainly not as the author of sin (as some Calvinist theologies have been obliged to maintain), but rather as the provider of resources for combating sin and evil. God is not damaged by sin except insofar as we are damaged; but God really is damaged by the damage we suffer since God is at risk in the world, wounded by the terrible wounds humans inflict on each other. We sin against God *indirectly*, but that is quite enough. We sin against God not so much by breaking a divine prohibition, as the Adamic myth emphasized (thus engendering a legalistic framework for interpreting sin), but rather by violating a relationship of trust not only with God but with our fellow creatures (thus Adam and Eve, knowing their nakedness, hid from God and passed the blame to each other and to the serpent).

One of the terms used by theological tradition to name this first form of sin was "concupiscence." According to scholastic theology,[43] concupiscence is any *excessive* desire, the object of which appeals to sense experience. Concupiscent love, for example, embodies no care for the welfare of the beloved but is wholly selfish, greedy, self-centered, lustful. It is self-love rather than love of the other. In psychological terms it is narcissism, aroused by a fear of otherness or difference and a quest for self-security, self-aggrandizement. This fear of the other, of difference, is what drives the dehumanizing -isms (racism, sexism, classism) and phobias (homophobia, xenophobia), all of which are forms of idolatry. Tillich defines concupiscence as "the unlimited desire to draw the whole of reality into one's self,"[44] thus freeing the term from any specific association with sensuality. This is advisable because it avoids the tendency frequently found in Christian tradition to associate sensual or erotic desire as such with sin, which it is not. We must distinguish, as Ricoeur points out, between the authentic human quests (having, power, worth) and their passional perversions (possession, domination, pride).[45] Only the latter are instances of concupiscent desire and thus of broken faith.

Flight (Fear)

Idolatry can be described as the "sin of infinitude" (Kierkegaard),[46] the apotheosis or "faulty infinite" of freedom, by which humans defy or deny the finite limits and conditions of their existence (Ricoeur).[47] Idolatry thus corresponds to one aspect of human fragility or disproportion, the polarity within us of freedom and nature, infinite and finite. In the case of idolatry, our infinitude attempts to outstrip, escape from, and deny its finite basis. It is an attempt at prideful overextension.

This correspondence between the structure of sin and human fragility suggests the existence of another form of personal sin, the diametrical opposite of the first, yet profoundly related to it: the sin of finitude, the denial of life and freedom, the apotheosis of death. Such a form of sin is indeed known to the Bible, and it can be described as flight, sloth,[48] failure, despair, surrender, submission. Such a nuance is already present in the Hebraic terms for sin: "missing the target," "a tortuous road," "going astray," "dereliction," "abandonment." Sin is a false, aberrant pursuit of life that not only issues in revolt against God and aggression against neighbor but also constitutes a way that leads to death. If we go astray in the pursuit of life, the result is the opposite of life, namely death.[49] Similarly with the New Testament image of anxiety: Anxiety is not only a false concern about worldly affairs, hence a perversion of the Creator-creature relation; it is also a debilitating fear of death and finitude that robs life of wholeness and power, as is evident from Jesus' sayings about persons of "little faith," and about anxiety, fear, doubt. The ultimate logic of anxiety is suicide, a flight from life and sacrifice to the god death.[50]

When this second form of sin is viewed in terms of interhuman rather than divine-human relations, it can be described as the sin of submission, that is, acquiescence in or accommodation to the domination of another, subjection in the face of abuse. Some feminist theologians believe that this is the form of sin most women experience, and the same might be said of racial and ethnic minorities. Others question whether it is appropriate to characterize such acquiescence as sin rather than victimization.[51] It clearly is victimization, but the question is how one comports oneself in the face of victimization or abuse. Does one resist or does one collaborate? If the option to resist is available (in any number of forms), then acquiescence is a form of flight. Survival is, of course, a fundamental human drive, but one must learn to survive by resisting, not by surrendering; otherwise one survives only to undergo an inward death. In speaking of submission as sin, it should be clear that we are referring to a human condition, not an act that merits blame or moral condemnation. Moralizing interpretations of sin are inappropriate because they presuppose a juridical framework and ignore the tragic dimension.

Flight is perhaps the primary form of sin in our time, one of whose symptoms is the widespread use of drugs, alcohol, and other chemical substances as a means of escape from reality, along with other distractions (cults, religions, therapy groups, popular entertainment, amusements, music, violence).[52] Not only flight but also idolatry seems to be rooted in a fundamental and pervasive fear—fear of vulnerability, otherness, difference, change, life itself, and ultimately death. The fear manifests itself in aggressive, repressive, and submissive attitudes. There surely is a connection between anxiety (an ontological condition) and fear (the concrete phobias that rob our lives of meaning), but it is difficult to establish a direct causal link between them. Vis-à-vis God, anxiety falsely interpreted takes the form of idolatry; vis-à-vis the world it takes the form of fear. Fear is the emotion that drives human beings to the most terrible of deeds. The world that God loves is converted into a field of hatreds, a killing field.

Alienation (Violation)

Idolatry and flight are closely related forms of primarily personal sin although each has interhuman implications and each is objectified in cosmic and social powers. There is in addition a form of sin that is characteristic of interpersonal relations, namely *alienation*. This is "malignant alienation," as distinct from the "benign alienation" that accompanies the incompatibilities intrinsic to interpersonal relations. Alienation becomes malignant (sinful) when relations are poisoned by violation and victimization.[53]

Violation, says Farley, "effects a malignant separation in relation." Individuals also engage in violating acts of domination and aggression, but these come and go, whereas malignant alienation is a structural feature of relation itself. "A relation itself is violative when its thous use the enduring materials of the relation against each other."

Primary examples are abusive marital or sexual relationships, domineering parent-child relationships, patterns of sexual harassment, situations of manipulation and deception, hierarchical relationships among workers or colleagues. In fact, all relationships of inequality are violative and thus alienating. They breed attitudes of resentment in the violated and guilt in the violator. Guilt arises from the awareness that relationships themselves have been wounded and that the damage cannot be repaired without building a new relationship. But individuals find themselves trapped within relationships, unable to attain a basis for rebuilding; the fact of violating and having been violated remains as a kind of stain that cannot be washed away or wound that will not heal. The feelings of guilt thus aroused are internalized by individuals and spread into the social world, where they infect institutional and legal relationships.[54]

Bondage of the Will

Guilt, according to Paul Ricoeur, expresses "the paradox toward which the idea of fault points—namely, the concept of a human being who is responsible *and* captive, or rather a being who is responsible for being captive—in short, the concept of the *servile will*."[55] Guilt is the "achieved internality of sin"; it is the subjective awareness of the objective situation of sin; it is sin raised to the level of moral consciousness or "conscience." We know that we are responsible, and this very knowledge has a binding, alienating effect. We are bound by the knowledge that we are responsible, bound by self-blame. We resort to various indirect ways of talking about this, using symbolisms of captivity such as flesh, infection, defilement, possession, because, says Ricoeur, "the paradox of a captive free will—the paradox of a *servile will*—is insupportable for thought. That freedom must be delivered and that this deliverance is deliverance from self-enslavement cannot be said directly; yet it is the central theme of 'salvation'."[56]

Thus the personal and interpersonal forms of sin—idolatry, flight, alienation—issue in something, namely a bondage of the will.[57] Sin becomes a hypersubjective reality or power, characterized as a quasi-personal force that possesses the sinner. The language of Paul in the letter to the Romans (chaps. 5–6) clearly suggests this: Sin, we are told, "came into the world" and "exercised dominion"; we are "enslaved" to it, sold under it, or place ourselves at its disposal, and we are paid wages by it. We experience sin as having the capacity of possessing and binding us.

Sometimes Paul uses the image of "flesh" (*sarx*), or of existence "according to the flesh" (*kata sarka*), to express this characteristic of sin as binding—a bondage to the flesh. This linkage of sin and flesh has had fateful consequences, for it has been used to give Christianity an anticorporeal bias, especially when linked with Neoplatonic ideas, as in the case of Augustine. But Paul is not suggesting that flesh as such is sinful. Rather *sarx* is one of the terms he uses to designate the human person or human nature as such. It is a term that calls attention to the embodied, corporeal, finite character of human beings; we are creatures belonging to the created world, sharing in its weakness, its transitoriness, but also in its basic thrust toward life.[58] Obviously *sarx*, the embodied human self, is not sinful or evil; it is good, and it wills the good, namely life. But the life that characterizes the world of *sarx* is not self-derived and self-sustained. It is the gift of the Creator. And the life toward which all flesh is pressing is not some organic core of the cosmos but the being of God, who is life. At this point Judaism and Christianity divide from Freud and all naturalisms, no matter how refined. Finite matter, erotic desire, are not ultimate. The human attempt to derive the source and goal of life from the life-process itself and to maintain life according to this standard and by this power are a delusion. Not flesh itself but existence *according to* the flesh is sinful because such a way of existing or comporting ourselves is a denial of the fact that God, not humanity—the Spirit of God, not the flesh of mortal beings—is the giver and preserver of life; it leads to rebellion against God and a life of defiance and boasting. That according to which we are to exist is the Spirit, not the flesh (*kata pneuma*, not *kata sarka*).

When we do exist according to the flesh, then we fall into bondage to precisely that which we think we can control and according to whose criterion we live, namely flesh itself. Thus Paul speaks of "flesh" as a quasi-personal being that exercises demonic power over us, just as he speaks of sin.[59] In both cases, the mythological language has already been demythologized in Paul's theology: "Flesh" is not an alien cosmic power, as the Gnostics believed, nor is it sensual lust; rather it is simply that when we try to live "according to" it, it rises up and ensnares us. Living *kata sarka* converts *sarx* from *eros* to *thanatos*, makes it into the binding power of death to which all mortal flesh is heir.

Cosmic and Social Objectifications of Sin: Structures of Evil

The fact that personal and interpersonal sin issues in a bondage of the will means that it has the capacity not only to alter the structures of the self but also to assume an objective power of its own vis-à-vis individual persons and interpersonal relations. The objectification of sin appears in the alteration of certain cosmic and social structures, which in turn profoundly affect individual and communal selves. I refer to this alteration as "structures of evil" or "structures of destruction."[60] The distinction between sin and evil is a tenuous one. Some theologians use the terms synonymously. However, I find it helpful to think of evil as not merely a consequence that follows upon sin but as a dynamic that demonically magnifies and reinforces it, converting it into something that cannot be remedied by a change of heart. Evil is a consequence that also precedes individual acts of sin; it becomes sedimented in the historical destiny that tempts to sin, thus adding a tragic dimension to moral responsibility.

To elucidate the structures of evil, the Pauline categories of law, death, and worldly powers may be put to good use. Death (in the sense of *thanatos*) is primarily a cosmic objectification of sin because it alters our way of being in the world as natural beings, while law and the powers are primarily social objectifications. It should be kept in mind that all of these forms of human evil flow ultimately from a violation or disruption of the fundamental human relationship, namely to God. Sin against God rarely appears as such; rather it appears as personal aggression (idolatry) and submission (flight), as interpersonal alienation, as cosmic evil (death), and as social evil (institutionalized alienation, ideologies, injustice).

Law: The Objectification of Alienation

In the Greek world, law was the indispensable precondition of freedom. The same remains true of any political concept of freedom, and the principle of "freedom under law" is essential to constitutional democracy, which limits political power by law, denying arbitrary or capricious rule to an individual, small group, or crowds. For the Hebrew Bible, however, the law is the consequence of the loss of freedom. Because human beings miss the good toward which they are striving, it takes on the character of demand. God's demand encounters the people in the law, the Torah, the purpose of which is to lead persons to the life they have lost. For Paul, the law has become an occasion of sin and therefore a form of bondage. Thus a progressive radicalization of the concept of law occurs: First it is a source of freedom, then it becomes a substitute for freedom, and finally it emerges as a threat to freedom. The ambiguity of law is that it is all of these.

From a religious perspective, law can be understood as the objectification of the consciousness of guilt. The "delicate and scrupulous conscience" (which is an element in most religious pieties) lives according to the law. The law is fulfilled not merely by clinging to scripture but by making it an actual divine teaching through an ongoing process of oral interpretation and supplementation. Through law the consciousness of guilt is objectified, rationalized, sublimated, and expunged by obedience. This is a heteronomous mode of existence, in which subjectivity and freedom are sacrificed for the sake of righteousness.[61]

Paul shares this religious view of the law, up to a point. He agrees that the law is the revelation of the will of God (in this sense "holy and just and good," Rom. 7:12), and that by means of it sin and guilt are brought to consciousness. But he does not agree that it is possible for humans to satisfy the demands of the law of God. Therefore, the law cannot be a means of salvation, and all that is left is its exposure of sin and the sacrifice of freedom to heteronomy. By this means, the law itself becomes one of the primary forms of bondage, a "law of sin and of death" (Rom. 8:2). The law not only awakens the knowledge that we are sinful (Rom. 7:7ff.), but evokes sin itself in order to bring us to grace: "Law came in, with the result that the trespass multiplied; but where sin increased, grace abounded all the more" (Rom. 5:20).[62]

The concept of "law" thus understood can be taken as a symbol designating the psychological, political, and social structures by which consciousness of guilt is objectified and rationally sublimated. The Freudian interpretation of civilization as a vast instrument for the repression of libidinal desire and the rationalization of this repression would fit here. The superego (the consciousness of guilt instilled by parental and cultural sanctions) has the function of "law" in the psyche, and the result is a deep alienation between psyche and society.

Turning from the psychological to the political and socioeconomic realms, it is clear that law takes on the form of alienation, which pervades all levels of corporate life. The patriarchalism that has characterized most societies, Western and Eastern, for millennia is a form of institutionalized alienation, the perpetual violation of women as subjects. The rules that accompany modern bureaucracies (states, agencies, legal systems, corporations, universities, churches) are intrinsically alienating since they treat persons as units of an impersonal process rather than as individual subjects, and they convert relations of equality into ones of hierarchy. Economic and marketing systems rely to a significant degree on manipulation. The positive function of law as the precondition of freedom in a constitutional democracy can be inverted into its opposite: The slogan "law and order" becomes a code language for oppression when dominant power groups are threatened by resistance. The legal structure of a racist society is a good example of how the consciousness of guilt over racial prejudice is rationalized and justified. Fascist, totalitarian, and communist regimes are inevitably highly legalistic; in most Western democracies, the systemic controls are more subtle and humane but no less real. In brief, law is an ambiguous factor in our corporate lives—necessary to social existence yet a ready seat for social evil.

Death: The Objectification of Flight

Death is the ultimate form of human bondage, infusing all the other forms. But what do we mean by "death"? The term itself has different levels of meaning. Death in the sense of mortality, physical perishing, is simply an aspect of our finitude, our bodily existence, and should not be regarded as a form of bondage any more than the body should be thought of as the prison house of the soul. Physical mortality becomes an oppressive, anxiety-laden event only when it becomes the occasion for flight from life and freedom. Sin, we have said, is a false, aberrant pursuit of life that not only issues in revolt against God and aggression against humans but also constitutes a way that leads to death. Thus Paul refers not only to *thnētos,* which is physical mortality, but also to *thanatos,* which is death in the sense of a binding power. *Thanatos,* he says, came into the world through Adam (1 Cor. 15:22), through Adam's sin (Rom. 5:12, 17–18); *thnētos* he associates with *sarx* or *sōma* (2 Cor. 4:11; Rom. 6:12; 8:11).[63] He is not speaking of two types of death, one physical and the other spiritual. Rather, *thanatos is* physical mortality *as* binding, "deadly." There is one death, physical death, which is, however, capable of taking on the quality of "deadliness." Human beings make their mortality, their perishable nature, into an event of "death" in the guise of *thanatos.* In this they seem to be unique among living creatures although there is a sense in which *thanatos* stalks the cosmos.

Why does mortality become a problem for human beings such that it becomes an occasion for sin? It does so when it is believed that each human being is an irreplaceable, unsubstitutable individual. Then mortality as such appears to become the enemy ("death") because it cuts the individual off from all life-sustaining relationships by which individual identity is preserved. But mortality is in fact the enemy only if it is *not* the case that God is the victor over mortal death, transforming and preserving each individual in God's life-giving presence. Not to believe that God is the victor is to live according to the flesh, to venerate the flesh (or mortality) as god. In that case, mortality becomes a binding power, which rises up and ensnares us; it then becomes death proper, *thanatos,* which is a form of sin. Paul describes this death both as the *punishment* for sin ("the wages of sin is death," Rom. 6:23—an older juridical concept that he sometimes adopts) and, more characteristically and profoundly, as a *fruit* organically growing out of sin ("if you sow to your own flesh, you will reap corruption from the flesh," Gal. 6:8). When mortality becomes death in this uniquely Pauline sense, then it becomes the ultimate form of bondage (Rom. 6:21-22; 8:2, 21).[64] Sin is "the sickness unto death."[65] The thing that enslaves or captures us above all else is our own mortality converted into death. Once this occurs, we are more likely to impose death on others or to justify killing. Death becomes a kind of god that fatally attracts us.

The paradox in all this is that as long as we live "according to the flesh" we will "die," and the only basis for not living according to the flesh is to believe that it is possible to live according to another power, which is the power of God. In this sense, the sin of death is the profound consequence of broken faith. To believe is precisely to know that mortality is not the ultimate power that cuts us off from God and life. It is to know that *thanatos* as such is an illusion, that the truth is not death alone but death-and-resurrection. The paradox is that we cannot speak properly of death without also speaking of resurrection from the dead. Resurrection does not cancel or deny mortality; rather it accepts it, assumes it, preserves and transforms it. It becomes, as suggested above (pp. 165–66), a moment in the life of God. Then it is no longer capable of being converted into "death," and in this sense the power of death (its "victory" or "sting," 1 Cor. 15:55) is destroyed. Paul never suggests in 1 Cor. 15:50–54 that we are already immortal and hence deathless in a Greek or Gnostic sense. Rather, in consequence of resurrection precisely from the dead, "we will be changed." What is mortal must "put on" immortality. First mortality, then and only then immortality. Death is undergone by each of us only once. Being raised from the dead, we shall never again die, and death has thus lost its dominion over us (Rom. 6:9); death is swallowed up in victory (1 Cor. 15:54), mortality by life (2 Cor. 5:4).

Is death a problem that afflicts only human beings, or is there also a death of nature? Paul does in fact assert that the whole of creation was subjected to "futility," to "bondage to decay" (Rom. 8:20-21)—and this seems to be precisely the death that comes from sin, *thanatos*, the sickness unto death. Such decay is not merely a natural process or the consequence of human exploitation and pollution although the latter is an urgently important aspect of the matter; rather there appears also to be a drift toward "futility" in nature itself, which can only be characterized as tragic if not evil. What that might mean will be considered later (chap. 18, pp. 319–23); for the moment I simply note that death is a binding power that pervades the cosmos and is not limited solely to human experience.

Worldly Powers: Objectifications of Idolatry

"World" (*kosmos*) designates for biblical thought the total world of creation, including both "heaven" and "earth," the latter being the stage on which human life is played. In 1 Cor. 8:4–5, the expression "in the world" is equivalent to "in heaven or on earth." More characteristically for Paul and John, the term "world" or "this world" contains a theological judgment: *Kosmos* designates the sphere of human possibilities and conditions in enmity toward God and in bondage to the "powers." Demythologized, these powers represent the forces of social evil that are primary expressions of idolatry and spread its destructive consequences throughout the human world. There are both "heavenly" powers (ideologies) and "earthly" powers (injustice, oppression).

Ideologies: Racism, Sexism, Classism, Naturism, Homophobia, Xenophobia

"Heaven" is not an otherworldly place, located somewhere above this world. Rather it is part of this world, that sphere or dimension of the world where the so-called "spirit powers" have their domain, by contrast to the sphere where human beings dwell ("earth"). Paul refers to these "spirit powers" in various ways: "angels," "rulers," "powers" (Rom. 8:38; 1 Cor. 15:24), "elemental spirits of the world" (Gal. 4:3, 9). While this is clearly mythological language, it should be observed that these spirit powers do not belong to a satanic world of darkness for Paul, as they did for the Gnostics, but rather to God's creation. They are powers by which God exercises dominion in the world, but they have been perverted into destructive powers by human defiance of this dominion. In this sense the powers really exist as demonic only "for us," and our situation is an enslavement to powers for whose corruption we ourselves are responsible. The heavenly powers seem to symbolize the fact that the reality in which humans find themselves is already one full of conflicts and struggles, a reality that threatens and enthralls.[66]

How might these powers be described in a contemporary nonmythological fashion? One would have to point to a parasociological, parapolitical structure of reality that is not physical or natural but psychological in character. What are frequently called *ideologies* in the pejorative sense are examples of such a parapolitical reality. An ideology is the rationalization of a practice by an uncritical set of beliefs that often have a deeply emotional or irrational basis. Like the personal sin of which they are an objectification, ideologies are driven by deeply seated fears, and they obscure or mask the true reasons for believing and behaving in a certain way. The -isms and phobias with which we are concerned today are all ideologies in this sense.

Take *racism*. It is the rationalization of economic and political exploitation by a theory asserting the inherent biological inferiority of persons whose skin color is different and generally darker than our own. It is a prime instance of idolatry, for it entails the apotheosis of one's own race and the negation of others; its logic is genocide although its practice is usually segregation. It is an extraordinarily resistant ideology because it is so deeply rooted in the archaic consciousness of light-skinned peoples: the association of darkness with stain, evil, malevolence. Long before economic conditions encouraged the enslavement of black Africans, beginning in the seventeenth century, white Europeans regarded Africans and Asians as inferior because they were different. When slavery became economically profitable, racial prejudice was ready-made to legitimate it. Racism is a "demon," a "spirit power," which holds us in its grip but is in fact an objectification of the primal sin of idolatry. Like all the -isms, it is driven by the fear of otherness, difference, and the desire to secure ourselves as the sole center and criterion by which everything is measured.[67]

Take *sexism*. Rosemary Radford Ruether speaks of it in very similar terms. It is rooted in the fundamental duality of self and other, which very early in human consciousness was correlated with a dualism of good and evil, superior and inferior, and male and female. Females were viewed by those in power, the males, as other and hence as inferior, just as body was believed to be inferior to mind, nature to spirit, the emotional to the intellectual, the feminine to the masculine. The ideology of sexism is driven by fear of otherness, and it is expressed in mechanisms of projection and exploitation, false naming and false relating. To fight it Ruether calls for a "conversion to the center" by which this and all other false dualisms might be overcome.[68] Mark K. Taylor identifies the fear in sexism as that of the mother; and the logic of matriphobia, he suggests, is matricide, just as the logic of racism is genocide. These are fears powerful enough to drive humans to acts of monster making and monster slaying.[69]

Take *classism*. It is an ideology that legitimates the institutionalizing of social differentiation and social inequality in a system of social stratification or "classes." An institutionalized system of inequality is not a normal human condition but one created by those who possess or gain power, wealth, privilege, and access in order to assure the retention of their advantages. Unlike race or gender, class is itself a form of evil, an objectification of the primal sin of idolatry, and it is intimately dependent on its legitimating ideology, classism. For this reason it is difficult to distinguish between class and classism, and the sociological literature rarely does so. But it is important to recognize the ideological dimension present in the creation and legitimation of class divisions. Religion has always played an important role in the legitimizing process. If it can be claimed that a patriarchal social structure and the division of classes is rooted in "natural law," willed by God and ordained to a higher end, and if future rewards are promised for those who accept their present calling, then the most powerful legitimation conceivable has been fashioned. Precisely this attitude is found throughout much of the history of the Western Christian church, Catholic and Protestant; and it is present in other religions as well (notably the caste system of Hinduism).

Another aspect of the legitimation process is the myth of equality of opportunity and competition allegedly present in democratic societies, a myth that can justify some of the most ruthless practices of capitalism. Here too religion has spread its "sacred canopy" of legitimation in the form of civil or patriotic religion, and beneath this canopy is a fear and suppression of social differences.[70]

Take *naturism.* This is an ideology that justifies the use and abuse of nature for human ends. It is deeply rooted in the Western tradition, and a biblical *locus classicus* provides support for it: "Be fruitful and multiply, and fill the earth and subdue it; and have dominion over the fish of the sea and over the birds of the air and over every living thing that moves upon the earth" (Gen. 1:28). The text is the product, of course, of an early agricultural society that struggled to survive in a fairly harsh environment and that lacked the power to damage it significantly. But there does seem to be something excessive about it: Why is it necessary for such a society to have dominion over the fish of the sea and the birds of the air in addition to domestic animals and food-bearing plants? An element of hubris reverberates in this text, which has only become more pronounced in the cultures that have been influenced by it. With the advent of acquisitive capitalism, modern technology, and exponential population growth, the admonition to "fill the earth and subdue it" becomes downright ominous, an invitation to disaster. Given the strategies of deception that accompany all ideologies, together with a lingering fear of nature, the danger is that naturism will not be recognized for what it is—a form of spiritual evil—until it is too late to avoid disaster.

Take *homophobia.* Here the idea of fear (phobia) is expressed in the very term itself, in this case fear of sexual orientations different from our own and the absolutizing of certain practices as normative. Taylor believes that the fear of sameness in sexual relations arises out of a devaluing of the body, sensuality, and friendship that one shares with those of one's own gender, and this may in turn reflect a self-hatred and an abstraction from one's concrete materiality.[71] Tolerance of a diversity of sexual orientations was more prevalent in the ancient world, especially among the Greeks and Romans, and not much attention was given to the issue of homosexuality in the Hebrew and Christian scriptures (what is condemned there are violent and perverted behaviors *contrary* to one's orientation, which is always assumed to be heterosexual).[72] Intolerance seems to have emerged in the Western world in the Middle Ages, and it is striking that the persecution of homosexuals, Jews, and, later, witches often went hand in hand, reflecting a widespread inability of Western societies to deal with the fact of difference.[73] The belief in witchcraft reveals just how easy it was to remythologize these spirit powers, to reify them into real demons.

Somehow we have remained in thralldom to these medieval superstitions for more than eight hundred years.

Take *xenophobia*. It exhibits a fear of strangers, foreigners, others (*xenos*), and is what drives nationalism, ethnocentrism, provincialism, parochialism, and other forms of human intolerance. Following the breakup of the Soviet empire, the resurgence of xenophobia in the form of ethnic cleansing and ethnic rivalries is one of the frightening manifestations of evil in our time. Xenophobia cannot be overcome by the totalitarian suppression of differences but only by building authentic human community through the free expression of differences. If xenophobia underlies all of the dehumanizing ideologies, then the latter, while on the surface manifesting the sin of idolatry, may be more deeply rooted in the sin of flight—in the fear of otherness, difference, materiality, death, ultimately of life itself.

Injustice: Political, Social, Economic, Environmental Oppression

The "earthly" powers, to continue the Pauline metaphor, are not parasociological and parapolitical, but precisely sociological and political. Paul did not pay as much attention to this type of worldly objectification of sin in structures of evil as he did to the other type, the spirit powers. He tended to treat institutionalized bondage under the category of law; and he did mention "the rulers of this age, who are doomed to perish" (1 Cor. 2:6, 8). Yet on the whole he did not seem to have been very sensitive to political or systemic forms of oppression. Among the most significant political facts of his day were the hegemony of Rome, the institution of slavery (which was based on economic and political factors, not racism), and the subordination of women. On all three of these issues Paul took what appear to us today to have been compromising stands.

Instead of speaking of earthly powers, the appropriate nonmythological reference is to the powers of *injustice,* which appear in the concrete practices of oppression and exploitation in the political, social, economic, cultural, and environmental domains.[74] These are connected to the legitimating ideologies but represent the concrete harm and suffering that are imposed on individuals and groups. Racism issues in slavery, apartheid, prejudice; sexism in patriarchalism and the subordination of women; homophobia in the victimization of gays and lesbians; classism in a system of stratification that withholds access to wealth and creates poverty; ethnocentrism in cultural conflict and domination; xenophobia in war. To these must be added the exploitation of nature and the recognition that human justice and ecojustice are intertwined.

These practices of injustice and oppression need to be analyzed in detail—a task for another book[75]—as yet further forms of human evil, perhaps the most terrible of all since they are so destructive, so widespread, so distant from what we ordinarily think of as personal sin. They spread a mantle of hatred and hostility over the world God created for the sake of love. We find ourselves hopelessly entangled in this mantle, in bondage to the interlocking dynamic of sin and evil. We cannot save ourselves. What is needed is a new incarnation of God's love, powerful enough to set us free from destructive practices, to break the grip of sin and death, to reconcile alienated groups, to engender justice.

15

CHRIST INCARNATE: THE SHAPE OF REDEMPTIVE LOVE

The Problem of Interpreting Jesus

The Christian faith believes that a saving incarnation of God's love has in fact occurred and that it is definitively, not exclusively, associated with a specific human being. Thus the focus shifts and narrows as we turn our attention from natural processes, anthropological structures, and mythic patterns to the concrete events of history. We are moving from the most universal to the most particular manifestations of God's love for the world—the same love no matter how different the forms in which it appears. Christ, cosmos, and history are part of a complex continuum that we only imperfectly understand. The tradition has known that Christ is not merely a historical figure but a symbol of cosmic proportions.

Access to a historical figure requires an interpretative framework. This framework becomes more decisive the more significant the figure is for our own lives. The hermeneutical problems involved in treating a sixteenth-century German pastor or a twentieth-century American preacher may be relatively simple, but they become quite complex when we are concerned with Martin Luther or Martin Luther King Jr. The interpretation of such figures is never completed; just because they are so important for us, each fresh angle of vision affords new insight. The events surrounding their lives and persons seem to remain contemporary. Here the interaction between past and present history is intensive because our own futures remain open and these past figures help to shape our futures.

A "figure" is in fact more than an individual human being. A figure is a representative of a particular shape or structure or paradigm of praxis, which spreads beyond the life of the individual person with whom it was first associated and which endures through time. We speak of historical "figures" in this sense; they are the ones who are remembered, the ones about whom history is written. The gestalt that is associated with them becomes more important than their individual lives, and it can grow or be modified beyond their original embodiment of it. With respect to such figures, their daily lives, personal idiosyncrasies, and intimate relations are not of ultimate significance (despite our curiosity about them), nor are such factors as their race, sex, ethnic identity, or geographical and temporal location. They become bearers of something that transcends them, which seems to make use of them, often rather cruelly. The great figures of history rarely lived happy, tranquil lives; they were at odds with conventions and accepted practices. The fate of those about whom history is *not* written is different but no less cruel: They are forgotten rather than crucified; they become statistics rather than figures. Neither for heroes nor for common folk does history as such offer much solace.

To say that the personal details in the existence of a historical figure are not of ultimate significance is not to suggest that they are insignificant. To be sure, the ultimate significance of a human life is not determined by the accidents of birth, race, gender, physical features, psychological characteristics, personal habits, etc. But these factors can be endowed with significance by concrete situations. For example, the fact that Jesus of Nazareth was a male is not irrelevant to his having challenged patriarchal domination to such an extent that it destroyed him. Elizabeth Johnson observes: "If in a patriarchal culture a woman had preached compassionate love and enacted a style of authority that serves, she would most certainly have been greeted with a colossal shrug. Is this not what women are supposed to do by nature? But from a social position of male privilege Jesus preached and acted this way, and therein lies the summons. . . . The heart of the problem is not that Jesus was a man but that more men are not like Jesus, insofar as patriarchy defines their self-identity and relationships."[1] Thus there is a sense in which Jesus' maleness was instrumental to his mission. The same is true of his Jewishness but in a somewhat different sense. He released one of the potentials (we cannot say *the* potential) present in Judaism in an astonishing new way. Only a Jew could do that. Because the followers of Jesus were forced out of the synagogues by the Jewish authorities, they assumed a new religious identity, and as a result the potential of Judaism instantiated by Jesus was released into the world and became a global, multi-ethnic reality. Jesus' Jewishness is significant in another sense too, since it identified him with an oppressed, once-enslaved, and again-to-be-enslaved people. Thus maleness and Jewishness were not incidental to the Christ-gestalt but became appropriate bearers of it, assuming that one of the features of this gestalt was to break the power of sexism, ethnocentrism, racism.

Tragically, however, in the course of Christian history maleness and Jewishness were twisted around in such a way as to block the gestalt. Jesus' maleness was used to support an ideology of male superiority, the subordination of women, and their exclusion from priesthood and ministry down to the present day. Jesus' Jewishness became a basis for claiming that the church is the new Israel while the old Israel was ruthlessly persecuted for having rejected the Messiah. The history of effects has cancelled whatever redemptive potential was present in the fact that Jesus was a Jewish male. In other words, his particularity proved to have both positive and negative significance in history, and thus it shares in the ambiguity of all history.

The details of a life, insofar as they can be known, do often show in revealing ways *how* a figure accomplishes his or her historical work or becomes the bearer of a historical shape, and they do reveal something of what the shape means. If we were to discover a profound contradiction between a personal life and a historical praxis, then questions would undoubtedly have to be raised about that praxis: Is it a deception, a cover, a falsification, a pretense?[2] Partial contradictions undoubtedly exist between the personal and the public existence of every historical figure; and the interesting question is how the figure handles these contradictions. A struggle undoubtedly occurs between personal fears, weaknesses, temptations, vanities, on the one hand, and a mission or vocation, on the other. We know that Jesus himself did not escape such a struggle.[3] Part of the hermeneutics of suspicion is to uncover such struggles and contradictions, but the presence of these factors does not of itself undermine the work of great figures; rather it illuminates it.

When we turn to the figure of Jesus of Nazareth, the situation becomes highly complex. For most Christians, he is not merely a significant figure of the historical past but a "saving event"—indeed, *the* saving event, which happened not just there and then but also happens here and now. This is what is meant by calling him "the Christ." The "here and now" of Christ as saving event is at the heart of what Christians believe about Jesus as risen from the dead. We entrust our salvation or redemption not simply to a past memory but to a present, contemporary reality. Thus in christology we start with a present experience of this figure as alive and at work in the world, which not only provides the framework for interpreting the historical testimonies concerning Jesus found in the New Testament but also appears to shatter all historical possibilities. It may be, however, that the presence of the risen Christ represents the most intensive actualization conceivable of the way in which a past historical figure can continue to live and have significance in the present, in which case the possibilities of history are not shattered but fulfilled in him. I shall return to this matter. The point now is that the question of frameworks or models for interpretation becomes absolutely crucial just because of the peculiarly intensive way that Jesus has been experienced as redemptively present by Christian communities, as involved in our own salvation.

Today the traditional models for interpreting Jesus as the Christ have come under severe attack. This is because the traditional models are perceived as ethnocentric, patriarchal, misogynist, anti-Judaic, exclusivist, and triumphalist. There is a good deal of truth to these criticisms, which will be examined more closely shortly. They point to the fact that Christian claims about Christ have always had a tendency to become over-inflated and idolatrous, perhaps just because of the tremendous vitality created by the experience of the risen Christ, the experience of being filled by the Spirit of Christ. Spirit-filled persons can change the world, but they can also become fanatic. An extreme solution would be to excise christology from theology entirely, but then we would no longer have distinctively Christian theology. A more viable option, and one that has been followed again and again by reform movements, is to turn back to the historical figure of Jesus as a corrective against the distorting ideologies by which he has been interpreted.

The difficulty is that we have no direct access to, and can never actually arrive at, the historical figure of Jesus. What we have, rather, are layer upon layer of interpretation, which can never be completely stripped away. On the basis of various analyses of early Christian tradition (form-critical, redactional, structuralist, literary), scholars may be able to construct a hypothetical picture of the pattern, shape, or "career" of the public activity of Jesus, which can lay reasonable claim to historical validity, although it always retains the character of a construct based on secondary evidence, evidence that is already interpreting what it is witnessing to. The elements of this career, by consensus, seem to include the following: baptism by John, independent proclamation of the inbreaking kingdom, gathering of disciples, parables and acts of healing, table fellowship with marginalized folk, conflict with religious and political authorities, journey to Jerusalem to celebrate the Passover, provocation, arrest, trial, condemnation, crucifixion. This is not much, but it is something with which to start.

Unavoidably, this very limited historical-critical construction of the figure of Jesus must be supplemented by a theological or christological construction, which introduces interpretative models in an effort to elicit the coherence and meaning of the figure of Jesus Christ for human existence today, and it does so in a more explicit, holistic fashion than a strictly historical sketch of what we can know about the public activity of Jesus will permit.[4] The theological construction relies not only on what can be learned from historical study but also on the experience of the Christian faith community in its ongoing encounter with the figure of the Christ, and it seeks to be faithful to the intention of early Christian kerygma in proclaiming Jesus to be the Messiah of God. Theology is a kind of fiction, an imaginative reconfiguration of what we know to be real. It is constrained by historical reality but not limited to it since it is seeking to elicit the possibilities for creative transformation hidden within events and figures of the past. The distinction between historical-critical and theological construction is a fluid one: The latter presupposes the former; and the former, if it is to achieve the coherence in the figure of Jesus that it seeks, will issue finally in the latter.

Rosemary Radford Ruether observes that we must "assume at the outset [a] hermeneutical circle between contemporary questions and interpretation of faith in Jesus as the Christ. Clarified hermeneutics lies in being conscious of the questions one brings from one's own situation and the response that one reads from the scripture." She goes on to say (referring to her own work) that

> the questions which are brought to the scriptures in these essays are those which the author believes to be most pressing and inescapable for our times. To avoid or finesse these questions by declarations of neutrality indeed helps to perpetuate the problems. These are the questions of political commitment in the light of poverty and oppression, the question of anti-Judaism and religious intolerance, the question of justice for the female half of the human race, and the question of human survival in the face of chronic environmental abuse.[5]

I shall now look at some of these questions more closely. They are the ones that must frame a contemporary christology. It will then become evident that classical christology constructed interpretative models of its own out of the questions *it* brought to bear upon the scriptural witness. While the mythological and metaphysical character of these models has become highly problematic for us today (to say nothing of their political, social, ethnic, and sexual implications), they do contain creative elements that can be retrieved and appropriated. Finally, as a means of revisioning the theme of incarnation, I shall construct a new model oriented to the idea of the "shape" or "gestalt" of Christ, a praxis of redemptive love incarnate in one filled by the Wisdom or Spirit of God, Jesus of Nazareth. This incarnation, culminating in crucifixion, symbolically completes the project of God's self-differentiation in the world. With the resurrection of Jesus from the dead and the fanning out of the Christ-gestalt into the world, the third and final figure of the divine life, that of the Spirit, comes into play, again symbolically since the Spirit has been at work since the beginning of creation (chap. 16). Christology forms the turning point and bridge between the second and third trinitarian spheres, the spheres of love and freedom, of differentiation and mediation: The world is poured into Christ, and Christ is poured out in the Spirit.

Postmodern Challenges to Christology

Religious Pluralism

Among the many issues involved with christology and religious pluralism, two will be our focus: rethinking Christian claims about Christ in light of the current "close encounter" of the religions, and enriching our thought about Christ through analogues to this figure in other religious traditions.

Paul Knitter points the way on the first of these paths in his attempt to fashion a theocentric christology. He says that all Christian models insist on some form of uniqueness with respect to Jesus. The question is whether this is to be understood as an *exclusive* uniqueness, "affirming that only in Jesus can true revelation or salvation be found"; or as an *inclusive* uniqueness, such that "God's revealing-saving action in Jesus includes all other religions, either as an anonymous, cosmic presence within them or as their final fulfillment." Against these traditional models, Knitter argues for a *relational* uniqueness for Jesus: This "affirms that Jesus *is* unique, but with a uniqueness defined by its ability to relate to—that is, to include and be included by—other unique religious figures. Such an understanding of Jesus views him not as exclusive or even as normative but as *theocentric*, as a universally relevant manifestation . . . of divine revelation and salvation."[6] Knitter works this out by showing that such an understanding of uniqueness is already present in the New Testament although the other patterns are there too, as would be expected from its historical-cultural context (a classicist understanding of truth and an eschatological-apocalyptic mentality) and from the confessional character of much early Christian language ("the language of lovers"). He thinks that the relational uniqueness of Jesus is best understood in the context of praxis. "Not knowing whether Jesus is unique, whether he is inclusive or normative for all others, does not interfere with commitment to the praxis of following him. Such questions may be answered in the future. In the meantime, there is much work to be done."[7]

Knitter concludes as follows:

> Christians, in their approach to persons of other faiths, need not insist

> that Jesus brings God's definitive, normative revelation. A confessional approach is a possible and preferred alternative. In encountering other religions, Christians can confess and witness to what they have experienced and come to know in Christ, and how they believe this truth can make a difference in the lives of all peoples, without making any judgments whether this revelation surpasses or fulfills other religions.[8]

After all, it is not very interesting to be told how or why one religion surpasses another, or what the deficiencies are of other religions from the point of view of the critic's own religion. All such talk is self-serving and parochial. Rather what is interesting is to learn what the genuine *points of contact* are and what the genuine *differences* are among religions, and thus to learn from all religions without passing judgment on any of them. Faithfulness to Christ demands openness to this kind of learning.

Mark K. Taylor suggests another approach to this first theme by arguing that certain features of the Christ symbol give it a "liminal character that is especially appropriate for formulating christology in relation to cultural plurality." The "dislocation" brought about by Jesus' proclamation and action has the effect of putting us at the margins of all established cultural worlds and of having to exist between them, "interstitially."[9]

The second way is offered by scholars who find analogues to the Christ figure in other religions, or who see complementary aspects of salvation thematized in different religions. Raimundo Panikkar goes so far as to speak of "the unknown Christ of Hinduism." Christ is present and active in the deepest mysteries of Hindu spirituality. Panikkar calls for a "homeomorphic" approach, one that finds corresponding functions within another setting. The goal is "mutual fecundation" or "mutual interpenetration." He thinks that the symbol "the Christ" is not simply identical with Jesus (we can say that "Jesus is the Christ," not that "the Christ is Jesus"), and he suggests that even if a symbol is primarily and directly meaningful in the environment in which it originated, it can be enlarged and deepened in such a way as to open up experiences and realities not yet intended in the actual symbol. "My contention is that in our present times a Christ-symbol valid only for Christians would cease to be a living symbol."[10]

Aloysius Pieris proposes the path of complementarity and convergence.[11] The "core" of any religion is the "liberative experience" that gave birth to it and that continues to be available through it. In Buddhism the core experience is that of "liberative knowledge"; in Christianity it is "redemptive love" (the term I have adopted to name the shape of Christ incarnate). Each of these alone is inadequate. "The movement of the spirit progresses through the dialectical interplay of wisdom and love." Such a dialectic is already going on in both religions, but it can be strengthened by contact with the other religion. Thus Pieris calls for "a christology that does not compete with buddhology but complements it by acknowledging the one path of liberation on which Christians join Buddhists in their *gnostic detachment* (or the practice of voluntary poverty) and Buddhists join Christians in their *agapeic involvement* in the struggle against forced poverty."[12] The reminder that wisdom is already an important motif in the Jewish and Christian tradition points in the direction of a sophia-christology as suggested by some feminists.

Feminist Critiques

The christological questions raised by feminist theologians go to the heart of the issues before us. As Ruether points out, the tradition (Jewish and Christian) quickly suppressed the female imagery associated with the idea of a messiah (the revivifying goddess, divine wisdom, etc.). The identification of Jesus with the Messiah of Israel was integrated into a "kingship ideology that provides the 'sacred canopy' over the existing political and social hierarchy. Likewise the Christological doctrine of Christ as *Logos* or ground of the created world is identified with the foundation of the existing social system. . . . Christology becomes the apex of a system of control over all those who in one way or another are 'other' than this new Christian order." Christological masculinism led to the notion that there must be a physical resemblance between the priest and Christ. "The possession of male genitalia becomes the essential prerequisite for representing Christ, who is the disclosure of the male God."[13]

This leads Ruether to ask whether a male Christ can represent redemptive personhood for women. We find in the Jesus of the Synoptic Gospels, she says, a figure who is remarkably compatible with feminism. He was (as portrayed in the Gospels) critical of established religion and social hierarchies; he aimed at a new reality in which hierarchy and patriarchy are overcome as principles of social relations; he revised God-language by using the familiar *Abba;* he spoke of the messiah as servant rather than king; he did not operate with a dualism of masculine and feminine; women played an important role in his movement. Theologically, Ruether concludes, the maleness of Jesus has no ultimate significance; in fact he represents the "kenosis of patriarchy." "Christ" is not necessarily male, nor is the redeemed community only women, but a new humanity, male and female. In terms rather like those used by Panikkar, Ruether argues that Christ as redemptive person and word of God need not be encapsulated once for all in the historical Jesus. Christic personhood continues in the community of sisters and brothers, and there have in fact been many female Christ-figures in the Christian tradition.[14]

This last line of thought is continued in an interesting way by Rita

Nakashima Brock.[15] Erotic power is the power of connection, a power that heals, makes whole, empowers, and liberates. It is the incarnation of divine love. This power, Brock argues, cannot be located in or restricted to a single individual. It is basically a communal reality, and she names it "Christa/Community" (an image based on a female crucifix called "Christa" found in the Cathedral of St. John the Divine in New York). Jesus participates centrally in Christa/Community, but he neither brings erotic power into being nor controls it. The salvific revelation of Christ is not limited to the historical Jesus. But Brock is by no means indifferent to the latter figure. She focuses on two aspects of the portrayal of Jesus in the Gospel of Mark, the first dealing with his exorcism and healing ("erotic power at work"), the second with his death ("erotic power in the shadows"). She makes the interesting point that Jesus not only gives power but is enabled to participate more fully in erotic power by others, notably the hemorrhaging woman (who takes away his patriarchal power) and the Syro-Phoenician woman (who shatters his religious exclusivity).[16]

African American Critiques

The black church in America has always had a powerful christological focus, partly because of its biblical basis, but also because the experience of the risen Christ has been a palpable one in the black community. James Cone brings this to theological expression in his various works. He argues that if it were correct to say that no one has a *present* experience of Christ as risen and exalted, as some theologians have claimed,[17] then the only conclusion could be that "black religion is nothing but an account of black people's subjective fancies." But the people testify otherwise: They could survive only because Jesus was present with them. It was Jesus who kept the community together and going, giving it courage to struggle on when it seemed a waste of time. Cone argues that "the only 'reasonable' and 'objective' explanation is to say that the people are right when they proclaim the presence of divine power, wholly different from themselves." Any other conclusion would violate the integrity of the black experience.[18]

Moreover, Cone contends, Jesus' presence in the social context of white racism means—if it is a real, not a docetic presence—that Christ must be *black* in order to remain faithful to the divine promise to bear the suffering of the poor. Christ's blackness is both literal and symbolic. It is literal in the sense that he truly becomes one with oppressed blacks, taking their suffering as his, being found in the history of their struggle. Christ really enters into the world where the poor, the despised, and the black are to be found. It is symbolic in that Jesus was a Palestinian Jew, not an African (and not, of course, a European)—but the soteriological meaning of the particularity of his Jewishness leads to the affirmation of his present blackness. This is not a denial of the universal significance of Christ for the salvation of all but a recognition that there is no universalism that is not also particular.[19]

In his study of African American theology, Theo Witvliet takes partial exception to Cone's christocentrism. He thinks that the focus of the black experience may be more *pneumatological* than christological, and that it is "the renewing power of the Spirit in the praxis of the black church and community" that "connects the liberating praxis of Jesus of Nazareth with black history and culture." "It is the Spirit which incorporates men and women into the messianic community of the exalted Christ. If that does not happen, . . . then a remarkably unhistorical element enters into the dialectical connection between incarnation and blackness." In support of this point, Witvliet refers to the work of the black South African theologian Takatso Mofokeng.[20]

This criticism seems to be well-taken. In his quite powerful appropriation of the christological language of the spirituals, Cone suppressed more than he realized (a by-product of his Barthian legacy?) the pneumatological language that is also present in them. The spirituals may in fact balance christological and pneumatological themes in exemplary fashion. They are after all "spirituals," and they are deeply rooted in the spirituality of African religions. Christology has been engrafted into them rather than vice versa.

This is where the work of African theologians like Mercy Amba Oduyoye will be increasingly helpful. She argues that the spirit world is a reality in Africa, and that Christianity needs to "have room for the concept of many Christs, persons in whom the Spirit of God dwells in all its fullness." Emphasis will be placed on the role of combat, healing, sacrifice, and the mediation of ancestors and companions. "In African Charismatic Christianity, the theology is christocentric but, with the emphasis being placed on the Holy Spirit, one reads a binitarian approach to the Godhead. In this theology, Christ and the Holy Spirit take the place of the spirit powers that are in the service of God in the traditional cosmology." Oduyoye mentions the writing of the Ghanan farmer and midwife Afua Kuma, whose poetry and prayers describe Jesus in immediate and powerful images: He is, for example, the pencil with which teachers teach knowledge to children, and a great hall that can accommodate all who come. The incarnation assumes many (unassuming) forms. The question Oduyoye leaves with us is similar to the one raised by religious pluralism and feminism: "The Christ for Africa is of course the Christ embodied in Jesus of Nazareth. But is that figure a *hapax* [a once and for all]? . . . Is God no longer incarnated for us today?"[21]

This line of thinking has been extended in an interesting way by James Evans. He suggests that a "figural" interpretation of Jesus as the

Christ accords well with African American religious thought and especially with the role of heroes in traditional African religions. The figura (or gestalt) of a liberating and mediating savior appeared in Jesus of Nazareth, but it continues to appear in cultic heroes and community leaders. The African epic hero provided a way for African American Christians to affirm the continuing efficacious presence of Jesus the messianic hero, who takes on the color of blackness, the social condition of the poor and disinherited, and (for womanist theologians) the gender of women. This christic figure functions both as a spiritual mediator or healer, like African ancestors, and as a personal and political liberator. A figural interpretation responds affirmatively to Oduyoye's challenge to give up the *hapax* and to think of many Christs. Just how such an approach might alter the interpretation of *Jesus* as the Christ, or clarify the sense in which *God* is redemptively present in the one Christ and the many Christs, is not worked out by Evans, but his ideas point the discussion in a fruitful direction and bring African American thought into proximity with an emerging postmodern consensus on the shape of a future christology.[22]

Jewish-Christian Dialogue

In an article reviewing recent works concerned with Jewish-Christian relations, Rosemary Ruether writes: "Christianity very much needs a theology that can affirm its experience of redemption in Christ without negating the Jewish people and its ongoing covenant with God."[23] Ruether concludes that such a theology has not been written. The primary work with which she is concerned in the review, that of Paul van Buren,[24] solves the problem, in her view, "by reducing Christianity to being simply the mediator of the covenant of God with Israel to the gentiles, in a way that allows for no significant new experiences of God to come through Christ." He also, she thinks, indulges in "an uncritical philo-semitism that is unable to face the significant ethical failures of the state of Israel." While concerned with present Israeli policies toward the Palestinians, Ruether, it should be kept in mind, has been one of the most consistent and powerful critics of Christian anti-Semitism.[25]

The question is whether we can allow for "significant new experiences of God to come through Christ" without falling into a "supersessionary" posture—the view that the "new covenant" inaugurated by God's incarnation in Christ somehow supersedes or completes the "old covenant" of God with Israel. This is the question raised by Peter Haas in a companion review on the same topic.[26]

The most ambitious attempt thus far to think through the christological aspects of this question is found in the work of John Pawlikowski. He states the dilemma by recognizing that, on the one hand, Christians can no longer claim that Jesus Christ has fulfilled the Jewish messianic prophecies or inaugurated the messianic age; while on the other hand, if no unique features are recognized in the revelation in Christ, Christianity would have no claim to being a major world religion.[27] His solution in part is to link Jesus very closely with Pharisaic Judaism (following the research of Ellis Rivkin, Michael Cook, and Jacob Neusner). Jesus furthered, indeed radicalized, the reforming tendencies present in Pharisaism, and many of the characteristic features of his message were already germinally present in Pharisaism. Pawlikowski then attempts to elaborate the uniqueness of Jesus in terms of a revised theology of incarnation, which in my view is both suggestive and puzzling. The suggestive part of it is the proposal that "what ultimately came to be recognized with clarity for the first time through the ministry and person of Jesus was how profoundly integral humanity was to the self-definition of God."[28]

What is puzzling is the claim that the Christ-event represents a culmination of the process of creation, "in which a part of the humanity in the Godhead broke out into a separate, though not fully separated, existence."[29] This could be intended as a restatement of the traditional doctrine of the incarnation of the divine Logos in the man Jesus, such that his "person" is divine, while his "nature" is human. The result is a mystical identity of the divine and the human that goes beyond the possibilities inherent in Judaism. Pawlikowski concludes that "Judaism and Christianity are essentially distinct religions, each emphasizing different but complementary aspects of human religiosity. . . . Authentic dialogue between them must start with the clear recognition of this difference."[30] Obviously any form of proselytism is out of the question, but mutual witness and dialogue are possible. "In the course of the dialogue which has been purged of all notions of superiority and all forms of proselytizing, Christians will try to convey to Jews why they feel that the Christ event carries a central meaning for the entire human family."[31]

Peter Haas thinks that Pawlikowski's solution still smacks of supersessionism. The close link of Jesus with Pharisaism does not really prepare Christians to deal with modern Judaism and modern Jews, who are as far removed from Pharisaism as are most modern Christians. Beyond this, however, the suggestion that Pharisaism is the group that has "seeded" Christianity implies "that while Christianity is thus the mature result of the seeding, Pharisaism (read Judaism?) is but the prior seed."[32] In other words, Christians tend to think of Judaism as locked into a permanently archaic stage and do not really relate to it as a living, changing religion. The same is true to some extent of Jewish understandings of Christianity, insofar as it is assumed that christology is locked into its orthodox, and from the Jewish point of view incredulous, formulations.

Is it possible to recognize a *difference* between Judaism and Christianity that does not become supersessionist? Without genuine difference, Christianity would either be the true Judaism (traditional Christian triumphalism) or a sect of Judaism, Judaism for Gentiles (van Buren). Pawlikowski is right in stressing the difference and the call for genuine dialogical mutuality. But his version of incarnation doctrine, as much as his interpretation of Pharisaism, subverts his intentions. He holds on to the *hapax,* stressing the ontologically unique and miraculous union of God and humanity through the incarnation of the "humanity in the Godhead," the divine Son or Logos, in a "separate existence," that of Jesus of Nazareth. A more plural and social understanding of incarnation, one that recognizes a multiplicity of shapes in which God appears, seems more promising. The shape of Christ itself is not one but many, and it does not supersede other shapes. Could we then say that Christianity actualizes *one* of the possibilities inherent in Judaism, but that there are other, equally authentic possibilities within Judaism, resources to which Judaism itself has turned in its own ongoing historical evolution? These possibilities are different, but there are also significant family resemblances between them, so much so that the diverse ways that have emerged out of biblical Judaism can continue to fructify each other through dialogue and collaboration in the larger human project.

In conclusion, these postmodern challenges suggest several important directions in which a contemporary christology should move. First, any interpretation of Christ must be genuinely pluralistic, open both to the diversity within the many cultural and ethnic expressions of Christianity and to the mediation of divine saving presence through other religions and figures. Second, it must be genuinely committed to the project of human liberation and to the vision of a just and sustainable social order. And third, it must find ways of appropriating and releasing the considerable saving resources of the Christian tradition. In pursuing these goals, christological reflection will, in William Schweiker's terms, find itself advancing claims about *Christ* rather than simply about Jesus as the Christ; accordingly, it "ought to be christomorphic—shaped by Christ—rather than christocentric in its orientation and perspective."[33]

The Dilemmas of Classical Christology

Mythological Patterns: Adoptionism, Kenoticism, Incarnationism, Docetism

A plurality of christological models, such as we encounter today, is nothing new for Christian faith. Such a pluralism is already found in the New Testament and other early Christian literature. The New Testament writings are not monolithic but part of the history of the formation of tradition, made up of a variety of competing interpretations and points of view. Thus we cannot speak of a single biblical christology but of the christologies of the pre-Pauline Palestinian-Jewish, Hellenistic-Jewish, and Hellenistic-Gentile communities, of Paul himself (who experimented with more than one model), of the four Evangelists, of Hebrews, of the deutero-Pauline and early catholic writers. Throughout the several layers of this tradition are found a variety of images borrowed from Judaism and Hellenistic religion—Messiah, Son of David, Son of Man, Son of God, Christos, Kyrios, Logos, Sophia, Sotēr—which have been applied to Jesus with different nuances of meaning, depending upon their milieu or context, and with different interpretative agendas. The issues that were being fought over, then as today, were political as well as religious: A messianic christology profoundly challenges political authority, while an imperial christology legitimates it.

From this matrix it is possible to identify several dominant patterns, and these patterns have influenced christological discussion ever since. Each of these patterns is "mythological." "Mythology" refers to an idealized form of narrative discourse that may or may not be rooted in actual historical events and that has the purpose of representing in story form the interaction of the divine and the human, the sacred and the profane, at the constitutive moments of human and cosmic process: birth and death, struggle and conflict, victory and defeat. Myths describe divine relations and actions in this-worldly, quasi-sensible terms. God and gods/goddesses are represented to act as though they were human agents. "Demythologizing" involves recognizing this mythical structure, recognizing that, in terms of literal descriptive reference, myths are not "true" as they were once thought to be, but recognizing also that, in terms of metaphorical, symbolic, "fictional" reference, they offer profound and subtle interpretations of basic aspects of human religious experience, interpretations that cannot be fully duplicated in more abstract, conceptual discourse.[34]

Maurice Wiles suggests that "the myth of God incarnate" is one of four basic myths that make up the structure of Christian faith: the creation, the fall, Christ's incarnation and work of atonement, the resurrection of the dead and the final judgment.[35] The incarnation myth differs from the others in that it is connected with, and offers an interpretation of, specific historical events relating to a specific historical figure, Jesus of Nazareth. We can press Wiles's point a step further and suggest that there are three (perhaps four) basic versions of the incarnation myth, only one of which is "incarnationist" in the strict sense. (A similar plurality attends the myths of beginning, fall, and end.) These three versions, in various combinations, provide the materials out of which most subsequent christologies have been built. Each has resources and limits. After exploring them, along with the classical christological doctrine they spawned, we shall have to ask whether it is possible to revision the myth of incarnation in nonmythological terms—since mythological thinking at the literal level is no longer possible for us but also since the incarnation mythos articulates a profound truth, the central and distinctive truth of Christianity.

It must be stressed that there is no simple normative truth about Jesus in relation to which all other interpretations are deviations. What is found rather are a variety of mythic patterns, none of which is literally true, but all of which offer insights into the redemptive significance of Jesus and the character of his relationship to God, the cosmos, and human beings: These are adoptionism, kenoticism, incarnationism (and docetism, which comes closest to being a deviation). They are not necessarily mutually exclusive myths; they overlap and incorporate each other but each has a distinctive logic. One finally has to decide whether the adoptionist mythos is more persuasive, or the kenoticist, or the incarnationist. All of these myths are in a broad sense "incarnational," that is, they are concerned to show the sense in which God becomes one with, or present in, an embodied human being and the corporate human community. As Elizabeth Johnson remarks, the "inner dynamic" of the doctrine of incarnation affirms "the transcendent God's capacity for embodiment, divine passion for liberation, and the constitutive nature of relation. . . . The living God is *capax hominis*, capable of personal union with what is not God, the flesh and spirit of humanity."[36] The question is how God does this.

Adoptionism[37]

The earliest christology is known as adoptionism. Its basic thesis was that Jesus, the holy and righteous one, who was crucified by lawless humans, God has raised up and exalted to a place of lordship, whence the Spirit is now being sent, and Christ himself will soon come to exercise the messianic functions. Jesus' distinctively divine action did not begin until after his death and resurrection. Two forms of the adoptionist pattern are discernible, the first of which was associated with the Palestinian Jewish-Christian community and the second with Hellenistic Jewish Christianity. In the first pattern, Jesus was not adopted as Messiah until his parousia or second coming; his earthly ministry was interpreted in terms of the Mosaic prophet-servant; and the present time following his death and resurrection was a brief period of inactive waiting (see Acts 3:20–21). In the second pattern, Jesus was adopted upon being exalted at the resurrection; he now reigns as Lord and Christ; and his earthly life was given a more positive assessment, becoming a preliminary stage of his messiahship since he was one filled by the Spirit and Wisdom of God (see Acts 2:32–36).

Kenoticism

The inadequacy of adoptionism was that it downplayed the significance of the earthly career of Jesus, and it made most sense when people still believed that Jesus would shortly return as heavenly Lord, bringing earthly existence as we know it to an end. As the parousia was delayed and the church's milieu shifted to that of a mission to Gentiles, the original story was made more adequate by adding a prologue: Back of the human career lay a divine preexistence or presence. What preexisted was the divine spirit (*pneuma*) or wisdom (*sophia*); it was not yet thought of as a preexistent divine person (an eternal Son or Logos) but as a divine power (*dynamis*), shape (*morphē*), or presence (*shekinah*). Spirit and Sophia were interchangeable ways of talking about the shape of God's empowering presence. According to an early Christian wisdom hymn quoted by Paul in Philippians, Sophia/Spirit "emptied" itself (*kenosis*) of divine power and took on the shape of a human being (Phil. 2:7–8). Jesus was "adopted" by this divine presence at birth rather than at death or second coming. Yet there was also an "incarnation," which occurred in the form of a divine emptying rather than a divine epiphany; divine power or spirit was present in the human Jesus without in any way divinizing his humanity; it was concealed or hidden, it honored the human shape. Thus kenoticism combined both adoptionist and incarnationist patterns, and in it the full structure of the incarnation mythos was evident for the first time:

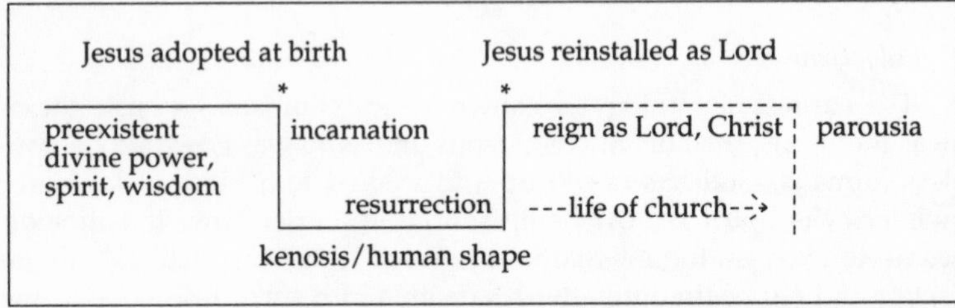

Even though kenoticism represents a hypothetical stage in the evolution of the incarnation mythos, it is a form of it that may be more retrievable for our purposes than the more fully developed incarnational theologies of the New Testament.[38] Among the canonical writings, the letters of Paul and Hebrews more closely approximated the kenotic pattern than any others. In some passages, Paul came close to primitive adoptionism (Rom. 1:4; Phil. 2:8–9); in others he assumed preexistence; and in yet others the two patterns were closely associated (Phil. 2:6–9). Sometimes Paul spoke of what preexists as the Spirit of God, other times as "Christ Jesus"; in any event, preexistence may have merely been implied for him by the postresurrection status of Jesus as Son of

God, and the latter was where his interest really lay. As to the human career of Jesus, Paul was aware only of contrasts between preexistence and the humiliated, suffering, earthly life of Jesus. Yet like Hebrews and the rest of the New Testament, he did not ascribe actual sinfulness to Jesus. Jesus was shaped into perfect obedience to God through the kenotically withdrawn divine dynamis.

Incarnationism

This is the christological pattern that characterizes most of the New Testament writings as we have them although Paul and Hebrews tend toward kenoticism while the Gospel of John in certain respects tends toward docetism. Incarnationism evolved out of kenoticism. The transitions were less sharp, forming an arc of descent and ascent of the divine Logos; the adoptionist motifs were eliminated; and what preexists now was thought of more clearly as a divine person or hypostasis (the Logos, the Son of God, Jesus Christ himself). The story about the human Jesus was adjusted to conform to the preexistence: The leitmotiv was no longer kenosis but epiphany, manifestation, glory; Jesus became a god-like man, a *theois anēr*, although Mark's messianic secret retained certain kenotic elements (only the demons recognized who Jesus really was, the Son of God incarnate). The importance of the resurrection diminished, notably so for the Fourth Gospel (in virtue of his preexistent divine glory, Jesus was *already* the resurrection and the life), while in Mark the resurrection accounts were a later addition.

Docetism

Docetism represented a logical working out of tendencies inherent in incarnationism. Often what we call heresies are simply more logical, consistent, and unambiguous rationalizations of mythological patterns. Here the eternal Logos never really departed the divine dwelling place, only seeming to appear (*dokein*) as a human being; incarnation and resurrection were themes of secondary importance; the parousia was eliminated; salvation occurred through gnosis. In short, we no longer have a story that involves changes. This fourth type is not on a par with the other three; it undercuts the incarnation myth and replaces it with the gnostic myth.

Chalcedonian Metaphysics: Two Natures, One Person[39]

The incarnationist pattern eventually prevailed in the history of the church although certain adoptionist and kenotic motifs were never completely lost and from time to time came into fresh prominence. The definition of the Council of Chalcedon in 451 represented a political and theological compromise between the schools of Antioch and

Alexandria. It affirmed two complete "natures" in Christ: a divine nature coessential (*homousios*) with the Father and a human nature coessential with us, being composed of a rational soul as well as a body (the Antiochene interest, stemming from a basis in adoptionism). But these two natures came together in a single person (*prosopon*) or hypostasis, which was that of the preexistent Son of God or divine Logos (the Alexandrine interest, which pressed incarnationism to the limit). Even though the human nature was technically complete as to soul and body, it derived or borrowed its hypostasis, its personifying and individuating principle, from the divine nature. In the jargon of post-Chalcedonian theology, it was "anhypostatic" (without its own hypostasis) or better "enhypostatic" (deriving its hypostasis from that of the incarnate Logos). In other words, the concrete personal self that appears in Jesus of Nazareth is divine, not human. Jesus, while retaining a full human nature, in some literal sense "is" God. An ontological identity exists between the personhood of Jesus and the Second Person of the Godhead. This was the so-called "Logos-flesh" christology, which originated with the Alexandrine theologians (Athanasius, Cyril of Alexandria), and which, despite the compromises of Chalcedon, became the backbone of Catholic and Protestant orthodoxy.

The difficulties with this way of thinking are all too evident today, and as a matter of fact the church has never succeeded in making much sense of it despite herculean efforts. The most important of these difficulties are the following: (1) Incarnationist christology diminishes the humanity of Jesus, robbing him of personal agency as a historical figure. The logical extreme of this position is docetism: Jesus Christ becomes a god disguised in human flesh. (2) It personifies or hypostatizes the Logos, regarding him as a gendered divine agent. To be sure, the ancient term *persona* originally referred to a functioning entity or mode of being rather than to personal agency, and "word" or "logos" is properly understood not as personal agency but as the power or event that constitutes personhood. But once *persona* terminology was introduced, personification became inevitable, along patriarchal lines of course. (3) It reifies Jesus' maleness (his contingent human particularity) into an ontological quality of Christ and God. Since the Second Person of the Godhead happens to be a male person (the Logos or Son), only male flesh could become the bearer of the incarnate Lord; obviously it would be absurd to have a male person in a female body. From this derives the ridiculous notion that only male priests can represent God. The argument works the other way as well in a vicious circularity: Since the Word of God incarnate is a male, so also must be the Word of God eternal and therefore God himself.

(4) Incarnationist christology thinks in terms not of relations or actions but of a duality of divine and human "natures," hierarchically dis-

tinguished from each other, connected in terms of "up-down" movements from one plane of reality to another and merging into a strange composite, the "God-man." Nothing is more characteristic of the classical mythological worldview, and this difficulty adheres as well to classical adoptionism and kenoticism. (5) It presupposes what today we seek to understand, namely, the "divinity" of Jesus. For modern persons it is by no means self-evident, as it may have been for ancients, to start with the triune being of God and ask how the Second Person of the Trinity has assumed a human nature. Rather we are able to speak about God, if at all, only by turning first to history and the historical figure Jesus. But this figure is obscured and passed over by the metaphysics of orthodox christology, which is unable to acknowledge the ways in which he too is limited and conditioned by historical context. (6) It limits God's incarnate presence in the world to a single, "once and for all" event, which is rendered ontologically distinct from all other events in which God may be present. This *hapax* lends itself to Christian absolutism.

The Shape of Christ: Revisioning a Theology of Incarnation[40]

Looking back over these materials—both the postmodern challenges and the dilemmas of classical christology—one begins to get some sense of what is needed if a theology of incarnation is to be revisioned.[41] (1) The connection between "Jesus" and "Christ" must be loosened or opened up. Following a suggestion of Panikkar, let us affirm that "Jesus is the Christ" but not that "the Christ is (simply) Jesus." What we mean by "Christ" is shaped in a definitive way by the concrete historical figure Jesus of Nazareth, but what we mean by it is not limited to this figure and in fact is enriched and extended by encompassing more than this figure. (2) A way must be found of avoiding the supernaturalism, patriarchalism, and docetism of the Logos-flesh christology, of moving beyond the impasse of the two natures doctrine entirely, and of preserving the full humanity of Jesus while at the same time affirming God's incarnate presence in him. (3) It must be explained how this "incarnation" is redemptive, that is, how it confronts and provides resources for dealing with the profound problem of human sin and its destructive consequences. The classical doctrine of substitutionary atonement, based on the juridical metaphor (guilt, penalty, satisfaction) and the assumption that it is primarily God who is injured by sin, is as little credible today as the classical doctrine of incarnation. A tall order indeed!

Maurice Wiles provides some helpful guidance in the attempt to demythologize, deconstruct, revision the mythos of incarnation. He says that in order to distinguish between true and false interpretations of myths such as the incarnation "there must be some ontological truth corresponding to the central characteristic of the structure of the myth." Orthodox christological doctrine understood this truth or reality in terms of an ontological identity between the personhood of Jesus and the Second Person of the Godhead. Wiles wonders if there is an alternative to this now highly problematic interpretation.

> The incarnation has never been proclaimed simply as an account of something that happened at a point in past history. It has also been seen as that which makes possible a profound inner union of the divine and the human in the experience of grace in the life of the believer now and more broadly in the life of the church as a whole. . . . Now if this union of divine and human at the heart of the human personality is a reality, however hard to identify or to describe, may that not be the ontological truth corresponding to and justifying a mythological understanding of the incarnation?[42]

The task then is to show how and why divine incarnation is linked in a special way with the historical figure of Jesus. Wiles thinks we can affirm three things: that Jesus' "own life in its relation to God embodied that openness to God, that unity of divine and human nature, to which the doctrine points"; that his relationship with fellow human beings was "a parable of the loving outreach of God to the world"; and that Jesus played and continues to play a special role in mediating "the full and effective realization of this union of divine and human nature" in the ongoing life of humanity as a whole.[43] While pointing in the right direction, these ideas are not elaborated in a reconstructed theology of incarnation and resurrection.

The Christ-Gestalt: An Incarnate Praxis

Wiles seems to suggest that God is not specifically active in the event of incarnation except in terms of a general availability, graciousness, or inspiration. The activity occurs solely in terms of Jesus' "openness to God." Such a view is problematic because of its abstractness and its removal *of God* from any sort of specific involvement in the process of incarnation and redemption. The argument I shall offer instead[44] is that God is redemptively present in the world, not as an individual human being (a "divine man") performing miraculous deeds (the traditional christological picture), nor as a distinctive sort of God-consciousness (Protestant liberal theology), nor as a uniform inspiration, lure, or ideal (Wiles and some forms of process theology), but rather in specific *shapes or patterns of praxis* that have a configuring, transformative power within historical process, moving the process specifically in the direction of the creative unification of multiplicities of acts into new wholes that build human solidarity, enhance freedom, break down systemic oppression, heal the injured and broken, and care for the natural world.

The English word "shape" (from the Anglo-Saxon *sceap*) means to carve with a sharp tool, to sculpt a shape into something, to inscribe, or "in-carnate." It seems a particularly apt metaphor for thinking about incarnation, which means literally to "en-flesh." The same aptness is true of the German word *Gestalt*, which has been accepted into English as a loan word through phenomenology and gestalt psychology: A "gestalt" is a pattern arranged, shaped, or structured from parts, producing a living, organic, plural unity—a unity of consciousness or of spirit—as opposed to a dead, mechanical identity.[45] Now the shapes or gestalts that I have in mind are not empirically visible but they have a real power to shape the world in which human beings dwell. "Shape" is a metaphor that refers not to literal physical objects but to structures or patterns of ethical life, practices of spirit. Yet it is clear that ethical shapes are not abstract but concrete, embodied, incarnate; they do, therefore, have a physical, carnal aspect to them, they employ the body toward distinctively human ends, they make something of nature. These ethical shapes occur at various levels of consciousness or awareness. At the most fundamental, preconscious level, they function as the structuring patterns and paradigms or values that underlie everything that we think and do and say. At the overt, conscious level, they serve as the actual shapes in which what we think, do, and say appears in the world.

The American civil rights struggle of the 1960s produced such a gestalt (the "civil rights gestalt"), which initially functioned overtly as the guiding ideal of the participants in the movement but which became woven into public consciousness in such a way that later attempts to subvert the gains of that struggle proved largely unsuccessful. Subsequently the methods and objectives of the American civil rights movement (nonviolent resistance, demonstrations and marches, songs and vigils, appeals to conscience) were adopted by the peoples of Eastern Europe in their successful effort at throwing off Soviet domination. The civil rights gestalt has become part of global consciousness and is echoed today in the peace and ecological movements as well as in continuing human rights struggles.

A shape or gestalt is not as impersonal as a universal influence or an abstract ideal since it connotes something dynamic, specific, and structuring, but it avoids potentially misleading personifications of God's action. What God "does" in history is not to intervene in the sequence of causes and effects in the form of special acts, or to become a god disguised in human flesh, or to speak literally through human speech, but to "shape"—to shape a multifaceted transformative praxis. God does this by *giving, disclosing, engendering,* in some sense *being*, the normative shape, the paradigm of such a praxis. This divinely given gestalt, in which God is really present, shapes the historical gestalts by which structures of freedom, compassion, solidarity, wholeness are built up. This gestalt is not a person or personal agent but a transpersonal structure of praxis that grounds personal existence and builds interpersonal relations since it itself is intrinsically relational, social, communicative in character. I shall call it the "Christ-gestalt," by which I mean what is for Christians the definitive shape of God in history.[46] If we wish to ask how God is active in this, my answer is that the Christ-gestalt is engendered by the Wisdom of God, which is a mode of God's spiritual presence in the world. God shapes spiritually and ethically, by indwelling, moving, empowering, instructing, inspiring human individuals and communities, and perhaps other forms of life as well. This points in the direction of a Wisdom christology, and it anticipates a theology of Spirit that cannot be fully developed until subsequent chapters. God's shaping activity is what I referred to earlier as the creative being, primal energy, or erotic power that God "has" absolutely. It is clearly an ethical, spiritual power, a wind of the Spirit that appears in the world as both a prevailing wind and many winds. Christ is for Christians the prevailing wind.

The Christ-gestalt is incarnate in the embodied personhood of Jesus, in the bodily as well as ethical/spiritual dimensions of his being. Crucifixion is something that is done to Jesus' *body*, and the most radical Christian claim is that it is *God* who dies on the cross, God who takes the negation, suffering, and death of the human condition into God's very being.[47] God is in Jesus as the Christ precisely in his *not*-Godness, his naturalness, his suffering and death, his contingency and limitation. In this sense his bodiliness is of significance for his identity as the Christ, as are his maleness and Jewishness, which are likewise aspects of his embodiedness. His physical body is significant not because it resembles divinity like a Greek statue but in its very *un*godliness, its finitude and mortality, its sexual and ethnic specificity, its susceptibility to suffering. It is not as though a divine nature (*physis*) enters into hypostatic union with a human nature, appearing as a divine man, a *theois anēr*. It is rather that the all-too-human, crucified nature of Jesus becomes a shape wherein God is definitively present in the world—the world that in its very not-Godness, its otherness from God, is affirmed as a moment within the life of God, remaining other even as it is incorporated by God.[48] There is suffering and tragedy in the divine itself, and this assumes vividly concrete form for Christians in the death of Jesus.

The Christ-gestalt is a shape or structure of incarnate praxis, the praxis of redemptive love and reconciliatory emancipation. This gestalt formed in and around the person of Jesus; his person in some sense became identical with it, and by means of it after death he took on a new, communal identity. The Christ-gestalt empowers the distinctive being of human being, which is a way of being in the world as a communion of free persons before God; hence the more radically Jesus is the Christ the more radically he is human. In this sense he is truly human as well as truly divine; these are not two natures in him but simply his identity as a bearer of the Christ-gestalt. His person played and continues to play a decisive role in mediating the shape of God in history, which is the shape of love in freedom. Jesus' personal identity merged into this shape insofar as he simply *was* what he proclaimed and practiced. But Jesus' personal identity did not exhaust this shape, which is intrinsically a communal, not an individual shape.

Mark K. Taylor offers a very similar approach when he speaks of the Christ-gestalt as a *dynamic*—a "sociohistorical dynamic of reconciliatory emancipation." This is an "intersubjective, communal dynamic" in which "Jesus was a necessary participant and contributor but not the only necessary one."

> The Christian mythos is a mythos of this sociohistorical matrix, the whole life-praxis within which Jesus was a historical part. The empowering mythos we need is not only a mythos displaying, telling, and retelling the story of an individual hero, Jesus. It needs to become, more than the tradition has allowed it to become, a mythos of Jesus *and* other lives touching and contributing to his as he touches and contributes to theirs.

In relation to this larger matrix, Jesus functions, in Taylor's view, as a "leaven" or "ferment," which permeates and enlivens the seething mixture of history but is dependent on other ingredients as well.[49]

Taylor wants to avoid any outright identification of Jesus with the divine gestalt, and he believes that my earlier formulations came too close to an identification.[50] I acknowledge the importance of maintaining a distinction between Jesus and the gestalt, so that if I speak of identification, it can only be dialectically—"in some sense," that is, a nonexhaustive or nonexclusive sense. My view is that Jesus was *a* bearer, not the sole and exclusive bearer, of the Christ-gestalt. I agree with Taylor that Jesus "was a necessary participant and contributor" to the Christ dynamic, "but not the only necessary one." The question on which Taylor must be pressed is precisely in what sense Jesus *was* a necessary participant or leaven. What did Jesus *distinctively* contribute to the sociohistorical dynamic without which it might have taken on a quite different configuration? Was this dynamic in fact shaped in distinctive ways by Jesus' embodiment and articulation of it? Was it *constitutively* associated with him even if not contained by him? By turning too quickly to the sociohistorical dimension of reconciliatory emancipation, Taylor's rich and innovative christology loses contact with the concrete figure of Jesus. A way of maintaining such contact is proposed in the following sections.

A subsequent conversation with Taylor helped both of us understand more clearly why the Christ dynamic/gestalt must become incarnate in a concrete human figure. It is because of the centrality of personal embodiment in human experience. Dynamics or gestalts become real for us only when they are actualized in concrete, embodied human persons. We relate primarily to persons, not ideas, in religious matters.[51] But we must remember that persons are not isolated but exist only in relation. Hence it is not Jesus' isolated body that is significant but his body interacting with other bodies. The corporate body generated by Jesus interacting with his contemporaries and with us is the incarnation of the Christ-gestalt.

The concept of the Christ-gestalt provides a way of addressing what William Schweiker describes as the central challenge facing postmodern christological reflection, namely that of affirming on the one hand that Christ acquires a specific identity through the narrative presentation of scripture, and on the other hand that Christ specifies a liberating power that radiates from the Jesus movement. He believes that these two approaches must be combined: "The title 'Christ' denotes a specific identity with the effective power to constitute communities of liberation. Only in specifying this can we properly explore the relation between the person of Christ (his identity) and the work of Christ (the effective power)." The difficulty we face in affirming this "is that we still labor with relatively crude ideas of identity and agency such that we hardly have the conceptual tools to explore the way in which a specific identity can have effective power."[52] I submit that the concept of gestalt offers such a conceptual tool: The Christ-gestalt names an identity that is transpersonal and interpersonal in character even as it is embodied in and configured by specific individuals, and it has the intrinsic quality of effective power since it names a pattern or paradigm of redemptive praxis. In the concept of the gestalt, the person and work of Christ are one and the same.

The Christ-gestalt is closely related to certain normative gestalts or "root experiences" of Judaism—exodus, covenant, prophecy, exile, messianic kingdom—which delineate the shape of God's presence in history as one of liberation, constancy, judgment, suffering, hope. It is also related to the normative gestalt of Christianity, which may be described as "ecclesia" or ecclesial existence—a mode of human existence transfigured in the direction of a nonprovincial, nonhierarchical, nonpatriarchal, nonethnic communion of persons, open to all without prior conditions, liberated from the power of sin, death, and oppressive structures by the grace of God, bound together in a solidarity and mutuality of love by the presence of God's Spirit. The ecclesial community is the "body" of Christ—the gestalt by which the love-in-freedom proclaimed and enacted by Jesus becomes intersubjectively efficacious in the ongoing history of Christian faith. The ecclesial gestalt is never adequately embodied in any empirical church or Christian group; it is rather a critical, productive paradigm of praxis by which the empirical churches are continually judged and transformed (see chap. 18, pp. 297–99). The Christ-gestalt takes shape out of the Judaic gestalt and merges into the ecclesial gestalt, but it is not identical with either of them. It has certain distinctive features of its own, acquired through association with a concrete historical figure.

God takes shape in other religions besides Judaism and Christianity. Their validity claims are as legitimate as ours. Yet the question remains whether there is a certain coherence or congruence among these multiple shapes, or whether they are utterly different from one another. Does something like the shape of love-in-freedom appear in other religions as well? Does the Christ-gestalt have analogues in Buddhism, Hinduism, Islam? It seems to me that it clearly does and that it can be enriched and better understood through encounters with them. In this encounter we must not obscure the significant and productive differences between the great religio-cultural shapes of redemption; the shape of Buddha, or Brahma, or Muhammad must in no way be subsumed under the Christ-gestalt. But at the same time we may hope for a convergence and mutual transformation of these distinctive shapes through dialogue and shared praxis in the face of common threats (see chap. 18, pp. 308–11).

Jesus of Nazareth: Shaped by the Wisdom of God

The text that underlies my approach has already been alluded to. In Philippians 2:5–11, Paul adopts an older christological hymn, which says that the "shape of God" (*morphē theou*) "emptied itself" and "took on" the "shape of a human being" (*schēmati . . . hōs anthrōpos*). This human shape, which was that of a servant (*morphē doulou*), entailed humility and obedience to the point of death but also exaltation and honor. In the version of the hymn that Paul gives, the subject of this activity (the one who was "in" the shape of God), was "Christ Jesus"—language that suggests a preexistent divine Son. But the christological language may well have been grafted onto what was originally a hymn to Wisdom, so that the original reference of the "who" in verse 6, a reference that is grammatically awkward, was not to Christ Jesus but to the Wisdom of God—this wisdom being the shape of God that took on human shape.[53] In connection with some recent feminist thought, I will explore the idea that the Christ-gestalt formed in Jesus of Nazareth through the distinctive presence in him of the Wisdom of God.

For biblical Judaism, Wisdom is one of three primary mediators, hypostases, or personifications of divine power and presence. The others are Spirit and Word. Wisdom is consistently feminine in grammatical gender across Hebrew (*hochmah*), Greek (*sophia*), and Latin (*sapientia*), while Word is consistently masculine (*dabar, logos, verbum*) and Spirit is mixed (feminine in Hebrew [*ruach*], neuter in Greek [*pneuma*], masculine in Latin [*spiritus*]). Wisdom is the most developed representation of God's presence and activity in Hebrew scriptures, appearing in Job, Proverbs, the Wisdom of Solomon, Sirach (the Wisdom of Jesus Son of Sirach), and Baruch. In these texts Wisdom is consistently female, "casting herself as sister, mother, female beloved, chef and hostess, preacher, judge, liberator, establisher of justice, and a myriad of other female roles wherein she symbolizes transcendent power ordering and delighting the world. She pervades the world, both nature and human beings, interacting with them all to lure them along the right path to life."[54] Thus it is appropriate to refer to her by her Greek name Sophia. "Sophia is Israel's God in female imagery," an imagery that places the stress on God's nearness, activity, and summons.[55] As such, she is a concrete manifestation or modality of God's Spirit. Spirit, like Sophia, was represented as a bird, a symbol of female deity; and in postbiblical Judaism, the Spirit of God came to be spoken of in the female symbol of the *shekinah,* meaning "to dwell." Feminine imagery of the Spirit is also found in the earlier Aramaic form of the Sayings Source of the Gospels and in Syriac Christianity. But in mainstream Christianity "the maternal imagery migrated away from the Spirit and accrued to the church, called holy mother the church, and to Mary the mother of Jesus."[56]

Only fragments of a Wisdom christology remain in the canonical writings of the New Testament. It is found in the Sayings Source (Q) believed to lie behind portions of the Gospels of Matthew and Luke, in 1 Corinthians 1—4, and in the hymnic settings of the earliest high christology such as those found in Philippians, Colossians, and Hebrews. Wisdom is also the provenance of the Gospel of John, which is suffused with wisdom themes. But in the Johannine Prologue, Wisdom is renamed the Word or Logos of God, and the process has begun of supplanting the female figure with a male hypostasis.[57]

It is possible to reconstruct this early Wisdom christology, relying especially on the Sayings Source.[58] References to Wisdom/Sophia are found in three of its passages. Against attempts to divide the followers of Jesus and John the Baptist, Jesus claims that "Wisdom is vindicated by *all* her children" (Luke 7:35). Wisdom is the one who sends "prophets and apostles, some of whom they [this generation] will kill and persecute" (Luke 7:49). In lamenting on Jerusalem, "the city that kills the prophets and stones those who are sent to it," Jesus remarks,

"How often have I desired to gather your children together as a hen gathers her brood under her wings, and you were not willing! . . . I tell you, you will not see me until the time comes when you say, 'Blessed is the one who comes in the name of the Lord'" (Luke 13:34–35). From these fragments (together with corroborating evidence from other wisdom sources) we may conclude that Sophia has many children, among whom are numbered the prophets and apostles, and Sophia's children are likely to suffer abuse and rejection at the hands of this world. Her children are presently scattered about, but she will gather them and be vindicated by them; she will outlast the powerful, and her children will be empowered to continue the struggle on behalf of God's project or inheritance (*basileia*).[59] Jesus is preeminent among these children because he proclaimed the inbreaking of God's project and engaged in a praxis of inclusive wholeness, gathering all who would follow. Sophia dwells in him fully but also transcends him, drawing him into contact with others, to whom he ministers and from whom he draws strength—women, tax collectors and sinners, Samaritans and Syro-Phoenicians, the sick and poor, children and old folk, ultimately the whole of humanity. Jesus' followers will carry on Sophia's mission and message despite—indeed because of—his death, which is not a death of "penal victimization" but of "heartbreaking empowerment."[60] His message or cause is the important thing, and Wisdom lives on in the continuing cause. Jesus is the Christ—the shape of God in human shape—because he is the power of God and the Wisdom of God although in the eyes of the world his power appears to be weakness and his wisdom foolishness (1 Cor. 1:18–25).

Jesus' cause is that of the kingdom, project, or inheritance of God, the *basileia tou theou*. Basileia, like Sophia, is a feminine image, and there are interesting connections between them, which can be formulated in different ways. James Robinson suggests that the basileia designates "the utopian goal, the ultimate," whereas Sophia is "the purity of intention, the commitment."[61] John Cobb argues that Wisdom combines the creative transformation envisioned by the basileia (the primordial nature of God, or "logos") with the suffering of God with us and the inclusion of all things in God (the consequent nature of God, or "truth").[62] In terms congenial to the present work, we could say that Wisdom names the constitutive power of the basileia—a rationality, discourse, or logos that is radically communicative, aimed at the overthrow and reshaping of all established structures and authorities. This is an eminently practical wisdom, issuing in communities of solidarity and mutuality. It engenders the praxis of its own substance, which is freedom. Paul captures this meaning of the basileia with his metaphor of the "Wisdom of God," which destroys all human power, wisdom, and boasting (1 Cor. 1:26–31).

The Wisdom of God is not to be thought of literally as a divine person, agent, or hypostasis any more than the Word or the Spirit of God are to be thought of in these mythological terms. The Wisdom of God is rather the logical substance (the *logos*) out of which the basileia is built, and it is the spiritual power that shaped Jesus into becoming the proclaimer and bearer of the basileia. The substance and power of divine Wisdom are what might be called "communicative freedom." Understood in this way, Wisdom encompasses yet transcends both Logos and Spirit. Jesus is the Word of God and the Spirit of God because he is the Wisdom of God, the incarnation of God's caring, truthful, communicative Sophia, which sets us free from the lying, foolishness, and boasting of this world.

We are tempted to ask how God does this. *How* does the Wisdom of God enter into and create the Christ-gestalt in Jesus of Nazareth? No theology can answer this question in the sense of providing a theoretical explanation. God, I am assuming, can appear in history, can enter into historical forms and shapes, but how God does this remains a mystery. It seems clear to me that God does not act in history in the mode of causality or of "possession." The former has collapsed with the discrediting of the logic of divine sovereignty; and the latter is unattractive because it suggests that human self-consciousness is replaced by the possessing spirit, whether divine or demonic.[63]

The Sophia-presence of God *is* a spiritual presence, but the question is how best to understand this—a question to which we shall turn in the last part of this work. In brief: Spirit indwells, empowers, instructs human spirit but does not displace it. Spiritual presence need not entail spiritual possession, even though it has often been understood in just such terms. Sophia defines the kind of Spirit that God's Spirit is—not a possessing, displacing, controlling Spirit, but a persuading, inviting, educing, communicating Spirit, acting in profound interaction with human spirit, indeed the whole cosmos. God's indwelling Spirit has the quality of wisdom rather than of raw force; and what God is spiritually present in are not simply individual human persons but the foundational paradigms by which human personal and social existence is shaped redemptively. God's Spirit "in-spirits" human spirit, which is a social and ethical matrix before it is an individual person, and it is the latter only in relation to the former. It is not on Jesus alone but on Jesus in interaction with all of Wisdom's children that the Spirit dwells.

Three powerful images associated with Jesus have become superimposed to form that complex shape, the shape of Christ, which serves as a paradigm of all Christian praxis as a world-transforming praxis. The three are *basileia, cross,* and *resurrection*. Among them there occurs an interplay of love and freedom by which God's redemptive presence in the world takes shape. Incarnation reaches its culmination in the crucifixion of the one who proclaimed God's inbreaking kingdom; basileia and cross together define "the shape of redemptive love." Resurrection launches into the world "the shape of reconciliatory emancipation": Crucified love takes on emancipatory force, which is already prefigured by the basileia message (and messenger). Thus our treatment of incarnation highlights love, of which freedom (redemption) is a qualifier; and our treatment of resurrection highlights freedom (emancipation), of which love (reconciliation) is a qualifier. This is because crucifixion seems to be the final, anguished act of God's love for the world, while resurrection means above all the victory of life and freedom over death and bondage. But these distinctions are highly nuanced and should not be pressed to the point of separating these themes—despite the caesura or break that exists between crucifixion and resurrection (marked in this work by a break between the second and third moments of the triune figuration).

The Shape of Communal Freedom: Basileia

The basileia, the kingdom, project, or inheritance of God, is the central image of Jesus' proclamation, especially in the form of parables. It is above all an image of freedom, a realm of freedom, a place or structure or world where freedom, communion, and truth prevail as the defining relationships among human beings instead of bondage, alienation, illusion. It is the power of God that establishes this parabolic clearing of freedom although God rarely appears within the clearing itself. The parables deconstruct the whole picture of monarchical-patriarchal-hierarchical rule to such an extent that the word "kingdom" is no longer usable and we are left without an adequate term for what is envisioned. I propose to let the Greek word stand without translation, hoping that it can be filled with a new meaning. Josiah Royce spoke of the "beloved community," as did Howard Thurman and Martin Luther King Jr.[64] We could add "liberated community" or "community of freedom"—or even "communicative freedom," which brings out more clearly the role of Wisdom in shaping the basileia. In the parlance of the North American civil rights movement and the Central American liberation theologies, we might speak of the basileia as "God's freedom project."[65] There is no single metaphor that will adequately grasp what is meant.

The world evoked by the parables is a strange world.[66] All the established economies that govern human behavior and relations of power are shaken to the core by Jesus' proclamation of the "nearness" of the basileia. The logic of domination, violence, reward, and punishment that prevails in the everyday world is challenged and replaced by a new logic, the logic of grace, compassion, freedom. The contents that make up this new world are familiar—banquets, wedding feasts, farms and farm workers, vineyards, royal households, merchants and stewards, noblemen and servants, public highways, law courts, the temple—but relations, values, behavior, consequences have been set strangely askew and intensified to the point of extravagance, paradox, hyperbole. The dislocation effected by these surrealistic qualities of the parables is an aspect of their liminality; and it is precisely in the liminal, marginal, interstitial spaces opened up by the parables that the gestalt of freedom forms. This is a gestalt that is "in" but not "of" the world; it forms between the closed systems that make up everyday life, opening them up, absolving them of their alienation, provincialism, false dichotomies, power struggles.

The gestalt of freedom, as it takes shape in the parables of Jesus, points unmistakably in the direction of a new kind of communal existence that is intrinsically open to the other, the stranger, those who are marginalized and oppressed, those who belong to an alien culture, people, or religion.[67] All of the false provincialisms break down—those based on race, class, sex, ethnic or national identity, religious piety, worldly success; none of these are relevant as conditions of God's redemptive presence, which is utterly gratuitous, open to all. This gestalt, found only at the margins of the everyday world, has a surreal quality without definable limits or boundaries. As such, it is able to serve as a paradigm or pattern of transformative praxis again and again in human affairs under radically different cultural conditions. This is how it works salvifically. There is nothing magical about it. It simply provides resources by which, again and again, we can break the grip of the dominant paradigms, battle against the debilitating fear that issues in the flight from life, or the dizzying illusion that we are godlike. With these resources at our disposal, we can find a purpose to life and even participate in the open-ended, always fragmentary project of building a new world.

Jesus embodied in his own personal existence the communal freedom of the basileia. He himself was a parable of that which he proclaimed. In this sense he became identical with the Christ-gestalt, but he did not exhaust or contain it. We can speak of three spheres of the "radical freedom" of Jesus: openness, community, selfhood.[68] These are, of course, the very spheres that constitute human being (chap. 14, pp. 199–208), but in the case of Jesus they have been rearranged in priority and importance. The central sphere is that of community or interpersonal freedom, the sphere of face-to-face relations, to which both openness and selfhood point in different ways.

1. It is appropriate to start not with Jesus' selfhood but with his *openness* to God. This openness cannot be grasped directly but is visible only in the communal and personal structures of his existence. There are only a few instances in the Synoptic tradition where his relation-

ship to God is made explicit in his own words: the references to God using the child's familiar name *Abba;* the "truly I say to you" and "but I say to you" formulations (implying a special authority to speak on behalf of God), and sayings such as those found in Matt. 12:28, "If it is by the Spirit of God that I cast out demons. . . ." The New Testament and Christian tradition referred to this special relationship by the notion of divine "sonship"—a notion that for us appears to be hopelessly mythological and patriarchal, and therefore no longer usable. Jesus spoke of himself not as "Son of God" but—if at all—as "son of humanity" (*huios tou anthrōpou*), which is a generic construction meaning "the (messianic) human being." In accord with the latter usage, we should stress that what is involved in this relationship is the *true humanity* of Jesus as it was completed in radical *openness* to God, a God whom he knew not as distant but as near, father- and motherlike. Openness to God is constitutive of true humanity; it does not add anything extra or supramundane or "divine" to it.[69] As the radically free person, Jesus is simply the fulfillment of human potentiality; he is the representative human being and *as such* the "son of God" but not God.[70]

Paul spoke of Jesus' openness in terms of "obedience," an "obedience unto death" (Phil. 2:8–9; Rom. 5:12–19). It should be noted, however, that Jesus also struggled against his fate and cried out in protest to God upon the cross (Matt. 27:46; Mark 15:34). The cry of God-forsakenness indicates Jesus' recognition that death is the final enemy, and it also marks an identification with sinful humanity's fear of mortality. Thus the openness or obedience maintained by Jesus was not, in the final analysis, a virtuous accomplishment but a gift of God, received in humility.

2. Jesus' gathering of a new and liberated human *community* about him was the concrete, positive form that his openness to God assumed, by contrast with the negative, self-surrendering character of his obedience. Today we are inclined to stress the former more than the latter. Jesus not only proclaimed the inbreaking basileia of God but enacted it under the specific conditions of his time and place. He condemned social injustice, religious arrogance, and political exploitation. He challenged the authority of the established religious leaders, pressing for a much more radical reading of their own scriptures. He identified himself with the poor, the powerless, the marginalized, having a table fellowship with them. He included women among his following, and they had a special relationship with him. He healed the sick and injured and liberated those possessed by demonic powers.

It is not surprising that the Gospels call attention to the "compassionate" character of Jesus' relationship to those whom he healed (Mark 1:41; Luke 7:13; Matt. 20:34), and to "the crowds" (Mark 6:34; 8:2; Matt. 9:36; 14:14). It is significant that the term "compassion" was used by Jesus himself to describe the Good Samaritan, the father of the prodigal son, and the king of the unforgiving servant (Luke 10:33; 15:20; Matt. 18:27)—parables of the basileia that mirror his own ministry. The term "compassion" is a strong one that goes beyond "sympathy." It means that Jesus took the misery and suffering that surrounded him literally into himself, his viscera, so that now it was more his misery than it was theirs who suffered it. His being became totally a being-for-and-with-others; the faces of others were reflected in his face, and his in theirs, so there formed around him a radical "community of the face."[71] Jesus also *received* compassion, care, erotic power from his companions. He not only ministered but was ministered unto, so that what came into being was a reciprocal communion of those bound together in solidarity and love, a solidarity unto death. He died for them, and *some* of his disciples—the women—stuck by him to the end.

This compassion not only took the form of an interpersonal communion but also had a fundamentally public, liberating character. For Jesus it seemed to involve three primary spheres of liberation: from law and religious piety, from death and the demonic powers of death, and from the earthly powers—precisely the worldly objectifications of sin that we have talked about (chap. 14, pp. 221–30). These are the spheres in which Jesus worked.[72] He attacked sin not only in terms of the inner corrosion of unbelief and broken (or "little") faith, but also, and perhaps primarily, in terms of its social objectifications and intensifications. He challenged the alienation and hypocrisy of religious practices; he healed those broken by sickness and possessed by demons, the powers of death; and he attacked the injustice reflected in wealth, poverty, captivity, patriarchy, and political tyranny although he was not a partisan of any political group. His ministry confronted the predominant forms of *evil* in his time and declared them to be fundamentally incompatible with God's "project" for humanity. The focus of his ministry was not on humanity's guilt-ridden disobedience of God, such as would require a substitutionary atonement, but rather on humanity's wounding of itself, its self-imposed and self-destructive bondage, which would require liberating power and redemptive healing.

3. This concentration on community does not mean that Jesus' personal identity was simply and totally dissipated into his interpersonal relations, even though for the most part his being-for-self came into view only in terms of his being-for-others. The Gospels do make it clear that Jesus exercised a remarkable *authority* (*exousia*), an authority that was the expression of his unique identity, an identity founded in openness to God and evident in the intense and direct character of his relationships with others. Yet this authority is not something Jesus laid claim to; it showed itself rather in the quality of his speech and actions.

His hearers (both friends and foes) recognized it—it was a quality predicated of him by the Evangelists many times—but he himself did not claim it (the term is found on Jesus' lips as a self-reference only four times, all of which are doubtless products of the tradition), nor did he suggest that it could be legitimated by some future event like the resurrection from the dead (as some theologians have argued[73]). The authority that marked Jesus' personal freedom already pointed away from himself; it was not a self-referential quality. His authority was really the authority of God on behalf of the basileia. Thus just as the new community he proclaimed and enacted was nonprovincial and nonalienating, so also the personal agency he exemplified was nonautonomous and not self-oriented. Rather it was oriented totally to others.

The Shape of Empowering Love: Cross[74]

What did this radical freedom, this parabolic enactment of the basileia, accomplish for him? Condemnation by the religious authorities on a charge of blasphemy and execution by the political authorities on a charge of agitation against the *Pax Romana*. This is the second powerful image or figure associated with Jesus, namely that of the *cross*, which is above all an image of love, of anguished, suffering, broken love. It is not that there is something essentially unique about Jesus' death; history has witnessed millions of executions, tortures, starvations, many more horrible than what Jesus suffered. It is rather that *this* death connected with *this* life generated a uniquely powerful and revelatory shape of God's presence in history.

The death of Jesus on the cross is the culminating moment in the act of love by which God posits a world that is other than God, for it signifies God's unity with perishability, God's struggle with the annihilating power of nothingness, taking that power into godself, converting its absolute negation into dialectical negation, enabling it thereby to become the possibility of the new (see chap. 11, pp. 165–66). This is the significance of the crucifixion of Jesus for God. It means the death of God, and that in turn means that suffering and tragedy are incorporated into the divine life.

But what is its significance for us? Of course at the core of its significance for us is precisely its significance for God. But beyond this, the cross has another significance for us: It means that all our historical projects of liberation will ultimately fail. Jesus' project of announcing the inbreaking kingdom of God failed; the transfigured world of the parables was interrupted and displaced by scenes of betrayal, false charges, political dealings, weakness and vacillation, an angry mob, and an ugly finale on Golgotha. It was not a beautiful death, not a "celebration of freedom" (as was said of Socrates' death). Jesus died with a question on his lips, "My God, my God, why have you forsaken me?" (Matt. 27:46). Did Jesus, who had proclaimed the saving nearness of God's basileia and had often spoken of God in intimate terms as *Abba*, experience the abandonment and remoteness of God at the moment of death? Was this not a falsification of the truth of his entire message, a negation of his very being?

The shape of the cross is a question mark or a cancellation sign, a large "X," which must be written across the shape of the basileia, reminding us that its vision of inclusive wholeness, of a liberated communion of free persons, will forever remain marginal in this world, unable ultimately to dislodge the economy of domination and violence but only to disturb it, to disclose it for what it is, to reduce its scope and hegemony, perhaps even to modify it, and above all to empower people to maintain a compassionate solidarity for and with each other in their struggle against it—as Jesus himself did, who died for the sake of all those who had joined or would join his cause, and indeed for those who would not. It reminds us that God will not rescue us from history or provide miraculous victories. Rather God suffers silently alongside us, so silently that we may not know that God is there. The shape of the cross *crosses*, is superimposed on, that of the basileia vision, lending it the realism, clarity, and toughness necessary for its endurance in history as a transformative factor. Freedom is infused with a compassionate, suffering, anguished love.

And yet, because the annihilating power of nothingness has been taken into God's being and converted there into the possibility of the new—because it has been historicized, made into a differentiating, generative factor rather than remaining an absolute negation—it is possible for human beings to go on after such defeats as the crucifixion of Jesus. "Out of death, new life arises"; from the "infinite anguish" of the cross there arises an "infinite love" and an "infinite freedom."[75] That death is not simply an end but a beginning, that it has the possibility of transforming human life and culture into new forms that open up new possibilities for consciousness and praxis that did not exist before—this is the profoundest meaning of the cross, which was not only the death of Jesus but the death of God by which God undergoes, incorporates, and transforms death. The meaning of the cross is the victory of life over death, the resurrection from the dead.

Spirit: Freedom

16

CHRIST RISEN: THE SHAPE OF RECONCILIATORY EMANCIPATION

Between Good Friday and Easter there occurs a break, a caesura, of three days. Theology must remain silent about these three days, for they represent the reversal that is the fundamental mystery of God—the turn or reversal from death to life, from defeat to victory, from suffering to joy. God lives through and sustains the process of differentiation and reunification; God does not come to a halt at the moment of anguished death but goes on, brings life out of death, creates anew out of what is spent and broken. God is an inexhaustible source of creative transformation. But how God does this remains the fundamental mystery about God. So theology remains silent in the interval between Good Friday and Easter, the interval between the second and third moments of the divine life, between differentiating love and reconciling freedom. I have marked this interval by a divisional break and a chapter break. Of course this interval, break, and reversal do not occur just once in history; they happen repeatedly in our individual and corporate lives. In the midst of suffering, defeat, despair, discouragement, we somehow find the resources to go on, to confront the challenges of life anew, to become engaged in the process of creative transformation, which is the divine process. This is the mystery of the resurrection—and of the coming of the Holy Spirit.

The Fused Shape of Love and Freedom: Reconciliatory Emancipation

From the fusion of the images of *basileia* and *cross* emerges a third primary christological symbol, that of the *resurrection* of Jesus from the dead. Through the death that put death to death, the shape of communal freedom imaged by the basileia passes from the limited ministry of Jesus and the basileia community that coalesced around him into the broad stream of human history, becoming a productive factor therein. The cross is the mediating link between the radical freedom of Jesus and "the glorious freedom of the children of God" (Rom. 8:21). As "resurrection," the fused, superimposed images of basileia and cross, of freedom and love, acquire the resiliency and realism necessary to endure in the midst of human tragedy, as well as the power to generate a continually transformative vision of a liberated communion of free subjects. The Christ-gestalt that came to speech in Jesus' proclamation and mission now "comes to stand" in the world as the productive paradigm of worldly praxis. It takes on the modality of "standing in the world" (*anastasis*), which is what "resurrection" means. Jesus, whose identity was first established by the gestalt that formed in and around his person, now assumes a new, communal identity as the risen Christ, the body of all those who share in and contribute to the transformation of the world wrought by suffering love. Resurrection takes place when basileia community forms under the conditions of the cross.

To characterize the shape of resurrection, I am borrowing Mark K. Taylor's expression "reconciliatory emancipation,"[1] by which he names the "Christ dynamic." Taylor does not distinguish between the manifestation of this dynamic in the historical figure of Jesus and in the community of the Risen One; for him it is one and the same dynamic. It surely is one and the same dynamic, but it is nuanced differently under the conditions of incarnation and resurrection—namely, the difference in nuance between redemptive love and reconciliatory emancipation. The latter expression is especially appropriate to characterize the resurrection event and experience, which is above all one of freedom—a setting free from the bondage of sin and evil, and a structuring of freedom in emancipatory practices. Etymologically, "emancipation" means to "deliver over" (*e-mancipare*) by taking something into hand (*manus*), namely a document granting title of ownership. It is a metaphor rooted in Roman legal practices, historically associated with the release of slaves from bondage and of women and children from patriarchal power. Taylor remarks that the release was "focused especially on the structural mechanism by which freedom is seized or granted and by which freedom is sustained. . . . Emancipation is structured and structuring freedom."[2] Thus the term is well-suited to express the public and social aspects of freedom with which we are concerned in the final part of this work.

If love had the primacy in the story of the Crucified One as the consummation of God's love for the world, and if basileia freedom served as the qualifier of this love, now freedom has the primacy in the story of the Risen One, but it is a freedom qualified by reconciliatory love. Taylor argues that these two elements, reconciliatory love and emancipatory freedom, must both be present in order to address two of the realities of the postmodern situation: on the one hand, "fragmentation, difference, lack of unity amid intense and recalcitrant pluralism," and, on the other hand, "oppression and systematic exploitation." The Christ-gestalt must provide resources both for achieving wholeness amid real differences and for combating oppressive forms of domination. In Taylor's view the latter objective is fundamental today, while the former serves as a necessary modification of it; hence the expression "reconciliatory emancipation."[3]

It is better, in my view, to regard the two elements as equally essential. I trace the elements not simply to features of the postmodern situation but to fundamental aspects of God's relation to the world. There can be no reconciliation without liberation, that is, without the radical change in social structures that overcomes injustice and inequality; otherwise reconciliation is a phony peace. Likewise there can be no liberation without reconciliation, that is, without the healing of divisive conflicts and the acceptance of genuine differences; if differences tear us apart, emancipation is a hollow victory. We must strive with equivalent zeal for both love and freedom, both wholeness and emancipation. When they come together, "resurrection" occurs.

The Meaning of "Resurrection"[4]

The New Testament uses two terms to interpret the experience that lies at the heart of Christian faith, the experience of the living presence of the Crucified One. The root sense of the first of these, *egeirein,* is "to awaken" or "to rise up," while the root sense of the second, *anastanai,* is "to arise" or "to stand up."[5] When applied to the resurrection experience, these terms can be interpreted in different ways. They can be construed in an apocalyptic direction, in which case they are taken to mean that Jesus "awakened from the dead" as from sleep, or "arose from death" as from sleep. This suggests the miraculous idea, common to the apocalyptic worldview, that dead people can be brought back to life or resuscitated, can literally rise up from death as they would from a deep sleep, such as Lazarus is supposed to have done. This is usually what these terms are taken to mean when applied to Jesus.

But another construal is possible, a functionalist one, which offers in my view a more adequate interpretation of what is involved in the experience of the presence of Christ and for which there is precedent in both the Septuagint and the New Testament. The meaning now would be that Jesus was "arising to an action" or was being "installed in a function"—for example, the reference in the letter to the Hebrews to "another priest," that is, Jesus, "arising" or being "installed" (*anistatai*) as "a priest forever" (7:15–17). Let us focus on the noun form of the word usually translated as "resurrection," *anastasis:* It means literally "coming to stand" (*stasis*) "in the midst of or throughout" (*ana*). That in the midst of which the risen Jesus stands is the world. Thus to say that Jesus is "risen from the dead" means that he "comes to stand" in the world as the agent or representative of God, engaged in a work of reconciliatory emancipation. Jesus' agency is not exercised in some remote, other-worldly realm but here and now, in our midst, on this earth. Resurrection means his coming, his presence, his efficacious agency on behalf of the shape of love-in-freedom, not his departure or removal from the scene.

A good case can be made that this functionalist interpretation of resurrection is the one that predominates in the New Testament after the stories of the empty tomb and appearances are left behind—that is, when we turn to the Pauline and Johannine writings and to the Epistle to the Hebrews. The focus of interest is not on the miracle of resuscitating a dead man but on the saving, life-giving, redemptively transformative work of the risen Christ. This is not to say that these authors do not assume that resurrection is an event that happened to Jesus of Nazareth. They do assume that, but they make no attempt to explain how it happened. It is a deep mystery and a primary experience of faith. The event insofar as it can be talked about has an effect on, becomes visible in, the community of faith, indeed is constitutive of this community. The resurrection happens to both Jesus and the community, or better between Jesus and the community, or even better between the small community that coalesced around Jesus (since Jesus is not comprehensible apart from that community) and the great global community of believers. This happening is a redemptive, salvific one.

Paul links in various ways the themes of salvation and resurrection. For him the event of salvation includes two elements, justification and newness of life, both of which are associated with the resurrection of Jesus from the dead. This is seen most clearly in two passages in Romans: Faith "will be reckoned to us who believe in him who raised Jesus our Lord from the dead, who was handed over to death for our trespasses and was raised for our justification" (4:24–25), and "Therefore we have been buried with him by baptism into death, so that, just as Christ was raised from the dead by the glory of the Father, we too might walk in newness of life" (6:4; see also 6:5–9). Likewise, for the Gospel of John, the resurrection is linked with the gift of eternal life, which has already been actualized in Jesus' earthly ministry and is evidenced by his life-giving power (11:25–26). Such life entails being "born anew . . . of the Spirit" (3:3–8), which means that the raising of Jesus is an upraising of the Spirit—a point to which we shall return.

The English word "resurrection" lacks the apocalyptic overtone of awakening from the sleep of death; rather its Latin root suggests something like "the surging forth (*surgere*) again (*re*) of life out of death." The surging forth of life out of death: This seems to be as good a way as any of expressing the fusion of basileia freedom and crucified love in resurrection. It captures precisely the sense of "new birth" or "rebirth" found in the Fourth Gospel. It is at the heart of what Christians mean by redemption.[6] The new life in question is transformed, faithful, liberated life. It is life in which fear is being overcome and idolatry rejected; life in which the alienation and oppression of our corporate existence is being healed; life in which the broken faith at the heart of sin is being reconstructed. H. Richard Niebuhr, in his posthumously published lectures, *Faith on Earth,* placed great stress on the transformative presence of the risen Christ, proposing that "the present Jesus Christ of faith is the companion who reconstructs the broken faith by which we have lived in the past."[7] The risen Christ is the companion who reconstructs.

This reconstruction issues above all else in a new birth of freedom—both personal freedom from sin, guilt, and death, and social liberation from alienating and oppressive powers. Christ, the Risen One, means freedom and gives freedom.[8]

Resurrection and Spiritual Presence

But, we are tempted to ask: How can this be? How can the past figure of Jesus serve not only as a historical model but as the living agent of the redemptive transformations and emancipatory practices we and our forebears have experienced in our own times and places? Or, to reiterate Nicodemus's blunt query: How can a person be born anew if he or she is old, dying, or dead (John 3:4)? As we have seen, the New Testament writings do not encourage speculation on this question, but the question does seem unavoidable nonetheless. Perhaps we can best approach it negatively. On the one hand, the resurrection of Jesus is something more than mere historical influence or memory or a mere psychological event in the minds of believers: This is a rationalist reduction of the resurrection experience. On the other hand, it is something other than a miracle of bodily resuscitation and quasi-physical immediacy, such as is implied by spiritualist visions or transubstantiation of the eucharistic elements: This is a supernaturalist distortion, against which the empty tomb stories protect in a negative way, discouraging speculation about what happened to Jesus' body. What is risen is not the corpse of a dead man but a gestalt, a sociohistorical dynamic that coalesced in and around a specific human being and with which this human being is still identified.

The resurrection experience seems rather to have something to do with the fact that the historical, remembered Jesus is *recognized* to be personally, efficaciously *present* in certain words, actions, and communal structures that evoke a new way of being human in the world, a way of faithfulness, liberation, and love. This is the positive significance of the appearance stories, especially as found in Luke 24: Jesus is recognized to be present in the breaking of bread, that is, in the act of communion, of sharing. Presence occurs when recognition is evoked. Jesus is recognized and thus present in a structure or gestalt of word and act with which his personal being has become paradigmatically identified. It is important to emphasize that what is recognized is not a human body per se but a shape of praxis embodied in a specific person in a quite unforgettable way; and it has to be reembodied in concrete persons ever anew for its emancipatory potential to be released into the world.

So the presence in question is a *spiritual-ethical* presence. That is, Jesus is no longer sensibly, physically present. The story in Luke 24 does depict a physical immediacy of Jesus with the disciples on the road to Emmaus, but he is not *present* to them because they have not yet recognized him, and when they do recognize him it is not because they have caught sight of his body but because they have shared in a structure of praxis with which he is identified. The Christ-gestalt becomes incarnate for them in this concrete action—and so it happens again and again. The recognition of Jesus in this gestalt is a spiritual recognition, not a sensible or physical recognition; in fact, once he is recognized he vanishes from their sight. What is recognized is something spiritual, an ethical action, and it is a recognition brought about by the inner witness or testimony of the Holy Spirit. This serves to remind us that, with the theme of the resurrection, we have moved from the second to the third figure of the divine life, that of the Spirit. The stress is no longer on differentiation, otherness, objective history, and physical embodiment, but on mediation and reunion, on God's indwelling presence and spiritual embodiment. It is still an embodiment but of a different character: corporate rather than individual, mediated rather than immediate.[9] Christology bridges the second and third figures, those of world and Spirit, differentiating love and unifying freedom. The transition from the one to the other is the transition from the shape of the historical Jesus to the shape of the risen Christ.

We now live "in the Spirit." But this is not any Spirit; it is the Spirit of Christ Jesus; and thus we can also say that we live "in Christ." This continued reference to Christ is important for we sense that the words, actions, and structures of the redeemed community in which we live are not our own doing but the doing of the one who is present through the gift of the Spirit and who defines or shapes that Spirit just as the Spirit is the power by which Christ is present. Christ (that is, the gestalt that coalesced in and around the figure of Jesus and with whom it is still identified) empowers these actions and lives on in them even though we are instrumental to this process as the immediate, embodied actors. We, individually and collectively, are the body of the risen Christ, while Christ is the true subject or agent of our words and actions insofar as they are liberating, salvific. That Jesus as the Christ continues to live on in the world in this agential fashion is the mystery of his resurrection from the dead.

A suggestive theological interpretation of this mystery is provided by Karl Rahner.[10] Already during its own lifetime, the individual human being exists in an open relation to the world, so that the world as a whole functions as the body of the individual, in addition to or as an extension of one's own body, and as the context for the latter. Through death and resurrection from the dead this world-relatedness is intensified and deepened: The human self becomes pancosmic, not acosmic. The world as a whole becomes its body although the relations to this body are qualitatively different from those to the individual empirical body. Perhaps this is a way of understanding what Paul means by a "spiritual body" as distinguished from the "physical body" (1 Cor. 15:35–50). Self-identity after death is preserved, not by individuated physical continuity, but by participation in a community or a spiritual realm of being in which the self is not lost but taken up into a higher unity or structure; there the self finds an identity that is founded outside itself. Such communal or world embodiment is spiritual in the sense that it consists of ethical relations and actions although of course it has a material substrate. Every human community, whether it is a family, a church, a club, a school, a business, a political party, or a state is in this sense spiritual, it is a spiritual body, a corporation.

Rahner suggests that the human self, "by surrendering its limited bodily structure in death, becomes open towards the universe and, in some way, a co-determining factor of the universe precisely in the latter's character as the ground of the personal life of other spiritual corporal beings."[11] If this theory is correct, then such a world presence or spiritual presence is possible for every human being after death; and indeed Rahner's point is that all human beings are in some sense co-responsible for the world and add something unique to it, in death as in life. The dead continue to have an effect on the living; resurrection brings what is dead and gone into play once again.

This is expressed in dramatic fashion by the Guatemalan poet Julia Esquivel in a collection of poems called *Threatened with Resurrection*.[12] She writes of those who have died in the struggle for liberation:

They have threatened us with Resurrection,
because they are more alive than ever before,
because they transform our agonies,
and fertilize our struggle.

Thus Jesus' resurrection from the dead seems to be a specific instance of a universal human promise and possibility, which is entirely consistent with what Paul says in 1 Cor. 15:12ff.: "Now if Christ is proclaimed as raised from the dead, how can some of you say there is no resurrection of the dead? If there is no resurrection of the dead, then Christ has not been raised." But Jesus' resurrection presence is more radical, and in that sense unique, by virtue of the absolutely fundamental way he co-determines the world, which in turn is a consequence of the fact that the Christ-gestalt took shape in and through his historical words, actions, and fate in a decisive way. The risen Jesus becomes a co-determining factor in the present constitution of the world whenever and wherever the Christ-gestalt (the fused shape of communal freedom and empowering love) takes shape anew. The identity of Jesus of Nazareth is borne through history by this gestalt—in so intensive a way that Jesus himself is felt to be personally present and active in the work of reconciliatory emancipation. All this takes place solely through the power of God. God contains within the divine life both the individual self and the world in which the risen self is newly embodied. Thus in rising into the world, we also rise into God.

The Socialization of Christ in the Ecclesial Community

The world as a whole, then, in its social, cultural, political fabric, functions as the embodiment of the shape of Christ. The Christian community of faith, the ecclesial community, is the place in the world where the recognition and hence the presence of *Jesus* as the Christ is brought to articulation by memory, cultic acts, proclamation, and mission. The community is the body of Christ in a more explicit, concrete sense but only because it is the place in the world where the world itself embodies the shape of Christ. It goes without saying, then, that the body in which the shape of Christ becomes incarnate is no longer the dead and decayed physical corpse of Jesus but the ongoing human community, and more specifically the community of those who connect this shape with the historical ministry of Jesus and who enact it in their own lives. For its worldly mediation, the shape of Christ is now dependent upon *our* words and deeds. This means that it is no longer embodied individually but rather socially, communally. To be more precise, even the original embodiment of the shape of Christ in Jesus of Nazareth was not simply individual. Bodies are not isolated; they exist only in relation. It was not Jesus' single body alone that was significant but his body interacting with other bodies. The corporate body generated by Jesus interacting with his contemporaries *and* with us *is* the incarnation of the Christ-gestalt. This means that the theme of incarnation is extended, not negated, by resurrection. Resurrection of the body is the extension of bodies-in-relation.

The individual person Jesus of Nazareth remains the necessary catalyst for resurrection just as he was for the basileia community that formed about him. In this sense he is indispensable for the unique kind of redemption experienced and proclaimed by Christians. At the same time he is experienced to be present in the many shapes or figures of Christ who have appeared and will continue to appear in the life of the ecclesial community. The many shapes of Christ are linked to the one shape, but the one does not contain or exhaust the many. The shape of Christ, which Jesus introduced and released into the world, lives on in a plurality of forms that continue to enrich the shape. One of the enrichments is the recognition that the shape is female as well as male, Gentile as well as Jewish, black as well as white, African and Asian as well as European and American, homosexual and bisexual as well as heterosexual and celibate. It appears in the shape of children as well as elders, of common folk as well as heroes, of sinners as well as saints. It is simply the human shape in its multiple manifestations, transfigured—if only momentarily—by love-in-freedom.[13]

As we move beyond the ecclesial community, we encounter shapes of God's presence in history that are not specifically linked with the shape of Christ, even though there may be analogies among these shapes. *We* may recognize in these other shapes a hidden form of the shape of Christ, but we have no right to impose this perception on others. Rather we can only hope that a convergence and transformation (but not a melding) of shapes may take place.

This is the point at which christology passes into ecclesiology, a theology of religions and history, and ultimately eschatology, these being increasingly broad interpretations of the third figure of the divine life, that of Spirit (see chaps. 18–19). In the treatment of the second figure, that of world, we moved with increasing specificity from nature, to human being, to the shape of Christ incarnate and crucified. God's love for the world comes to focus at this point. Now we open out, through concentric spheres of freedom, from the shape of Christ risen, to the ecclesial community, to religions, to history and eschatology. With this opening out, we move from christology to pneumatology—a theology of the Holy Spirit.

17
THE SPIRIT AND FREEDOM

The Meaning of "Spirit"

Loss and Recovery of Spirit

The doctrine of the (Holy) Spirit is the most difficult and uncertain of Christian doctrines. The ancient creeds are not very helpful in clarifying what the Spirit is, and in systematic or constructive theologies the doctrine of the Spirit is often treated as an embarrassing appendage. It was for many years an appendage in the course from whose lectures this book evolved. Only recently have I discovered its power and begun to have some sense of its meaning. Reasons for its neglect are not hard to find. In Western theology and philosophy the very concept of "spirit" has for the most part been fraught with difficulties, conveying something vapid and dualistic, implying a separation of and a hierarchy between the mental and the physical, the soul and the body, the human and the natural, the male and the female, the holy and the profane. The hierarchy reflects a suspicion and fear of the suppressed poles: nature, the body, the feminine. Spirit had to be detached from these and controlled by means such as spiritualism and institutionalism, that is, through esoteric practices and male-dominated ecclesiastical office. Subordination of the Spirit, marginalization of women, and exploitation of nature have gone hand in hand in the history of the church.[1]

This traditional theological attitude toward the Spirit has been compounded in modern times by what Joel Kovel describes as a "despiritualization" of culture, brought about by technocracy, the destruction of nature, the loss of a sense of the sacred, the turn to utilitarian and hedonistic values, the breakup of organic wholes into isolated fragments, the displacement of self-sustaining human communities by socioeconomic and political systems oriented to production, consumption, control, and the concentration of power and wealth. Kovel believes that a symptom of this despiritualization is found precisely in the multiplicity of fragmented, sometimes bizarre or destructive spiritualities that litter the cultural landscape today. We are like the protagonists of Kafka's novels, he says, "engaged in doomed, endless spiritual quests."[2]

Yet, surprisingly, we may be experiencing a rebirth of the Spirit today. In the void of despiritualization, winds of the Spirit are stirring, and people are discovering that, far from being vapid and dualistic, Spirit is the clue to the energy and wholeness of life. Feminist, ecological, and charismatic-Pentecostal movements have been harbingers of this rebirth, reinforced by the spiritualities of Native American, Latin American, African, and Asian peoples, newly encountered through interreligious dialogue and the ecumenical movement. The theme of the 1991 Assembly of the World Council of Churches in Canberra, Australia, "Come, Holy Spirit—Renew the Whole Creation," provided a powerful symbol of what is happening.[3] The resources for a theology of Spirit are rich and diverse, ranging from Eastern Orthodoxy and classical Western spirituality to New Age movements, folk and tribal religions, feminist, ecological, and liberation theologies, and new philosophies of spirit. Very little of this has as yet been absorbed by theology. A new paradigm in pneumatology has not yet emerged, says Jürgen Moltmann. Yet there are beginnings, and it does seem right to suggest, as he does, that we are witnessing a transition from an anthropocentric to a holistic pneumatology, one that embraces the whole creation and recognizes in the Spirit the symbol of wholeness, relatedness, energy, life.[4]

Metaphors of Spirit

Biblical and classical metaphors of spirit represent it as a fluid, pervasive, intangible energy whose fundamental quality is vitality and freedom and whose fundamental purpose is to create, shape, and enliven. Four natural elements have traditionally been associated with spirit: air, fire, light, water. These are material images of an immaterial vitality. The image of wind, moving air, and breath or breathing lies linguistically at the root of the words for spirit in Semitic and Indo-European languages: *ruach* (Hebrew), *pneuma* (Greek), *spirare* (Latin). God's wind (*ruach*) swept over the face of the waters, and God breathed the breath of life (*ruach*) into human beings (Gen. 1:2; 2:7). Germanic *Geist* (English "ghost") differs slightly since it suggests the idea of being moved powerfully, as in fear or amazement, a movement associated with the sudden drawing in or expelling of breath. The inhaling and exhaling of air is the essential condition of life for mammals, and it is the most direct means by which they are linked with the natural world. Moreover, through little explosions and transmissions of air, human beings communicate by means of language, which is the most mysterious and powerful of all invisible forces. It is not surprising that Anaximenes identified the world substance as air, which is both the prime stuff and the prime movement.[5]

The God of Israel is the God not only of wind but of fire, light, and water, which are in the Psalmist's imagination closely related elements:

> You are clothed with honor and majesty,
>   wrapped in light as with a garment.
> You stretch out the heavens like a tent,
>   you set the beams of your chambers on the waters,
> you make the clouds your chariot,
>   you ride on the wings of the wind,
> you make the winds your messengers,
>   fire and flame your ministers (Ps. 104:1–4).

God's essential nature is described as a "devouring fire" in Deut. 4:24, yet in Ex. 3:2 the divine fire burns but does not consume. The "rushing wind" of Pentecost appears also as "tongues of fire" that make human tongues incandescent with language (Acts 2:2–4). Fire is produced by the rapid union of wind/air/oxygen with other substances, and it in turn produces heat and light. Spirit is a fusion that releases an incredible energy.

The first of God's creative acts was to separate light from darkness: As the Spirit swept over the waters, God said, "Let there be light," and there was light (Gen. 2:3–4). As Hegel observes, God "needed only a breath [a word] and there was light, light that is only a breath."[6] This light *is* God—a light that illuminates us by its radiance ("in your light we see light," Ps. 36:9) and saves us by its steadfastness ("the light shines in the darkness, and the darkness did not overcome it," John 1:5). This light, called into being by God's breathing/speaking/igniting, is a figure of both the Spirit of God and the Word of God.

It should not be assumed that darkness is primarily a symbol of evil or negation in the Hebrew and Christian scriptures, despite the deeply rooted tendency of light-skinned peoples to regard it as such. Light presupposes darkness and is nothing without it: A universe that is all light would be the opposite of Hegel's night in which all cows are black.[7] Darkness is the matrix, the fertile abyss, out of which everything is created; and creation involves the separation of light from darkness, not the elimination of darkness. "The light shines *in* the darkness": This assumes that darkness remains, that light did not overcome it any more than that darkness has the power to overcome light. Truth and beauty are in fact generated by the *interplay* of light and darkness. In this interplay, light is the symbol of God's Spirit (or Word) and darkness the symbol of God's world across which Spirit sweeps; both are needed for revelation to occur. To be sure, for the Gospel of John, darkness is the symbol of a world that is fallen and needs redemption, but it is presumed that the world is worth saving, that it is not utterly evil.

In Psalm 36:9 God is also described as "the fountain of life," which makes a connection to the metaphor of water. As Moltmann observes, the Spirit operates "from below" (as source, fountain, spring) as well as "from above" (light). Water together with air and light are essential for life. God is "the fountain of living water" (Jer. 2:13), and Jesus gives "a spring of water gushing up to eternal life" (John 4:14). Water is what is "poured out," and the "pouring out" of Spirit is one of its most powerful images in the Hebrew Bible and the New Testament, suggesting its fluidity and pervasiveness.[8]

If we move back slightly from these metaphors, we can say that Spirit is an immaterial vitality that enlivens and shapes material nature: It is the *energeia* that infuses all that is. For this reason Krister Stendahl proposes the metaphor of energy as best suited for the Spirit. "Energy," he says, "is a better word than power. Power is for ruling. Energy is for living."[9] This is a helpful corrective. Following Tillich I have spoken of God's creative being as the "power" of being, but I went on to say that in relation to the natural world this power manifests itself as "primal and all-pervasive energy." Energy is simply that mysterious power that is active and at work in things (*en + ergon*, work)—and that power (which need not be understood as ruling power) is God as Spirit.

Related to energy are other metaphors of Spirit that suggest an activity of creating living space for all things and shaping the concrete configurations of life. In the creation story of Genesis, God prepares appropriate spaces for living: heaven and earth, air, land, and water. This is the work of the Spirit that moves across the face of the waters and calls into being the realms in which creatures dwell.[10] Creation is a work of distinguishing, shaping, configuring, and so too is redemption. The Apostle Paul says that we are "formed" by God's Spirit—that is, we are to be "conformed" (*summorphous*) to Christ, the "firstborn" of God's children (Rom. 8:29); we are to be "transformed" (*metamorphous*) by the renewal of our minds (Rom. 12:2). The Spirit, the shaper of forms, is the agent of metamorphosis, of transformation.

Human Spirit

Spirit is not only the primal energy, the power of being, that infuses and enlivens all beings and that can be vividly represented by natural images. It is also the distinctive essence of human being. In humans, remarks Paul Tillich, spirit unites the power of being (or life) with the meaning of being.[11] That is, the life-giving power also gives, or rather is, wisdom, intelligibility, reason. That is why in the Hebraic tradition spirit (*ruach*), wisdom (*hochmah*), and word (*dabar*) are so closely linked,[12] a linkage contained also in the German *Geist*, which means "mind" as well as "spirit." Spirit is intrinsically wise, rational, linguistic power; and wisdom, logos, language are spiritual in the sense of breathing knowledge and will into materiality.[13]

When spirit enlivens human nature, the result is *consciousness*, which is at once physiological and psychological: It is founded in an embodied brain yet engenders language, freedom, communication, centered personhood, self-relatedness mediated through other-relatedness. Today we are inclined to say that the essence of consciousness or selfhood, and hence also of human being as spirit, is relationality. As personal selves or conscious subjects we are an infinitely complex network of relationships—to our own bodies, to the material world through our bodies, to our past experiences through memory, to other personal spiritual beings through acts of recognition and intentionality, to the sociocultural world in which we are nurtured, to the universal power of being and meaning. Spirit is no one thing in this network but the network itself, pure relationality; or as Steven Smith says, "the perfect void yawning between me and others," "the open place across which the wind of spirit blows"; or in Kovel's terms, spirit is "no-thing in itself" but "rather the relatedness, the coming together of separated elements of being."[14] This is the immateriality of spirit, but its materiality is precisely the energy of nature shaped into meaningful patterns by relationships.

Far from being dualistic, then, spirit is a *mediating* term: It is the rational manifested in the material, intelligibility in consciousness, language in speech; it is the unity of freedom and nature, self and body, individual and society, Creator and creation. Spirit overreaches all these dichotomizing distinctions and levels the hierarchy between them. It is the relationality that holds things together even as it keeps them distinct, it is a desire or eros at once intellectual and sensuous. It posits and presupposes a material world but is itself immaterial and intangible, the ideality of reason, which itself is nothing but relationality. Spirit is rationality or wisdom *as embodied in consciousness.* If spirit entails consciousness, there can never be spirit without the embodying medium, nature.

Divine Spirit

The embodiment of Spirit is as true for divinity as for humanity. God is "Spirit" insofar as God is present to, active in, embodied by that which is other than God, namely the natural and human worlds. Thus in scripture "Spirit" refers to that modality of divine activity whereby God indwells, empowers, energizes the forces of nature, the people of Israel, the ecclesial community, and individual persons. The Spirit is the indwelling power of God that brings the natural and human worlds to consummation by bringing estranged and fallen beings back into everlasting, liberating communion with the one God, whose true and proper name is now Spirit.[15]

Although in some sense personal (a matter to be considered in the next section), God's Spirit is not gendered. The word "spirit" is grammatically feminine in Hebrew (*ruach*), neuter in Greek (*pneuma*), and masculine in Latin (*spiritus*)—a circumstance that signified for the Latin theologian and biblical translator Jerome "that God transcends all categories of sexuality and is indeed Spirit."[16] In any event, the translation of pronominal references to the Spirit as "he" in the English Bible is completely unjustified on both grammatical and theological grounds. In fact, in biblical literature the role of the Spirit is often found in activities associated with maternity and femininity: inspiring, helping, grieving, sheltering, enveloping, bringing to birth, nurturing, instilling wisdom (*sophia*). The Spirit is commonly represented as a dove or some other species of bird, and these are conspicuously feminine images in ancient Near Eastern religions and Greek mythology. The association of the Spirit with divine wisdom (*sophia*) and presence (*shekinah*) connects it with feminine symbols. Thus it is appropriate, as Johnson says, to speak about Spirit "in analogy with women's historical reality, not exclusively but legitimately."[17] As she recognizes, it is misleading to suggest that the Spirit represents a "feminine principle" in the Godhead, for this implies that there is also a masculine principle (or principles, Father and Son). Rather the Spirit gives us a way of speaking of God that is not patriarchal or gender-specific, and it should become the model for all talk about God, who is personal yet neither male nor female. The God of Joel's prophecy declares: "I will pour out my Spirit on all flesh; your sons and your daughters shall prophesy" (Joel 2:28; compare Acts 2:17).[18]

When God's Spirit pours out, it engenders love and freedom. Love has long been associated with the work of the Spirit by the theological tradition. In the Augustinian and Thomistic trinities, the Spirit was identified with love, love "breathed forth" or "spirated," "love proceeding," the "mutual love" of Father and Son, God and world. The imagery of fire was often used to express the energizing and fusing power of love. Hildegaard of Bingen connects fire with the Holy Spirit (*ignis Spiritus*) and with love (*ignis caritatis*), and one of Charles Wesley's hymns beseeches the Holy Spirit to "kindle a flame of sacred love" in us.[19]

The Apostle Paul links the Spirit with both love and freedom in such a way that these become virtually indistinguishable qualities. It is through the Holy Spirit that "God's love has been poured into our hearts" (Rom. 5:5); and "the fruit of the Spirit is love" (Gal. 5:22; compare

Rom. 15:30; 1 Cor. 4:21). At the same time we are told that "the Lord is the Spirit, and where the Spirit of the Lord is, there is freedom" (2 Cor. 3:17). This is Paul's way of saying that the presence of God is no longer to be sought on Mount Sinai but in the Spirit and that this presence liberates us from the law and all else that veils God from us. This is "the freedom of the glory of the children of God," our being set free from subjection to "futility," which Paul describes as "the first fruits of the Spirit" in Rom. 8:21–22. Johannine imagery can be mixed with Pauline to suggest that when the Spirit of God is poured out it engenders not only love but also a "new birth of freedom." The Spirit is the power by which one is "born anew" (John 3:3–7), and the life into which one is newly born is a symbol of freedom. Life is linked to freedom through the category of truth (John 8:32; 14:6), which means that it involves a liberation from "falsehood"—the Johannine equivalent to the Pauline "futility" as a characterization of the world's bondage.[20]

In sum, God's love is a liberating love, and God's freedom is a reconciling freedom. If love posits difference for the sake of union, freedom consummates relationships for the sake of a whole in which each particular is respected. The latter is the special work of the Spirit, but it presupposes the work of love, which is the work of the one filled by the Spirit, Jesus Christ.

Perhaps the theology of Spirit has gone into recession in our time because it is centrally concerned with God's presence, whereas it is just God's presence that has become so doubtful, so deeply questioned by the cultural emptiness and the critical philosophies of our time. God may once have been present, we say, but surely no longer in the world *we* experience. Our problem is that we sophisticated Westerners really cannot believe in such a thing as the Holy Spirit, cannot believe that a Paraclete is at work in the world, or that the world will attain its consummation in God. Perhaps then it is not so surprising that it is among the powerless, oppressed, and marginalized that the Spirit is pouring itself out afresh—upon those for whom authentically liberating power can come only from God, not from humanity. The Spirit is arising for us today from the underside of history.[21]

The Emergence of Spirit

Following insights from Michael Welker and Marjorie Suchocki, I am arguing that the Holy Spirit is not something that exists in advance as a supernatural person of the Godhead. There are no such preexisting persons in God but rather potentials for relations that become actual when God creates the world as other than God. God does have a primordial self-relatedness, an inner complexity of identity-difference-mediation, but this should not be hypostatized into subsistent persons.

Thus the Spirit is an *emergent* person (not an individual but a social person), generated out of the interaction of God and the world, in the process of which the world is liberated and God is perfected. "The Spirit proceeds not from 'Father' and 'Son' alone, but also from the world: Spirit names God *and* the world." The Spirit comes into being through the "outpouring" of God in the world.[22]

The ancient biblical metaphor of "pouring" (Joel 2:28; Acts 2:17) accords nicely with this process notion of Spirit as emergent, and the latter accords with the idea of God advocated in this work (chap. 11), namely that Spirit mediates between God as God and God in the world, emerging out of the interaction between them, completing God by bringing God back to godself enriched and enlivened by worldly difference. God *becomes* Spirit in and through relationship with the world. The appropriate trinitarian formula is God-World-Spirit, or God as World-Spirit, or God-in-the-World-as-Spirit. Like the fire that does not consume (that is, does not reduce the other to the same), Spirit is a fusion of God and world. The Spirit proceeds out of the emerging *love* between God and the world, and the Spirit then becomes the power of reconciling *freedom* within this differentiated love. "God's love has been poured into our hearts through the Holy Spirit that has been given to us" (Rom. 5:5). Spirit is generated precisely in the process of pouring; it does not preexist the pouring as a kind of prepackaged *persona* or *dynamis*. Wind cannot be boxed; it happens in the happening. The verb used in Joel 2:28 is active and future: "I *will pour* out my Spirit on all flesh," says the Lord. This is not to suggest that the pouring has not begun. It began with creation and will continue as long as there is a relationship between Creator and creation. While the mediating "third," the Spirit is not simply last in relation to God and Christ but contemporaneous. The Spirit both precedes and follows Christ.

Even if it is not a preexistent hypostasis, is God's Spirit in some sense personal? Jürgen Moltmann says that in the Spirit we experience God as both "pure presence" (*Gegenwart*) and as "counterpart" (*Gegenüber*), that is, as someone over against us. "In the flow between counterpart and presence, a personhood comes into being with permeable frontiers, in energy-charged relationships." This appears to mean that the Spirit is not a preexistent *persona* of the Trinity but emerges into a personal identity through its relations with the world. Like that of all other persons, the personhood of the Spirit is concrescing. Such a reading is confirmed by Moltmann's summary definition: "The personhood of God the Holy Spirit is the loving, self-communicating, out-fanning and out-pouring presence of the eternal divine life of the triune God." Yet Moltmann in his critique of modalism retrojects the personhood of the Spirit into the immanent Trinity and speaks of the eternal interaction among the three divine Persons: Father, Son, and Holy Spirit.[23]

My view by contrast is that the innertrinitarian relations take on the character of personal subjects only in relation to the world. Christ is an individual historical subject although engaged in a network of relationships; the Spirit is a social subject, a community of subjects. God as a whole is personal, the one true and perfect person and the power of personhood, "the personifying person," as Barth expresses it. What God "personifies" is not only God's creatures but God's own self, and this divine self-personification is taking place through the evolutionary process, the emergence of human beings, the appearance of Christ, and the sending of the Spirit. God is already and not yet personal: "already" in the sense that real relations subsist within the oneness of God, "not yet" in the sense that the wholeness of God is an emergent sociality of which the Spirit is the preeminent figure. My objective is to articulate a social understanding of God that is neither modalistic nor tritheistic.

The Relations of Spirit

These "relations" are phases in the emergence of Spirit or elements of the world out of which God-as-Spirit is pouring forth. Spirit is nothing without relations; it is precisely relationality, the moving air that permeates and enlivens things, the open space across which the wind of Spirit blows. The open space is the condition of possibility of relations; without it, everything would collapse into sameness. By entering into relations, Spirit loses its vagueness, takes on specificity and shape: It is this to which the language of "person" is pointing.

Divine Spirit and Natural Spirits

God's Spirit takes on the shape of *many* created spirits: not just the spirits of living persons but of ancestors and animals as well as the spirits of plants, trees, rivers, mountains, storms and earthquakes, stars and planets. Belief in such spirits as intermediaries of both divine and demonic power is widespread in the folk religions, African, Asian, and American, and it is presupposed by the Bible.[24] Sophisticated Westerners dismiss such belief as superstitious, but it reflects the conviction that God is universally present and works through instrumentalities that are appropriate to concrete situations. Rather than overriding natural powers, God acts through them in ways that are complex, mysterious, and hidden. Thus God honors the integrity of the natural world while exercising sovereignty in it. This sovereignty is not absolute since there are also demonic and destructive forces at work in the world, and humans become involved in the struggle between good and evil. On the whole this is a portrayal that, while mythological, is subtle and realistic.[25]

It is the very universality of God's spiritual presence that requires recognition of the insight contained in such belief. Such recognition has not often been forthcoming among modern theologians. Ernst Troeltsch was an exception. In view of the immeasurability of the universe, he recognized that the human race could no longer be regarded to stand at the center of all things. There must occur a decentering of the human, a recognition of the "multiplicity of spiritual realms besides the human one," an affirmation that "subspiritual creatures" also have a goal, and in general a shift from an anthropocentric and even a geocentric to a cosmocentric perspective. By the act of love, God's "essence is reproduced and multiplied in innumerable realms of spirit, and in those very realms reclaims itself. God is thus construed, in terms of a universal theism, as the one who allows the light of [God's] goodness and love to shine upon all spirits in their several contexts and circumstances." Implicit in such a conviction, Troeltsch observed, is that God's Spirit must be present in primitive and prehistorical peoples as well as under conditions of human impairment (mental illness, severely deformed children) and in animals. "An animal is no machine, but a spirited [*geistiges*] organism. But if animals are not mere automatons, then we must ask, What is the relationship between the spirited power incarnate in animals and our concept of the highest goal? The answer that animals exist for the sake of human nourishment will not suffice. Theologians, of course, are not supposed to ask these sorts of questions, but this does not make them any less necessary."[26]

Theologians are not supposed to ask such questions. They have too long avoided them, and the present author is no exception. What has been avoided is thinking of the Holy Spirit as World Spirit—Hegel's *Weltgeist*.[27] It is just this thought that is required if the Spirit really emerges out of the interaction between God and the world—the whole world, not just the human part of it. But what does it mean? "World Spirit" does not mean "Spirit World," a special world or realm of spirits, preternatural beings hidden in natural things. Rather it means that the *whole* world is animated by Spirit and that Spirit proceeds from the whole world as God's body. It means that Spirit manifests itself in nature, that Spirit slumbers in nature and nature cries out to Spirit ("the very stones . . . cry out," Luke 19:40).

Can this be thought nonmythologically? Joel Kovel suggests that the manifestation of Spirit in nature is *eros* or *desire*—the great binding force of the universe, the cosmic law that all beings are connected, the longing to annihilate what cannot be annihilated, namely finitude and difference, "the roiling of indwelling nature striving toward spirit."[28] Eros makes itself known through bodily desire, or sexuality, a wanting of and sharing in the other as belonging to an original yet separated unity, but it appears as well in other forms of desire, intellectual, ascetic, aesthetic, religious. Perhaps the natural spirits are all expressions of this cosmic eros or allurement in modes appropriate to specific forms of life. Diverse parts of the universe are calling and reaching out to each other in a thousand different voices. They are the voices of Spirit concrescing, of spirits witnessing to Spirit; but in nature Spirit has not yet found a fully spiritual counterpart.

Divine Spirit and Human Spirit

Such a counterpart is found with the evolution of human beings as free and self-conscious persons. Both God and humans are quintessentially "spirit," but they are so in different ways, and they relate to each other differently. The difference is described by Tillich as follows. Whereas the divine Spirit "dwells" and "works in" the human spirit, the human spirit "stands out" from itself in a state of ecstasy under the impact of the divine Spirit. "If the divine Spirit breaks into the human spirit, this does not mean that it rests there, but that it drives the human spirit out of itself. The 'in' of the divine Spirit is an 'out' for the human spirit."[29] Both of these expressions—"dwelling in," "standing out"—are metaphorical; we have no other way of expressing the mystery of the relationship of the divine and the human. The "dwelling in" of the divine Spirit has the character of an utterly gratuitous gift; it cannot be compelled or controlled by us, it is something that comes upon us in seemingly miraculous fashion. The "standing out" or *ecstasis* of the human spirit does not destroy or dispossess its structure as a centered self but turns it from self-centeredness to reality-centeredness, to connection with an elemental vitality.[30]

Tillich suggests that "Protestant moralistic personalism . . . is distrustful of the ecstatic element in the Spiritual Presence and drives many people, in protest, toward an apersonal mysticism."[31] Over against this distrust, with its accompanying christocentrism, he wants to recapture and emphasize the spiritual dimension of theology—a dimension preserved in Eastern Orthodoxy and in the so-called Spirit-movements of the West (the Montanists, the radical Franciscans, the Anabaptists, the Quakers and Shakers, the Pentecostals, etc.). For Tillich this takes the form of a theology of "Spiritual Presence," elaborated in the fourth part of his system. He argues that the Spirit-movements were correct in claiming that the Spirit is not bound to any of its manifestations (in word and sacrament), but they were wrong in believing that Spirit does not need any sociocultural mediations whatsoever and is simply immediately present as a private "inner word." The latter could lead to an unchecked, illusory enthusiasm. The Spiritual Presence is essentially a social and communal rather than an isolated, private presence.[32] The divine Spirit does indeed indwell individual human beings, but this experience almost always occurs in a communal, interpersonal context, which lends structure, meaning, and checks to the experience.

What actually happens when divine Spirit dwells within or pours out upon human spirit? Something happens, says José Comblin, that cannot be wholly explained in normal human terms. People experience an empowerment by an unknown strength. "This *is* a human strength, but a human strength that suddenly comes upon people unprepared for it." The Holy Spirit acts in the form of human activity and is dependent on us to actualize itself. When it does so, however, we have what Comblin describes as "experiences of an unexpected transformation. People feel themselves taken hold of by new strength that makes them do things they had never thought of doing. Individuals and communities that had been downhearted, lacking in dynamism, resigned to the endless struggle for survival, discover themselves to be protagonists of a history far greater than themselves."[33]

Comblin is speaking of experiences of liberation that come upon oppressed and powerless people in Latin America, but the experience of the Spirit is similar for all people. When we find available the resources and power to go on when we have reached the end of the rope, when we are filled with hope in the midst of despair, when we are given the courage to act in the face of fear and discouragement—then we know that the Spirit has been "poured out" upon us and that we are "standing out" into God. This is life in the Spirit, and it is what spirituality is all about. It is the most fundamental of all religious experiences, the experience of a renewing and empowering power. Comblin describes it as the experience of action, freedom, speech, community, and above all life itself—the bringing of new life out of death.[34]

The Spirit and Christ

The relationship between Christ and the Spirit is a reciprocal one: Each encompasses and is dependent on the other but in distinctive ways. There is both "the Christ of the Spirit" and "the Spirit of Christ."[35] Precisely how this reciprocal relationship is to be understood constitutes an ancient and ongoing debate in Christian theology.

1. Christ is dependent on the Spirit in a twofold sense. First, according to the adoptionist and kenotic christologies (which are more retrievable today than strict incarnationism), what makes Jesus to be the Christ is the indwelling of the divine Spirit. His spirit was shaped by the divine Spirit (Sophia/Spirit, according to the earliest traditions) in ways regarded as disclosive and normative by the Christian community. It is the Spirit that engenders the Christ-gestalt in Jesus of Nazareth.[36] Stendahl makes the interesting observation that in the Synoptic Gospels the Spirit is not represented as the source of specific

divinely inspired words of Jesus. Rather the Spirit engenders and energizes Jesus' *action* in the form of a ministry of liberation, healing, and justice (see Luke 4:18–19). Jesus is not so much an inspired prophet who speaks divine words ("Thus says the Lord . . .") as he is a Spirit-filled agent of worldly transformation.[37]

Second, the shape of the risen Christ is no longer historical and sensible but present and spiritual. The Spirit is the instrument of Christ's contemporaneous presence to communities of believers, the means by which the Christ-gestalt fans and flames out to embrace the whole world. "Christ" is no longer incarnate in the individual body of Jesus of Nazareth but rather is infused into the world by the Spirit, which shapes corporate bodies of redemptive praxis (chap. 16, pp. 274–75). Thus Jesus cannot be the Christ without the Spirit, and the Christ cannot become redemptively efficacious for the world without the Spirit.

2. The Spirit is dependent on Christ in one fundamental sense: The Spirit known by the Christian community of faith is not any spirit or a multiplicity of spirits but the Spirit defined, profiled, discerned, interpreted (see 1 Cor. 2:13–14) by the concrete configuration of the Christ-gestalt in Jesus of Nazareth. The Spirit is "the Spirit of Jesus Christ." For Paul, who uses this expression, being "in Christ" and being "in the Spirit" are one and the same thing.

Just how this latter dependence is to be understood makes a considerable difference. Much of the Western church, and Reformed Protestantism in particular, have emphasized that "the function of the Spirit is essentially subservient and instrumental to the work of the incarnate Christ."[38] The Spirit comes after Christ in the divine economy according to both the Lukan and the Johannine accounts: "For as yet there was no Spirit, because Jesus was not yet glorified" (John 7:39). Jesus must withdraw from the scene in order for the Spirit to make its appearance. Paul draws this distinction in terms not of a temporal sequence but of the respective spheres of operation of Christ (objective) and the Spirit (subjective). According to George Hendry, who is a good modern representative of this view, the primary danger is that the presence of the Spirit will come to be viewed as superseding the presence of Christ; this is "the spiritualist heresy which has plagued the Church repeatedly from the time of Montanus onward." To guard against this heresy, a modification of the Nicene Creed was adopted at the Third Synod of Toledo in 589, specifying that the Holy Spirit proceeds "from the Father *and from the Son* (*filioque*)"—a modification not accepted by the Eastern church. This *filioque* assured the subordination of the Spirit to the Son in the West, guarding, according to Hendry, against "the danger of an undefined, unregulated, and, in the final count, unevangelical spirituality."[39]

With Paul Tillich, the emphasis is different. He agrees that "in the divine economy, the Spirit follows the Son," but adds, "in essence, the

Son *is* the Spirit." This can only mean that Spirit is the more fundamental and inclusive symbol of divine presence than the Son. The Spirit indwells and empowers the Son, not vice versa, but at the same time for Tillich the figure of Jesus as the Christ serves as the criterion of every new manifestation of the Spiritual Presence. Indeed, Tillich goes so far as to claim that "more than one manifestation of the Spiritual Presence claiming ultimacy would deny the very concept of ultimacy." In response it might be said that no single manifestation of the Spiritual Presence can claim ultimacy. Tillich is walking a tightrope on this issue. On the one hand he maintains the necessity of having a single central manifestation of the Spiritual Presence and warns against the danger of a "direct theocentric mysticism." On the other hand, he warns against any legalistic circumscription of the freedom of the Spirit such as has occurred in the Western church (Catholic and Protestant) through a scholastic application of the *filioque*. The impulse of his *Systematic Theology* is in the direction of the Spirit-movements and religious pluralism, but it is held in check by a lingering christocentrism shared with the other theologians of his generation.[40] Jürgen Moltmann provides a more thoroughgoing critique of the *filioque*, regarding it as destroying the reciprocity of relationships between the Son and the Spirit. "The Spirit *accompanies* the Son, *rests* in the Son, and *shines* from the Son." This, he says, "corresponds much better to the Spirit-history of Christ and the Christ-history of the Spirit" than any one-sided procession.[41]

We too must find a way of walking this tightrope, guarding against the dangers of both subordinationism (of the Spirit to Christ) and supersessionism (of Christ by the Spirit). The greater threat today for most Euro-American Protestants remains the former. The challenge is to work out a theology of the Spirit that embraces and empowers the Christ-gestalt without superseding it. The figure of Christ, we have said, represents the turn from the second to the third moment of the divine life, from worldly difference to spiritual mediation. The figure of Christ, for Christians, lends definition to both God-in-the-world and God-as-Spirit; thus Christ is essential to both but is not as inclusive as either of these moments.

Although subordinationism poses the greater threat to the vitality of the church in our time, and although a new emphasis on the Spirit provides a way of responding to concerns raised by feminism, ecology, and religious pluralism, we must also clearly recognize the danger of supersessionism. Ernst Troeltsch warned against a purely spiritual religion of the "third kingdom" (Joachim of Fiore's age of the Spirit): The problem is that such a kingdom, cut off from historical reality, will never arrive.[42] Or, if such a kingdom does arrive, it may do so in a fanatic, destructive form such as the Nazi "Third Reich."[43]

Nazism was in fact a fascist form of spirituality that held considerable appeal to those looking for a spiritual rejuvenation in the context of the crisis afflicting Germany and late-bourgeois culture. Philosophers such as Martin Heidegger and theologians such as Emanuel Hirsch and Friedrich Gogarten found in it an affirmation of spiritual and social harmony oriented to the distinctive needs of the German people, in contrast to the materialism, individualism, and anarchy of their time. They were basically authoritarian in their politics and believed that a strong leader was needed to give the people direction, unity, and purpose.[44] It is striking that the most fanatic ideologies (not only fascism but white supremacism, nationalism, communism, xenophobia, the samurai) often have a spiritual quality, and their leaders sometimes seem to be possessed by the spirit. There are in fact many spirits at loose in the world—false and evil spirits, perhaps demonic and destructive spirits. This fact is not attributable to an evil god, a real Satan or Devil, or to an evil principle within the godhead. Rather spirit is a potency whose specific character is determined by the elements with which it reacts. It readily can be distorted by human sin, and sin becomes objectified in structures that take on a demonic, spirit-like quality. Evil mimics the good, the demonic mimics the divine, destructive spirits mimic the Holy Spirit. Human beings strive to be "like God," and they are remarkably successful at this deception.

Because of this mimicry, this pervasive deception, it is necessary to be able to *discern* the spirits. For Christians, the shape of Christ incarnate and risen is the basis for discerning a Spirit that is true and holy, a Spirit of suffering love and reconciling freedom. But it is naive to think that this Christ, supposedly revealed in an authoritative scripture, provides an absolute criterion by which to judge history, for Christ is known and interpreted only through the witness of the Spirit in concrete situations.[45] It is the complex interplay of Christ and Spirit that enables Christians to make always ambiguous and relative judgments in history. There is no absolute guarantee against illusion and self-deception, no sacred authority to which to appeal, but rather a constant struggle of interpretation. The Spirit is our companion in that struggle, but how we use the Spirit is up to us. It behooves us to use it critically, suspicious of all claims to authority, rather than in a state of uncritical enthusiasm, whether for Christ or for nation. The critical principle is the true spiritual principle.[46]

In arguing for the emergence of the Spirit out of the interaction of God and the world, I have advocated a kind of double procession. The Spirit proceeds not from the Father and the Son but from God and the world. Thus there can be no question of a subordination of the Spirit to Christ, but does not such a proposal face the reverse danger of an uncritical spiritualism? The world produces many spirits, both good and evil. I offer two observations. First, the world that is the figure of God in the element of difference is not just any world but (from a Christian perspective) the world in process of being shaped and configured by Christ. Hence the world out of which the *Holy* Spirit proceeds is a christomorphizing world. The world does not outgrow Christ but grows into Christ, and it does so through the Spirit, which both precedes and follows the historical figure around whom the shape of Christ coalesced. The Spirit emerges neither independently of Christ nor in sole dependence on him. The relationship is one of a thoroughgoing reciprocity.

Second, the theological tradition thought only in terms of the opposition between Christ and Antichrist. There surely are Antichrists, and Hitler was one of them. But there are also those who are *other* than Christ, different from Christ without being antagonistic toward Christ. Today we must recognize a plurality of saving shapes of divine presence, and we should be able to affirm that the Spirit proceeds from this plurality, not from Christ alone. Ethical judgments about what is truly *anti-* (anti-human, anti-cosmic, anti-christic, anti-spiritual) are not thereby eviscerated but arise from a communicative consensus rather than from a solitary revelation.

The Work of the Spirit: The Liberation of the World, the Perfection of God

Two functions or activities have been attributed to the Spirit of God in traditional theology: (a) The Spirit as Paraclete, Illuminator, and Comforter is the power that inwardly mediates God's saving, liberating presence in the world both to individual human beings and to the human community, calling to us as an advocate or intercessor (*paraclesis*), illuminating us from within,[47] comforting and sustaining us through the struggles of life. If Christ is the figure of God's objective and individual presence, then the Spirit is the figure of God's (inter)subjective and communal presence. As Paraclete the Spirit is also an Interpreter (Josiah Royce) and a Transformer (H. Richard Niebuhr)—functions to which I shall refer in chapter 18. (b) The Spirit as Sanctifier and Perfecter is the power that brings all things to completion in God and thus completes the divine life itself. Here the Spirit is the figure of God's eschatological presence and as such is the quintessence of divine freedom, of God's being in-and-for-self.

We can express these two aspects of the being and activity of the Spirit of God as the *liberation of the world* and the *perfection (or freedom) of God*. They are the subject of the next two chapters.

The expression "liberation of the world" gathers up the whole process of the return of the world from alienated otherness and separateness to its end in the divine life: It is the process of redemption that constitutes history as a meaningful though always incomplete and ambiguous process. The return does not entail a reduction of the other to the same; precisely in redeeming it God allows the world to remain different from God, namely world. The Spirit is the indwelling power or *energeia* by which this process is engendered and sustained. "Come Holy Spirit—renew the *whole* creation." We can analyze this process in terms of concentric spheres of liberation: the Christian ecclesial community, the religions of the world, and the process of history as a whole, meaning both natural and human history. The spheres are concentric in the sense that they exist within and around each other and represent increasingly broad domains of the activity of Spirit. Many other themes could be included within a spirituality of liberation, which if fully developed would require a book in itself. At minimum a constructive theology needs a theology of the church, of religions, and of history, and only a brief sketch of these can be provided within the confines of the present work. Through all of these spheres a common thread of spirituality can be detected, namely (in Kovel's terms), "an overcoming of egoic relations of being," and a seeking of the whole through and beyond all the particular forms of creed, religion, nature, and history. Such a whole clears the world of idols and is the ground of true liberation.[48]

The expression "perfection of God" or "freedom of God" identifies the goal of this process in terms of what it means for the divine life itself (the triune figuration of God) and for the consummation of the world in God, its sanctification. The first work of the Spirit is cosmological and historical, while the second work is eschatological and eternal. Through both of these works the Spirit emerges as a distinct modality of the divine life: The Spirit does not preexist but comes into being as the world is liberated and God is perfected. The person of the Spirit is formed by the work of the Spirit.

18

THE LIBERATION OF THE WORLD: ECCLESIA, RELIGIONS, HISTORY

Ecclesia: Liberated Communion

Spirit and Community

Spirit is a community-creating power; spiritual presence engenders spiritual community. The intrinsic sociality and relatedness of Spirit is a central theme of modern philosophy from Hegel on. Hegel understood Spirit (*Geist*) to be the result or accomplishment of reciprocal recognition, and therefore to be essentially a holistic, social, intersubjective category. The individual subject is at most a phase in the development of Spirit, an abstraction from the larger concrete social whole. Individuals are not ontologically prior to the social but are always already embedded in and dependent on a social matrix. This matrix, which Hegel sometimes referred to as "objective Spirit," is not something mysterious and mystical, such as a group mind or consciousness, but is simply the "spiritual air . . . in which we breathe," the sphere in which we are situated and nurtured by culture, customs, language, ideas, values.[1]

According to Hegel, there are two kinds of community or two ways of conceiving community. One is an aggregate of atomic individuals who exist mostly in isolation and from whom social unity must be coerced, so that community is essentially heteronomous, limiting autonomous freedom. The other is a communion of freedom, a community of free communicative praxis, in which individuality is not suppressed but elevated to a higher cause, that of freedom and truth, the consciousness of a free people.

Only the latter is a spiritual community. It is spiritual because it is grounded in acts of mutual forgiveness and releasement, allowing the other to be other while remaining in relation to the other. God as Absolute Spirit *is* the event of reciprocal forgiveness, releasement, and love that makes community possible. Love is at one with its object, neither dominating it nor being dominated by it. In love the separate remains but in union. Hegel in his *Logic* describes the Absolute or the Universal as "the free power; it is itself and overreaches its other, but not in a dominating or forceful way. . . . It could also be called free love and limitless blessedness, for it is a relating to its other only as itself. In its other it has returned to itself."[2] Robert Williams comments: "Love transcends the standpoint of domination, and allows the other to be free. In such absolving love, there is no reduction of the other to the same or exclusion of difference from totality, but rather solidarity with the other. Self-recognition in other presupposes and requires that the other remain distinct, even as it is no longer purely other. Love transforms identity into a holistic conception that not only preserves, but requires otherness."[3]

The holism that constitutes Spirit entails a triadic rather than a monadic or dyadic social structure. It is not a matter of an absolute ego (I=I) positing the other as merely the self-othering of the ego, such that the other is reduced to the same. This is the received opinion about Hegel, but it is a false reading, a confusion of Hegel's position with that of a Kantian transcendental idealism. Nor is it a matter of an I and a You standing in infinite, irreducible otherness to each other (I vs. You). This is the position adopted by Emmanuel Levinas over against what he terms an Hegelian "totality." Rather it is a matter of a triple mediation in which I and You remain other yet related in a third, a We (I–You–We). The Spirit is the third, the We, the community. The We is no undifferentiated fusion of persons but a reciprocity of recognition that produces a new kind of differentiated wholeness, a liberated communion of free persons. This is the authentically Hegelian philosophy of Spirit.[4]

What God does in the world as Spirit is to engender spiritual community. The term "spiritual community," while a central concept for Paul Tillich,[5] was earlier employed by the American philosopher of religion Josiah Royce, who in turn borrowed and refined it from Hegel. Royce has a very suggestive theory of community. Communities depend on acts of interpretation, and interpretation involves a triadic process, namely, the introduction of a third, comparative idea or deed into a dyadic relationship, a third perspective that creates a unity of consciousness and action in the form of insight or vision. Creative insight comes from those who first compare and then mediate, who first see two great ideas at once, and then find a new third idea that mediates between and illumines them.[6]

Now God, according to Royce, is "the Interpreter who interprets all to all," the infinite Third that is present in every mediating idea.[7] The divine Spirit is the third reality, the living power unifying the many into a one, while the members as such remain individually distinct. A divine unifying power seems to be needed because of the individuality and conflicts that pervade the human social world. A unity that does not destroy but embraces finite entities, healing their mutual hostility, bringing good out of evil, seems to be attributable only to a transcendent cause, not to immanent human resources. An Interpreter is needed who breaks through the blockages and isolation of human existence and interprets "all to all." "Interpreter" is Royce's ingenious equivalent for the traditional name of the Holy Spirit, "Paraclete"—an advocate, intercessor, intermediary, interpreter (1 Cor. 2:13; 12:30; 14:13). It needs only to be added that such interpretation has not only a reconciling but also an emancipatory effect in the world since it is above all conditions of systematic exploitation that block communication. Thus the spiritual community is not only a beloved community (an expression borrowed from Royce by Howard Thurman and Martin Luther King Jr.) but also a liberated, free community.

Ecclesial Community as Spiritual Community[8]

The church is such a community. It exists in and through "the communion (*koinōnia*) of the Holy Spirit" (2 Cor. 13:14).[9] To articulate the connection between the community of those who confess Jesus to be the Christ and the work of the Holy Spirit, Paul and his followers made use of several images of building or shaping. What the Spirit does is to build, upbuild, shape a community, an "ecclesia" (in Greek the word means "assembly"). Our words "communion" and "community" derive from Latin roots meaning to "build" or "fortify": A community is a mutual building, a building for service (*munus*), an upbuilding through love. The ecclesia is described variously as "God's temple" (1 Cor. 3:16); a "spiritual house" (1 Peter 2:5); the "household of God" (Eph. 2:19); a "dwelling place for God" (Eph. 2:22).

The last two passages are from a text, Eph. 2:12–22, that contains a rich store of ecclesial images. The author (a Paulinist but not Paul himself) argues that the division of Jews and Gentiles into alien communities has been overcome "by the blood of Christ." Christ's purpose was to "reconcile both groups to God in one body through the cross." This "one body" is described in terms of the building images that have been referred to, and the "one Spirit" of God is active in the building process. "So then you are no longer strangers and aliens, but you are citizens with the saints and also members of the household of God, built upon the foundation of the apostles and prophets, with Christ himself as the cornerstone. In him the whole structure is joined together and grows into a holy temple in the Lord; in whom you also are built together spiritually into a dwelling place for God." If Christ is the cornerstone, the builder or shaper is the Spirit, and the edifice is the ecclesia in which the "dividing wall" of hostility has broken down and "one new humanity" is in process of being fashioned.

In this way, several ecclesial images found in the New Testament—people of God, body of Christ, communion of faith and love, creation of the Spirit—are gathered together and modified. The new people of God is not to exist at enmity with the old; both peoples are to be incorporated into one body, founded on the blood of Christ. This body is a true communion or fellowship, in which there are no longer aliens and strangers but fellow citizens, members of God's household. And the bond or matrix of this building, household, temple, is the redemptive presence, the indwelling, the upbuilding, creative work of God as Spirit. Ecclesia, in brief, is the community of the Spirit, the spiritual community, and God in the Spirit is God existing as community.

In the doctrinal tradition, Augustine was the first to expand upon this image in a profound way. The Holy Spirit is the bond of love and as such is the "soul" that indwells and quickens the mystical body, which is a fellowship of love. The idea of the Spirit as the "soul" of the body that is the church was employed by Thomas Aquinas in his attempt to moderate the ecclesiology of papal primacy. The image was put to similar use by the Tübingen school in nineteenth-century Catholicism and by the French *nouvelle théologie* in the twentieth century. This was the background of the innovative ecclesiology of the Second Vatican Council, of which Hans Küng is one of the best contemporary representatives.[10]

In modern Protestant theology, the idea of the church as a spiritual community originated with Schleiermacher and Hegel and became the centerpiece of Tillich's ecclesiology.[11] Among these innovative thinkers, Hegel is especially suggestive. The essence of the spiritual community, he said, is a unique, transfigured intersubjectivity, distinguishable from all other forms of human love and friendship. Privatistic and exclusivistic modes of existence are set aside, as are distinctions based on mastery, power, position, sex, and wealth. In their place are actualized a truly universal justice and freedom. The name Holy Spirit signifies the unifying and liberating power of the "infinite love that arises from infinite anguish," the same love that was objectively represented on the cross of Christ but that now works inwardly, subjectively, building up a new human community: "This is the Spirit of God, or God as the present, actual Spirit, God dwelling in God's community." Thus "the community itself is the existing Spirit, the Spirit in its existence, God existing as community." God in the modality of Spirit *is* the redemptive, transfigurative power that indwells and constitutes a new human intersubjectivity, an intersubjectivity shaped by the paradigmatic love of Christ, which is an "infinite love in infinite anguish." This love, when shed abroad in the world, engenders a communion of free people. Such a communion is the church, but in Hegel's view it is not to be restricted to the church; its mission is to become the substance of the world.[12]

Definition of the Ecclesial Community: Liberated Communion[13]

Ecclesia is a transfigured mode of human community, an image of God's project for the world embodied in a diversity of historical churches, comprising a plurality of peoples and cultural traditions, founded upon the life, death, and resurrection of Christ, created by the redemptive presence of God as Spirit. It is a community in which privatistic, provincial, and hierarchical modes of existence are challenged and being overcome, and in which is fragmentarily actualized a universal reconciling love that liberates from sin and death, alienation and oppression.

Several implications of this definition will be explored.

1. Ecclesia is an anticipatory sign and sacrament of God's project—the basileia vision of Jesus, the vision of a new community brought into being by God's saving, transformative presence, the productive ideal of a new way of being communally human in the world and before God, a liberated communion of free subjects, an inheritance of freedom imaged in the ecclesia of freedom. This productive ideal works within history as a power—not a causal power but a creative, luring, shaping power that creates new life and actualizes redemption in a variety of historical forms, social and individual. But this ideal transcends history precisely as it works within history; it cannot be identified with an actual or a future state of affairs; it can only be anticipated, never grasped or finished.

When the actualization of redemption occurs in and through the historical churches, the result is ecclesia, which is a determinate form of basileia—the shape it takes when faith in Jesus as the Christ and relationship to the life, death, and resurrection of Jesus are explicit and establish the specific contours of redemption. Ecclesia thus understood is, like Spirit itself, a mediating reality: It participates in both the ideality of the basileia and the reality of the historical churches. It does not exist as an entity beside the churches but is their inner essence and telos, the source of everything that makes them churches. As a mediating, spiritual reality, ecclesia is unambiguous but fragmentary: It participates in the saving power of the basileia (God's world-transforming redemptive presence), disclosing it unambiguously but actualizing it only fragmentarily because the instruments of actualization are historical and finite.

As a critical principle, ecclesia is unambiguous; as a practical principle, fragmentary. Hence the definition says that distorted modes of existence "are challenged and being overcome" in the ecclesial community; in it liberating love is truly envisioned but only "fragmentarily actualized." In brief, ecclesia links together basileia vision and real churches: Without their ecclesial essence, the churches would be merely human, social institutions; and without the ecclesial community, God's freedom project would become historically actual only in diffused, anonymous forms.

2. The definition incorporates several biblical images of the church—people, body, communion, Spirit—allowing these ancient symbols to help establish the lineaments of a new ecclesiology. Ecclesia is the people of God, one people yet drawn from a plurality of peoples and cultural traditions. It is the body whose unique intersubjectivity is shaped by the life, death, and resurrection of Christ. It is a transfigured mode of human community, a koinonia of faith, hope, love. And its source of vitality is the creative, upbuilding work of the Spirit of God.

3. The definition also incorporates the classic doctrinal marks of the church—one, holy, catholic, apostolic—while attempting to reformulate them in light of new expectations. The church's unity is fashioned out of plurality and seeks the common ground not only of Christian faith but of the many human modes of apprehending the holy. Its catholicity, its inner wholeness or integrity, resides in its overcoming privatistic, provincial, and hierarchical modes of existence and in its orientation to the universal redemption of humanity. Ecclesia has a peculiarly self-surpassing character: It knows no ethnic, spatial, or temporal boundaries and is intrinsically nonprovincial. There are no absolute strangers, for God's redemption has no specific cultural conditions. It is radically universal, available in and through any cultural wrappings. The wrappings do not disappear, but they are relativized: This is the true meaning of catholicity. The church's holiness consists in its ecclesial essence as a liberated communion of free subjects under the grace of God; it exists by grace alone, but is a communion of sinners as well as of saints. And its apostolicity takes the form of witness to Christ and mission in his name; it exists by Christ alone, but its mission, its apostolic mission, entails service in and to the world and a sharing in common struggles against dehumanization, alienation, and oppression.

4. The definition responds to the exigencies of our time. I am attempting to understand the church in terms oriented to the praxis of liberation. Ecclesial community is human community transfigured in the direction of liberation—liberation through Christ from all provincialisms and oppressions based on race, sex, sexual orientation, class, dogma, ideology, location, culture; liberation from personal and social forms of sin, from the burdens of law and guilty conscience, from the

ultimate emptiness and alienation of death. Freedom is the critical mark of ecclesia in our time. The definition hints also at our ecumenical, global context by suggesting that the ecclesial community encompasses a plurality of peoples and cultural traditions and is but one of several religio-cultural shapes assumed by what Christians call the "kingdom of God" but what other religions give other names.

It should be clear that this definition with its particular way of retrieving and integrating the images and marks of the church reflects the ecumenical, liberative, and critical exigencies of our time. In this respect, it is a contingent, relative definition that has no pretense of being perennially valid.

5. Of course, no actual church adequately embodies the elements of this definition, but when an actual church asks itself what it ought to be, it cannot avoid reflecting upon itself in some such fashion as this unless it is willing to give up the question of its essential being. Without the discipline of critical self-reflection, the church would succumb to its persistent tendency to lose its ecclesial essence—to drift into becoming a privatistic, alienated, merely human association serving certain social functions such as the disburdening of individuals and the maintenance of authority structures. We know all too well that churches can fail miserably as ecclesial communities, can in fact become positively antiecclesial. It is all the more important, therefore, to be able to specify what the essential and constitutive features of ecclesia are, in order to have a critical principle against which these distortions can be measured.

No definition can of itself combat the distortions. If we were to remain at the stage of definition, the definition itself would be falsified: The church must become in praxis what it understands itself to be in essence, and often it only discovers in praxis what it ought to be in essence. True praxis requires a critical theory, and the latter is only a theory of praxis. By entering into praxis, we are entering into the realm of historical struggle, conflict, and compromise. An abstract or rigid idealism at this point does no good at all. The very purpose of having a productive or practical ideal such as that of the ecclesia of freedom is to realize it in historical forms. Such an ideal can in fact be a tremendously powerful factor in the historical process. But the process is a continuing one, requiring constant vigilance and a recognition that all historical realizations of ecclesial freedom are incomplete.

Elements of the Ecclesial Community

Necessary to the praxis of the church are a leadership and certain structured activities—interpretation, sacramentality, caring and justice, ecumenical and world openness—that assume an institutional character without which the church could not survive in history or have an effect on it.[14]

Leadership

The fundamental role of ministry is that of leadership—leadership in the community of Jesus Christ.[15] The words "priest" and "presbyter" derive from an Indo-European root similar to the Sanskrit *purugava,* meaning "guide" or "leader." This was the original and most fundamental function of ministry; only later did sacerdotal, substitutionary, hierarchical functions accrue to the office. What authorizes ministry is not the possession of jurisdiction, office, consecration, or special "call," but rather the possession of knowledge, skill, commitment, and character. Certainly commitment is a kind of "call," but it need not be a direct and identifiable personal experience, nor does it alone make one competent for ministry. Ordination is basically a matter of recognizing and certifying the possession of such knowledge, skill, commitment, and character. It does not confer sacral power or authority, and it should not lead to a separate clergy class.

I am proposing a democratic-participative-secular model of ministerial office as distinguished from a hierarchical-authoritarian-sacerdotal model. Not only is this model closer to the practice of the early church, as numerous studies have shown,[16] but also it is required by the context of ministry today. The minister as leader should empower the common ministry of the whole people. True leadership is not simply management or administration, and it cannot be accomplished through the application of management skills. Ministerial leadership involves at heart articulating a vision of what the church is, its essential being, its purpose, and enabling this vision to become a productive ideal that infuses all church activities and all participants. Above all, true leadership is the antithesis of clericalism, which Rosemary Radford Ruether defines as "the separation of ministry from mutual interaction with community and its transformation into hierarchically ordered castes of clergy and laity."[17]

One of the features of clericalism is the preservation of ministry as a (celibate) male caste. Nothing could be a deeper perversion of what "ministry" is about, namely ministration, service, *diakonia,* nurture. It is self-evident that women often have special gifts of ministry, and their exclusion from this office has been a terrible scandal and loss. It also is likely that women will play a major role in the future leadership of the church, Catholic as well as Protestant. It is a matter of time, struggle, courage in the Spirit—and large quantities of each will be needed, considering the depth of lingering resistance.[18] Resistance is even greater to the ordination of gays and lesbians, who also often bring gifts of ministry. This is an injustice that contradicts the very essence of the ecclesial community. If one of the features of this community is its nonprovinciality, its openness to all persons regardless of race, culture, class, gender, or sexual orientation, then the same openness must apply to its leadership. The only relevant criteria for the latter are knowledge, skill, commitment, and character. It should not have to be said that gender and sexual orientation have nothing to do with these criteria.

Interpretation

The church maintains its identity over time, as well as adjusts to the demands of new times, through processes of interpretation and reenactment. These processes have a double referent: to the objective repres entation of meaning in the documents, symbols, and rites of the community, and to the internalization of meaning by its individual members. A community, says James Gustafson, is essentially a time-process: a community of memory and expectation, a community that has an objective spirit by means of which it is able to make the lived experience of the past its own lived experience, a community in which the past comes alive through the communication of significant symbols.[19]

Interpretation refers to the meaning side of this process and includes such activities as preaching, teaching of scripture and tradition, doing scholarly research and constructive theology, interpreting the present situation. The resources of the tradition for redemptive transformation are enormously rich. But they must be interpreted, used critically, appropriated in what Paul Ricoeur calls a "second naïveté."[20] A relationship of immediacy or first naïveté to scripture and tradition is no longer feasible once people have been exposed to historical consciousness and modern science. (It is, of course, possible to forget this exposure when it comes to religion and thus to live in two worlds, one precritical and mythical, the other scientific and secular.) In a postcritical context, the power and meaning of texts can be released only through interpretation, but they can indeed be released quite powerfully in this way.

The ecclesial tradition includes a great deal more than the Hebrew and Christian scriptures. These are undoubtedly the norm, the classic, the center, but it would be an impoverishment to insist that they are the whole and sacrosanct. Protestant preaching has almost always been based solely on biblical texts, but it is not self-evident why this should be the case, why it should be deemed inappropriate to draw upon texts from the great postbiblical tradition, which has its own classics, along with scriptural texts. Even churches that are relatively sophisticated in the study of scripture generally share a vast ignorance of Christian theology throughout the history of the church. Of course, there is no canon of tradition, at least for Protestants, but canonical status finally does not resolve anything with respect to the meaning and truth of biblical texts either. There is no avoiding the risk, the conflict, and the interplay of interpretations. Truth is strong, and it will win out in such a process. Part of the hard work of ministry is to guide and nurture the interpretative process. There is in fact a hunger among people for genuine learning and instruction, and a willingness to go much further than is generally thought possible. The problem in part is lack of leadership, an inability to conceive and construct a total educational program in which every facet of congregational life becomes an appropriation and reconfiguration of the tradition.

Sacramentality[21]

Sacramentality refers to the ritual and reenactment side of the process of maintaining ecclesial identity through time. Human beings live by rites and symbols as well as words and ideas. If the community is the embodiment of the risen Christ, then the community itself is embodied by ritual actions that mark its distinctive identity in the world. Virtually all Christian churches recognize at least two sacraments, baptism and the Lord's Supper, which signify the initiation and renewal of one's participation in the transfigured life of the community of faith. Both are associated with the shape of Christ incarnate in Jesus of Nazareth, the shape of anguished love and reconciling freedom. By partaking of the body and blood of Christ, we become one with his death and resurrection; by sharing in his baptism we are born anew of the Spirit. Roman Catholic and Eastern Orthodox churches recognize additional sacraments—confirmation, penance, extreme unction, ordination, matrimony—all of which mark significant stages in the pilgrimage of a Christian. Augustine regarded the preaching of the word as a sacrament. By contrast, the Quakers acknowledge no sacraments other than silence, the need for openness in the presence of the Holy Spirit.

Beyond specific sacraments, the whole of the liturgy is sacramental in the sense of evoking God's spiritual presence in embodied form—singing and praying, praising and thanking, moving and dancing, partaking and sending. Sacraments are an affirmation that the sensuous is spiritual and the spiritual sensuous. Like the Spirit they emerge out of the interaction of God and the world, and thus they are intrinsically spiritual in character. They are worldly shapes of God's sanctifying grace. Everything in the world has the potential to become a sacrament, a mediation of the sacred. We need have only eyes to see and ears to hear. Our eyes and ears are trained by the rituals and liturgy of the church.

Caring and Justice

The "sending" that is part of the liturgy (*leitourgia*, the "work of the people," the "service of God") points to other forms of enactment that are equally essential to the life of the community. These may be broadly described as caring for specific and individual human needs, and engaging in the work of social justice by which the community ministers to the needs of the world. These are ways in which the distinctive intersubjectivity of the ecclesial community—its intrinsic nonprovinciality and openness—is put into practice.

The church's praxis is multifaceted, encompassing personal healing and piety, eucharistic and liturgical celebration, and world-transforming mission. This praxis must be seen as a whole; alienation occurs when it is fragmented. Many congregational and individual problems stem from this fragmentation: Personal crises are often related to a loss of meaningful context, of objective purpose in life; eucharist without human solidarity is an empty gesture; praxis without spiritual purpose is ideology. The minister's role is to nurture a wholeness of vision in which these things fit together in a productive way. Most middle-class Christians think of social ministry in terms of works of charity or philanthropy rather than in terms of systemic change or structural reform. It is of course both—a matter of both love and justice, of both responding to immediate, concrete needs and working for long-term reforms. But it is all too easy (because less threatening) to concentrate on the former while forgetting the latter. Most congregations—most of us!—could benefit from a good deal of consciousness-raising with respect to the facts of social injustice, structural oppression, racism, sexism, classism, homophobia. We must come to see these evils as part of the totality of sin and to see their combating as related to the confession of faith in God—for to know God *is* to do justice. This too is part of the hard work of ministry.[22]

Ecumenical and World Openness

The fundamental thrust of Christian faith is a movement beyond provincialism in all forms toward a universal community of redemption. Everything culture-specific in Christianity is relativized without being discarded. We have the universal, the divine, only in and through the particular, but the particular is not an ultimate end in itself: It is the bearer of, and points beyond itself to, the universal. The church is a work of the Spirit in a specifically christic "domain of resonance,"[23] but it is oriented to more encompassing global domains.

The work of ministry faces several sets of problems at this point, among them the need to challenge local, regional, and denominational parochialism. Because of limited experience, people tend to think that the way they do things is the best or only way, that what they believe is alone right and true. It is all too easy to be absorbed by what is familiar and ready to hand. Horizons need to be opened up, stretched, expanded. The fact is that distinctive denominational or confessional traditions are not very relevant in today's world. The real issues cut across the traditions and are not much illuminated by them—issues such as the credibility of belief in God, the meaning of Jesus' death and resurrection, the nature of human sin, the threat of nuclear and environmental holocaust, the perplexities of personal crisis, the shock of massive poverty.

Ministerial leadership requires helping people come to terms with two further facts. The first is that Christianity is a world religion, largely non-Protestant, increasingly non-Western, encompassing a great variety of cultures and traditions, with enormous potential for both good and ill.[24] The institutional expression of this awareness is the ecumenical movement, but it is one that is downplayed by today's churches. The second fact is that Christianity is only one of the great religious and ethical systems of humanity, that it cannot expect to evangelize or prevail over the others, that all claims to superiority are parochial, that the survival of all may depend on finding new bases for spiritual unity that transcend anything we now know. Here the institutional expression is interreligious dialogue, but again it is one that is not on the agenda of most local churches. Helping people to appreciate that this twofold recognition is part of the very process of deepening ourselves in the truth and validity of our own faith is one of the severest, noblest works of ministry.

Religions: Plurality and Solidarity

Plurality

Chapter 8 described one of the postmodern quests as "dialogical" and examined this theme in its application to interreligious dialogue. There I summarized the transition to a pluralistic theology of religions as advocated by a number of scholars whose essays are published in *The Myth of Christian Uniqueness* (1987) and also looked briefly at some of the questions about religious pluralism raised by contributors to *Christian Uniqueness Reconsidered* (1990) as well as by others. I concluded by agreeing with John Cobb that the objective of interreligious dialogue is to avoid religious essentialism (the assumption that there exists a common essence of religion) on the one hand and conceptual relativism (the view that religious truths are totally context-dependent) on the other hand. The alternative is to affirm both the plurality and the solidarity of the religions.

This task can be addressed by first considering more closely the arguments of the most radical critics of religious pluralism and global theology. These are ably represented by three of the contributors to *Christian Uniqueness Reconsidered:* J. A. DiNoia, John Milbank, and Kenneth Surin.[25] They make several claims: (1) that the discourse of "pluralism" and "dialogue" is actually a Western form of domination that obscures the truth of difference; (2) that religions are unique cultural-linguistic-social systems that construct their own worldviews and cannot be integrated into new hybrids; (3) that the propositional force of doctrines must be preserved since only this provides a basis for debating the truth of religious claims; (4) that the so-called "praxis solution" (collaboration based on practical goals rather than theoretical agreement) presupposes the values articulated by Western secular liberalism (justice, freedom, equality, etc.) and ignores any theological basis of reconciliation; (5) that the material conditions for a global theology are lacking in light of new manifestations of Western hegemony and colonialism (multinational corporations, the ideology of free markets, etc.); (6) that since the likely goal of conversation is conversion, it must be subject to the hermeneutics of suspicion; (7) and in general that the global project homogenizes differences, systematically overlooks real and persistent asymmetries of power, and allows for no intractable otherness.

These are serious and weighty objections that must not be passed over lightly. It is clear, in the first place, that these critics are no advocates of Christian inclusivism or exclusivism; they themselves belong in the pluralist camp but are pressing for a more radical pluralism—a pluralism of separation rather than of solidarity. They are engaged in the deconstruction of dialogue rather than in a return to cultural domination or religious absolutism. They rightly highlight the difficulties of dialogue across deep cultural and religious differences; their warnings against naïveté, optimism, essentialism, power imbalances, and homogenization are well-taken. At the same time they have a tendency to caricature the pluralist position and not to acknowledge its own recognition of these complexities. The categories of dialogue, pluralism, justice, freedom, equality, etc., may well be Western in provenance, but that in itself does not invalidate them; they represent a Western contribution to human self-understanding and well-being. Besides, as Aloysius Pieris points out,[26] Asia has always been pluralistic, and its religions are seeking liberation in a variety of forms. To claim these categories as simply Western is itself a form of cultural imperialism.

The argument that the propositional force of doctrines must be preserved since only this provides a basis for debating the truth of religious claims is advanced in detail by Paul Griffiths.[27] While appreciating the brilliance with which he makes the case, I am not persuaded by it. The propositional view of language and truth is subject to serious objections if it claims to be solely valid. Griffiths argues for not only a negative apologetics (defense against a critique of one's own truth-claims) but also a positive apologetics (designed to show that the doctrine-expressing sentences of a particular religious community are cognitively superior to those of another religious community). Yet in his own example of "apologetics in action" (Buddhists and Christians on human selfhood), he himself scarcely engages in positive apologetics, seeming to shy away from its aggressiveness. He offers primarily a negative apologetics, a defense of the Christian doctrine of soul, couched in very traditional, classic terms. Buddhist and Christian anthropologies seem to be static, unchanging in their essential features. He insists that both kinds of apologetics are "occasional," but one wonders how this could be if religious differences are as widespread, deep, and intractable as he claims. It would seem rather on his model that apologetics would be a constant feature of interreligious discourse. Griffiths states that the proper goal of apologetics is one not of vindication and victory but of problem-solving, learning, modifying previously held views, gaining heuristic insight, and so on. But it would seem that such goals, which are incompatible with the assertion of cognitive superiority, would be more readily attained by nonapologetic dialogue. This does not, of course, exclude vigorous debate over truth-claims.

All human beings have language and a capacity for communication. When people come together from radically different cultural contexts, the natural tendency is for conversation to ensue and a certain common "shaky ground"[28] to be fashioned. Truth and values are capable of *emerging* out of difference through dialogue rather than being imported a priori. The only precondition is the willingness to talk and listen. If we do not talk, we are likely to fight. Dialogue is the conversion of conflict from violent to nonviolent forms. Despite the distortions and agendas present in it, dialogue can become a kind of solvent that opens new possibilities and converts contradictions into differences.

In the final analysis, the postpluralists do not offer a credible alternative to dialogue. They keep their own theological, ethical, and hermeneutical agendas well-concealed. Is it to be a matter of mutual suspicion? Conversion-oriented apologetics? Total conceptual relativism? Aesthetic reveling in heterogeneity and indecipherable particularities? Nihilistic wallowing in the realities of dominance and hegemony? Or ceaseless conflicts between cultural-linguistic systems, sometimes erupting into violence and religious wars?

I affirm the quest for a more radical pluralism, but let it be a pluralism of solidarity rather than of separation. Anything less than this not only threatens human survival in an interdependent, nuclear world but betrays a lack of faith. Confidence in the possibility of mutual transformation through dialogue is properly grounded not in an optimistic humanism but in a realistic theology of spiritual presence: Spirit is the third, the Interpreter who interprets all to all.

This Spirit must be understood as in some sense plural or pluriform—a whole emerging out of the inexhaustible diversity of the world fused with the incomprehensible oneness of God. The universe is a whole without a single center, yet it works together as a system through an interplay of centers. This sort of unitive pluralism or plurality-in-unity can be understood theologically in trinitarian terms, as I have attempted to do throughout this work. Or it can be understood in apophatic terms as the nonbeing, silence, and mystery of God.[29] Both approaches affirm the radical relativity of God, which means that God shares in the plurality and solidarity of the religions that know God, and even of those that know no God. The many religions reflect the manifoldness of God, who is inexhaustible and incomprehensible. The solidarity of religions hints at the wholeness of God, who is one in and through the most radical diversity.

Solidarity: Criteria of Dialogue

Solidarity is achieved through dialogue, not apologetics, but this does not mean that it excludes rigorous argument about meaning and truth. To the contrary, as Paul Knitter points out, dialogue must be based on personal religious experience and firm truth-claims. What is really experienced to be true cannot be true "only for me." At the same time, dialogue must be based on the recognition of the possible truth in all religions, and this presupposes that there must be some common ground and goal for all religions, even if this ground itself has the character of diversity and can be known only in a plurality of ways. Finally, says Knitter, dialogue must be based on openness to the possibility of genuine change or conversion—not conversion to another faith but to a deeper and broader understanding of one's own faith.

Following John Dunne, Knitter suggests that the method of interreligious dialogue involves a process of passing over to the standpoint of another culture, way of life, or religion, and then coming back with new insight to one's own culture. Passing over and coming back require the exercise of a sympathetic and constructive imagination, the ability to project ourselves sympathetically into the life and thought of others and then to think constructively about how our own perspective (and perhaps that of the other) is modified and enriched through encounter. The capacity for such imagination is found in all the great cultures and religions. Dialogue presupposes a new model of truth, whose criterion is not that of exclusion but rather that of the ability to relate to other expressions of truth and to grow through these relationships. Truth-through-relationship enables us to affirm that each religion has a particular grasp of divine truth, and that religions relate to each other in terms not of contradictions but of dialogical tensions and creative polarities. Truth is by nature dialectical: Every discovery and insight must be balanced by its opposite, every statement is both true and not true. Each religion needs what the others can give. All this cries out for theological interpretation—that is, for a global theology or a theology of religions.[30]

Toward a Global Theology of Religions

Paul Tillich was among the first to recognize the need for a global theology of religions. In his last public lecture he called for an "interpenetration of systematic theological study and religious historical studies," and he set forth several systematic presuppositions of a theology of religions: (1) Revelatory experiences are universally human and mediate saving powers that transcend humans. (2) All revelation is limited by finite and estranged situations, hence no revelation is fully transparent and comprehensible. (3) There is a revelatory process in history that subjects all revelation to criticism. (4) There *may* be a central event that unites the positive results of the critical developments and makes possible a universal theology of religions, but this central event must be assumed to be the *goal* of an emerging common history of religions, not some past event belonging to a particular religion. (5) History of religions belongs together with history of culture since the sacred does not lie beside the secular but is its depth as the creative ground and critical judgment of the secular.[31]

In sum, Tillich is pointing to "a dynamic historical process in which the various religions mutually criticize and correct each other,"[32] possibly converging toward a central and as yet unknown goal. Thus a theology of religions seems to have two tasks, one critical and the other constructive, which I described earlier as "exposing idolatries and drawing out convergent truths" (chap. 8, pp. 106–8). I would imagine that the Spirit is at work in both of these tasks as a "refining fire" that burns away the evil present in all religions and as an "attracting wind" that draws the religions into mutually enriching dialogue and practices. Where the Spirit is leading on this adventure no one knows. I do not believe it is toward a monolithic world religion but rather toward the discovery of a liberative and compassionate core of spiritual truth present in the great religious traditions. I believe there can and will be a heightened appreciation of both plurality and solidarity among the religions. Solidarity arises through a mutually correcting coalescence of diverse interests and insights rather than by the imposition of totalitarian claims. The plurality will frequently remain recalcitrant, resistant to easy unification; and when solidarity is achieved under such conditions it is a spiritual gift.

Theology of religions, Tillich also says, is part of a larger concentric circle, that of a theology of culture and history. The waters across which the Spirit is sweeping include all of history, natural as well as human history; the religions represent the depth dimension of history; and one religion, the Christian, provides the vantage point from which "we" (the author and presumably most of the readers of this book) view the whole. Thus the religions form a bridge between ecclesia and history as spheres comprising the liberative work of the Spirit. This is not just a formal bridge; interreligious dialogue sheds light on our understanding of both ecclesial community and world history.

Let us now consider more closely the critical and constructive components of a theology of religions. Idolatry involves the confusion of our images of divinity (our "idols" or "icons") with divinity itself, and thus the worship of the idols (images, doctrines, scriptures, cultural-linguistic systems) rather than the divinity.[33] All religions fall into idolatry, and all must be continually liberated from it. The reason is that on the one hand ultimate reality is elusive and mysterious, while on the other hand we humans crave security and certainty. Thus the temptation to claim that *our* system of beliefs and values is alone true and absolute proves irresistible. Difference is necessary in religious matters because the universal can be revealed only in a plurality of particular, concrete configurations; but we blind ourselves to this fact and instead seek to reduce the other to the same (*our* same). This reduction often assumes violent and destructive forms. Tragically, the history of religions is the history of violence—a violence waged both externally, against other religions, and internally, against deviation from established and self-legitimating authorities. The violence takes both physical and psychological forms and is directed against both individuals and groups. A current example of psychological violence within the Christian religion is the exclusion of women, gays and lesbians from ordained ministry; other religions make similar exclusions. One task of a theology of religions is to expose this violence with its accompanying dogmatism and sectarianism, to combat what Joseph Kitagawa calls "the self-authenticating circularity common to religious traditions." Critical dialogue among the religions can serve as a refining fire that burns away what is false, evil, and idolatrous in each of them. If, at the beginning of the third millennium of the common era, something like this does not happen, humanity is likely to consume itself instead.[34]

The constructive component is that of enhancing solidarity by drawing out convergent truths and common practices. This can be likened to the attracting power of the wind of Spirit that draws us into its source, a source that we can never see or grasp. Human beings do have, or discover, the capacity for breaking the impasse of incommensurability and violence, for recognizing and criticizing their own idolatry. This capacity is the gift of the Spirit. There is within us as humans, says Julius Lipner, a generic open-endedness and a capacity for constructive imagination, an ability to break out of our own frameworks and confessional identities. It is in fact possible to share in the praxis of another religion and to shape a common spirituality; this is happening today among Buddhists and Christians in Sri Lanka at the dialogue center directed by Aloysius Pieris. Yet we must be cautious. The goal is not syncretism or synthesis but symbiosis—living together in mutual interdependence. The objective is not assimilation but appreciation, not conversion but mutual transformation.[35]

Several steps toward a global theology that builds solidarity have been taken by thinkers in our generation. It is fitting that there is a plurality of such approaches and that they cannot be readily synthesized although common themes emerge. The pioneer is Wilfred Cantwell Smith.[36] Major contributions have been made by Raimundo Panikkar, John Cobb, John Hick, Paul Knitter, and Aloysius Pieris.[37] More recently Robert Neville has essayed a "comparative theology," focusing on Chinese religions and Christianity.[38] Ross Reat and Edmund Perry have co-authored a "world theology" that fashions the concept of a "central spiritual reality of humankind" out of comparative religious studies.[39] David Krieger has developed a "global theology" based on a Wittgensteinian theory of "universal discourse."[40] Each of these studies merits close attention, and others are sure to follow. For the sake of brevity I will consider Krieger's work and then, by way of offering some concrete examples of global theology, conclude with a brief look at Buddhist and Christian views of community, history, and eschatology.

Krieger starts from Wittgenstein's conviction, expressed in his later writings, that the meaning of language derives from its use, and that the usage which gives language meaning cannot be private. Rather it must be intersubjective and communal, and the community in which linguistic praxis takes place cannot be arbitrarily limited. Every language-game presupposes and points toward a universal community of discourse where it is subject to correction and supplementation. Corrigibility and openness to a community of discourse that is unlimited in principle is a condition of all meaningful speaking and thinking. The form of life of such a universal community is one shaped by the intenticnality of communication, of sharing meaning, of dis-closure. Krieger believes that such a community provides the foundation for a "pragmatics of cosmotheandric solidarity," a "universal horizon of encounter," a mutually interdependent "global form of life."[41]

Following Raimundo Panikkar, Krieger distinguishes among three levels of discourse: (1) within a culture, a "morphological" discourse, which argues about states of affairs; (2) with a past culture, a "diachronic" discourse, which overcomes the distancing and alienation of meaning through time; and (3) between contemporary cultures, a "diatopical" discourse in which radically different horizons (or *topoi*) of meaning may encounter one another. Diachronic discourse, by projecting unity, totality, universality, is a discourse of closure. Interreligious dialogue occurs primarily at the third level, in the diatopical space that precedes all identity, a space of difference, of dis-continuity, of dis-closure. On the one hand, it is a discourse of *difference*, which lets the difference between transcendent faith and particular beliefs appear (corresponding to the ontological difference between Being and beings). On the other hand, it is a difference of *discourse*, a discursive difference, a difference that issues in dialogical solidarity rather than apologetic antagonism. It moves beyond primal violence and social resistance to a pragmatics of nonviolence, a horizon of encounter that transforms the violence of exclusion into a solidarity from which speech may arise. It opens human existence to the cosmic and the divine, thus grounding a cosmotheandric solidarity.[42]

Mahatma Gandhi termed the pragmatic conditions of such a universal discourse *satyagraha*, a quiet and irresistible pursuit of truth. *Satya*, truth/the true (God), requires *ahimsa*, nonviolence, and *tapas*, suffering. Nonviolence is necessary because no one possesses absolute truth, only fragments of truth, and thus no one is allowed to force his or her partial truth on others. Nonviolence is capable of instituting community because it participates in the power of truth, a power greater than all violence. Suffering is needed because the only way to break the ideological absolutization of a particular worldview is by solidarity with the enemy and voluntary suffering. Nonviolent resistance and voluntary suffering break the logic of suspicion, condemnation, self-justification, and make it possible for conflicts to be carried on within the domain of discourse.[43]

It is significant that Gandhi called this pursuit of truth "soul force" or "spiritual force." It is the power of the Spirit, not the power of weapons and wealth, that engenders a universal community of discourse. Spirit has the power to open a truly global, noncoercive community of communication, of cosmotheandric solidarity, in which differences are honored and all sides are turned toward truth.[44]

Buddhist and Christian Views of Community, History, and Eschatology

Implications for a theology of ecclesial community are immediately evident from Gandhian *satyagraha* and the accompanying theory of a universal community of discourse. Surely the Christian church, of all human institutions, ought to be such a community, a liberated communion of free people; yet it rarely is. Here resources from the Hindu tradition on which Gandhi drew might be tapped to help the church become what it is meant to be. In the process Hinduism and Christianity, precisely by realizing their own universal meanings more truly and radically, might become more alike.

Similar resources are found in Mahayana Buddhism. Gautama,

John Cobb points out,[45] taught that we suffer because we are attached to things, and that when we relinquish this attachment we become free. The result is a freedom for all things because it is a complete freedom from all things. This detachment is more radical than anything we know in the West; it is both a total emptiness and a total fullness. Christian faith approximates this sense of total detachment, but it is hindered by our Western cultural heritage of possession, ownership, self-activity, and individual fulfillment. What Buddhism calls detachment, Christianity calls grace—God's salvific gift that can never be claimed or possessed but can only be accepted in thankfulness and given to others. It is an emptiness that is a fullness. Living by grace is a complete letting go, not a holding fast, an openness to what presents itself, a gaining of life only by losing it. Such grace appears to be the basic condition and constitutive reality of the ecclesial community, which is a community of reciprocity, solidarity, and mutuality of recognition, of intending the other for the sake of the other, and of mediating grace for others without preconditions or expectations. But such a community is almost a utopian ideal in our consumer-oriented, materialist, individualist culture. Perhaps Buddhism can help the Christian church to be a community of grace in a graceless culture by showing more clearly what it means to have faith without attachment, to find fulfillment in utter emptiness, to become a communal self by giving up private selfhood. In the process Buddhists and Christians will move a little closer to each other. Spirit as it attracts is drawing us together without dissolving us into one.

But toward what end is the Spirit drawing us? The Zen Buddhist Masao Abe, in his seminal essay "Kenotic God and Dynamic Sunyata,"[46] says that in Buddhism time and history are without beginning and end; they are neither linear nor circular nor irreversible. Each moment embraces the whole process of time. We are not moving from life to death in history but are enveloped in the unchanging process of living-dying. There is neither creation nor final judgment but rather endless samsara, transiency, in the midst of which nirvana can be realized. But history as such is not meaningless, Abe insists, if we take seriously the compassionate and dynamic aspect of the ultimate reality, sunyata, its emptiness and self-emptying. Because the process of time is totally concentrated in each moment, every "now" is realized as the eternal Now of the absolute present (which is also the absolute void, no-thingness). But the unawakened are not yet aware of this basic reality, and there will always be unawakened ones. Hence the "process of actualizing the compassionate aspect of sunyata is endless. Here the progress of history toward the future is necessary and comes to have a positive significance. . . . At this point, history is no longer a 'history of karma' in which persons are transmigrating beginninglessly and endlessly. It becomes a 'history of vow and act' in which wisdom and compassion are operating to emancipate innumerable sentient beings from transmigration." What they are emancipated to, however, is not any sort of future eschatological consummation. Rather it is a matter of "a completely realized eschatology, because in the light of wisdom everything and everyone without exception is realized in its suchness, and time is thereby overcome." We are released from the burden of the past and the uncertainty of the future—from entangling memories and false hopes—to live fully in each present moment.

A number of questions can be raised about this fascinating effort on Abe's part to respond to, and even partially incorporate, Western criticisms of the Buddhist view of history.[47] I will focus on Charles Strain's appropriation of Abe and other thinkers of the Kyoto School in his attempt to bring Buddhism into critical dialogue with the sort of theology of history I have been advocating in this work and elsewhere.[48]

One is tempted at the beginning of this dialogue to throw up one's hands in despair at the apparent incommensurability between the categorial frameworks of Western ontology (even when deconstructed) and Buddhist emptiness (sunyata). When the latter is formulated in terms accessible to Westerners, as it is by Abe, it appears paradoxical to the point of unintelligibility. No distinctions seem to apply to sunyata, yet what is being proposed is not a simple identity but a dynamic realization of everything in its suchness. The particularities of history seem to be swallowed up in an ethical and ontological indifferentism, yet there is a call for the "compassionate healing of the web of relationality." Surely within its own categorial framework these paradoxes disappear, but to enter into that framework would entail a crossing over from one religio-cultural and linguistic system to another. I stress "linguistic" since I suspect that it is not really possible to understand what is being said without understanding the language in which it is being said. Is it possible to cross over and then come back in such a way that our own ways of viewing and experiencing history are not simply deconstructed but reconstructed? This is a project of immense importance as well as immense difficulty.

One of the central questions raised by Strain is whether it is possible to affirm, as I do, an open teleology with its many partial and ambiguous histories of freedom without falling into the "karmic web" of a multitude of "autotelic movements" that are "fatally blind" and "purely tragic" in their self-centeredness. Sunyata offers a radical deliverance from this self-centeredness through an understanding of nothingness as "absolute mediation," a circularity of unceasing mediation that delivers us from both a unilinear teleology and a destructive autoteleology. It does this in the form of a realized eschatology, the eternal Now in which all reality interpenetrates and co-originates, nirvana in the midst of samsara. According to Abe, this realized eschatology also generates an open teleology because the compassion that emerges from the wisdom of enlightenment is oriented to the process of awakening others in history, to saving all sentient beings, and that is an endless task. Out of the completely realized moment of self-emptying arises an open-ended trajectory of historical action.

My own version of this insight is as follows. Without revelatory moments of fulfillment, insight, self-emptying, history would indeed devolve into an endless sequence of autotelic movements, diverse expressions of the will to power. This is why I believe it is necessary to identify a paradigmatic gestalt of God's presence in history, which for Christians is associated with Jesus of Nazareth, the radically self-emptying one, the one in whom God is emptied out into history. This too is why we must affirm a transhistorical consummation of freedom in God (chap. 19) as well as a history of freedom within history (see next section). The former, which does not occur in the form of a chronological terminus of history but in every lived moment, alters the horizon in which historical praxis is interpreted. It is the dimension of depth, of spirituality, that funds the work of liberation. Does the Buddhist version of realized eschatology allow for a more radically open and less dualistic teleology than the Christian version? I cannot answer that question definitively, but I do know that in my own theology of history the eschatological dimension, while not absent, needs to be strengthened, and that the dialogue with Buddhism can contribute to that effort.

Yet at the end Strain suggests that the concept of even an open teleology must be questioned in light of the Buddhist deconstruction of both God and history. If "history" remains as a category, it will be an "empty" history, like a bush with a profusion of flowers (a sheaf of possibilities), or like an ecosystem (a self-transforming matrix with feedback loops), and freedom becomes, in Gary Snyder's phrase, "the practice of the wild."[49] Strain thinks that my insistence that it is *not* enough "to speak only of more or less random configurations of freedom and not also in some sense of a *history* of freedom, a history of transfigurative praxis,"[50] may reflect a "residual clinging." Perhaps so. But I ask in turn how Buddhism then avoids falling back into a destructive web of autotelic movements. In the wild, Snyder still wants to "improve the campsite, teach children, oust tyrants." By what criteria does one do these things? Strain points out that Buddhism does provide some criteria for emancipatory praxis, and these are quite helpful: a mindful practice that attends to quiet, imperceptible transformations; a nonretributive justice that eschews "weighted polarizations"; a commitment to nonviolence; a detachment from clinging to a utopian future that robs us of the present. Moreover he suggests that a new cultural synthesis may be emerging through the alliance of Buddhism with a number of Western movements: ecology, sustainable economics, holistic medicine, peace, feminism. The matrix does not seem to be quite empty; the bush does not seem to be simply a patternless profusion of flowers.

Jesus also compared the kingdom of God to a bush, a mustard bush, which grows from the smallest of seeds but then "becomes the greatest of all shrubs, and puts forth large branches, so that the birds of the air can make nests in its shade" (Mark 4:32). We need a bush in which we can make nests. Is that still clinging? Without such a bush, we would be exposed to the merciless heat of the sun and the relentless cold of night; we would be prey for the predators of history. And yet—this sheltering bush will not allow us to rest for long. It is also the bush that burns but is not consumed, the bush that mediates the flaming presence of God's Spirit in history (Ex. 3:2). Like Moses, we are commanded to go into Egypt and liberate God's people.

History: The Transformation of Futility into Freedom

The lowly bush, with which Jesus compared God's project, is a metaphor of history. The evolution characteristic of history—of natural history as well as human history—is not linear or unidirectional. Rather it opens out into an incredible diversity, like a bush with many branches.[51] Within its encompassing reach, God's creatures find shelter and are sent forth upon a multitude of adventures. The objective is not to use the bush as a ladder by which to climb into the sky but to realize in full the potential for life it gives here on earth.

By "history" I mean world history, which must now be understood to include the history of nature as well as of human culture. It is the history of the whole cosmos, the most encompassing of the spheres of liberation: "The creation itself will be set free." One of the lessons of modern science is that nature has a history; it changes and evolves through time in ways that can be comprehended. We suspect that there is greater continuity between natural history and human history than we yet understand, and that the patterns we detect in the human story may be deeply ingrained in the cosmos. So this section addresses the impossible task of sketching a theology of world history, focusing first on the human aspect, which I call the history of freedom within history, and then on the cosmic aspect, the redemption of creation. A text from the letter to the Romans links these two aspects.

The phrase "the history of freedom within history" suggests that there is also a history of freedom beyond history, or, as I prefer to call it, "the consummation of freedom in God." What is the end or purpose of history? The English word *end*, like the Greek *eschatos*, means both "aim" or "purpose" (*telos*) and "boundary" or "limit" (*terminus*). Taken in the first sense, it refers to an *innerhistorical* process that is both goal-oriented and open-ended. Taken in the second sense, it refers to a *transhistorical* consummation of all things in God. God and God alone is the ultimate terminus or limit of world history—not a chronologically future terminus but an ever-present one, a terminus that is also a transition, a passing over into a new and unimaginable historicality, the triune figuration of the One who loves in freedom.[52]

There are connections between these two senses of "end." The consummation of the world and the world's freedom in God is also an aim or telos of world history, but it is one that lies beyond the boundary distinguishing history from God, and it is not an aim that can be accomplished by historical process and praxis. The innerhistorical process is the proper object of *theology of history*, of God in history, and it is the theme addressed in the present section, focusing on the liberation of human and natural history as the broadest spheres in the Spirit's liberation of the world. The transhistorical consummation, which is the proper object of *eschatology*, of history in God, alters the horizon in which historical process and praxis are interpreted. It is the topic of chapter 19, the perfection of God.

Throughout we are concerned with the question of the meaning, purpose, and redemption (or liberation) of world history. Tillich says that the most encompassing of the Christian symbols for this redemption is "kingdom of God." It includes on its innerhistorical side the symbol of "spiritual presence" (the Spirit of God as the presence of the divine life within creaturely life) and on its transhistorical side the symbol of "eternal life" (the conquest of the ambiguities of life in the eternal divine life).[53] This shows both the connection and the distinction between theology of history and eschatology, and it indicates that the former belongs within the domain of Spirit, the liberating work of God in history, while the latter involves a transition into what we can only faintly imagine, the eternal divine history.

The History of Freedom Within History[54]

Hints of a theology of history responsive to the experience of the liberation movements and theologies are found in chapter 6. In the face of widespread suffering, poverty, and systemic oppression, we need an understanding of God who suffers with the oppressed yet combats oppression, and a theology of history that attends to both the interruptions and the transformations of history. We need a realistic theology that recognizes that definitive and final events of liberation do not occur in history but that affirms that God provides resources for attaining partial victories over racial, sexual, social, and ethnic injustices, and for maintaining a continuous struggle against them. We must learn to avoid once-and-for-all thinking while working to achieve livable humane balances.

The liberation theologies teach us that there is no triumphal march of God in history, no special history of salvation, but only a plurality of partial, fragmentary, ambiguous histories of freedom. History is an open-ended, never-finished process of shaping new cultural syntheses on both large and small scales, ranging from great civilizations to base communities. At their best, these syntheses have the quality of constructing domains of freedom and wholeness in a world of violent, conflicting, and fragmented forces, but the syntheses break down after a while or can be subverted into oppressive structures. History takes on a cyclical character although advance toward novelty occurs. Each synthesis represents a certain kind of completion in history, but history dissolves all these syntheses in an endless flux. Perhaps a trajectory of such syntheses takes shape such that we can indeed speak of "the history of freedom within history." Such a history is the ever unfinished work and generation of the Spirit. It remains irreducibly plural, multiform, fragile, yet it has certain recognizable qualities, about which there may even be an emergent consensus.

These qualities, for our time, seem to include the combating of suffering, poverty, and prejudice, the protection of individual rights, the enhancement of democratic institutions, the articulation of integrative purposes and values for a people, the fashioning of sustainable and just economic systems, the repudiation of violence as a means of settling conflicts (while recognizing the tragic necessity of force to restrain the violence of tyrants and criminals), the liberation of the earth from ecological devastation, the promotion of dialogue and shared concerns among the religions, the creation of a truly global communication community in which national and ethnic differences are both honored and transcended. Any such trajectory of practices remains highly fragile, subject to setbacks and reversals; it does not advance along a steadily progressive line; the struggle against the systems of domination and alienation, to say nothing of personal sin and pathological destruction, is endless.

History takes on the character of an "open wholeness" and of a "helical spiral."[55] There is a wholeness in history, but it is not closed, final, or total; rather it is open, preliminary, and partial. The work of art is a model of the kind of wholeness that can be achieved in history. Perfection is found in art not just once but again and again in a plurality of manifestations. The beauty of an art work does not exhaust perfection but reflects in a compacted fullness an unattainable wholeness. The same perfection characterizes works of love or the practice of love in freedom. In such acts, history reaches completion again and again, yet it remains ever incomplete since the wholeness of such acts does not close off but opens out into an infinite inexhaustibility and leaves the future undetermined.

The movement of history is neither linear nor cyclical but spiral. History advances and does not repeat itself, but the advances are not unidirectional and they take on a cyclical pattern—the pattern of splitting and overcoming splitting,[56] of constructing and deconstructing syntheses, harmonies, balances, on both microhistorical and macrohistorical scales. At the end of each cycle there is a return to a point that is analogous to the starting point but also different; what has happened between the two points constitutes the difference. The best spatial metaphor by which to envision this process is that of the spiral—not an inward or outward spiraling in a single plane, but a coiling through constantly changing planes, which is the shape of a helix. The helix of history does not come to a point at the apex of a cone, nor do its coils remain of constant diameter. Rather the coils decrease and increase in a wavelike fashion, perhaps like the radiation of energy in subatomic quanta or the double helix of the genetic code. The analogy with nature suggests that the deep structure of history may replicate that of nature in a way that is only dimly perceived. While there are significant advances and declines in history, moments of kairos[57] and of futility, of disclosure and of closure, and while certain kinds of progress are evident, the question of an innerhistorical consummation remains open. Historical process will undoubtedly at some point come to an end like everything finite, but whether that termination will be a consummation of freedom or an apocalyptic failure of the human project is unknown.

Can we speak then in any sense of a goal of history? For Christians there is such a goal. It is the shape of God in history, the shape of love in freedom, incarnate in the life and death of Jesus, fanning and flaming out into the world through the power of the Spirit. The shape takes on a multitude of forms in history, appearing in many figures of Christ, many manifestations of the Christ-gestalt, all of which are partial and incomplete, none being able to prevail in any final victory over evil, but there nonetheless, quietly at work in ordinary human beings. The Spirit is drawing us toward this shape, and it is our responsibility to discover what that means in our particular time and place, how this gestalt might take shape in our little sphere of action, how we might, for the time being, become a bearer of the christic paradigm, knowing that it is not we who act but the Spirit in us. Our task and opportunity is to join the history of freedom within history, to get on board this train,[58] to ride it for a while and make our contribution to it, to learn from the mistakes and achievements of the past, to prepare ourselves to face new challenges with courage and hope, knowing that our final hope is in God and not in history.

This is my attempt at avoiding a destructive autoteleology without clinging to a totalizing mythos of salvation history. I doubt that I have succeeded in a way that will be convincing to Buddhists. I do hope that through dialogue the Christian symbol of the kingdom of God might be deepened in its transhistorical dimension (a task to be addressed in the next chapter), while the Buddhist symbol of nirvana might be deepened in its innerhistorical dimension, such that Buddhists might join with Christians on the paths of freedom in history—not a single triumphal march but numerous paths with peoples of every creed and color, paths through thickets and clearings, paths with detours and obstacles, but paths nonetheless, paths from futility to freedom for all of God's children. The freedom is found on the way, in the journeys, not simply at the destination, and whether the paths ultimately converge remains a mystery of history as yet undisclosed.

The Redemption of Creation

Let us now expand the discussion to a cosmic horizon:

> The creation waits with eager longing for the revealing of the children of God; for the creation was subjected to futility, not of its own will but by the will of the one who subjected it, in hope that the creation itself will be set free from its bondage to decay and will obtain the freedom of the glory of the children of God. We know that the whole creation has been groaning in labor pains until now; and not only the creation, but we ourselves, who have the first fruits of the Spirit, groan inwardly while we wait for adoption, the redemption of our bodies (Rom. 8:19–23).

"Futility" (*mataiotēs*) is a state of emptiness, purposelessness, vanity, hopelessness, depression, bondage to decay (*phthoras*). The term is found occasionally in the Greek translation of the Psalms and is used nearly forty times in Ecclesiastes ("Vanity of vanities, says the Teacher. . . . All is vanity," 1:2). It seems to afflict the whole of creation, according to Paul, not just human beings and their history. And it seems to arise from the fact that all of creation is finite, subject to mortality or death, combined with the fact that sinful estrangement has infected this condition, turning death into a form of bondage, an occasion for despair and fear. It is, in Paul's terms, the death that comes from sin (Rom. 6:23), or in Kierkegaard's terms, the "sickness unto death." I have argued that such death is the ultimate form of human bondage, infecting all the other forms (chap. 14, pp. 224–25). And not just human bondage: The creation as a whole was "subjected" to futility and will be set free from it.

Paul speaks in this passage of the "children of God" and seems to mean *all* of God's creatures, not just human beings but animals and plants, lakes and mountains, stars and planets, the whole of creation, every creature in the heavens and on earth. He says that "all who are led by the Spirit of God are children of God" (Rom. 8:14), and indeed this whole chapter of Romans is concerned with the work of the Spirit. It is the Spirit that makes God's creatures "children," that is, brings them into a living, redemptive, "adoptive" relationship to the Abba God (8:15–16). If we live "according to the flesh," we will die, submit to the "spirit of slavery," "fall back into fear" and futility. But if we live "by the Spirit," we will put death to death and receive a "spirit of adoption" (8:13, 15). This is the "very Spirit bearing witness with our spirit that we are children of God," children of freedom (8:16, 21).

The Spirit, then, is the transformer of futility into freedom: This is the work of God in history, in the whole of history, cosmic as well as human. The language of "transformation" (*metamorphōsis*) is found in Romans 12:2: "Do not be conformed to this world, but be transformed by the renewing of your minds." This, we are told, is our "spiritual worship" (12:1), and it is clearly the Spirit bearing witness with our spirit that brings it about. We have already received the "first fruits of the Spirit" but await full adoption, "the redemption of our bodies," "the freedom of the glory of the children of God" (8:23, 21). The freedom that we are to share with the whole of creation entails not only a renewing of our minds but the redemption of our bodies, that is, a liberation from bondage to decay, from the futility of death. Redemption of the whole cosmos means some sort of transformation of material existence, a "glorification."

But what does this mean? We can understand readily enough what it means to say that "futility" is the problem beneath all the problems in human history and that the Spirit works in history as the transformer of futility into freedom. This is what makes it possible for there to be a history of freedom within history, and it explains why this history is partial, ambiguous, and incomplete: The problem of futility will not go away as long as there is history. "Futility" is a biblical analogue to the Buddhist notion of "samsara," endless transiency, dying in the process of living.

But what does it mean to say that futility is the ultimate problem of *cosmic* history and to allude to the redemption of the whole of creation, including especially its material aspect, through the transforming power of the Spirit? This is a very difficult question and one for which little guidance is provided by the theological tradition. It is easy enough to say that nature must be saved from the encroachment and destructiveness of human activity: That is what the environmental crisis and the ecological movement are about. And it is true to say that, since human evolution is a product of nature, human sin contributes to evil in nature and human salvation is also a salvation of nature. But there seems to be more at issue than that, a deeper and more difficult problem. An element of tragedy, if not of evil in the strict sense, seems to be present in nature, a tragic dimension that is not attributable to human sin and that does not simply reflect a human perspective and human interests. I believe it is advisable to speak of "tragedy" rather than of "evil" at this point since evil implies moral and hence human responsibility even if sedimented in objective structures, while tragedy points to a conflict or vulnerability that is intrinsic to a situation. What might this mean?[59]

The Pauline text gives us a clue: "We know that the whole creation has been groaning in labor pains until now" (Rom. 8:22). The cosmos is in process of being born, and birth is a painful, messy, sometimes violent business. The attempt in an earlier chapter to sketch a theology of nature led to the conclusion that there is a tendency in nature for the necessary thrust toward difference and differentiation (which is what birth is all about) to overreach itself, to disintegrate into rivalry and violence, to engender chaos and disorder, to move toward death rather than life. Difference under the conditions of finitude tends to become rupture, separation, estrangement, self-centeredness. The struggle for life tends to be excessive, to go beyond what is actually necessary for survival. At the same time there is a drive toward stagnation and decay; entropy is the scientific version of the Pauline "bondage to decay." The elements of creation tend to move against each other, to encroach upon each other destructively. There is in the world an indeterminacy, capriciousness, or "waywardness," which is the condition of possibility for the emergence of freedom, but which also drifts into disorder, encroachment, destructiveness.[60]

Tillich says that life in all of its dimensions—inorganic, organic, and spiritual—falls into "ambiguity" because of the estrangement that invades the structural elements of being. In the framework of his ontology, life has three basic functions: self-integration, self-creation, and self-transcendence (a striving toward ultimacy). Under the conditions of existence, self-integration falls into disintegration, self-creation into destruction, and self-transcendence into profanization or violation. Disintegration, destruction, and violation are all present in nature as well as in human culture. Ambiguity results from the conflict between integration and disintegration, creativity and destructiveness, striving toward ultimacy and falling back into profanity. Tillich provides detailed analyses of each of these conflicts. In inorganic and organic life there is a striving toward centeredness that is countered by forces of disintegration and disorder (for example, entropy, disease). There is also a struggle between the forces of life (creativity) and death (destruction); the same cellular constitution that gives a being the power of life drives toward the extinction of this power. Finally, "the holiness of a living being, its greatness and dignity, is ambiguously united with its profanization, its smallness, and its violability. . . . All organisms live through the assimilation of other organisms. . . . This is radical profanization." These ambiguities are replicated with greater intensity and complexity in the dimensions of spirit and history.[61]

This is the presence of tragedy in the cosmos, which arises from the juxtaposition of finitude and creativity. For there to be a finite cosmos in which creative powers are at work, tragic conflict and wayward drift seem to be inescapable. They are endemic to the divine project of having a world that is other than God but that images the divine creativity. In that sense "the creation was subjected to futility, not of its own will but by the will of the one who subjected it, in hope that the creation itself will be set free from its bondage to decay" (Rom. 8:20–21). The whole of creation groans in travail and cries out for redemption.

But what does redemption mean for the natural world? This question is no easier to answer than that concerning the meaning of its futility. Paul says only that it has something to do with entering into an "adoptive" relationship with God such that creation will obtain "the freedom of the glory of the children of God." How God brings about such a relationship with natural creatures we can only faintly imagine. This is essentially an eschatological vision. The word "glory" (*doxa*) signifies a participation in the radiance or glory that is the essence of divinity; it points toward eternal life in and with God rather than temporal life. Thus Paul says: "I consider that the sufferings of this present time are not worth comparing with the glory about to be revealed to us" (Rom. 8:18). Paul did not attend to history because he believed that the eschatological age was at hand, arriving within the present generation. We know that it is not so and that we must attend to history, even if we believe that in every moment there is also a relationship of immediacy to God, a participation in God's glory. Thus the question remains concerning the meaning of the redemption of nature during the long aeons of cosmic history. Is the Spirit at work as the transformer of futility into freedom for nature as well as for spirit? What does freedom mean in the natural world, if it has any meaning there at all?

Earlier I proposed (chap. 13, pp. 194–96) that God's Spirit is present and active in all dimensions of the cosmos as creative, shaping, alluring, energizing eros. The fundamental quality of this eros is allurement, drawing all things to itself, sustaining and cherishing all things in relationship to it. Without it, the universe would fly apart, disintegrate; its creativity would cease to be serendipitous and become self-destructive. God lets the world go, but God also loves the world and does not abandon it to its own devices. God draws things toward godself and out of their isolation. Perhaps this is what Paul means by speaking of entering into an "adoptive" relationship with God such that the creation itself "will obtain the freedom of the glory of the children of God." Freedom is a function of being in a loving, sustaining, nurturing relationship with God, of being "heirs of God and joint heirs with Christ" (Rom. 8:17). Paul seems to envision this familial relationship as a possibility for all of creation and as the condition of possibility of its freedom. Without it, there would be nothing but futility. We must insist that the Spirit is already at work as the transformer of futility; this is a present reality and not simply something to be awaited in hope.

How the Spirit works in nature we cannot directly know. It is enough to say that it works through the cosmos's own dynamism and not by direct divine maneuvering. The spiritual eros that empowers and attracts has determinate features (working to produce order, purpose, freedom, enhancement of value), but it is everywhere present and available. Whether the possibilities that it offers are actualized depends on the contingency of each situation and the free play of conflicting forces. This is as true for natural history as for human history, in modalities appropriate to each. God is a *factor* in the way the world goes, but precisely where and how it goes is not controlled by God. God is at risk and suffers in the world but also rejoices in the emergence of everything that is good.

19
THE PERFECTION OF GOD: ESCHATOLOGY

The Spirit and the Triune Figuration of God

I have been arguing in various ways that the Spirit is an emergent persona of God, generated in the act of outpouring, dependent upon worldly activity for its actualization. Thus Spirit is the final and consummate figure of the divine life, the mediation of identity and difference, of God's primordial self-relatedness and worldly other-relatedness. Spirit is the divine freedom that completes or perfects God's love for the world. This freedom presupposes love's positing of distinction and completes love's act of reunion. Love without emancipatory freedom is mere anguish, and freedom without compassionate love is mere capriciousness. The divine freedom is not sheer indeterminacy but a freedom determined by and bound to compassion for the world. Because this compassion is an aspect of the divine freedom, it is not left hanging in the anguish of death and separation but is completed by overcoming estrangement, negating the annihilating power of death, re-establishing communion by the "subjection" and return of all things, "that God may be all in all" (1 Cor. 15:28). Just as love signifies the immanence of God in the world, so freedom signifies the immanence of the world in God. In freedom, God comes back to godself as an enriched, suffering, embodied, spiritualized God. The perfection of God is eschatological rather than archeological; it is God as omega, not alpha.

Tillich believes that an authentic trinitarianism is persuasive because it corresponds to the intrinsic dialectics of experienced life: Life is the process of going out from itself and returning to itself. "If God is experienced as a living God and not as a dead identity, an element of nonbeing must be seen in [God's] being, that is, the establishment of otherness. The Divine Life then would be the reunion of otherness with identity in an eternal 'process.'" (In saying this Tillich is very close to Hegel, but that is not important—what is important is the power of the insight.) Spirit is the moment of reunion and thus the most comprehensive of the trinitarian symbols because it encompasses the other two. God *is* Spirit (see John 4:24) in a way that God is not simply Father or Son, power or meaning, abyss or logos.[1]

By returning to godself as Spirit, God incorporates the world's historicality within the divine life. In the process historicality itself is transfigured. It becomes a historicality in which there is both temporality and yet the utter coinherence of the modes of time. God's eternity is not a static timelessness but a more radical and infinite temporality, a concordance of time without discordance, of which we have at best only faint intimations in our own experience.[2] The dialectic of identity-difference-mediation spirals back upon itself in an eternally complete process of becoming. Negativity, destruction, evil, death remain present only as conquered, rejected, refined away. Eternal blessedness is not an immovable perfection but the eternal conquest of the negative and the sublation of the positive in a process of essentialization or glorification. The identity of worldly creatures is preserved by being taken up into, embodied by, a whole that is radically communitarian.

These statements are highly paradoxical because they are an attempt to introduce the world into God, the finite into the infinite, the temporal-historical into the eternal. The concept of an "eternal divine history"[3] is paradoxical, but it is a necessary thought if we are to take seriously the historicization of God in and through God's self-involvement in world process. The inner preworldly life of God is a dynamic process, the logical ground of historical process, but not yet itself a historical process. God becomes historical in relation to the world, but what this means for God's eternal life we can only faintly imagine. "God, as eternal, has neither the timelessness of absolute identity nor the endlessness of mere process. [God] is 'living,' which means that [God] has in [godself] the unity of identity and alteration which characterizes life and which is fulfilled in eternal life."[4]

This is the divine eschatology. Tillich describes it as an "eschatological panentheism." The temporal referent in 1 Cor. 15:28 is clearly future: After all things have been subjected to God, God *shall* be "all in all." Now is the time of difference, separation, conflict, resistance. Even now the world is "in" God, in the sense of its ontological dependence, "the inability of anything finite to be without the supporting power of the permanent divine creativity—even in the state of estrangement and despair." The world is also "in" God in the sense of its creative origin in the ground of being. But the "in" of 1 Cor. 15:28 is eschatological; it is the "in" of "ultimate fulfillment, the state of essentialization of all creatures," which is accomplished through a process of "subjection." "This threefold 'in-ness' of the temporal in the eternal indicates the rhythm both of the Divine Life and of life universal. . . . It is the way from the merely potential through actual separation and reunion to fulfillment beyond the separation of potentiality and actuality."[5]

In God this rhythm is eternally complete and yet eternally open, spiraling forward into novelty as long as there remains a world other than God. The third moment is both already and not yet. Perhaps the model of a triadic holism is more adequate than that of eschatological panentheism to describe a divine process in which, even in the moment of fulfillment, subjection, or essentialization, the other is not reduced to the same. If it were reduced to the same, then in the final analysis world process would count for nothing for God, and the eternal divine history would collapse into static identity. Rather, in the third, eschatological moment, the world retains the element of difference that makes God a whole rather than a one, a We rather than an I. God continues in a process of triune figuration rather than coming to rest in a state of bliss. "Eternal blessedness" in any event is not a state of immovable perfection but "blessedness through fight and victory."[6] What this might mean is further explored below.

The Consummation of the World in God

The divine eschatology is also a world eschatology: The end (telos) of God is the end (telos *and* terminus) of the world and the world's history. We are speaking now of the transhistorical consummation of all things in God, who is the ultimate limit or terminus of world history, but this consummation is also the ultimate goal or telos of world history.

If there is to be a consummation of all things, it must be in God because the liberation of the world is never accomplished within world history itself. The kingdom of God never arrives in history as an earthly utopia; it is always "coming," both absent and present. This planet will someday become uninhabitable, either through human action (nuclear war, environmental destruction) or natural processes (collision with a comet, the next ice age, expansion and overheating of the sun); at the end the whole cosmos may blow apart or collapse in on itself. As John Cobb says, "Our resurrection cannot be here or on any other planet revolving around some other sun. It must be in God."[7]

But is there to be a consummation of *all* things? Or is it rather to be of only *some* things, either those chosen by God in an eternal decree or those that prove themselves worthy of inclusion? Is it possible to conceive, as an alternative to eternal life, an "eternal death" or "death away from eternity" (Tillich's terms) as a possible destiny for some, perhaps a large number of human beings, to say nothing of all the other creatures of the cosmos? Here there is a great divide in the history of doctrine between the orthodox majority who think that such a conception is both possible and necessary for the sake of ethical and educational seriousness (Augustine, Aquinas, Calvin), and a heterodox minority who think it is not possible because it finally proves to be unethical and makes God into a demon (Origen, Socinus, Schleiermacher). The choice ultimately is between Calvin's double predestination (some condemned by God's decree, others saved) and Origen's restoration of all things (*apokatastasis pantōn*, Acts 3:21). Tillich stands with the heterodox minority (as indeed I think we must) but not in such a way as to claim that the incertitude about our ultimate destiny can be removed. Both, he says, have to be denied—both the threat of eternal death and the security of the return. There *is* a return, but it is a process that continues through and beyond life and the outcome is not certain. It has to be "worked out" in the case of each and every person, and some, perhaps many, remain stubbornly resistant to it. It is not a matter of worthiness, for all are unworthy. Rather it is a matter of defiance and illusion for the return cannot be coerced.[8]

When does the consummation occur? Only at the end of time or in every moment of time? The theological tradition has usually understood it to be the former, by way of a chronologically future package of "last things." Not only is the notion of an abrupt and catastrophic end a literalized and misleading myth (the cosmos is more likely to die a slow death), but also it devalues the present. I think we must affirm that God is not merely a chronologically future terminus of world history but an ever-present one, a terminus that is also a transition, a passing over into the eternal historicality of God. We experience this transition both in the fullest moments of our living and in the final moment of our dying. God is always there, always available. This is the dimension of depth, of spirituality, that funds liberation and alters the horizon in which historical praxis is undertaken.

This is what the dialogue with Buddhism calls us to affirm in a much more radical way: sunyata as absolute mediation, the eternal now in which all reality interpenetrates and co-originates, nirvana in the midst of samsara, freedom in the midst of futility (see chap. 18, pp. 311–15). In affirming this, we must not lose the sense of temporal process and historical change.[9] We are empowered to struggle for a better tomorrow *just because* we are sustained by God's amazing grace, suffused by divine presence, today. The transhistorical horizon invigorates the historical field. Within Christianity, valuable resources for this affirmation are provided by Western mystics and Eastern Orthodox theologians: Even now, they say, we experience the mystery of *theosis* or glorification; by the Spirit we are being transformed into the image and glory of God (2 Cor. 3:18).[10]

But what does all of this *mean?* How does the consummation or restoration or transition take place and what happens to finite beings in the process? Obviously we have no way of adequately describing the eschaton since all our categories presuppose worldly distinctions and relations. Here theological language becomes paradoxical and poetic. The imagery of the eschatological banquet in the New Testament is an example. My own imagination falters at this point, and I have found the most helpful guidance from Tillich, who virtually alone among contemporary theologians has addressed these questions with both imagination and conceptual rigor.

He says that the ongoing "end" of the temporal-historical process has three aspects to it: the elevation of the temporal into eternity, the exposure of the negative as negative, and the final conquest of the ambiguities of life. The first two are closely related. God elevates the positive content of history into eternity and at the same time excludes the negative from participation in it. Nothing that has been created in history is lost but is liberated from the negative element with which it has become entangled in existence.[11]

The exposure and annihilation of the negative as negative is the meaning of the symbol of "ultimate judgment." God, or God's Spirit, is represented as a refining fire that burns away the negative (evil) and purifies the positive (good). The negative does not simply disappear; it remains in the eternal memory of God as that which is conquered and thrown out into its nothingness. The positive is retained in God's eternal life in its true, essential reality; it is restored to what it essentially is or was created to be. Borrowing a category from Schelling, Tillich describes this as "essentialization," and it becomes his version of Origen's *apokatastasis*. Essentialization can be taken in two senses. It can mean the return to the state of mere essentiality or potentiality, including the removal of everything that is real under the conditions of existence, as is characteristic, Tillich believes, of the India-born religions in contrast to the Israel-born ones. Or it can mean that the new that has been actualized in time and space adds something to essential being. God unites essential being with the positive that is created within existence, thus producing the *ultimately* new beyond all fragmentation and ambiguity.[12]

We need not assume that these two senses must remain statically opposed to each other. We have seen Masao Abe's attempt to introduce a dynamic and open dimension into the Buddhist conception of sunyata. This is the beginning of a difficult and important dialogue.

Just as the symbol of nirvana may contribute to a deepened understanding of the eternal presence of the eschaton for Christians and Jews, so also the symbol of the kingdom of God may contribute to a deepened understanding of the positive meaning of history for Buddhists and Hindus.[13]

The third meaning of the "end" of the temporal-historical process is the final conquest of the ambiguities of life. They are conquered in the eternal life that is God's own life enriched by worldly life. As we have seen (chap. 18, pp. 321–22), life according to Tillich has three basic functions that appear in history only ambiguously: self-integration falls into disintegration, self-creativity falls into destructiveness, and self-transcendence falls into profanization. In eternal life the first of these ambiguities is conquered by the divine centeredness or love, the second by the divine creativity, and the third by the divine freedom.[14]

God is the eternally creative One who loves in freedom. As such God does not remain an isolated one but becomes a whole, a We, who includes others within God without destroying their otherness. The divine centeredness does not annihilate individuality but unites it with perfect participation or communion. The divine creativity balances the polarity of dynamics and form, and the divine freedom brings about a union of freedom and destiny. God is a tensive harmony rather than a static identity.

This provides a basis for addressing our last question, which concerns the destiny of individual persons in the consummation or restoration of all things in God. Christian theology has used two symbols to express the idea of individual participation in eternal life: immortality and resurrection. If immortality means that the soul is incapable of dying and can be separated from its mortal body, then it must be rejected. But it can also be used to express negatively what the term eternity conveys positively: not a continuation of temporal life after death but a quality that transcends temporality.[15] For example, when Paul says that "this mortal body must put on immortality," and that thereby "death has been swallowed up in victory" (1 Cor. 15:54–55), he means that we must first die, we must first go through dying, and then and only then may we put on immortality—not as a natural quality of our souls but as a spiritual gift, the gift of eternal life.

The symbol of resurrection avoids the misleading connotations of immortality but introduces problems of its own. Resurrection of the body does not mean the coming back to life of a dead body, a corpse (see chap. 16). Rather it means taking up an action or function by which one's identity is preserved in a new kind of communal, corporate embodiment that is spiritual in character. Self-identity after death is preserved, not by individuated physical continuity, but by participation in a community or spiritual realm of being in which the self is not lost but taken up into a higher unity of structure. There the self finds an identity that is founded outside itself. In this way one's life surges forth again after the hiatus of death. The hiatus is marked by the two kinds of embodiment: the human self "is sown a physical body, it is raised a spiritual body" (1 Cor. 15:44). The spiritual body is a spiritual community, a community created by the Spirit. The ultimate spiritual community into which we are raised is God's own communal being as the whole or all that encompasses all that is, but we are also raised into the world as God's body, so that our embodiment after death becomes pancosmic rather than acosmic. Because we are raised into the world, and because the world is taken up into God, we are raised into God. Individual destiny and universal destiny are wrapped up together. We obtain some sense of what this might mean from the resurrection of Jesus, whose personal identity is preserved by his presence in and to the community that becomes his body, and which he empowers to become a liberated communion of free subjects. But then, when all things are subjected to him, he too will be subjected to (raised into?) God, so that God may be "all in all."

Tillich arrives at a similar position via the theory of essentialization. When applied to individuals, it means that what is to be valued (the positive as opposed to the negative) in each and every personal identity will be preserved in relation to a larger totality. This includes the positive essence of the least actualized beings (for example, distorted and aborted forms of life) as well as that of the most fully actualized individuals. God finds what is positive in each and elevates it into the divine life, thus affirming the eternal significance of each human person, perhaps of every sentient creature.

But is it going too far to say that the self-conscious *self* or *subject* is included in God's eternal life? Tillich thinks it is possible to answer this question only in the form of two negative statements: The self-conscious self cannot be excluded from eternal life, yet the self-conscious self in eternal life is not what it is in temporal life. The first is true because eternal life is not an undifferentiated identity, and there can be no participation in it without individual centers to participate. The second is true because the participation of the centered self in eternal life "is not the endless continuation of a particular stream of consciousness in memory and anticipation." Self-consciousness as we know it requires temporal change and spatial differentiation, but these are no longer applicable in eternal life. So it is not possible for us to know in any positive sense how the centered self participates in eternal life.[16] What we can know, by faith, is that God preserves each and every thing of value in this world and that God does so in a way that is appropriate both to the thing and to God.

The perfection of God and the consummation of the world are two aspects of the same reality. God achieves perfection only through the world, and the world attains its consummation only in God. Both are works of the Spirit, which is co-generated by God and the world. Spirit is the wind that draws and drives the world toward its goal, and Spirit is the refining fire that purifies without consuming. God becomes a whole in which otherness is not reduced to the same, even in the eternal divine history. This history is the history of love in freedom. Our vocation is to be a small part of it.

20
A PERSONAL EPILOGUE

In a response to my book *God in History* for a panel sponsored by the American Academy of Religion, Mark K. Taylor wondered why it is that I and others like me tend to avoid the sort of "self-implicating or self-involving discourse" that would counter the illusion of speaking from an elevated plateau and might reveal something of the author's social location. "Is it a lingering respect for disembodied ideals of 'objectivity' . . . ? Or is it the academic reserve that feels such a discourse somehow is necessarily narcissistic or individualistic?" Probably both of these, together with a wariness about exposing one's vulnerabilities. In any event, I found myself doing a bit of what Taylor is calling for on recent occasions of teaching the course from which this book has emerged. I noticed that each of the chapters in one of our assigned texts, *Lift Every Voice: Constructing Christian Theologies from the Underside,* begins with a section called "Context and Commitment." The editors, Mary Potter Engel and Susan Brooks Thistlethwaite, expected their contributors to identify their social location and personal commitment. This was a valuable exercise, and I decided therefore to conclude my lectures with "a personal statement."

This proved to be a painful and revealing task. Not only was it helpful to me personally, but it seemed to put a kind of perspective and closure on the course. Some of the facts about me are pretty much to be expected: white, male, Protestant (Presbyterian), middle class, Midwesterner, Midsoutherner. I had to acknowledge that I have lived in the South most of my life although I have never thought of myself as a Southerner, having been born in Chicago. I experienced the rigid segregation of the deep South in Memphis during the

1940s, and I remember having questions that could not be asked or answered.

By the time I was ready for college my family had moved to Baltimore, and I attended Princeton University, where I majored in history and was heading toward law but was captivated by religious and ethical questions. In 1955 I visited Union Theological Seminary along with other college students. There I heard Paul Tillich and Reinhold Niebuhr and toured the East Harlem Protestant Parish—all of which had a powerful impact. I wondered how one could be a minister in a comfortable suburb in face of such pressing social needs. Unwilling, perhaps, to confront that question directly, I enrolled a year and a half later in Yale Divinity School, where I received a rich theological education. My teachers included H. Richard Niebuhr, Robert Calhoun, Julian Hartt, Hans Frei, George Lindbeck, James Gustafson, Claude Welch, Paul Schubert, Paul Minear, and Paul Meyer. My central interest was theology, but the three Pauls of the New Testament faculty awakened in me an interest in biblical studies. The theologians who had the greatest impact on me at the time were Augustine, Calvin, Schleiermacher, Kierkegaard, Troeltsch, Barth, Bultmann, and Tillich.

In the spring of 1958 I enrolled in Robert Calhoun's course in systematic theology. Recently I have reread my lecture notes from that class and am astonished to realize how much of their spirit and substance have been absorbed into my own thinking. Calhoun, one of the old Yale liberals, lectured without notes and wove a brilliantly textured mosaic that was intellectually rigorous, ethically passionate, religiously committed, and historically resonant. I am embarrassed by the poverty of my own efforts in comparison. For the required credo I wrote a 75-page synthesis of Calvin and Tillich. The fundamental problem with which it was concerned was—lo and behold!—the meaning of history and God's redemptive action in it. The problem presents itself, I said, in three fundamental forms: the threat of nonbeing or death, the dilemma of sinful estrangement, and the subjection of the whole of creation to futility. In response to the last of these, God is revealed as "the transformer of futility" (Rom. 8:20-23; 12:2). When I looked at my credo again a few years ago and came across these words, I thought to myself, "That's an interesting idea!" I have incorporated it into the theology of history offered in chapter 18.

This Yale theology did not sit well with the Presbytery of Baltimore, and my ordination caused something of a disturbance although at the time I was pretty much a straightforward Barthian. My own identity as a Presbyterian has been a complex matter since I have found myself both attracted and repelled by Reformed theology, and I have taught most of my career in an ecumenical theological school. I decided to publish this book with Westminster/John Knox Press because I wanted to put in a claim to be doing a kind of Reformed theology—not the kind that is ordinarily thought of today as being Reformed. It has puzzled me that the Reformed tradition, with its high valuation of theology, has produced so few truly major contemporary thinkers. I believe that the way to be faithful to this tradition is not to repeat what has gone before but to address the theological task quite differently: *theologia semper reformanda.* The greatest Reformed theologians were visionaries in their own time: Calvin, Edwards, Schleiermacher, Bushnell, Barth, the Niebuhrs.

Fast-forward my life by ten years from the spring of 1958 to the spring of 1968. In the interim I completed my divinity and Ph.D. degrees, was married and ordained, taught two years in Texas, and came to Vanderbilt Divinity School in 1965. The spring and summer of 1968 saw the assassinations of Martin Luther King Jr. and Robert Kennedy, the urban riots resulting from the unfulfilled promises of the civil rights movement, the escalation of the war in Vietnam, and the Soviet invasion of Czechoslovakia (on the day that my family and I arrived in Germany for a year's leave). My comfortable late modern world was beginning to crumble. I was deeply affected by these events and began looking for a way to connect theology with political and social issues. In the spring of 1970 and for several years thereafter I offered a course called "theology of freedom" in which we read some of the literature from the counterculture movement and from the early political and liberation theologies. It was at this time that I first encountered the work of James Cone, Rosemary Radford Ruether, and Gustavo Gutiérrez. Their thought had a profound impact on me, and I devote considerable attention to them in chapter 6.

The spring semester 1970 came to an early end with protests and teach-ins over the shootings at Kent State University. The following fall I became involved in the unsuccessful reelection campaign of Senator Albert Gore, Sr., who had become a prominent war critic; and in the spring of 1971 I taught jointly with James Lawson and Thomas Ogletree a course on "theology and the black experience"—the first such course ever at Vanderbilt, where eleven years earlier Lawson had been expelled for leading the Nashville sit-ins. This course changed my life in many ways since it exposed me to the history and literature of black religion in America and made me aware of the depth and intransigence of racism.

In 1974 I published a little book that came out of readings and lectures for that class, *Children of Freedom: Black Liberation in Christian Perspective.* The motto was the same passage from Romans that had figured prominently in my credo, which in the meantime had been forgotten (or perhaps half-forgotten): "The creation itself will be set free from its bondage to decay and obtain the glorious freedom of the children of God." Shortly after this book was published, I was made painfully aware of my own complicity in the very racism I thought I was combating. I had arranged for my family to spend a summer in Marin County near San Francisco at the beginning of another leave. Without being aware of it, we had rented a house in a poor black community and did not stay long. This was the leave during which I wrote *New Birth of Freedom: A Theology of Bondage and Liberation*, and I was constantly aware of the deep ambiguities (maybe even hypocrisy) involved in my addressing this topic. But I could not leave it alone. I would describe this period in my life from 1968 to 1974 as the loss of innocence. It was my second theological education.

By then I was forty years old, and the next twenty years brought some difficult transitions to middle age and now to *late* middle age. I did not handle these transitions very well. I became addicted to alcohol and experienced periods of depression, even while I was working feverishly on Hegel and then on ecclesiology and theology of history. Ironically, I seemed to be doing creative work while escaping from reality. Perhaps "futility" was knocking at the door, which I attempted to slam shut, and I also shut myself off from healing resources for too long. This phase of my life is past, but I am still dealing with its aftereffects on myself and my family.

What partly triggered the difficulties I experienced may have been uncertainty about my own theological identity and personal future. My attempt to contribute to the emerging liberation theologies drew a decidedly mixed reaction. One reviewer of *New Birth of Freedom* wondered why "the two-edged sword of liberation has to be packed in the cotton balls of German romanticism or German idealism." I felt isolated, an out-of-place academic liberal, a white male who lacked a community of discourse and practice that might have contextualized and funded his work. So I turned back to what I was most familiar with, the nineteenth century, this time with a concentrated focus on Hegel, where, surprisingly, I discovered new resources. The cotton ball of Hegelianism proved to be a cannon ball that propelled me into a fresh engagement with my own context. I found myself on a bridge between enlightenment and liberation, modernity and postmodernity, my first and second theological educations. I have not gotten all the way across and doubt that I ever will. This bridge is my theological and also my social location. A bridge may not be a very chic place to be these days, but I suspect that most of us find ourselves on one sort of bridge or another, never quite reaching the promised land. I may even have a good deal of company on this particular bridge.

My interest in Hegel goes back to a college course on nineteenth-century philosophy taught by a brilliant but eccentric visiting professor. The opening words of the first lecture, without any explanation, were from one of the most difficult passages in the *Phenomenology of Spirit*, a passage, so the professor claimed, that is the clue not only to Hegel's thought but also to the meaning of history and the challenge of modernity. I was totally baffled and utterly intrigued—and probably (without knowing it) hooked. Unfortunately the professor was under the mistaken impression that this was a two-semester course. In December he was still lecturing on Hegel, and the class covered the remainder of the nineteenth century during three weeks in January. Someone has observed that Hegel has a Puck-like capacity to make sober people lose their senses.

I wrote my doctoral dissertation on Ferdinand Christian Baur, a nineteenth-century historical theologian deeply influenced by Hegel, but I did not seriously study Hegel on my own until the mid-1970s. This was partly motivated by a course I was teaching on nineteenth-century theology. But I was also searching for a philosophical framework in relation to which I could think theologically. I was attracted for a while to Heidegger and the new hermeneutic (as evidenced in my early book, *Jesus—Word and Presence*), and I still find resources there, but they proved to be inadequate as my interests turned to liberation theology and questions of praxis. The formal categorical scheme of process philosophy did not seem to work well with my basically historical mentality, but I began to view myself as a kind of process thinker, and I have been influenced especially by John Cobb.

Hegel offers a holistic vision that is at once ontologically radical and socially transformative. This is the cannon ball I discovered in Hegelianism. The ontological radicalism provides a way of reconstructing the concept of God in light of the critiques of modernity and postmodernity—a reconstruction that avoids the dualism of classical theism, the monism of modern atheism, and the fragmentation of postmodern deconstruction. The social transformation is rooted in a vision of freedom as the nisus of history and in a dialectical method that demands a critique of all existing forms of thought and praxis. Perhaps there is something providential in my having become occupied with Hegel texts and translations during the winter of my discontent. Resources were laid away that would prove indispensable when I returned to constructive theology, for I discovered that precisely what is called for today is a holistic reconstruction of the concept of God and of God's relationship to the world in the context of social, ecological, and dialogical transformation. Hegel can help with this project although it is one that must be carried through on its own terms and in light of contemporary issues.

The theologian who is cited most frequently in these pages, Paul Tillich, developed an original philosophical vision, which however was influenced by the Hegelian tradition as mediated through Schelling and

Kierkegaard. Theology, Tillich showed, is not obliged simply to accept a prefabricated philosophy; it is free, rather, to reshape it in accord with its own interests, insights, convictions, and commitments so long as it argues its views publicly. In his own way, Barth held a similar view, with Hegel especially in mind. This is what I have attempted to do from a Hegelian base with the help of Tillich, Barth, and others, acutely aware of the modesty of my effort as compared with these great thinkers.

During the past decade I have become more deeply engaged with feminist theology through the influence of colleagues and students, and with issues related to ecology and interreligious dialogue, as part of an effort to contextualize theological reflection for students enrolled in constructive Christian theology. All of these influences, together with African American and Latin American theology and philosophical postmodernism, have had the effect of deconstructing my old identity as a white middle-class liberal male. I have not felt as isolated and threatened by this as I once did. I see it now as an opportunity for growth, often painful to be sure, and I have found support in the process. The Workgroup on Constructive Theology, which my colleagues and I at Vanderbilt helped to organize a good many years ago, and which has published three introductory texts resulting from collaborative work, has in recent years become an intergenerational group with a younger and more diverse membership. Some of the early members like myself have stayed with the group and are enriched and nurtured by it.

I am finding that it is not easy to go through the transitions life demands, both intellectually and physically, and that doing so requires inner spiritual resources as well as close personal relationships. These are abundantly available if one opens oneself. I recognize more clearly that life is a continuous pilgrimage, requiring courage, commitment, purpose, supporting communities, and good friends. Perhaps my personal experiences help to account for the emphasis I place on the reality of fear that lies at the heart of sin, as well as on a theology of spiritual presence. I have experienced the fear, and I need the help of the Spirit.

One thing that has sustained me is a love for lakes and sailing inherited from childhood. Sailing, with its serenity and exhilaration, rhythms and dangers, joys and frustrations, its attunement to forces of nature and its intimations of a spiritual presence, has become for me a metaphor of theology and indeed of life itself. Memories of good times sailing with students linger over the years—even of those times when all got soaking wet or when not a breath of wind stirred. The Spirit indeed blows where and how it chooses.

NOTES

Full bibliographic information for frequently cited works is not repeated in every chapter. These works are included in the bibliography, which provides a convenient reference for publication facts.

Chapter 1. Thinking Theologically

1. These expressions are used by theologians influenced by Rudolf Bultmann and Martin Heidegger, notably Gerhard Ebeling and Ernst Fuchs. See Ebeling's *Introduction to a Theological Theory of Language*, trans. R. A. Wilson (Philadelphia: Fortress Press, 1971).

2. *Praxis* is the Greek word for "action." It delineates a distinctively human form of action, action that involves speech and is essentially political or relational in character, as opposed to activity in the form of "labor," which is physical in character and involves the struggle for survival, and activity in the form of "work," which is the fabrication of things with our hands. See Hannah Arendt, *The Human Condition* (Chicago: University of Chicago Press, 1958), parts 3–5. Our word "practice" derives from Greek *praxis*, but in English "practice" often has the sense of acquiring proficiency through repeated performance or exercise. To avoid the ambiguities in the words "action" and "practice," the term "praxis" has come into common usage as a loan word in English.

3. This expression derives from Jürgen Habermas. See *The Theory of Communicative Action*, trans. Thomas McCarthy, 2 vols. (Boston: Beacon Press, 1984, 1987).

4. I acknowledge that this statement reflects a Western logocentric perspective. In Buddhist meditation, the objective is to achieve a state of utter thoughtlessness and wordlessness, to empty oneself of compulsive thinking so as to attain an awareness of reality beyond thought. Is it possible to attain awareness

without thought and without words? Perhaps so, but any reflection upon or communication of the experience requires thought and language. The Buddha as the fully aware one has the task of awakening others. Only a linguistic being is capable of renouncing language and knowing the renunciation.

5. See Paul Ricoeur, *The Symbolism of Evil*, trans. Emerson Buchanan (Boston: Beacon Press, 1969).

6. This is an Hegelian way of understanding the relationship between metaphor or symbol (what Hegel called *Vorstellung*) and concept. See G. W. F. Hegel, *Lectures on the Philosophy of Religion*, 3 vols., trans. and ed. Peter C. Hodgson et al. (Berkeley and Los Angeles: University of California Press, 1984, 1985, 1987), 1:396–414. See also Paul Ricoeur, *The Rule of Metaphor*, trans. Robert Czerny et al. (Toronto and Buffalo: University of Toronto Press, 1977), study 8, "Metaphor and Philosophical Discourse."

7. See *The Westminster Dictionary of Christian Theology*, ed. Alan Richardson and John Bowden (Philadelphia: Westminster Press, 1983); *A New Handbook of Christian Theology*, ed. Donald W. Musser and Joseph L. Price (Nashville: Abingdon Press, 1992); *Christian Theology: An Introduction to Its Traditions and Tasks*, ed. Peter C. Hodgson and Robert H. King, 3d ed. (Minneapolis: Fortress Press, 1994); and Dorothee Sölle, *Thinking about God: An Introduction to Theology* (Philadelphia: Trinity Press International, 1990).

8. In the Reformed tradition the church is spoken of as *ecclesia reformata et semper reformanda*, "the church reformed and always reforming." The origin of the slogan is unknown; it may go back to the period of Reformed orthodoxy, but it may also have originated in the nineteenth century. See Gyula Bárczay, *Ecclesia semper reformanda: Eine Untersuchung zum Kirchenbegriff des 19. Jahrhunderts* (Zürich: EVZ-Verlag, 1961). It is within the spirit of the Reformed tradition to transfer this expression to theology itself. The present work claims to stand in the Reformed tradition not so much in the sense of an identifiable doctrinal content but in the more profound sense that theology is "always reforming." Obviously this does not mean that theology simply invents new content since what is involved is precisely an *interplay* of root revelatory experience, texts and traditions, and contemporary context.

9. Søren Kierkegaard, *Fear and Trembling* and *Repetition*, ed. and trans. Howard V. Hong and Edna H. Hong (Princeton: Princeton University Press, 1983), 131. Kierkegaard alludes to the Greek idea that all knowing is a recollecting, and he argues that similarly all life is a repetition. I would add: not *mere* repetition or sameness but repetition with variation and difference. The appropriate image is not a circle but a spiral.

10. The theoretical basis for the model of the hermeneutical circle presented here is found in the later philosophy of Martin Heidegger; see especially the essays contained in *On the Way to Language*, trans. Peter D. Hertz (New York: Harper & Row, 1971); and *Poetry, Language, Thought*, trans. Albert Hofstadter (New York: Harper & Row, 1971). However, my presentation is nontechnical, and the development and application of the model differ considerably from Heidegger. I have also been influenced by Hans-Georg Gadamer and Paul Ricoeur. See Gadamer, *Truth and Method*, 2d ed., trans. rev. by Joel Weinsheimer and Donald G. Marshall (New York: Crossroad, 1989); Ricoeur, *Interpretation Theory* (Fort Worth: Texas Christian University Press, 1976); and Ricoeur,

Hermeneutics and the Human Sciences, trans. John B. Thompson (Cambridge: Cambridge University Press, 1981).

11. This expression is used by Emil L. Fackenheim; see *God's Presence in History: Jewish Affirmations and Philosophical Reflections* (New York: New York University Press, 1970), 8–14.

12. See David Tracy, "Theological Method," in *Christian Theology,* esp. 42–43, 45, 49. Tracy is relying here on the hermeneutical theories of Hans-Georg Gadamer and Paul Ricoeur.

13. The terms "analysis," "criticism," and "interpretation" all have a similar meaning—analysis: to resolve (*ana-lysis*) a whole into parts; criticism: to cut (*krinein*) or separate; interpretation: to go between (*inter-pretari*) or mediate between parts.

14. It might be objected that my interpretation of this metaphor reflects an aesthetic rather than a utilitarian perspective: sailing for sailing's sake rather than for the transport of goods. I believe there is truth in both perspectives. It *is* true that sailing is for sailing's sake: A ship becomes a ship when it is on its own, moving, under sail; the act of sailing gathers a space of truth, freedom, beauty; the meaning is in the sailing. At port, in dry dock, or on land, the ship is out of its element and is dysfunctional. It is also true that the purpose of sailing is to transport goods and people. We have no other option if we wish to move across the water. (Today, of course, the image of the ship must be extended to include mechanically-powered vessels and flying ships known as airplanes, nautical imagery having been taken over into aviation.) The seas can be brutal, the work is hard and risky, and lives are lost. The goal is partially achieved when the ship reaches port, but it must head out again. In water-based cultures (e.g., Polynesia) there are no ports and the only home is on boats. We are a land-based culture, but we recognize that the sea is a metaphor of the whole of history; the flood has not yet subsided. As Thales remarked, everything is fluid, everything is made of water.

15. H. Richard Niebuhr, *Radical Monotheism and Western Culture* (New York: Harper & Bros., 1960), 15.

16. This is one of Karl Barth's great themes. See *Church Dogmatics,* ed. G. W. Bromiley and T. F. Torrance, vol. 1: *The Doctrine of the Word of God* (Edinburgh: T. & T. Clark, 1936, 1956).

17. See Ricoeur, *Hermeneutics and the Human Sciences,* chap. 4.

18. It has become fashionable today to substitute the word "faith" for "theology" where it is considered embarrassing or inappropriate to use the latter, e.g., in religious studies departments. When this is done, it is assumed that theology like faith makes confessional claims in contrast to the critical approach of religious studies. But theology, while related to faith, is not the same as faith; nor is it the same as religious studies.

19. Rebecca Chopp, *The Praxis of Suffering: An Interpretation of Liberation and Political Theologies* (Maryknoll, N.Y.: Orbis Books, 1986), 139–42.

20. Edward Farley, *Theologia: The Fragmentation and Unity of Theological Education* (Philadelphia: Fortress Press, 1983), 31–44, 165–69.

21. In Hodgson and King, eds., *Christian Theology,* chap. 1 (quotation below from 36). This is developed more fully in *Blessed Rage for Order: The New Pluralism in Theology* (New York: Seabury Press, 1975). A refinement of Tracy's

hermeneutics is offered by Francis Schüssler Fiorenza's theory of a "wide reflective equilibrium" that correlates the reconstruction of traditions, retroductive warrants derived from present experience and praxis, and background theories. The latter seem to be concerned primarily with the reality status of what I am calling root experiences or "pre-text." I believe that my approach is generally consistent with Fiorenza's, although formulated in rather different terms. See *Foundational Theology: Jesus and the Church* (New York: Crossroad, 1984), 301–11.

22. Paul Tillich, *Systematic Theology*, 3 vols. (Chicago: University of Chicago Press, 1951, 1957, 1963), 1:59–66. "Correlation," says Tillich, can designate the "correspondence of different series of data," the "logical interdependence of concepts," and "the real interdependence of things or events in structural wholes"; and it is used by theology in all three senses. I employ the concept of correlation rather loosely and primarily in the third sense.

23. See David Tracy, *Plurality and Ambiguity: Hermeneutics, Religion, Hope* (San Francisco: Harper & Row, 1987).

24. I adopted this model from Robert C. Calhoun's way of teaching systematic theology at Yale Divinity School when I was a student there in the 1950s. I have told students that they should use my lectures as *one* of the resources provided by the course, along with the readings, group discussions, etc. I have urged them to think about the lectures, argue with them, disagree with them, and begin to shape their own theological stance. I have tried to persuade them that, as far as assessing student work is concerned, there is no acceptable position, no party line, no right theology. The school in which I teach does have commitments, and I have commitments; but it is not the school's intention, nor is it my intention, to impose these commitments on anyone. I have told students that the worst thing they could do with my lectures is to take them as the established dogma of the course. I want them to learn to think theologically on their own, and I expect only two things of them: (1) to show a reasonable mastery of the materials they have been studying; (2) to articulate their own views in a publicly defensible way, that is, by means of argument, analysis, dialogue, persuasion, not hesitating to acknowledge where they are confused, uncertain, in a state of transition, but not hesitating either to state forthrightly where they stand. This ideal has not been perfectly achieved. To the extent that a consensus about commitments builds up, in an institution or a class, it places pressure on students to conform to it. And I have found it difficult to evaluate fairly the work of students who oppose in principle the model of pluralistic inquiry.

25. Information of this sort is provided by books such as Hodgson and King, eds., *Christian Theology: An Introduction to Its Traditions and Tasks.*

26. David Tracy first introduced this expression; see *Blessed Rage for Order*, 32–34.

27. See especially the contributors to Mark A. Noll and David F. Wells, eds., *Christian Faith and Practice in the Modern World: Theology from an Evangelical Point of View* (Grand Rapids, Mich.: Wm. B. Eerdmans Publishing Co., 1988).

28. Ibid., 93–108.

29. See above, n. 8.

Chapter 2. The Resources of Theology

1. Hodgson and King, eds., *Christian Theology: An Introduction to Its Traditions and Tasks*, 61–87. I draw on materials from that chapter in what follows. Used by permission of Fortress Press. See also Edward Farley, *Ecclesial Reflection: An Anatomy of Theological Method* (Philadelphia: Fortress Press, 1982).

2. See David Tracy on the idea of a "classic" in *Christian Theology*, ed. Hodgson and King, 46–52. See also Tracy, *The Analogical Imagination: Christian Theology and the Culture of Pluralism* (New York: Crossroad, 1981), chap. 3.

3. See chap. 15, pp. 241–43.

4. See Gerhard Ebeling, *Theology and Proclamation*, trans. John Riches (Philadelphia: Fortress Press, 1966), 25–26; and *The Problem of Historicity in the Church and Its Proclamation*, trans. Grover Foley (Philadelphia: Fortress Press, 1967), chap. 2.

5. Rosemary Radford Ruether, *Sexism and God-Talk: Toward a Feminist Theology*, with a new introduction (Boston: Beacon Press, 1993), chap. 1.

6. Ferdinand Christian Baur, *On the Writing of Church History*, ed. and trans. Peter C. Hodgson (New York: Oxford University Press, 1968), esp. 336–41. Adolf Harnack, *History of Dogma*, trans. Neil Buchanan (New York: Dover Publications, 1961), vol. 1, introduction.

7. For a good sampling of this diversity, see the essays in *Lift Every Voice: Constructing Christian Theologies from the Underside*, ed. Susan Brooks Thistlethwaite and Mary Potter Engel (San Francisco: Harper & Row, 1990). See also *Reconstructing Christian Theology*, ed. Rebecca Chopp and Mark K. Taylor (Minneapolis: Fortress Press, 1994).

8. Tillich, *Systematic Theology*, 1:39.

9. See chap. 8 and chap. 18, pp. 304–15. See also Tillich, *Christianity and the Encounter of the World Religions* (New York: Columbia University Press, 1963), 95–97; and *The Future of Religions*, ed. Jerald C. Brauer (New York: Harper & Row, 1966).

10. Tillich, *Systematic Theology*, 1:39.

11. Ruether, *Sexism and God-Talk*, 22, 41–45.

12. Tillich, *Systematic Theology*, 1:3–6.

13. See chap. 6, pp. 72–77.

14. Paul F. Knitter, *No Other Name? A Critical Survey of Christian Attitudes Toward the World Religions* (Maryknoll, N.Y.: Orbis Books, 1985), 7.

15. Tillich, *Systematic Theology*, 1:40–46.

16. David H. Kelsey, *The Uses of Scripture in Recent Theology* (Philadelphia: Fortress Press, 1975); and "The Bible and Christian Theology," *Journal of the American Academy of Religion* 48 (1980): 385–402.

17. See *Christian Theology*, chap. 2.

Chapter 3. The Dimensions of Theology

1. See Ernst Troeltsch, "Religion and the Science of Religion," in *Writings on Theology and Religion*, trans. and ed. Robert Morgan and Michael Pye (Louisville, Ky.: Westminster/John Knox Press, 1990), 82–123.

2. For example, R. G. Collingwood says that the historian weaves a "web of

imaginative construction," the test of which is its coherence, continuity, and persuasiveness, not simply its correspondence to empirical data; see *The Idea of History*, ed. T. M. Knox (Oxford: Clarendon Press, 1946), 244 (see 231–49). Hayden White claims that every historical interpreter makes conceptual decisions on ideological grounds at a metahistorical level—decisions with respect to the figurative use of language, modes of employment, principles of coherence and combination. Ultimately, he suggests, the only validity tests of a historical interpretation are those of representational persuasiveness and ethical implication. See *Metahistory: The Historical Imagination in Nineteenth-Century Europe* (Baltimore: Johns Hopkins University Press, 1973), chap. 1. No historian is able to avoid the ethical implications, the implications for praxis, of his or her work. Most modern secular historical work implicitly embraces a tragic vision of the human condition and employs irony as its basic linguistic protocol. White is seeking a "way beyond irony" because of its "inherent skepticism," "moral agnosticism," and pretensions of scholarly objectivity and neutrality. If historical study promotes moral agnosticism, for example, then it has certain effects on responsible historical praxis today. The Christian view of history cannot be primarily tragic, nor is it primarily comic; rather it is tragicomic. See chap. 18, pp. 315–23; and Peter C. Hodgson, *God in History: Shapes of Freedom* (Nashville: Abingdon Press, 1989), 147–68.

3. See Bernard Cooke, *Ministry to Word and Sacraments: History and Theology* (Philadelphia: Fortress Press, 1976), part 1. See also my discussion of these matters in *Revisioning the Church: Ecclesial Freedom in the New Paradigm* (Philadelphia: Fortress Press, 1988).

4. I provide a brief discussion of church and ministry in chap. 18, pp. 297–304.

5. I am influenced in these formulations by Thomas W. Ogletree, "Dimensions of Practical Theology: Meaning, Action, Self," in *Practical Theology*, ed. Don S. Browning (San Francisco: Harper & Row, 1983), 83–101. This collection of essays is one of the best theological discussions of practical theology. Edward Farley's contribution, "Theology and Practice Outside the Clerical Paradigm," 21–41, applies what he has to say about theology as a *habitus*, a practical wisdom (see chap. 1, p. 15), to the concept of practical theology.

6. God is also the water that supports (and threatens) the ship. The metaphor of wind is more congenial to my approach, but wind and water together are metaphors of the Spirit (see chap. 17, pp. 277–79). For Tillich water and the sea were powerful symbols of the abysmal character of the divine. God's Spirit is both energy (wind) and source or fount (water).

Chapter 4. Revisioning the Constructive Task of Theology

1. See Baur, *On the Writing of Church History*, 266–69.

2. For a history and defense of the use of the term "dogmatics," see Gerhard Ebeling, *The Study of Theology*, trans. Duane A. Priebe (Philadelphia: Fortress Press, 1978), chap. 10.

3. Ibid., 125–26. Ebeling argues that the concept "systematic theology" is broader than that of "dogmatics," which was distinguished from ethics, because

of its tendency "to embrace everything in theology methodologically oriented to the question of contemporary validity and the testing of the claim to truth."

4. Tillich, *Systematic Theology*, 1:58.

5. Ibid., 1:59.

6. James A. Weisheipl, *Friar Thomas D'Aquino: His Life, Thought, and Works* (Washington: Catholic University of America Press, 1983), 321.

7. This example is cited by Hegel, *Lectures on the Philosophy of Religion*, 1:224, 320.

8. At Thingvellir, site of the ancient Icelandic parliament, located on the mid-Atlantic rift, temporary shelters called booths were constructed, made of wood, grass, turf, canvas—metaphorically, straw. Where the earth moves and the climate is harsh, where resources are scarce and the time is limited to a midsummer's fortnight, there are no permanent structures; yet laws and traditions were established in this place and a people formed a nation.

9. Deconstruction is a literary and philosophical movement that has been influenced above all by the writings of Jacques Derrida. But it can be taken more broadly as a description of the condition of postmodern culture. See Jonathan Culler, *On Deconstruction: Theory and Criticism after Structuralism* (Ithaca: Cornell University Press, 1982); and Jean-François Lyotard, *Toward the Postmodern*, ed. Robert Harvey and Mark S. Roberts (London: Humanities Press, 1993). Its theological representation is best found in Mark C. Taylor, *Erring: A Postmodern A/theology* (Chicago: University of Chicago Press, 1984). For a theological response, see Edward Farley, *Good and Evil: Interpreting a Human Condition* (Minneapolis: Fortress Press, 1990), 10–26.

10. Catherine Keller, "Piling Up and Hopefully Saving: Eschatology as a Feminist Problem" (Paper presented to the Work Group on Constructive Theology, October 1989), 10. A different, published version of this paper is found in Irene Diamond and Gloria Orenstein, eds., *Reweaving the World: The Emergence of Ecofeminism* (San Francisco: Sierra Club Books, 1990), 249–63.

11. Just such a variety is appearing on the scene today in increasing numbers. Among the most recent are: James H. Evans, *We Have Been Believers: An African-American Systematic Theology* (Minneapolis: Fortress Press, 1992); Francis Schüssler Fiorenza and John P. Galvin, eds., *Systematic Theology: Roman Catholic Perspectives*, 2 vols. (Minneapolis: Fortress Press, 1991); Paul K. Jewett, *God, Creation, and Revelation: A Neo-Evangelical Theology* (Grand Rapids, Mich.: Wm. B. Eerdmans Publishing Co., 1991); Daniel L. Migliore, *Faith Seeking Understanding: An Introduction to Christian Theology* (Grand Rapids, Mich.: Wm. B. Eerdmans Publishing Co., 1991); Sallie McFague, *The Body of God: An Ecological Theology* (Minneapolis: Fortress Press, 1993); Robert C. Neville, *A Theology Primer* (Albany: State University of New York Press, 1991); Ted Peters, *God—the World's Future: Systematic Theology for a Postmodern Era* (Minneapolis: Fortress Press, 1992); Ninian Smart and Steven Konstantine, *Christian Systematic Theology in a World Context* (Minneapolis: Fortress Press, 1991); Dorothee Sölle, *Thinking about God: An Introduction to Theology* (Philadelphia: Trinity Press International, 1990). This list reveals a new phenomenon, the growing popularity of confessional or thematic systematic theologies: African American, Roman Catholic, neo-Evangelical, Reformed, Lutheran, global, comparative, pluralist, postmodern, liberationist, feminist, ecological, etc. While this is a sound way to avoid overly

ambitious or pretentious efforts, there is something disappointing about it to the extent that it reflects the loss of an ecumenical or holistic vision and of the effort to keep the boundaries between cultural-linguistic systems open. For a new work that does exhibit some of the latter characteristics, see Gordon D. Kaufman, *In Face of Mystery: A Constructive Theology* (Cambridge, Mass.: Harvard University Press, 1993). My own project attempts to move in a direction similar to Kaufman's on this score but with quite different results (which might be seen as the difference between Kant and Hegel replayed in a new key). With a few exceptions, I have not attempted to take these recent theologies into account in the present work. Smart and Konstantine make the helpful point that systematic or constructive theology is similar to "what the Indian tradition calls *darśana*, a viewpoint or vision of reality," a "worldview." Such worldviews are multiple, perspectival yet holistic, oriented to ultimate reality, and not demonstrable in a logical or empirical sense. The "soft epistemology" of worldviews need not, however, lead to relativism, for "life in fact demands, pragmatically, the adoption of a worldview," and good reasons can be given for choosing certain worldviews rather than others—reasons oriented to paradigmatic narratives, ethical criteria, religious experience, political and social fruits. See *Christian Systematic Theology in a World Context*, 17–18, 82–93.

12. Tillich, *Systematic Theology*, 1:28–34.

13. Karl Rahner is the greatest modern representative of this approach. See his *Foundations of Christian Faith: An Introduction to the Idea of Christianity*, trans. William V. Dych (New York: Crossroad, 1978). See also Francis Schüssler Fiorenza, *Foundational Theology: Jesus and the Church*.

14. See John Macquarrie, *Principles of Christian Theology* (New York: Charles Scribner's Sons, 1966), 50. Macquarrie calls this "philosophical theology" or a "new style natural theology." Gordon Kaufman's new work, *In Face of Mystery*, devotes considerable attention to foundational theological questions.

15. This was Hegel's interpretation of the proofs; see *Lectures on the Philosophy of Religion*, 1:414–41. See also Paul Tillich, "The Two Types of Philosophy of Religion," in *Theology of Culture* (New York: Oxford University Press, 1959), 10–29.

16. John Macquarrie uses "symbolic theology" in this sense; see *Principles of Christian Theology*, chap. 8.

17. Langdon Gilkey, *Message and Existence: An Introduction to Christian Theology* (New York: Seabury Press, 1980), 24–25, 33–36.

18. Sallie McFague, *Models of God: Theology for an Ecological, Nuclear Age* (Philadelphia: Fortress Press, 1987), 32.

19. Raimundo Panikkar, "The Jordan, the Tiber, and the Ganges," in *The Myth of Christian Uniqueness: Toward a Pluralistic Theology of Religions*, ed. John Hick and Paul F. Knitter (Maryknoll, N.Y.: Orbis Books, 1987), 109–10. Panikkar also uses the term "cosmotheandric," which he notes is "rather more euphonic" than "theanthropocosmic." See *The Cosmotheandric Experience: Emerging Religious Consciousness* (Maryknoll, N.Y.: Orbis Books, 1993), 54–55. See chap. 8, pp. 108–12.

20. McFague, *Models of God*, chap. 1.

21. In her most recent book, *The Body of God: An Ecological Theology*, McFague places anthropology at the beginning of her discussion of theological topics, believing that it is necessary for theology to start its thinking about the human

place in the scheme of things with what we know about ourselves as creatures of the earth rather than as creatures of God, thus avoiding the spiritualization of theological anthropology. By contrast, I have placed anthropology in the middle. In the middle is cosmos, world, that which is not God, and human beings are a part of cosmos, formed of dust as well as created in the image of God. I want to affirm that human beings are spiritual but without spiritualization, and material but without materialization. Locating anthropology in the middle rather than at the beginning serves (for me) as an effective reminder that we humans are part of a larger whole, not that whole itself or its foundation. In the beginning is God, not the self. In responding to similar concerns, McFague and I have moved in different directions. Probably neither move in itself is decisive but rather what is said about human beings wherever they are discussed.

22. Calvin struggled with the question how to start theology. He offered two initial propositions: "Without knowledge of self there is no knowledge of God"; "Without knowledge of God there is no knowledge of self." But he concluded: "However the knowledge of God and of ourselves may be mutually connected, the order of right teaching requires that we discuss the former first, then proceed afterward to treat the latter." John Calvin, *Institutes of the Christian Religion*, trans. Ford Lewis Battles (Philadelphia: Westminster Press, 1960), book 1, chap. 1, 35–39. This is the order I have decided to follow. It is the trinitarian order.

23. Karl Barth, *Church Dogmatics*, vol. 2/1: *The Doctrine of God* (Edinburgh: T. & T. Clark, 1957), § 28.

24. See Hegel, *Lectures on the Philosophy of Religion*, 1:307–9, 323–24; 3:271–74, 291–94. For Hegel's logical deep structure, see the editorial introduction to the one-volume edition of this work (Berkeley and Los Angeles: University of California Press, 1988), 11–14. This matter is further discussed in chap. 11, pp. 151–57.

25. In his PBS television conversations with Bill Moyers.

Chapter 5. The Challenge of Postmodernity

1. This section utilizes material from the Introduction to my book *Revisioning the Church: Ecclesial Freedom in the New Paradigm* (Philadelphia: Fortress Press, 1988). Used by permission. It has, however, been extensively revised.

2. See Gustavo Gutiérrez, *The Power of the Poor in History*, trans. Robert R. Barr (Maryknoll, N.Y.: Orbis Books, 1983), chaps. 7, 8. Gutiérrez's expression "theology from the underside of history" was suggested by Dietrich Bonhoeffer (see 231).

3. Such is the proposal of Langdon Gilkey in "The New Watershed in Theology," in *Society and the Sacred: Toward a Theology of Culture in Decline* (New York: Crossroad, 1981), 3–14. See also his "Events, Meanings, and the Current Tasks of Theology," *Journal of the American Academy of Religion* 53 (1985): 717–34. An international symposium was held at the University of Tübingen in 1988 on this topic; it was published in a volume edited by Hans Küng and David Tracy, *Paradigm Change in Theology: A Symposium for the Future*, trans. Margaret Kohl (New York: Crossroad, 1989).

4. See Thomas Kuhn, *The Structure of Scientific Revolutions*, 2d ed. (Chicago: University of Chicago Press, 1970), esp. 150.

5. On the Enlightenment and the age of modernity viewed in theological terms, see Robert H. King in *Christian Theology: An Introduction to Its Traditions and Tasks*, ed. Hodgson and King, 10–21; John Polkinghorne, *One World: The Interaction of Science and Theology* (Princeton: Princeton University Press, 1986), chap. 1; and Rebecca Chopp, *The Praxis of Suffering* (Maryknoll, N.Y.: Orbis Books, 1986), 29–33.

6. See Jürgen Habermas, "Modernity—An Incomplete Project," reprinted in *The Anti-Aesthetic: Essays on Postmodern Culture*, ed. Hal Foster (Port Townsend, Wash.: Bay Press, 1983), 3–15. See also Habermas's *The Philosophical Discourse of Modernity*, trans. Frederick Lawrence (Cambridge, Mass.: MIT Press, 1987); and Jean-François Lyotard, *Toward the Postmodern*, ed. Robert Harvey and Mark S. Roberts (Atlantic Highlands, N.J.: Humanities Press, 1993).

7. Hal Foster in *The Anti-Aesthetic*, xii.

8. For the following analysis I am indebted to Langdon Gilkey (see n. 3); John B. Cobb, Jr., "Revisioning Ministry for a Revisioned Church," paper presented to a Lilly Foundation conference on the future of ministry, Vanderbilt Divinity School (1992); Nelson Pallmeyer, "Summary of the Kairos USA Process," unpublished paper (1992); James H. Evans, Jr., Mark K. Taylor, and Susan Brooks Thistlethwaite, presentations and discussion at a meeting of the Workgroup on Constructive Theology, Yale University (1992).

9. Gilkey, *Society and the Sacred*, 6.

10. See the reference below to Mark C. Taylor, n. 22.

11. Gilkey, *Society and the Sacred*, 8.

12. For a detailed analysis and suggestions, see Herman E. Daly and John B. Cobb, Jr., *For the Common Good: Redirecting the Economy toward Community, the Environment, and a Sustainable Future* (Boston: Beacon Press, 1989). On the despiritualizing effect of capitalism, see Joel Kovel, *History and Spirit: An Inquiry into the Philosophy of Liberation* (Boston: Beacon Press, 1991), 6–13.

13. Al Gore, *Earth in the Balance: Ecology and the Human Spirit* (New York: Houghton Mifflin, 1992).

14. I am especially indebted to John Cobb (see n. 8) at this point.

15. This is Mark C. Taylor's expression (see below, n. 22). Not many theologians have followed Taylor's path into "a/theology," but it is the prevailing stance in other disciplines of the academy, where a tragic or ironic view of life prevails, notably philosophy, literary criticism, the social sciences.

16. This is an option pursued especially by feminist critical theory. See Chris Weeden, *Feminist Practice and Poststructuralist Theory* (Oxford: Basil Blackwell, 1987); Drucilla Cornell, *The Philosophy of the Limit* (New York: Routledge, 1992); Sharon D. Welch, *A Feminist Ethic of Risk* (Minneapolis: Fortress Press, 1990).

17. In the paper referred to in n. 8. Again I am indebted to his insightful analysis.

18. This is the option associated with the so-called Yale School, which has enjoyed wide influence through the work of George A. Lindbeck (*The Nature of Doctrine* [Philadelphia: Westminster Press, 1984]) and Hans W. Frei (*Types of Christian Theology*, ed. George Hunsinger and William C. Placher [New Haven: Yale University Press, 1992]). It has been carried on by their students, notably William Placher and Stanley Hauerwas. It is also the position with which many present-day Reformed and Neo-orthodox theologians align themselves, those

who have been influenced by Karl Barth and his critique of Protestant liberalism, as were Lindbeck and Frei. In terms of H. Richard Niebuhr's famous typology, this is "Christ and culture in paradox" (*Christ and Culture* [New York: Harper & Bros., 1951]). Renewal is a worthy option, and as Cobb notes, from a transformationist perspective it is the best that is possible for many Christians who are not prepared to accept transformation. However, some younger scholars schooled in this theology are clearly moving in the direction of transformation; e.g., Kathryn Tanner, *The Politics of God: Christian Theologies and Social Justice* (Minneapolis: Fortress Press, 1992).

19. These are the theologians David Tracy identifies as "revisionist" (*Blessed Rage for Order* [New York: Seabury Press, 1975]). They include process, existentialist, and hermeneutical thinkers as well as many feminist, liberation, and pluralist theologians. They are heirs of a prophetic and critical liberalism that can be traced back to Schleiermacher and Hegel in the nineteenth century and that has been mediated through Troeltsch, Tillich, Rahner, and H. Richard Niebuhr in the twentieth. In the latter's typology, this is "Christ the transformer of culture."

20. See William Hamilton, "The Death of God Theologies Today," in *Radical Theology and the Death of God*, ed. Thomas J. J. Altizer and William Hamilton (Indianapolis: Bobbs-Merrill, 1966), 23–50.

21. Thomas J. J. Altizer, *The Gospel of Christian Atheism* (Philadelphia: Westminster Press, 1966). There is also a strongly apocalyptic element in Altizer's thought; see *Genesis and Apocalypse: A Theological Voyage toward Authentic Christianity* (Louisville, Ky.: Westminster/John Knox Press, 1990).

22. Mark C. Taylor, *Erring: A Postmodern A/theology*. For the following summary, see 3–18, 36–39, 47–51, 71–72, 105–7, 114–17.

23. Sallie McFague, *Models of God*, 25–26.

24. See Robert McAfee Brown's introduction to the volume edited by him, *Kairos: Three Prophetic Challenges to the Church* (Grand Rapids, Mich.: Wm. B. Eerdmans Publishing Co., 1990), 1–14. The original *Kairos Document* was issued in South Africa in 1985, followed by similar documents coming from Central America in 1988, and from the collaboration of South African, Central American, and Asian theologians in 1989. The draft of *Kairos USA* document, prepared by Nelson Pallmeyer, circulated in 1992. The authors of these documents argue that we are in a time of *status confessionis*, a "confessional situation" in which bold opposition and clear statements are called for, comparable to the situation of the Confessing Church in Germany in the 1930s.

25. In the paper referred to in n. 8.

26. In a presentation to a conference on biblical interpretation and social location, Vanderbilt Divinity School (1993). See also Chopp's book, *The Power to Speak: Feminism, Language, God* (New York: Crossroad, 1989).

27. Mark K. Taylor, *Remembering Esperanza: A Cultural–Political Theology for North American Praxis* (Maryknoll, N.Y.: Orbis Books, 1990), 20–21, 31–45.

Chapter 6. The Emancipatory Quest

1. See the tribute to Gutiérrez's work in the collection of essays presented in honor of his sixtieth birthday, *The Future of Liberation Theology*, ed. Marc

Ellis and Otto Maduro (Maryknoll, N.Y.: Orbis Books, 1989). Theologians from around the world contributed to this volume, which is an excellent reference for the current discussion of liberation theology. The Latin American literature is extensive. In addition to Gutiérrez, the writings of María Clara Bingemer, Leonardo and Clodovis Boff, José Comblin, Enrique Dussel, José Míguez Bonino, Juan Luis Segundo, Jon Sobrino, and Sergio Torres should be noted.

2. Gustavo Gutiérrez, *A Theology of Liberation: History, Politics, and Salvation*, 15th anniversary ed., trans. and ed. Caridad Inda and John Eagleson (Maryknoll, N.Y.: Orbis Books, 1988), chap. 10. This book was first published in Spanish in 1971 and translated into English in 1973. One section of the new edition has been rewritten, and the text has been reedited to employ inclusive language. An introduction called "Expanding the View" surveys the evolution of liberation theology and identifies present and future themes. In answer to the question whether he would write it differently today, Gutiérrez responds, "My book is a love letter to God, to the church, and to the people to which I belong. Love remains alive, but it grows deeper and changes its manner of expression" (xlvi).

3. "The gospel proclaims God's love for every human being and calls us to love as God loves. Yet recognition of the fact of class struggle means taking a position, opposing certain groups of persons, rejecting certain activities, and facing hostilities. . . . The universality of Christian love is . . . incompatible with the exclusion of any persons, but it is not incompatible with a preferential option for the poorest and most oppressed. When I speak of taking into account social conflict, including the existence of class struggle, I am not denying that God's love embraces all without exception. Nor is anyone excluded from our love, for the gospel requires that we love our enemies; a situation that causes us to regard others as our adversaries does not excuse us from loving them." Ibid., 159–60.

4. Ibid., 86; see chaps. 5, 9.

5. Ibid., 104.

6. Gustavo Gutiérrez, *The Truth Shall Make You Free: Confrontations*, trans. Matthew J. O'Connell (Maryknoll, N.Y.: Orbis Books, 1990), 2–4. This point is reinforced by his most recent book to appear in English, *The God of Life*, trans. Matthew J. O'Connell (Maryknoll, N.Y.: Orbis Books, 1991). This is a biblically-based introduction to theology that focuses on the love of God, the coming of the kingdom proclaimed by Jesus, and the inspiration of the Spirit.

7. *The Truth Shall Make You Free*, 7–11, 55–57. Gutiérrez's spirituality of liberation is developed more fully in *We Drink from Our Own Wells: The Spiritual Journey of a People*, trans. Matthew J. O'Connell (Maryknoll, N.Y.: Orbis Books, 1984).

8. *The Truth Shall Make You Free*, 155–60, 172. See *The God of Life*, 9–19.

9. *The Truth Shall Make You Free*, 155–56.

10. Aloysius Pieris, *An Asian Theology of Liberation* (Maryknoll, N.Y.: Orbis Books, 1988), 69. Other important Asian theologies to which I am unable to attend are the Korean Minjung and the writings of Asian women. For helpful anthologies and surveys see C. S. Song, *Theology from the Womb of Asia* (Maryknoll, N.Y.: Orbis Books, 1986); David Kwang-sun Suh, *The Korean Minjung in*

Christ (Hong Kong: Christian Conference of Asia, 1991); *Asian Christian Spirituality: Reclaiming Traditions*, ed. Virginia Fabella, Peter K. H. Lee, and David Kwang-sun Suh (Maryknoll, N.Y.: Orbis Books, 1992); *We Dare to Dream: Doing Theology as Asian Women*, ed. Virginia Fabella and Sun Ai Le Park (Maryknoll, N.Y.: Orbis Books, 1990); and Chung Hyun Kyung, *Struggle to Be the Sun Again: Introducing Asian Women's Theology* (Maryknoll, N.Y.: Orbis Books, 1990).

11. Pieris, *An Asian Theology of Liberation*, 120–24. See Gutiérrez, *A Theology of Liberation*, 163–71.

12. Aloysius Pieris, "The Buddha and the Christ: Mediators of Liberation," in *The Myth of Christian Uniqueness*, ed. Hick and Knitter, 175. See also his *Love Meets Wisdom: A Christian Experience of Buddhism* (Maryknoll, N.Y.: Orbis Books, 1988), chap. 10.

13. Pieris, *An Asian Theology of Liberation*, 59; *The Myth of Christian Uniqueness*, 162.

14. Pieris, *An Asian Theology of Liberation*, 62, 85.

15. James H. Cone, *God of the Oppressed* (New York: Seabury Press, 1975). In this work Cone achieved a synthesis of his earlier thinking, which was influenced by black power and a radical reading of Karl Barth, with his subsequent study of resources from the African American religious tradition (spirituals, blues, black preaching, etc.). He described the development of black theology and the changes in his own thought in *For My People: Black Theology and the Black Church* (Maryknoll, N.Y.: Orbis Books, 1984). Other important writings of African American theologians during the past two decades include J. Deotis Roberts, *Liberation and Reconciliation: A Black Theology* (Philadelphia: Westminster Press, 1971); William R. Jones, *Is God a White Racist? A Preamble to Black Theology* (Garden City, N.Y.: Doubleday, 1973); Gayraud S. Wilmore, *Black Religion and Black Radicalism: An Interpretation of the Religious History of Afro-American People*, 2d ed. (Maryknoll, N.Y.: Orbis Books, 1983); Cornel West, *Prophesy Deliverance! An Afro-American Revolutionary Christianity* (Philadelphia: Westminster Press, 1982); *Prophetic Fragments* (Grand Rapids, Mich.: Wm. B. Eerdmans Publishing Co., 1988); and *Race Matters* (Boston: Beacon Press, 1993); Katie Cannon, *Womanist Ethics* (Atlanta: Scholars Press, 1988); Jacqueline Grant, *White Women's Christ and Black Women's Jesus: Feminist Christology and Womanist Response* (Atlanta: Scholars Press, 1989); James H. Evans, Jr., *We Have Been Believers: An African-American Systematic Theology* (Minneapolis: Fortress Press, 1992); Dwight N. Hopkins, *Shoes that Fit Our Feet: Sources for a Constructive Black Theology* (Maryknoll, N.Y.: Orbis Books, 1993). An excellent sourcebook covering the period from 1966 to 1992 is edited by Cone and Wilmore, *Black Theology: A Documentary History*, 2 vols. (Maryknoll, N.Y.: Orbis Books, 1993). The first volume of this anthology has been substantially revised since it was first published in 1979, while the second volume contains selections from many of the new voices in black theology.

16. Cone, *God of the Oppressed*, 10; see 39–44.

17. Ibid., 45–52.

18. Ibid., 97.

19. Ibid., 50. See Cone's recent study, *Martin and Malcolm and America: A Dream or a Nightmare?* (Maryknoll, N.Y.: Orbis Books, 1991).

20. *God of the Oppressed,* 45, 95.

21. Ibid., 92.

22. Ibid., 37–38.

23. This expression was used by Hegel and Lessing, but it can be traced back to the twelfth century. See M. D. Chenu, *La théologie au douzième siècle* (Paris: J. Vrin, 1957), 361.

24. Cone, *God of the Oppressed,* 102–7.

25. Ibid., 111–12. James Evans arrives at a similar position from a different approach; see *We Have Been Believers,* chap. 2.

26. Cone, *God of the Oppressed,* 55, 70, 99.

27. Jones, *Is God a White Racist?,* esp. chaps. 1–4, 5, 11–12.

28. Emil L. Fackenheim, *God's Presence in History: Jewish Affirmations and Philosophical Reflections* (New York: New York University Press), chap. 3.

29. Jones examines the works of earlier black theologians—Joseph Washington, Albert Cleage, Major Jones, Deotis Roberts—as well as Cone's second book, published in 1970, *A Black Theology of Liberation* (*Is God a White Racist?,* chaps. 6–10).

30. Jones, *Is God a White Racist?,* 115–17.

31. Cone argues to this effect in *The Spirituals and the Blues: An Interpretation* (New York: Seabury Press, 1972), chap. 4, and in *God of the Oppressed,* chap. 8, where he deals with questions raised by Jones (see 187–92). Cone's most direct response to Jones, found in a note to this chapter on 267–68, is in terms of a firm insistence that Jesus Christ is the "decisive historical event beyond which no one needs to appeal." But in the text of the chapter, as well as in *The Spirituals and the Blues,* he develops a more nuanced approach, showing how this event has been actually experienced as redemptively efficacious in the African American community. I anticipate here an argument developed more fully in later chapters, and I also draw on ideas contained in *God in History,* chap. 4.

32. Evans, *We Have Been Believers,* chap. 3. Dwight Hopkins offers another variation on this theme. He argues that a "faith in freedom" is the central reality in African American religious life. Freedom is something that must be struggled and hoped for; it has not yet arrived and thus is the object as well as the substance of *faith.* Blacks need "shoes" to walk the rocky road toward freedom, and these shoes are fashioned in the crucible of the African American experience—that of slaves, of women, of folk culture, of the black church, and of political and religious leadership. These are the primary sources for constructing a black theology. Shoes that fit our feet are needed for the long walk to freedom. See Hopkins, *Shoes That Fit Our Feet,* 1–10.

33. Rosemary Radford Ruether, *Sexism and God-Talk: Toward a Feminist Theology,* with a new introduction (Boston: Beacon Press, 1993), xv. Ruether's more recent book, *Gaia and God: An Ecofeminist Theology of Earth Healing* (San Francisco: HarperSanFrancisco, 1992), does not really develop the God-concept further except for a brief section on an "ecofeminist theocosmology," to which I shall refer.

34. Sallie McFague, *Models of God,* and *The Body of God;* Rita Nakashima Brock, *Journeys by Heart: A Christology of Erotic Power* (New York: Crossroad, 1988); Elizabeth A. Johnson, *She Who Is: The Mystery of God in Feminist Theological Discourse* (New York: Crossroad, 1992). I make use of all these works in

subsequent chapters. McFague (especially in her later work) and Johnson do cover a broad range of topics and in this respect offer constructive feminist theologies.

35. E.g., Sharon D. Welch, *Communities of Resistance and Solidarity: A Feminist Theology of Liberation* (Maryknoll, N.Y.: Orbis Books, 1985); Catherine Keller, *From a Broken Web: Separation, Sexism, and Self* (Boston: Beacon Press, 1986); Rebecca Chopp, *The Power to Speak.*

36. Especially the works of Elisabeth Schüssler Fiorenza, *In Memory of Her: A Feminist Theological Reconstruction of Christian Origins* (New York: Crossroad, 1983); and *But She Said: Feminist Practices of Biblical Interpretation* (Boston: Beacon Press, 1992).

37. Ruether, *Sexism and God-Talk,* xvi. These include lesbian voices: Carter Heyward, *Touching Our Strength: The Erotic as Power and the Love of God* (San Francisco: Harper & Row, 1989); womanist voices: Jacquelyn Grant, *White Women's Christ and Black Women's Jesus* (see n. 15); Mujerista voices: Ada María Isasi-Díaz and Yolanda Tarango, *Hispanic Women: Prophetic Voice in the Church* (San Francisco: Harper & Row, 1988); Asian, African, and Latin American voices: Virginia Fabella and Mercy Amba Oduyoye, *With Passion and Compassion: Third World Women Doing Theology* (Maryknoll, N.Y.: Orbis Books, 1988); Elsa Tamez, *Through Her Eyes: Women's Theology from Latin America* (Maryknoll, N.Y.: Orbis Books, 1989); Virginia Fabella and Sun Ai Park, *We Dare to Dream: Doing Theology as Asian Women* (see n. 10); Chung Hyun Kyung, *Struggle to Be the Sun Again: Introducing Asian Women's Theology* (see n. 10); Jewish voices: Judith Plaskow, *Standing Again at Sinai: Judaism from a Feminist Perspective* (San Francisco: Harper & Row, 1990); Buddhist voices: Rita Gross, *Buddhism after Patriarchy: A Feminist History, Analysis, and Reconstruction* (Albany: State University of New York Press, 1992).

38. Ruether, *Sexism and God-Talk,* 47–61.

39. Ibid., 61–66, 135–38.

40. Ibid., 49.

41. Ibid., 71.

42. Ibid., 85–87.

43. Ibid., 253–54.

44. Ruether, *Gaia and God,* 247–53, also 4–5. This is as far as Ruether is willing to go by way of constructing a theoretical God-concept. The chapters on God/ess and eschatology in *Sexism and God-Talk* end with similar tantalizing allusions. Ruether is dependent here on hints from Teilhard de Chardin and process theology (see *Gaia and God,* 242–47), but she does not really deliver the promised "ecofeminist theocosmology" (247). I believe it would prove difficult to develop such a cosmology using the paradoxes of Nicholas of Cusa; a more promising route might be through Hegel's dialectical holism (see chap. 11) or Whitehead's relational categories (in, e.g., the work of Marjorie Hewitt Suchocki). But Ruether avoids philosophical theology, preferring instead to focus on the function of God-concepts in human history and experience.

45. Ruether, *Sexism and God-Talk,* 237, 243–46.

46. Ibid., 252–53.

47. Ibid., 254–56.

48. Ibid., 232–34. A similar vision is offered in *Gaia and God,* chap. 10. In this

work Ruether does not speak of democratic socialism but rather of "building local communities of celebration and resistance." Her political critique is iconoclastic: She does not seem to believe that working through the political process or attempting to bring about systemic political changes will accomplish much.

49. *Sexism and God-Talk*, 258.

Chapter 7. The Ecological Quest

1. A number of helpful books have been published that not only explore these recent developments in lay terms but also open a new dialogue between natural science and religion that is promising to be exceedingly fruitful. The pioneer in this dialogue is the physicist and theologian Ian Barbour, whose *Issues in Science and Religion* (Englewood Cliffs, N.J.: Prentice-Hall, 1966) opened the discussion, and whose recently published Gifford Lectures, *Religion in an Age of Science* (San Francisco: Harper & Row, 1990), provides a comprehensive overview of its current stage. Several British scientist-theologians have contributed to the discussion in imaginative ways: Paul Davies, *God and the New Physics* (New York: Simon & Schuster, 1983), and *The Cosmic Blueprint: New Discoveries in Nature's Creative Ability to Order the Universe* (New York: Simon & Schuster, 1988); Arthur Peacocke, *Creation and the World of Science* (Oxford: Clarendon Press, 1979), and *Theology for a Scientific Age* (Oxford: Basil Blackwell, 1990); and John Polkinghorne, *One World: The Interaction of Science and Theology* (Princeton: Princeton University Press, 1986), and *Science and Providence: God's Interaction with the World* (Boston: Shambhala Publications, 1989). A valuable collection of essays is contained in a book produced by scholars associated with the Center for Theology and the Natural Sciences in Berkeley and edited by Ted Peters, *Cosmos as Creation: Theology and Science in Consonance* (Nashville: Abingdon Press, 1989). In addition to these works specifically on the relation of science and religion, books continue to appear from scientists, philosophers, and journalists on new aspects of cosmology (Stephen Hawking, Stephen Toulmin, Brian Swimme), astrophysics (James Trefil), molecular biology (Jacques Monod), chaos theory (Ilya Prigogine and Isabelle Stengers, James Gleick, Stephen Kellert).

2. Polkinghorne, *One World*, 8–9, 16, 25, 64, 85, 97.

3. Peacocke, *Creation and the World of Science*, 61–63.

4. See Polkinghorne, *One World*, 43–44.

5. See Jerry H. Gill, *Faith in Dialogue: A Christian Apologetic* (Waco, Tex.: Word Books, 1985), 27–32, 58; and Polkinghorne, *One World*, 86.

6. Polkinghorne, *One World*, 88, 92ff.

7. See Ian Barbour, "Creation and Cosmology," in *Cosmos as Creation*, ed. Peters, 116–20; Barbour, *Religion in an Age of Science*, 125–29; and James S. Trefil, *The Moment of Creation: Big Bang Physics from Before the First Millisecond to the Present Universe* (New York: Macmillan, 1983), chap. 1.

8. Barbour, in *Cosmos as Creation*, ed. Peters, 120–21, 126–27, 141.

9. Ibid., 122, 142. See chap. 12, pp. 175–79.

10. Ilya Prigogine and Isabelle Stengers, *Order out of Chaos* (New York: Bantam Books, 1984).

11. See James Gleick, *Chaos: Making a New Science* (New York: Penguin Books, 1987). Lorenz is discussed on 11–31. For a recent and careful assessment, see Stephen H. Kellert, *In the Wake of Chaos: Unpredictable Order in Dynamical Systems* (Chicago: University of Chicago Press, 1993).

12. An example. Let's say I go out to sail on a windy day and a gust of wind capsizes the boat. This would not have happened if the boat had not been on the lake in a particular place at a particular time. Why was it there at that precise instant? An exceedingly complex and open-ended sequence of causes comes into play. Among other things, it has to do with the fact that I drove to the lake a little faster and encountered less traffic than normally. While rigging the boat I forgot to install the battens, which slowed the process down by thirty seconds. The wind shifted and made it more difficult to tack out of the harbor. And so on. Then there is the matter of the causal sequences leading to a strong puff of wind at just that point in time and space, and the contributing effect of a large wave that swamped the boat as it heeled sharply. Sailing is definitely a nonlinear activity.

13. Gleick, *Chaos*, 213ff.; Davies, *The Cosmic Blueprint*, 21–22, 30–31, 42, 52–55.

14. "The role of chance is what one might expect if the universe were so constituted as to be able to explore all the potential forms of organization of matter, both living and non-living, that it contains. . . . The mutual interplay of chance and law, the operation of chance in a lawlike framework, is creative. It is the combination of the two that allows new forms to emerge. On the one hand, if all were lawlike and regular, then the system would be ossified. It would always repeat itself. On the other hand, if all were chance, then we would have chaos. . . . It is chance and law *together* that produce a universe in which new forms emerge, a universe that has creativity built into it." Arthur Peacocke, "Theology and Science Today," in *Cosmos as Creation*, ed. Peters, 39.

15. See Polkinghorne, *Science and Providence*, 2, 25, 28–31.

16. See Davies, *The Cosmic Blueprint*, 200–203. Davies and some other scientist-theologians tend to overstate the scientific evidence in quasi-religious form. We must be cautious at this point and recognize that theological claims represent a religious *interpretation* of empirical evidence. See chap. 13, pp. 183–86.

17. McFague, *The Body of God*, 56–57. See Stephen Toulmin, *The Return to Cosmology: Postmodern Science and the Theology of Nature* (Berkeley and Los Angeles: University of California Press, 1982), 272.

18. Thomas Berry, *The Dream of the Earth* (San Francisco: Sierra Club Books, 1988), 41–42.

19. Ibid., 37–39.

20. Charles Birch and John B. Cobb, Jr., *The Liberation of Life: From the Cell to the Community* (Cambridge: Cambridge University Press, 1981), esp. 79–96. This is a seminal text for the subsequent development of ecological theology. I have also been helped by Thomas Berry, *The Dream of the Earth;* Jay B. McDaniel, *Of God and Pelicans: A Theology of Reverence for Life* (Louisville, Ky.: Westminster/John Knox Press, 1989); *Earth, Sky, Gods and Mortals: Developing an Ecological Spirituality* (Mystic, Conn.: Twenty-Third Publications, 1990); Charles Birch, William Eakin, and Jay B. McDaniel, eds., *Liberating Life: Contemporary Approaches to Ecological Theology* (Maryknoll, N.Y.: Orbis Books,

1990); Al Gore, *Earth in the Balance* (New York: Houghton Mifflin, 1992); Ruether, *Gaia and God;* McFague, *The Body of God.*

21. See McDaniel, *Of God and Pelicans,* chap. 3.

22. Birch and Cobb devote the later chapters of *The Liberation of Life* (chaps. 7–10) to devising strategies for meeting this multifaceted challenge. For a clear description of the challenge, see Gore, *Earth in the Balance,* Parts I-II; for Gore's prescriptions, see Part III. Gore openly acknowledges the difficulties faced by politicians in confronting the environmental crisis. He refers to "the failures of candor, evasions of responsibility, and timidity of vision that characterize too many of us in government," and he wrote the book about this challenge partly "to summon the courage to make a full and unreserved commitment to see it through" (11, 16). Now that he is in an unexpectedly good position to see it through, he will discover, I fear, that environment gets pushed down the list of priorities by other urgent and more immediately visible crises. As he learned in the campaigns of both 1988 and 1992, the environment is still too abstract an issue for most people to grasp. When they *are* able to grasp it, it may be too late.

23. "The Peace of Earth is not some fixed condition, but a creative process activated by polarity tensions requiring a high level of endurance. This creative process is not a clearly seen or predetermined pattern of action; it is rather a groping toward an ever more complete expression of the numinous mystery that is being revealed in this process." Berry, *The Dream of the Earth,* 220–21; cf. 36–38, 197, 206–8, 216–23.

24. R. W. Sperry, quoted in *The Liberation of Life,* ed. Birch and Cobb, 176.

25. Ibid., 177–79.

26. Ibid., 183–93.

27. Ibid., 189.

28. Ibid., 195–97.

29. Ibid., 197–98.

30. Peacocke, *Creation and the World of Science,* 356–57.

31. Brian Swimme, *The Universe Is a Green Dragon: A Cosmic Creation Story* (Sante Fe, N.Mex.: Bear & Co., 1984), 43–50, 56–61, 64, 87–88.

32. McDaniel, *Of God and Pelicans,* 21.

33. Ibid., 24, 31–41, 89–92.

Chapter 8. The Dialogical Quest

1. See Jürgen Habermas, *Knowledge and Human Interests,* trans. Jeremy J. Shapiro (Boston: Beacon Press, 1971); *Communication and the Evolution of Society,* trans. Thomas McCarthy (Boston: Beacon Press, 1979); *The Theory of Communicative Action,* 2 vols., trans. Thomas McCarthy (Boston: Beacon Press, 1984, 1987); *The Philosophical Discourse of Modernity,* trans. Frederick Lawrence (Cambridge, Mass.: MIT Press, 1987). I discuss the ideas of Habermas and some of his followers and critics in *God in History,* 219–29.

2. Jürgen Habermas, "Dialectics of Rationalization: An Interview," *Telos* 49 (1981): 7.

3. Richard J. Bernstein, *Beyond Objectivism and Relativism: Science, Hermeneutics, and Praxis* (Philadelphia: University of Pennsylvania Press, 1983), 181; on Habermas, see 182–96.

4. The sort of theology that is possible on the basis of deconstruction is well-represented by Kevin Hart, *The Trespass of the Sign: Deconstruction, Theology and Philosophy* (Cambridge: Cambridge University Press, 1989). I believe that an apophatic moment is necessary in theology since negation is a necessary element of the divine life, but it should not control the logic of theological discourse.

5. John B. Cobb, Jr., "Beyond 'Pluralism,'" in *Christian Uniqueness Reconsidered: The Myth of a Pluralistic Theology of Religions,* ed. Gavin D'Costa (Maryknoll, N.Y.: Orbis Books, 1990), 85–86. See also Cobb's earlier work, *Beyond Dialogue: Toward a Mutual Transformation of Christianity and Buddhism* (Philadelphia: Fortress Press, 1982).

6. John Hick and Paul F. Knitter, eds., *The Myth of Christian Uniqueness: Toward a Pluralistic Theology of Religions* (Maryknoll, N.Y.: Orbis Books, 1987). The title was deliberately provocative, recalling an equally provocative book edited by Hick and published a decade earlier, *The Myth of God Incarnate* (Philadelphia: Westminster Press, 1977). The provocation called forth a sharp rejoinder, edited by Gavin D'Costa, *Christian Uniqueness Reconsidered: The Myth of a Pluralistic Theology of Religions.* A year before the Claremont conference, Knitter published a seminal work, *No Other Name? A Critical Survey of Christian Attitudes Toward the World Religions* (Maryknoll, N.Y.: Orbis Books, 1985). He summarized the major works on the subject up to that time (by such pioneers as Ernst Troeltsch, Karl Rahner, Paul Tillich, Wilfred Cantwell Smith, Raimundo Panikkar, Stanley Samartha, John Hick, and John Cobb), and gave the discussion a new agenda, namely the acceptance of "religious pluralism" as a viable and more authentic Christian option than either "exclusivist" or "inclusivist" postures toward other religions. Subsequently Knitter became general editor of the "Faith Meets Faith" series of Orbis Books, which has published a continuous stream of valuable and innovative works. Several of these and other works are discussed in chap. 18, pp. 304–11, where I return to this topic in relation to a theology of the Spirit. In addition to Hick and Knitter, I have been especially influenced by the work of John Cobb, Joseph Kitagawa, David Krieger, Raimundo Panikkar, Aloysius Pieris, Wilfred Cantwell Smith, and Paul Tillich.

7. Knitter, Preface to *The Myth of Christian Uniqueness,* viii.

8. John Hick, "The Non-Absoluteness of Christianity," *The Myth of Christian Uniqueness,* chap. 2; for the following paragraph see esp. 17–19.

9. Ibid., 20–22.

10. Ibid., 22–23.

11. Knitter provides a detailed account of these developments in *No Other Name?,* chaps. 2–8. His own work in no small measure contributed to the pluralist flood.

12. Hick and Knitter, eds., *The Myth of Christian Uniqueness,* ix.

13. Ibid., chaps. 1–3 (Gordon Kaufman, John Hick, Langdon Gilkey). My version of God's relative absoluteness is found in chap. 10.

14. Ibid., chaps. 4–7 (Wilfred Cantwell Smith, Stanley Samartha, Raimundo Panikkar, Seiichi Yagi). Knitter explores the christological implications of pluralism in *No Other Name?,* chap. 9. See also chap. 15, pp. 236–38.

15. Ibid., chaps. 8–11 (Rosemary Radford Ruether, Marjorie Hewitt Suchocki, Aloysius Pieris, Paul Knitter).

16. "Problems in the Case for a Pluralistic Theology of Religion," *The Journal*

of Religion 68 (October 1988): 493–507. Ogden has expanded this critique in a recently published book, *Is There Only One True Religion or Are There Many?* (Dallas: Southern Methodist University Press, 1992). Here he develops a fourth option (beyond exclusivism, inclusivism, and pluralism), according to which "the possibility of salvation is constituted solely and sufficiently by the primordial and everlasting love of God. Thus, not only Christians but all human beings always already have the *possibility* of salvation, and there *can be* (whether or not pluralists are right that there actually *are*) as many true religions as there are religions that so respond to God's love as to be constituted by it and representative of it." This, he says, might be called "*pluralistic* inclusivism" as opposed to the more customary "*monistic* inclusivism" (see the preface). The nuances here differ slightly but importantly from what Knitter calls "unitive pluralism." Ogden would, I think, have to acknowledge that what he offers is a Christian formulation of the inclusive ground of all that is, and that other religions offer different formulations. The meaning of such terms as "God," "love," "salvation," "primordial and everlasting," etc., could only be determined, not on the basis of one religion, but in open and unending dialogue. It seems to me that the answer to the question posed by the title is paradoxical: There is no true religion (none is *truly* representative of God's love); there are many true religions (God's love is ambiguously mediated by many religions). Ogden's position, however, is that since there *is* one true religion (Christianity, for which the universal and all-embracing love of God is decisively re-presented in Christ), there can also be many true religions (see 104).

17. Cobb in *Christian Uniqueness Reconsidered*, ed. D'Costa, 81, 83–92.

18. I offer here the foundations for an argument that is further developed in chap. 18, pp. 308–11.

19. Cobb writes: "My goal is to transform contradictory statements into different but not contradictory ones. My assumption is that what is positively intended by those who have lived, thought, and felt deeply is likely to be true, whereas their formulations are likely to exclude other truths that should not be excluded. . . . Alongside all the errors and distortions that can be found in all our traditions there are insights arising from profound thought and experience that are diverse modes of apprehending diverse aspects of the totality of reality. They are true, and their truth can become more apparent and better formulated as they are positively related to one another." *Christian Uniqueness Reconsidered*, ed. D'Costa, 93–94.

20. Joseph M. Kitagawa claims that a "quest for human unity" is at the heart of each of the great religions although none of them has shown sufficient wisdom to guide humanity very far toward this unity. Each religion is part of a "religious-cultural-social-political synthesis," which achieves a unity of its own but in terms limited to that synthesis. Each religion also has a certain capacity for self-transcendence by which it recognizes the existence and even validity of other cultures and religions. This is the "outer meaning" of a religion, and without it there would be no means of combating "the self-authenticating circularity common to religious traditions" when they view themselves only internally. The objective of interreligious dialogue is best achieved, in Kitagawa's view, neither by religious imperialism (whether exclusivist or inclusivist) nor by the surrender of distinctive particularities in a lowest common denominator of reli-

giousness, but rather by holding in balance the inner and outer meanings of religions—striving for an interaction among the outer meanings and a discovery of the truth of the inner meanings of other religions. There are a number of historical instances from the past when this was accomplished rather well, Kitagawa believes, and today he sees a new synthesis emerging based on the "Easternization" of the world, which will encourage a pluralist rather than a monolithic temper. See *The Quest for Human Unity: A Religious History* (Minneapolis: Fortress Press, 1990), especially the introduction and chap. 5.

21. Knitter, *No Other Name?*, 166.

22. Ernst Troeltsch, *Christian Thought: Its History and Application*, trans. and ed. Baron F. von Hügel (London: University of London Press, 1923), 35.

23. Knitter, *No Other Name?*, 7.

24. See his essay, "The Jordan, the Tiber, and the Ganges: Three Kairological Moments of Christic Self-Consciousness," in *The Myth of Christian Uniqueness*, ed. Hick and Knitter, chap. 6.

25. Ibid., 90–92, 103, 107.

26. Ibid., 109. See Pannikar's recently published *The Cosmotheandric Experience* (Maryknoll, N.Y.: Orbis Books, 1993). While the essays in it date from the mid- to late seventies, it contains Panikkar's fullest discussion of this theme. "Cosmotheandric" is a more euphonic version of "theanthropocosmic" although it could give the mistaken impression that *cosmos* rather than *theos* is the encompassing reality for Panikkar.

27. *The Myth of Christian Uniqueness*, ed. Hick and Knitter, 109–10.

28. Aloysius Pieris, "The Buddha and the Christ: Mediators of Liberation," in *The Myth of Christian Uniqueness*, ed. Hick and Knitter, chap. 10; see 171–72.

29. See Rowan Williams, Gavin D'Costa, and Christoph Schwöbel in *Christian Uniqueness Reconsidered*, ed. D'Costa, chaps. 1–3. A similar myopia afflicts Ted Peters's *God as Trinity: Relationality and Temporality in Divine Life* (Louisville, Ky.: Westminster/John Knox Press, 1993). Peters surveys the trinitarian theology of Karl Barth, Karl Rahner, Claude Welch, Jürgen Moltmann, Wolfhart Pannenberg, Eberhard Jüngel, Robert Jenson, and Catherine Mowry LaCugna. He concludes that the primary scriptural witness to and Christian experience of God in terms of Father, Son, and Holy Spirit is "settled," and that therefore it is possible to move on to the question of the connection between the economic Trinity in time and the immanent Trinity that is timeless. He writes as though the feminist critique of patriarchy, the deconstructive critique of ontotheology, and the pluralist critique of Western monotheism do not exist.

30. See David Tracy, "Kenosis, Sunyata, and Trinity: A Dialogue with Masao Abe," in *The Emptying God: A Buddhist-Jewish-Christian Conversation*, ed. John B. Cobb, Jr., and Christopher Ives (Maryknoll, N.Y.: Orbis Books, 1990), 135–54.

31. See chap. 10, pp. 145–50.

Chapter 9. Faith, Reason, and Revelation

1. See chap. 4, pp. 44–46.

2. H. Richard Niebuhr, *Faith on Earth: An Inquiry into the Structure of Human Faith*, ed. Richard R. Niebuhr (New Haven, Conn.: Yale University Press, 1989), chap. 3.

3. Hegel referred to this as the "speculative" insight into the truth of religion. Religious faith is not simply our consciousness *of* God but God's own self-consciousness. Thus religion is not a human projection but "the self-knowing of divine spirit through the mediation of finite spirit." Hegel, *Lectures on the Philosophy of Religion*, 3 vols., ed. and trans. Peter C. Hodgson et al. (Berkeley and Los Angeles: University of California Press, 1984, 1985, 1987), 1:314–19 (quotation from 318 n.120). This theme is emphasized especially in Hegel's 1824 lectures against the philosophy and theology of subjectivity (Kant, Schleiermacher). The insight is "speculative" because speculation grasps the relationship of mirroring (*speculum*) between the divine object and the human subject: divine revelation is "reflected" in human faith.

4. See George Stroup, "Revelation," in *Christian Theology: An Introduction to Its Traditions and Tasks*, 3d ed., ed. Peter C. Hodgson and Robert H. King (Minneapolis: Fortress Press, 1994), chap. 4.

5. Ibid., 122.

6. Immanuel Kant, *Religion within the Limits of Reason Alone*, trans. T. M. Greene and H. H. Hudson (New York: Harper & Bros., 1960); *Critique of Practical Reason*, trans. Lewis White Beck (New York: Liberal Arts Press, 1956).

7. Friedrich Schleiermacher, *On Religion: Speeches to Its Cultured Despisers*, trans. Richard Crouter (Cambridge: Cambridge University Press, 1988), esp. Second Speech (96–140); and *The Christian Faith*, ed. H. R. Mackintosh and J. S. Stewart (Edinburgh: T. & T. Clark, 1928), esp. § 10 (44–52).

8. Hegel, *Lectures on the Philosophy of Religion*, esp. 3:63–64, 170–71, 251–53.

9. Paul Tillich, *Systematic Theology*, 1:94–97. "Reason and Revelation" is the first of the five main parts of Tillich's system.

10. Ibid., 1:71–106.

11. Ibid., 1:81–83.

12. See Immanuel Kant, *Critique of Pure Reason*, trans. Norman Kemp Smith (London: Macmillan, 1929), 297ff.; and Emmanuel Levinas, *Totality and Infinity: An Essay on Exteriority*, trans. Alphonso Lingis (Pittsburgh: Duquesne University Press, 1969), sec. 1.

13. It was Hegel who named God "the whole" (*das Ganze*). God is not merely the object of consciousness but the whole that encompasses both consciousness and its object. This whole is not an abstract totality but is itself consciousness, *infinite* subjectivity, which means that it is a nexus of relationships in which difference is preserved and novelty is generated in an endless process. This is what it means to speak of God as *Spirit*. See *Lectures on the Philosophy of Religion*, 3:62; the theme of wholeness recurs many times in the lectures. On open wholeness, see also the discussion below of "the history of freedom within history" in chap. 18, pp. 316–19.

14. Tillich, *Systematic Theology*, 1:105.

15. Ibid., 1:83.

16. Jürgen Habermas, *The Theory of Communicative Action* (Boston: Beacon Press, 1984, 1987); Richard J. Bernstein, *Beyond Objectivism and Relativism* (Philadelphia: University of Pennsylvania Press, 1983); Helmut Peukert, *Science, Action, and Fundamental Theology*, trans. James Bohman (Cambridge, Mass.: MIT Press, 1984).

17. See Michel Foucault, *Power/Knowledge* (New York: Pantheon Books, 1980).

18. Tillich, *Systematic Theology*, 1:83.

19. Tillich offers a similar definition; see *Systematic Theology*, 1:108–10.

20. See Gerhard Ebeling, "Existence between God and God: A Contribution to the Question of the Existence of God," *Journal for Theology and the Church* 5 (1968): 150–54; John Dillenberger, *God Hidden and Revealed* (Philadelphia: Muhlenberg Press, 1953); and Karl Barth, *Church Dogmatics*, vol. 2/1, § 27.

21. See Hegel, *Lectures on the Philosophy of Religion*, 1:382, 3:280; and Tillich, *Systematic Theology*, 1:108–9.

22. Tillich, *Systematic Theology*, 1:110–17.

23. Ibid., 1:125, 2:166–67.

24. See chap. 17, pp. 277–79.

25. See Levinas, *Totality and Infinity*, sec. 3.

26. See McFague, *The Body of God*, 131–35.

27. See above, n. 16.

28. See chap. 15, pp. 259–63. The expression "God's project" is borrowed from the liberation theologians of Central America, who have used the dynamic phrase *el proyecto de Dios* to indicate what is meant by *basileia tou theou*. I am indebted to Sharon H. Ringe for this reference.

29. H. Richard Niebuhr, *The Meaning of Revelation* (New York: Macmillan, 1941), 109.

30. Ibid., 93.

31. Ibid., 110.

32. Tillich, *Systematic Theology*, 1:133–34, 147.

33. Niebuhr, *The Meaning of Revelation*, 115–16.

34. Knitter, *No Other Name?*, 171–72.

35. Tillich, *Systematic Theology*, 1:156–57.

36. I develop this idea in a more theoretical way in *God in History*, 83–92. The image of the potter is an important one in African American folklore; see James H. Evans, Jr., *We Have Been Believers: An African-American Systematic Theology* (Minneapolis: Fortress Press, 1992), 76.

37. See my *God in History*, 194–215, esp. 205.

Chapter 10. The Creative Being of God

1. Tillich, *Systematic Theology*, 1:235, 238–39. The so-called proofs of the existence of God are based on these questions and really represent approaches to God, or ways of thinking about God, rather than proofs in the strict sense. See 204–10.

2. Elizabeth Johnson, *She Who Is* (New York: Crossroad, 1992), 236–39.

3. The texts of the sermon are Jer. 4:23–30; Is. 24:18–20; Is. 54:10. See Paul Tillich, *The Shaking of the Foundations* (New York: Charles Scribner's Sons, 1948), 1–11.

4. Tillich, *Systematic Theology*, 1:235–38.

5. Langdon Gilkey, *Message and Existence: An Introduction to Christian Theology* (New York: Seabury Press, 1980), 90–95. See also Gilkey's *Maker of Heaven and Earth* (Garden City, N.Y.: Doubleday, 1959); *Reaping the Whirlwind: A Christian Interpretation of History* (New York: Seabury Press, 1976); and his chapter on "God" in *Christian Theology*, ed. Hodgson and King.

6. McFague, *Models of God*, 66–67.

7. In her discussion of the models, McFague does not provide much help in understanding how God is actually embodied in and relates to the nonhuman world. Her metaphors focus rather on the most basic *human* relationships. These human relationships—mother, lover, friend—involve, to be sure, human embodiment. But it would be odd to speak of God as the mother of atoms and genes or the friend of trees and plants. We can say perhaps that God befriends animals and loves the world, but in saying this we tend to speak anthropomorphically and/or abstractly. As powerful and as appropriate as McFague's metaphors are, they are not really adequate for speaking about God's relationship to the natural world, nor does she represent them as being adequate for this purpose. She addresses this task in her next work, *The Body of God*. I refer to this work in chaps. 12, 13.

8. See chap. 7, pp. 86–92. The following summary is based especially on Arthur Peacocke, *Creation and the World of Science* (Oxford: Clarendon Press, 1979), 61–63, 65–68; and John Polkinghorne, *One World* (Princeton: Princeton University Press, 1979), 43–44, 51, 86.

9. See chap. 6, pp. 78–81; and Ruether, *Sexism and God-Talk* (Boston: Beacon Press, 1993), 49–52.

10. Ibid., 85–87. These ideas are developed more fully in Ruether's *Gaia and God* (San Francisco: HarperSanFrancisco, 1992); see esp. chaps. 2, 9.

11. G. W. F. Hegel, *Lectures on the Philosophy of World History*, Introduction: *Reason in History*, trans. H. B. Nisbet (Cambridge: Cambridge University Press, 1975), 47–48; and *Encyclopedia of the Philosophical Sciences*, part 2, *Hegel's Philosophy of Nature*, trans. A. V. Miller (Oxford: Clarendon Press, 1970), §§ 247–52; and part 3, *Hegel's Philosophy of Mind*, trans. William Wallace and A. V. Miller (Oxford: Clarendon Press, 1971), § 385.

12. Ancient religions knew that God is not literally a great womb or sun or mountain; rather God is *like* these natural phenomena in their mystery and power. God is essentially spiritual power, but this power is represented in natural images. Hegel pointed this out in his treatment of nature religion; see *Lectures on the Philosophy of Religion*, 2:531.

13. Jacques Monod, *Chance and Necessity: An Essay on the Natural Philosophy of Modern Biology* (New York: Vintage Books, 1971); see esp. 112–17.

14. Ibid., 138.

15. This is the argument of the Anglican archbishop and chemist John Habgood in a review of Monod's book in *The Expository Times* 84 (December 1972): 90–91.

16. The British scientist-theologians Arthur Peacocke and John Polkinghorne argue to this effect. See Peacocke, *Creation and the World of Science*, 69–71, 77–84, 356–57; and Polkinghorne, *One World*, 79.

17. See David A. Pailin, *God and the Processes of Reality: Foundations of a Credible Theism* (London and New York: Routledge, 1989), for a summary and critique of this theory. See also John B. Cobb, Jr., *A Christian Natural Theology: Based on the Thought of Alfred North Whitehead* (Philadelphia: Westminster Press, 1965), chaps. 4–5.

18. John B. Cobb, Jr., *God and the World* (Philadelphia: Westminster Press, 1969), 54–55. Italics mine.

19. The preceding paragraphs and the following section draw on ideas I first worked out in *Jesus—Word and Presence: An Essay in Christology* (Philadelphia: Fortress Press, 1971), chap. 3.

20. This ambiguity is rooted in the Greek participle *ōn,* "being," which can appear either as a substantive noun, *ta onta,* "beings," or as a verbal noun, *ousia,* "being." The same ambiguity is found in the German verb *sein,* "to be," which can be used as a substantive noun, *Seiende(s),* "a being" or "entity," or as a verbal noun, *Sein,* "being." The ambiguity is the basis for Heidegger's so-called "ontological difference" between being (*Sein*) and beings (*Seiende*), and it is employed in Hegel's philosophy. See Martin Heidegger, *Hegel's Concept of Experience* (New York: Harper & Row, 1970), 105–7.

21. Paul Tillich, *The Courage to Be* (New Haven, Conn.: Yale University Press, 1952), 182–90. For Hegel's critique of the ideas of the "supreme being" and "spurious infinite," see *Lectures on the Philosophy of Religion,* 1:116–17, 124, 127, 308, 422–23.

22. See, e.g., Karl Barth, "Philosophie und Theologie," in *Philosophie und christliche Existenz,* ed. G. Huber (Basel: Helbing & Lichtenhahn, 1960), 93–106; and Rudolf Bultmann, "The Historicity of Man and Faith," in *Existence and Faith,* trans. and ed. Schubert M. Ogden (New York: Meridian Books, 1960), 92–110.

23. Karl Rahner, *Hörer des Wortes: Zur Grundlegung einer Religionsphilosophie,* ed. J. B. Metz (Munich: Kösel-Verlag, 1963), 66, 69; see the whole of chap. 4. An English translation of this work exists, but it is very poor: *Hearers of the Word,* trans. Michael Richards (New York: Herder and Herder, 1969), 48–50.

24. This understanding of the term "absolute" is based on my reading of Hegel. See Hodgson, *God in History,* 62, 69, 172–73, 178.

25. The text is formulated in the first person because God is the speaker, but YHWH is actually a third person verbal form. Elizabeth Johnson observes that Thomas Aquinas (*Summa theologica* I, q. 13, a. 11) translated the name into Latin as *qui est,* "He who is," "who is," or "the One who is." But "He who causes to be" or "the One who lets be" comes closer to the active sense of the Hebrew verb. Johnson then proposes a feminist gloss on the name, arguing that the "who" is open to inclusive interpretation. Thus she arrives at the title of her book. *She Who Is,* 241–42.

26. See Gilkey, *Message and Existence,* 101; and McFague, *Models of God,* 78–87.

27. Masao Abe, "Kenotic God and Dynamic Sunyata," in *The Emptying God,* ed. Cobb and Ives, 16.

28. See David Tracy in *The Emptying God,* 139.

Chapter 11. The Triune Figuration of God

1. The model of the Trinity offered here was first developed in my book *God in History,* chap. 2 (esp. 93–112). Much of what is presented in this chapter is a revision and elaboration of what is found in that work and is used by permission of Abingdon Press. The conceptual underpinning for the model comes from Hegel's interpretation and appropriation of the doctrine of the Trinity in his *Lectures on the Philosophy of Religion.* My reading of Hegel on the Trinity is found in *God in History,* 60–70. Another primary source for the model is the

doctrine of God set forth in Karl Barth's *Church Dogmatics*, esp. vol. 2/1, although I have serious reservations about the way in which Barth develops certain aspects of his conception (see *God in History*, 97–98, 109–10). Finally, I am influenced by process theology but also have questions about some aspects of its understanding of God as they bear upon trinitarian reflection (70–83). For a brief survey and critique of the classic doctrine of the Trinity, see 52–60. For my use of the metaphors "figure," "shape," "figuration," etc., see 83–92 (also above, p. 135, and below, p. 251).

2. The term *oikonomia* means the management (*nomos*) of a household (*oikos*); more generally, it is an arrangement or a plan. In classical theology, the expression "economic Trinity" referred to God's arrangement of and involvement in the world's salvation through the creative work of the Father, the redemptive work of the Son, and the sanctifying work of the Spirit; whereas the "immanent Trinity" referred to God's internal self-relations prior to and apart from the world.

3. The process of retrieving the Trinity in a feminist conceptuality is just beginning. See especially Elizabeth A. Johnson, *She Who Is*, chap. 10 (discussed below, see esp. n. 45); and Sallie McFague, *Models of God*, 181–87. McFague's three models of Mother, Lover, and Friend correspond precisely to the three figures of the One, love, and freedom in the model proposed here. She acknowledges that "the pattern of three is appropriate for expressing the unity, separation, and reunification that have been the central theme of this [book's] experiment" (184). McFague's models are personal, whereas I prefer cognitive-existential concepts and praxis-oriented figures. The concepts are needed to correct the mythological as well as the patriarchal deficiencies of the old doctrine. The way *not* to proceed, in my judgment, is to identify a "feminine principle" in the Godhead, e.g., the Spirit, and play it off against the masculine principles, the Father and Son. This leaves us with a gender dualism and a mythological way of thinking. Catherine Mowry LaCugna's *God For Us: The Trinity and Christian Life* (San Francisco: HarperSanFrancisco, 1991), is a major scholarly study, but it does not represent a feminist reconstruction, nor does it fundamentally question traditional trinitarian conceptualities.

4. See Jürgen Moltmann, *The Spirit of Life: A Universal Affirmation*, trans. Margaret Kohl (Minneapolis: Fortress Press, 1992), 290ff.

5. The primary representatives of modalism in contemporary theology are Karl Barth (*Church Dogmatics*, vol. 1/1 [Edinburgh: T. & T. Clark, 1936], § 9) and Karl Rahner (*The Trinity*, trans. Joseph Donceel [New York: Herder and Herder, 1970]), while the primary representatives of a social trinitarianism are Jürgen Moltmann (*The Trinity and the Kingdom of God*, trans. Margaret Kohl [San Francisco: Harper & Row, 1981]) and Leonardo Boff (*Trinity and Society*, trans. Paul Burns [Maryknoll, N.Y.: Orbis Books, 1988]). See the discussion of their views in Johnson, *She Who Is*, 205–9.

6. This is the logical deep structure that, according to Hegel, underlies all thought and all life. See *God in History*, 60–65. The primary text is Hegel's *Logic*. See G. W. F. Hegel, *The Encyclopaedia Logic*, trans. T. F. Geraets, W. A. Suchting, and H. S. Harris (Indianapolis: Hackett Publishing Co., 1991), esp. §§ 181–93 (the syllogism). The three moments or figures of Hegel's syllogism are universality (identity), particularity (difference), and individuality or singularity (mediation).

7. Barth, *Church Dogmatics*, vol. 2/1, § 28, "The Being of God as the One Who Loves in Freedom." According to Barth, the oneness of God is God's being in act, specifically the act of living and revealing. The love of God means that God "seeks and creates fellowship between himself and us." The freedom of God refers to "the freedom of the Lord, who has his life from himself" without us (2/1:257). My interpretation of the formula differs from Barth's in important respects, as will become evident. A similar formulation is found in Hegel's *Logic*. The "universal" (the One) is the "free power" and "free love" since "it is a relating to its other only as itself," but "not in a dominating or forceful way." Love means to *relate* to the other as to oneself; freedom means to be "at home with oneself [*beisichselbst*]" in the other. See G. W. F. Hegel, *Science of Logic*, trans. A. V. Miller (London: Allen & Unwin, 1969), 603; see also Robert R. Williams, *Recognition: Fichte and Hegel on the Other* (Albany: State University of New York Press, 1992), 211.

8. Karl Rahner writes: "The 'economic' Trinity is the 'immanent' Trinity and the 'immanent' Trinity is the 'economic' Trinity." *The Trinity*, 22. The "is" is not intended as a sheer identity, however, but as an "axiomatic unity" (21–24). Rahner's primary concern in this context is with the isolation of the traditional treatise on the Trinity; rather "there *must* be a connection between Trinity and [humanity]. The Trinity is a mystery of *salvation*." The connection is one of "permanent perichoresis" between the two Trinities (21). I agree with Rahner in principle, but in his determination to establish the connection he minimizes the difference and ultimately tends to absorb the immanent Trinity into the economic (see 101–3).

9. See Williams, *Recognition*, 267–70; and G. W. F. Hegel, *Phenomenology of Spirit*, trans. A. V. Miller (Oxford: Clarendon Press, 1977), 10–11, 18–19. Williams believes that Hegel's reversal of the tradition on this point (the immanent Trinity within the economic rather than the economic within the immanent) is one of his greatest contributions. He comments that Hegel's "system is both closed in respect to its categorical structure (the logic), and open with respect to its correspondences with the empirical realm, even to the point of allowing the latter's contingencies to reflect back into the former" (267). The system is not the logic alone but the "super-triad" of logic-nature-spirit, the elements of which stand in a nonfoundationalist mutual mediation (268).

10. Johnson, *She Who Is*, 229.

11. See Barth, *Church Dogmatics*, 2/1:297–321.

12. Johnson, *She Who Is*, 234–35; McFague, *Models of God*, chap. 6. The words "freedom" and "friendship" have the same Indo-European root.

13. This is one of the important differences between the Hegelian and Whiteheadian systems. See *God in History*, 67–68, 74–75. Robert Neville argues for the assymetry on a different basis, namely the logic of creation *ex nihilo*. See *Behind the Masks of God: An Essay toward Comparative Theology* (Albany: State University of New York Press, 1991), 89–97.

14. Johnson, *She Who Is*, 220–21. She is drawing on the ideas of John Damascene and Edmund Hill as well as modern biology.

15. Barth, *Church Dogmatics*, vol. 2/1, §§ 29–31.

16. Augustine, *De trinitate* 1.1, 4; 5.11; et passim.

17. The formulations in this paragraph are deeply indebted to Robert

Williams, *Recognition*, esp. 221–22, 224, 255–56, 259–61, 264–71. Williams argues that Hegel's system is properly interpreted not as idealism but as a triadic holism or social ontology. For this reading, the preface, introduction, and concluding chapter of the *Phenomenology of Spirit* are especially important, as are many passages in the *Lectures on the Philosophy of Religion* (e.g., 3:62 for the idea of God as "the whole" and 3:292 for the idea of the "absolute" as "releasing") and the whole of the *Encyclopedia of the Philosophical Sciences*. See *God in History*, 65–70; also chap. 9, n. 13.

18. See n. 6 and Hegel, *Lectures on the Philosophy of Religion*, 3:15–16, 28, 39–40, 77–86, 189–98, 275–90. See also *God in History*, 66–68.

19. Barth, *Church Dogmatics*, 2/1:263.

20. Augustine, *De trinitate*, 8–15.

21. Barth, *Church Dogmatics*, 2/1:284–97.

22. See Johnson, *She Who Is*, 215–23, and our discussion above of perichoresis.

23. Moltmann, *The Spirit of Life*, 302–5. The reference to the "stream of life" is from K. Kronseder (345 n.67).

24. Paul Ricoeur, "Religion, Atheism, and Faith," and "Fatherhood: From Phantasm to Symbol," in *The Conflict of Interpretations: Essays in Hermeneutics*, ed. Don Ihde (Evanston, Ill.: Northwestern University Press, 1974), 440–67, 468–97; see esp. 441, 467, 481–97.

25. See Joseph Campbell, "The Mystery Number of the Goddess," in Joseph Campbell and Charles Musès, eds., *In All Her Names: Explorations of the Feminine in Divinity* (San Francisco: HarperSanFrancisco, 1991), 55–129.

26. McFague, *Models of God*, 116. For a recent discussion of the metaphor of God as Mother, see Johnson, *She Who Is*, chap. 9; on the limitations, 234–35. She suggests that all three of the trinitarian figures may be spoken of in female metaphors, 211–15.

27. See McFague, *Models of God*, 36.

28. Ruether, *Sexism and God-Talk*, esp. 68–71.

29. For Hegel, Judaism played a key role in the history of religions because it was the first to attain the true idea of God as "spiritual subjective unity." In comparing Judaism and Hinduism, he insisted that God must be understood as "the personal One" (*der Einer*) as opposed to "the neuter One" (*das Eine*). See *Lectures on the Philosophy of Religion*, 2:128–30, 339–40, 669.

30. Hegel, *Lectures on the Philosophy of Religion*, 3:292–93: In the immanent Trinity "the act of differentiation is only a movement, a play of love with itself, which does not arrive at the seriousness of other-being, of separation and rupture." Yet "it belongs to the absolute freedom of the idea that, in its act of determining and dividing [i.e. creating], it releases [*entlassen*] the other to exist as a free and independent being. This other, released as something free and independent, is *the world* as such." The "other" that is within God "also obtains the determinacy of other-*being*, of an actual entity." See also *Phenomenology of Spirit*, 10–11 and 19: "The life of Spirit is not the life that shrinks from death and keeps itself untouched by devastation, but rather the life that endures it and maintains itself in it. It wins its truth only when, in utter dismemberment, it finds itself." Williams notes that Hegel's *entlassen* is similar to Meister Eckhart's *Gelassenheit*, "releasement" (*Recognition*, 164 n.33). It defines the absolute as "absolving" rather than dominating, static, cut off.

31. On Hegel's concept of tragedy, see Williams, *Recognition*, chap. 10.

32. Hegel, *Lectures on the Philosophy of Religion*, 2:573.

33. Ernst Troeltsch, *The Christian Faith*, trans. Garrett E. Paul (Minneapolis: Fortress Press, 1991), 179.

34. Hegel, *Lectures on the Philosophy of Religion*, 3:131–41. Williams notes that Hegel "identifies divine love not with reconciliation so much as with death: 'death is what reconciles. Death is love itself; in it absolute love is envisaged' [3:220]." Williams, *Recognition*, 239.

35. Eberhard Jüngel, *God as the Mystery of the World: On the Foundation of the Theology of the Crucified One in the Dispute between Theism and Atheism*, trans. Darrell L. Guder (Grand Rapids, Mich.: Wm. B. Eerdmans Publishing Co., 1983), 185ff., 204, 210–19.

36. Ibid., 219.

37. Williams, *Recognition*, 264.

38. See H. Richard Niebuhr, *The Purpose of the Church and Its Ministry: Reflections on the Aims of Theological Education* (New York: Harper & Bros., 1956), 44–46.

39. See Karl Barth, *Church Dogmatics*, vol. 3/2 (Edinburgh: T. & T. Clark, 1960), § 45.1, esp. 211; and vol. 4/2 (Edinburgh: T. & T. Clark, 1958), 180–92.

40. Barth, *Church Dogmatics*, vol. 2/1, § 28.3.

41. Ibid., 2/1: 313–14.

42. Ibid., 2/1: 317, 320.

43. See Tillich, *Systematic Theology*, 1:249–52.

44. Hegel, *Lectures on the Philosophy of Religion*, 3:370; cf. 323n–324n.

45. This is one of Elizabeth Johnson's most valuable insights. Thus she names the three persons of the triune God in female metaphors, recognizing that God transcends gender: Spirit-Sophia, Jesus-Sophia, Mother-Sophia (*She Who Is*, chaps. 7–9). She also reverses the traditional order, starting with the Spirit, "God's livingness subtly and powerfully abroad in the world" (121–23, 211–15). This is where the experience of women (and men) start in knowing God. This "inductive" approach starts where the "ontological" approach ends. Both approaches are valid, and they share the recognition that the consummate manifestation of God is as Spirit.

Chapter 12. Creation of the World

1. See Dietrich Bonhoeffer, *Creation and Fall: A Theological Interpretation of Genesis 1–3* (London: SCM Press, 1959), 9–18, 47–57.

2. "The doctrine of creation is not the story of an event which took place 'once upon a time.' It is the basic description of the relation between God and the world. It is the correlate to the analysis of human finitude. . . . It discovers that the meaning of finitude is creatureliness." Paul Tillich, *Systematic Theology*, 1:252.

3. See Ian Barbour, *Religion in an Age of Science* (San Francisco: Harper & Row, 1990), 131–32, 144–45.

4. See Hegel, *Science of Logic*, 82ff. See also above, chap. 11, pp. 165–66.

5. Robert C. Neville offers a unique analysis of the logic of creation *ex nihilo* in *Behind the Masks of God*, 89–97. He argues that *nothing* is the ground or source, of which the world is the product or creature, while creation itself is the result of

creating. The ground becomes creator only in the act of creating. There is no antecedent agent; rather the agent comes into being in the act of, and as the result of, creation. Thus God, apart from creating, is literally nothing. This argument does link nothing with God, thus avoiding dualism, and it does so in such a way as to avoid emanationism, but at the price of reducing God to nothing apart from the act of creating. Thus the immanent Trinity seems to disappear into the abyss. My view is that nothing is a *moment* of the divine life but not the totality of that life; God's fundamental quality is that of *becoming*, the unity of being and nothing, not sheer nothingness. On Neville's model, it is hard to understand how nothing ever gets the project of creation under way; there seems to be no dialectical ferment out of which something might be generated. But his model has the advantage of approximating Buddhist and Confucian understandings of creation and thus of providing a basis for comparative theology. For another version of Neville's argument, which is found in all his works, see *A Theology Primer* (Albany: State University of New York Press, 1991), chaps. 3–4.

6. Sallie McFague makes the distinction between procreation and production in *The Body of God*, 151–57. McFague herself thinks that "ex nihilo" points to a source other than God, and thus she criticizes the doctrine, but I believe it really means "out of God," out of no-thing other than God.

7. See Barbour, *Religion in an Age of Science*, 133–34, 144. See also the discussion in chap. 13, pp. 183–84 of the distinction between natural theology and theology of nature.

8. Ibid., 127–28. See also James J. Trefil, *The Moment of Creation: Big Bang Physics from before the First Millisecond to the Present Universe* (New York: Macmillan, 1983), chap. 9; and Brian Swimme and Thomas Berry, *The Universe Story* (San Francisco: HarperSanFrancisco, 1992), chap. 1; they refer to the Big Bang as the "primordial flaring forth."

9. Its nonbeing is, to employ Tillich's distinction, *me-ontic* or relative, the sort of nonbeing that participates in being, not *ouk on*, the absolute nonbeing or *nihilo* out of which God creates in the beginning. *Systematic Theology*, 1:187–88.

10. Bonhoeffer, *Creation and Fall*, 19–21.

11. See Barbour, *Religion in an Age of Science*, 130–31. See also chap. 7, pp. 86–92, and chap. 13, pp. 193–96.

12. Barbour, *Religion in an Age of Science*, 125–28; Trefil, *The Moment of Creation*, chap. 2.

13. James Gleick, *Chaos: Making a New Science* (New York: Penguin Books, 1987).

14. McFague, *The Body of God*, 45–47, 55, 78–79. McFague does not, however, accept the notion of a quasi-teleological "serendipitous creativity," which has been advanced by Gordon Kaufman; see the brief summary of his views in chap. 13, pp. 191–92.

15. Errol E. Harris, *Cosmos and Anthropos: A Philosophical Interpretation of the Anthropic Cosmological Principle* (Atlantic Highlands, N.J.: Humanities Press International, 1991), 1–9, 154–59, 169–70. See also J. D. Barrow and F. J. Tipler, *The Anthropic Cosmological Principle* (Oxford: Oxford University Press, 1986), 16, 21–23.

16. Barbour, *Religion in an Age of Science*, 147, 194–95.

17. Ibid., 147.

18. McFague, *The Body of God*, 108–10.

19. Barbour, *Religion in an Age of Science*, 190–91; Swimme and Berry, *The Universe Story*, chaps. 8–9.

20. Barbour, *Religion in an Age of Science*, 194–99; Harris, *Cosmos and Anthropos*, 107–9. See the discussion of dimensions in chap. 13, pp. 188–90.

21. Barbour, *Religion in an Age of Science*, 135–36.

22. Harris, *Cosmos and Anthropos*, 47–59, 60–61, 80–82. Harris refers to Barrow and Tipler's calculation that the odds against the spontaneous assemblage of the human genome as falling between $10^{-12,000,000}$ and $10^{-24,000,000}$.

Chapter 13. Nature

1. In this chapter I presuppose the discussion of postmodern science, the new cosmology, and ecological sensibility in chap. 7. I have drawn on a number of specific points in that discussion and have tried to avoid too much repetition. My knowledge of this material is limited, and I have relied heavily on secondary sources; however, the constructive proposals set forth here are my own. What is offered in this chapter is not so much a theology of nature as a series of theological reflections on features of the new cosmology. A fully developed theology of nature would require for its foundation a *philosophy* of nature that represents a step beyond postmodern cosmology. The principal philosophies of nature of the twentieth century (Whitehead, Collingwood, Leclerq, etc.) need to be revised in light of scientific developments during the last third of the century. Errol Harris is cognizant of these developments and much of his work is suggestive although philosophically derivative from Hegel. Creation of a new philosophy of nature adequate to our time will require speculative genius comparable to that of Whitehead or Hegel. Unless and until it appears, theology of nature will be hampered, forced to rely on earlier models and to improvise as best it can.

2. The first and second steps are addressed in this chapter, and the third step in chap. 14.

3. Ian Barbour, *Religion in an Age of Science*, 144, 183–85.

4. Sallie McFague, *The Body of God*, 65–66, 78ff.

5. Ernst Troeltsch, *The Christian Faith*, 81, 91, 97, 195–98.

6. Barbour, *Religion in an Age of Science*, 43–44.

7. Brian Swimme and Thomas Berry describe the rise of modern and then of postmodern science as "a momentous change in human consciousness, . . . among the most significant changes since the emergence of human consciousness in the Paleolithic period, a change of such significance in its order of magnitude that we might think of it as revelatory, meaning by this term a new awareness of how the ultimate mysteries of existence are being manifested in the universe about us." *The Universe Story*, chap. 12 (quotation from 223).

8. Barbour, *Religion in an Age of Science*, 218–21. See also Arthur Peacocke, *Creation and the World of Science* (Oxford: Clarendon Press, 1979), 61–63; and John Polkinghorne, *One World* (Princeton: Princeton University Press, 1986), chaps. 1, 4.

9. Errol E. Harris, *Cosmos and Anthropos*, chaps. 2–10, 12; for the following summary see esp. 17–28, 98–99, 167–70.

10. See Charles Birch and John B. Cobb, Jr., *The Liberation of Life: From the Cell to the Community* (Cambridge: Cambridge University Press, 1981), 79–96. See also above, chap. 7, pp. 92–94.

11. G. W. F. Hegel, *Philosophy of Nature,* ed. and trans. M. J. Petry, 3 vols. (London: Allen & Unwin, 1970), §§ 247–48. Hegel was an organic thinker but inherited a mechanical view of nature from Newtonian and pre-evolutionary science; thus there is a fundamental tension in his philosophical interpretation of nature. J. N. Findlay argues that while Hegel's philosophy of nature was antiquated in its scientific detail, it was deeply right in its interpretative principles; see "Hegel and Whitehead on Nature," in *Hegel and Whitehead: Contemporary Perspectives on Systematic Philosophy,* ed. George R. Lucas (Albany: State University of New York Press, 1986), 155–66. See also R. G. Collingwood, *The Idea of Nature* (Oxford: Clarendon Press, 1945), 121–32. Errol E. Harris has in effect rewritten Hegel's philosophy of nature in light of postmodern science, with which it is much more congruent; see the summary below of Harris's multidimensional analysis in *Cosmos and Anthropos,* chaps. 3–10.

12. See Carolyn Merchant, "Nature as Female" in *The Death of Nature: Women, Ecology, and the Scientific Revolution* (San Francisco: Harper & Row, 1983), xxiii–xxiv, 1–41. See also Ruether, *Sexism and God-Talk,* 49; and above, chap. 6, pp. 78–81.

13. See the previous note.

14. I was forcefully reminded of this during a visit to Iceland, where the fluid forces of nature are dramatically displayed: the drift of the continental plates, the shaking of the earth, the eruptions of volcanoes, the flow of lava, the play of the aurora borealis, the sudden shifts of weather patterns, the relentless power of wind and water, fire and ice.

15. See G. S. Kirk and J. E. Raven, *The Presocratic Philosophers: A Critical History with a Selection of Texts* (Cambridge: Cambridge University Press, 1957), 87, 144, 199.

16. Barbour, *Religion in an Age of Science,* 96, 98–106, 109–10; John Polkinghorne, *One World,* 43–44, and *The Quantum World* (London: Longman, 1984); James J. Trefil, *The Moment of Creation,* chap. 4.

17. Barbour, *Religion in an Age of Science,* 111–12, 126–27, 138–40; Trefil, *The Moment of Creation,* chaps. 5–7.

18. Harris, *Cosmos and Anthropos,* 31–44; quotation from 34.

19. Barbour, *Religion in an Age of Science,* 108–11.

20. McFague, *The Body of God,* 45–47, 55, 99–102.

21. See Jerry H. Gill, *Faith in Dialogue: A Christian Apologetic* (Waco, Tex.: Word Books, 1985), 27–32, 58; Polkinghorne, *One World,* 86, 92ff.; Barbour, *Religion in an Age of Science,* 114–17, 123–24, 167–69, 171–72.

22. This is a summary of the thesis of the central chapters of Harris's *Cosmos and Anthropos;* see esp. 63–66, 74, 103–9, 149–51, 167–70.

23. Collingwood, *The Idea of Nature,* 9–13, 174–77.

24. See Barbour, *Religion in an Age of Science,* 110, 123, 143. Swimme and Berry make much of this point, arguing that the recognition that the universe has a history that can be told in narrative form is the "single greatest achievement in the entire scientific venture from Copernicus to the present" (*The Universe Story,* 236).

25. Gordon Kaufman makes this claim in the work referred to below in n. 29. He argues that we must now learn to think in "biohistorical" terms.

26. Paul Davies, *The Cosmic Blueprint* (New York: Simon & Schuster, 1988), 2, 5–6, 19–20, 198. On negentropy see Gregory Bateson, *Steps to an Ecology of Mind* (New York: Ballantine Books, 1972), esp. 456–57, and Juan Luis Segundo, *An Evolutionary Approach to Jesus of Nazareth*, trans. John Drury (Maryknoll, N.Y.: Orbis Books, 1988), esp. 113–18. See also chap. 7, pp. 89–92.

27. See Arthur Peacocke, "Theology and Science Today," in *Cosmos as Creation*, ed. Ted Peters (Nashville: Abingdon Press, 1989), 39; and *Creation and the World of Science*, 69–71, 104–11.

28. See James Gleick, *Chaos* (New York: Penguin Books, 1987); Davies, *The Cosmic Blueprint*, 21–22, 30–31, 42, 52–55; Harris, *Cosmos and Anthropos*, 33–36.

29. Gordon D. Kaufman, *In Face of Mystery: A Constructive Theology* (Cambridge, Mass.: Harvard University Press, 1993), chaps. 19–23. This book, one of the most creative of the new systematic theologies, came into my hands too late to be used extensively in the present study. While in agreement with Kaufman on many issues of substance, my overall approach to constructive theology is quite different from his.

30. See Barbour, *Religion in an Age of Science*, 148–50.

31. Harris, *Cosmos and Anthropos*, 170–72.

32. See McFague, *The Body of God*, 79. I return to the metaphor of the bush in chap. 18, pp. 314–15.

33. See chap. 7, pp. 94–98.

34. See Barbour, *Religion in an Age of Science*, 172–75, 210–11, 231–34, 236, 260–61, 269; McFague, *The Body of God*, chap. 5; Peacocke, *Creation and the World of Science*, 137–46; and "Theology and Science Today" in *Cosmos as Creation*, ed. Peters, 28–43; John Polkinghorne, *Science and Providence* (Boston: Shambhala Publications, 1989). On God as Spirit and the meaning of spiritual presence, see chap. 17. In a somewhat different vein see Erazim Kohák, *The Embers and the Stars: A Philosophical Inquiry into the Moral Sense of Nature* (Chicago: University of Chicago Press, 1987). Kohák speaks of the sense of God's "incoercible presence" in nature as the ground of its moral meaning, which has to do with the incarnation of eternal value in the intense particularities of nature and time.

35. See chap. 7, pp. 94–98.

36. Brian Swimme, *The Universe Is a Green Dragon: A Cosmic Creation Story* (Santa Fe, N. Mex.: Bear & Co., 1984), 43–50, 56–61, 64, 87–88.

37. Gleick, *Chaos*, 119ff.

38. See above, chap. 10. Ernst Troeltsch stressed the importance of affirming the immediacy of God's presence to every creature as well as a universal divine world-governance (*The Christian Faith*, 208–11, 215, 218–22).

39. Sigurdur Árni Thordarson, *Liminality in Icelandic Religious Tradition* (Ph.D. Diss., Vanderbilt University, 1989), 56–67.

40. This matter is discussed more fully in chap. 18, pp. 319–22.

Chapter 14. Human Being

1. My first attempt at a theological anthropology is found in *New Birth of Freedom: A Theology of Bondage and Liberation* (Philadelphia: Fortress Press,

1976), 122–65. I still affirm the basic approach of that work, but the details have been thoroughly revised. My earlier work was deeply influenced by Paul Ricoeur's philosophy of will: *Freedom and Nature: The Voluntary and the Involuntary*, trans. Erazim V. Kohák (Evanston, Ill.: Northwestern University Press, 1966); and *Fallible Man: Philosophy of the Will*, trans. Charles Kelbley (Chicago: Henry Regnery Co., 1967). The revisions of my earlier approach are primarily prompted by Edward Farley's *Good and Evil: Interpreting a Human Condition* (Minneapolis: Fortress Press, 1990), which is the most significant theological anthropology of our time. Other important resources for my thinking are found in Hegel's philosophy of spirit and in twentieth-century philosophical and theological anthropologies (Edmund Husserl, Martin Heidegger, Karl Jaspers, Gabriel Marcel, Jean-Paul Sartre, Maurice Merleau-Ponty, Max Scheler, Hannah Arendt, Emmanuel Levinas, Alfred Schutz, Karl Rahner, Paul Tillich, Wolfhart Pannenberg). These resources have been assimilated through a variety of readings and for the most part are not specifically noted.

2. These correspond to what Friedrich Schleiermacher identified as the three dogmatic forms of Christian theology: descriptions of the *self*, utterances about the *world*, and conceptions of *God*. See *The Christian Faith*, ed. H. R. Macintosh and J. S. Stewart (Edinburgh: T. & T. Clark, 1928), § 30. Schleiermacher proposed to organize the whole of theology according to these forms, which gave his work a distinctly anthropological cast. By contrast, I see a correspondence, not an identity, between this form and the trinitarian form, and it is the latter that organizes the whole of theology. It is true that there is a concealed trinitarianism in Schleiermacher's structure: the Son corresponds to the self, the Spirit to the world, and the Father to God.

3. It is at this point that my approach to theological anthropology differs most sharply from Farley's. Farley identifies three spheres of the human: the interhuman, the social, and the personal. He does refer to an "eternal horizon," which is an implicate of the elemental passions that pervade the personal sphere, but the eternal horizon is not a term for God; it only permits the question of God. The eternal horizon appears as an actual, sacred presence, i.e. God, only in relation to the experience of redemption mediated by determinate communities of faith. See *Good and Evil*, 28–29, 111–13, 144–46. By contrast, I claim that relatedness to God is intrinsic to and constitutive of human being apart from both sin and redemption. This is what makes it possible to understand sin as the idolatrous disruption of a relationship and to affirm that divine redemption is both possible and necessary for human well-being. This difference reflects an underlying difference in strategy between a trinitarian and an anthropological approach to theology. It is the difference between Hegel and Schleiermacher replayed in a contemporary key. The difference helps to expose fundamental issues in a productive way, and, as will be evident, I have learned a great deal from Farley's approach.

4. Farley, *Good and Evil*, chaps. 1–2. Farley also proposes to offer a theology of the human condition oriented to "historical freedom." But for him freedom does not designate a structural component of human being; rather it "gather[s] up and unif[ies] the vocabulary of salvation in Hebraic and Christian symbolism" (117). It refers to redemption rather than to human being as such. For redemption I use such terms as "liberation," "emancipation," "reconciliation"—

meaning thereby the *re*construction and consummation of human freedom—and it seems to me more plausible to understand redemption as liberation when it has been established that freedom is the fundamental condition in which human beings have been created and from which they have fallen. Farley correlates the analysis of sin (evil) and redemption (freedom) under each of the three spheres of the human. In this way he incorporates redemption into a theological anthropology, whereas I treat redemption in relation to christology and pneumatology. From Farley's perspective the latter are "cosmic narratives" that do not add anything essential to the Christian "paradigm" of good and evil (see *Good and Evil*, 117, 140). In this he is very close to Schleiermacher. Again, the difference between a trinitarian and an anthropological approach to these questions is evident.

5. I am indebted to Eleazar Singson Fernandez for raising some critical questions about my project at this point. Farley addresses the question of ontological reflection in the Introduction to *Good and Evil*, 1–26. In *New Birth of Freedom*, I employed the category of autonomy.

6. Farley, *Good and Evil*, 28–29, 282–84. Farley does allow a distinctive form of primacy to the interhuman since it is the sphere that engenders the criterion, "the face," for the workings of the other spheres. What is manifested through the face, however, is the sacred (287–89); and in my approach the primacy of the interpersonal yields to the primacy of the transpersonal. Farley's "community of the face" (289–93) corresponds anthropologically to what I name theologically the "community of the Spirit."

7. On the personal, biological, and passional aspect of human being, see Farley, *Good and Evil*, chaps. 3–5. See also Ricoeur, *Freedom and Nature*, parts 1 and 2.

8. See Farley, *Good and Evil*, chap. 1. He uses the term "interhuman" to include the elements of alterity, intersubjectivity, and concrete interpersonal relations. I have not maintained this distinction between "interhuman" and "interpersonal." The primary work of Emmanuel Levinas upon which Farley draws is *Totality and Infinity: An Essay on Exteriority*, trans. Alphonso Lingis (Pittsburgh: Duquesne University Press, 1969). Other important resources are found in Husserl, Heidegger, Buber, Merleau-Ponty, Marcel, Scheler, and Theunissen. Hegel was profoundly aware of the interhuman dimension and regarded recognition (*Anerkennung*) as the clue to the meaning of human being as spirit (*Geist*), which is intrinsically interpersonal and social. See Robert R. Williams's interpretation in *Recognition: Fichte and Hegel on the Other* (Albany: State University of New York Press, 1992), chaps. 7, 9, 11, 12. The theme of interpersonal communion is discussed more fully in connection with that of ecclesial or spiritual community, chap. 18, pp. 293–97.

9. Farley, *Good and Evil*, 47–48; for what follows, see the whole of chap. 2.

10. G. W. F. Hegel, *Philosophy of Right*, trans. T. M. Knox (Oxford: Oxford University Press, 1952), § 4. Aristotle *Politics* III.4 1279a21. On the *polis* as a realm of freedom, see Hannah Arendt, *The Human Condition* (Chicago: University of Chicago Press, 1958).

11. This is one of the points at issue with Farley. See above, n. 3.

12. This is demonstrated by Scheler, Heidegger, Jaspers, Rahner, and Pannenberg, among others. For detailed references see *New Birth of Freedom*, 159–65.

13. On limit: Hegel, *The Encyclopaedia Logic* (Indianapolis: Hackett Publishing

Co., 1991), §§ 92, 103. On boundary experience: Paul Tillich, *On the Boundary: An Autobiographical Sketch* (New York: Charles Scribner's Sons, 1966). On religion as limit experience: David Tracy, *Blessed Rage for Order* (New York: Seabury Press, 1975), chap. 5. On limit experience and liminality: Mark K. Taylor, *Beyond Explanation: Religious Dimensions in Cultural Anthropology* (Macon, Ga.: Mercer University Press, 1986).

14. Farley, *Good and Evil*, 146–50.

15. Ricoeur, *Freedom and Nature*, part 3.

16. On faith, Farley, *Good and Evil*, 150–53. On hope, Paul Ricoeur, *History and Truth*, trans. Charles A. Kelbley (Evanston, Ill.: Northwestern University Press, 1965), 93–97; and *Freedom and Nature*, 479–80. On despair as sin, see n. 65.

17. I am influenced on this matter by Hegel's critique of Schleiermacher: Religion entails not the feeling of utter dependence but the feeling of radical freedom. See *Lectures on the Philosophy of Religion*, 2:158, 218–19, 443–44, 508; 3:93–94.

18. The discussion of the fall, sin, and evil in the next three sections is based on an approach first worked out in *New Birth of Freedom*, chap. 4 (168–206). As presented here, the material has been considerably revised. In these sections I rely rather heavily on biblical materials (especially from the Hebrew Bible and Paul) because the specific themes under discussion are derived from the symbols and myths of the Jewish and Christian traditions rather than from a more general anthropology. I also rely on the work of several contemporary theologians and philosophers of religion: Paul Ricoeur, *Fallible Man*, and *The Symbolism of Evil*, trans. Emerson Buchanan (Boston: Beacon Press, 1969); Edward Farley, *Good and Evil*; Paul Tillich, *Systematic Theology*, esp. vol. 2; Reinhold Niebuhr, *The Nature and Destiny of Man*, 2 vols. (New York: Charles Scribner's Sons, 1941); Søren Kierkegaard, *The Concept of Anxiety*, ed. and trans. Reidar Thomte (Princeton: Princeton University Press, 1980); Rudolf Bultmann, *Theology of the New Testament*, trans. Kendrick Grobel, 2 vols. (New York: Charles Scribner's Sons, 1954–55).

19. See Ricoeur, *Fallible Man*, esp. xx, 6–7, 29–57, 204–5, 208. A description of fallibility along Ricoeurian lines: In the fragile synthesis that human being is, autonomous agency seems to have a seductively disproportionate attraction vis-à-vis communal relations, and the involuntary vis-à-vis the voluntary. With respect to agency: Our tendency is to draw everything into the autonomous self and to make other persons functions of our own agendas, thus violating otherness by reducing it to the same, rupturing and destroying community, and turning the social world into a system of domination and alienation. Is there a primordial egoism or narcissism at the heart of human being? With respect to the involuntary: Our tendency is to infinitize bodily needs and desires far beyond what is actually required to exist, and to absolutize death as the final and inescapable necessity of finite existence. Is there a primordial, fatal attraction to the involuntary at the heart of human being, a giving up on the human project, a death wish? We are an unstable mix of finitude and freedom, each pulling in opposite and potentially destructive directions. When this potential is actualized, fallibility becomes fault.

20. Farley, *Good and Evil*, 29. For what follows, see 43–46, 56–61, 72–75, 89–96, 109–11.

21. Ibid., 94.

22. Ibid., 43–45.

23. Ibid., 57–60.

24. On the myths of origin, see Ricoeur, *The Symbolism of Evil*, part 2.

25. Tillich, *Systematic Theology*, 1:198–201, 2:33–36.

26. Niebuhr, *The Nature and Destiny of Man*, 1:182.

27. Kierkegaard, *The Concept of Anxiety*, 32–34, 111–13.

28. Tillich, *Systematic Theology*, 2:41–42.

29. Niebuhr, *The Nature and Destiny of Man*, 1:150, 242.

30. In view of the inevitability or universality of sin, Tillich's reference to the "coincidence" of creation and fall makes sense. As soon as essential being is actualized as something existent (in other words, as soon as it is "created"), it falls into estrangement or alienation. Creation and fall are transitions—transitions from essence to existence, from fallibility to fault—which occur simultaneously. But while these transitions are coincident, they are not identical, not simply one and the same thing. Estrangement is not a necessary condition of creation; on the contrary, it is a distortion and disruption of what is essentially good. The possibility of nonestranged existence is not excluded. In fact, according to Tillich, there is at least one instance of nonestranged existence: the power of New Being in Jesus as the Christ. Here the disruptions of existence are conquered in a life that is unambiguous but still fragmentary—hence still subject to ontological anxiety and historical temptation. *Systematic Theology*, 2:39–44, 125–35; 3:144–49.

31. The other sort of logic is Hegelian logic. Kierkegaard questioned whether it or any logic could really grasp the paradoxes of life, yet he incorporated much of it in his own dialectic of existence. See Søren Kierkegaard, *Philosophical Fragments*, ed. and trans. Howard V. Hong and Edna H. Hong (Princeton: Princeton University Press, 1985). Hegel remained profoundly convinced that logic and life are not contradictory, that truth is historical and history meaningful. See Stephen Houlgate, *Freedom, Truth and History: An Introduction to Hegel's Philosophy* (London and New York: Routledge, 1991).

32. Farley is rightly critical of the judicial metaphor and the suggestion that suffering and mortality follow upon evil as punishment, not only because of what this implies about God (a law-giving monarch) but also because it seems to diminish the element of the tragic in the origin of sin. See *Good and Evil*, 127–29. But there are internal tensions in the story at this point since it also presupposes that human beings are already mortal and are driven to seize immortality and unlimited knowledge by their anxious condition. Tragic and juridical-moralistic motifs are found alongside each other.

33. See Ricoeur, *The Symbolism of Evil*, 253–54.

34. Ibid., 256.

35. Ibid., 257–59 (translation altered for purposes of inclusivity).

36. See Phyllis Trible, "Depatriarchalizing in Biblical Interpretation," *Journal of the American Academy of Religion*, 41 (March 1973): 39–41.

37. Gerhard Kittel and Gerhard Friedrich, eds., *Theological Dictionary of the New Testament*, trans. Geoffrey W. Bromiley (Grand Rapids, Mich.: Eerdmans Publishing Co., 1964–74), 1:267–316 (*hamartanō, hamartēma, hamartia*). See Ricoeur, *The Symbolism of Evil*, 70–73; and Bultmann, *Theology of the New Testament*, 1:224–25, 241–42.

38. Farley, *Good and Evil*, 127–28, 140–43.

39. Ibid., 126, 233–35, 143–44.

40. Tillich, *Systematic Theology*, 2:47–49.

41. H. Richard Niebuhr, *Faith on Earth* (New Haven, Conn.: Yale University Press, 1989), chap. 5, esp. 68ff.

42. See Mary Potter Engel, "Evil, Sin, and Violation of the Vulnerable," in *Lift Every Voice: Constructing Christian Theologies from the Underside*, ed. Susan Brooks Thistlethwaite and Mary Potter Engel (San Francisco: Harper & Row, 1990), 152–64.

43. Thomas Aquinas, *Summa Theologica* IaIIae, q.77, a.4.

44. Tillich, *Systematic Theology*, 2:52; see 51–55.

45. Ricoeur, *Fallible Man*, 161–91. The equation of sensuality with sin was made by Niebuhr, *The Nature and Destiny of Man*, 1:228–40, although it is clear that by sensuality he meant "lust," which is a form of concupiscence and also of flight.

46. Søren Kierkegaard, *The Sickness unto Death*, ed. and trans. Howard V. Hong and Edna H. Hong (Princeton: Princeton University Press, 1980), 29–35.

47. Ricoeur, *Freedom and Nature*, 29, 354, 444–46, 463, 477.

48. Karl Barth described this second form of sin as "sloth." "Sin has not merely the heroic form of pride but also, in complete antithesis yet profound correspondence, the quite unheroic and trivial form of sloth. . . . It has the form, not only of evil action, but also of evil inaction; not only of the rash arrogance which is forbidden and reprehensible, but also of the tardiness and failure which are equally forbidden and reprehensible." See *Church Dogmatics*, 4/2:403ff.

49. Bultmann, *Theology of the New Testament*, 1:246.

50. Sin in the form of flight bears similarities to the Freudian theory of repression, just as idolatry is analogous to aggression. According to Freud, the id (libido, instinctive energy) must be repressed because the primary instincts—life and death, eros and thanatos—are mutually destructive and because the scarcity of the external world prohibits unrepressed gratification of our desires. The perpetual repression of eros weakens the life instinct and strengthens its opposite, the death instinct: Civilization seems to be moving toward its own annihilation. See Sigmund Freud, *Civilization and Its Discontents*, trans. James Strachey (New York: W. W. Norton & Co., 1962). Of course, the Freudian theory of repression differs from the biblical interpretation of flight. For the latter, life and death instincts are not locked in mortal combat. Rather the disproportion between our bodily nature and our freedom is a weakness that leaves us open to the temptation to abandon freedom and sink down into the securities of the flesh, especially when the failures of freedom become evident. For the Bible, desire for death is not a natural instinct but a form of bondage, an objectification of the sin of flight.

51. See Engel, in *Lift Every Voice*, ed. Thistlethwaite and Engel, 152–64; James H. Cone, *A Black Theology of Liberation* (Philadelphia: Lippincott, 1970), 186–96; Henry Highland Garnet in *A Documentary History of the Negro People in the United States*, ed. Herbert Aptheker, vol. 1 (New York: Citadel Press, 1951), 226–33.

52. See Farley, *Good and Evil*, 137–38.

53. Ibid., 234–35. Tillich uses alienation or estrangement as a modern concept

for the totality of sin. In this he stands in a powerful philosophical tradition going back to Hegel and Marx, which understood the human condition to be alienated, that is, disrupted by the split between the way human beings exist and what they essentially are and ought to be. Since sin involves a complex rupturing of relationships, this is a compelling interpretation. But alienation does not capture the personal aspect of sin as well as other terms. See *Systematic Theology*, 2:44–47.

54. Farley, *Good and Evil*, 238–42.

55. Ricoeur, *The Symbolism of Evil*, 101 (translation altered); cf. 100–106.

56. Ibid., 152.

57. There is a form of human bondage that is not bondage of the *will*, that is, a bondage in which both voluntary and involuntary elements play a role. This is pathological bondage, in which sociological, psychological, and/or physiological disturbances are such that no element of responsible freedom is present. Here medical treatment and therapy are required, not salvation. The distinction between sin and pathology is often not clear-cut, however, since in many concrete instances they are both present and may even feed into each other (e.g., a condition of abuse may be partly pathological, partly sinful). See Farley, *Good and Evil*, 137.

58. Bultmann, *Theology of the New Testament*, 1:233–34, 246.

59. Ibid., 1:236–46.

60. The latter expression is used by Tillich, *Systematic Theology*, 2:60. Tillich identifies the doctrine of evil with "existential self-destruction," which follows upon "existential estrangement" or the state of sin.

61. Ricoeur, *The Symbolism of Evil*, 118–39; Bultmann, *Theology of the New Testament*, 1:259–60, 262–63.

62. See Ricoeur, *The Symbolism of Evil*, 139–50; and Bultmann, *Theology of the New Testament*, 1:259–69.

63. See Rudolf Bultmann, "Death in the New Testament," in *Bible Key Words*, vol. 5, part 2 (New York: Harper & Row, 1965), 87–90, 101–2. This material is also available in *Theological Dictionary of the New Testament*, 3:15–16, 21–22.

64. See Bultmann, *Theology of the New Testament*, 1:246–47.

65. Kierkegaard describes despair, which "before God" is sin, as "the sickness unto death." *The Sickness unto Death*, 13ff., 77ff.

66. Bultmann, *Theology of the New Testament*, 1:257–59.

67. See George D. Kelsey, *Racism and the Christian Understanding of Man* (New York: Charles Scribner's Sons, 1965), 32. See also the works cited in Peter C. Hodgson, *Children of Freedom: Black Liberation in Christian Perspective* (Philadelphia: Fortress Press, 1974), 19–20, 23–30.

68. Rosemary Radford Ruether, *Sexism and God-Talk*, chap. 7.

69. Mark K. Taylor, *Remembering Esperanza: A Cultural-Political Theology for North American Praxis* (Maryknoll, N.Y.: Orbis Books, 1990), 80–82, 114–15, 140ff.

70. See Susan Brooks Thistlethwaite and Peter Crafts Hodgson, "The Church, Classism, and Ecclesial Community," in *Reconstructing Christian Theology*, ed. Rebecca Chopp and Mark K. Taylor (Minneapolis: Fortress Press, 1994).

71. Taylor, *Remembering Esperanza*, 115–16.

72. See James B. Nelson, *Body Theology* (Louisville, Ky.: Westminster/John Knox Press, 1992), 58–62.

73. See John Boswell, *Christianity, Social Tolerance, and Homosexuality* (Chicago: University of Chicago Press, 1980).

74. See Farley's helpful discussion of "subjugation" as the structure of social evil in *Good and Evil*, chap. 14. Subjugation is rooted in the "social tragic" (benign victimization) (253–54). The act of subjugation entails malignant victimization and "is a social entity's *utilization* of another targeted group by means of *violence*" (259–61). This process is institutionalized in normative culture, property and state, and regimes of power (262–64).

75. Taylor offers the beginnings of such an analysis with his theory of an "infrastructure of oppressions" in chap. 4 of *Remembering Esperanza*. Using a different approach, Kathryn Tanner, in *The Politics of God: Christian Theologies and Social Justice* (Minneapolis: Fortress Press, 1992), argues that hierarchy, oppression, intolerance, and other forms of social injustice are based on idolatrous misconstruals of God's transcendence and world-relatedness, leading to a violation of the respect owed all creatures of God. She thus provides a theological basis for political critique and social action.

Chapter 15. Christ Incarnate

1. Elizabeth A. Johnson, *She Who Is: The Mystery of God in Feminist Theological Discourse* (New York: Crossroad, 1992), 160–61; see also 151–52.

2. The possibility of discovering such a contradiction is one of the risks that had to be faced by the so-called quest of the historical Jesus.

3. In the absence of reliable information on this subject, the imagination can create a false or distorting picture, as in the novel and film *The Last Temptation of Christ* by Nikos Kazantzakis.

4. Ernst Troeltsch makes it clear that theological propositions are not simply historical-critical ones, even though history provides a basis (but no proof) for claims of faith about Jesus as the Christ. He also shows why, for psychological and sociological as well as religious reasons, people need to experience redemption not as some abstract force, idea, or dynamic, but as embodied in concrete persons and personal relationships. He argues, moreover, that a redemptive personality must become a living "principle" that continues to work efficaciously in history. The concept of the "Christ-gestalt" is similar to Troeltsch's "Christian principle," and my approach to christology has been influenced by him in a variety of ways. See *The Christian Faith*, trans. Garrett E. Paul (Minneapolis: Fortress Press, 1991), 24–25, 29, 41, 74–75, 84, 87–91, 98–100, 274–75.

5. Rosemary Radford Ruether, *To Change the World: Christology and Cultural Criticism* (New York: Crossroad, 1983), 3.

6. Paul F. Knitter, *No Other Name?* (Maryknoll, N.Y.: Orbis Books, 1985), 171–72.

7. Ibid., 196.

8. Ibid., 205.

9. Mark K. Taylor, "In Praise of Shaky Ground: The Liminal Christ in a Culturally Plural World," *Theology Today* 43 (1986): 44ff.

10. Raimundo Panikkar, *The Unknown Christ of Hinduism: Toward an Ecumenical Christophany*, rev. ed. (Maryknoll, N.Y.: Orbis Books, 1981), 4–20.

11. Aloysius Pieris, "The Buddha and the Christ: Mediators of Liberation,"

in *The Myth of Christian Uniqueness*, ed. John Hick and Paul F. Knitter (Maryknoll, N.Y.: Orbis Books, 1987), chap. 10; and *Love Meets Wisdom: A Christian Experience of Buddhism* (Maryknoll, N.Y.: Orbis Books, 1988).

12. Pieris, in *The Myth of Christian Uniqueness*, 162–63, 175.

13. Ruether, *Sexism and God-Talk*, 125–26; see the whole of chap. 5 and *To Change the World*.

14. Ruether, *Sexism and God-Talk*, 135–38.

15. Rita Nakashima Brock, *Journeys by Heart: A Christology of Erotic Power* (New York: Crossroad, 1988).

16. These are just two examples of the work being done in christology by feminist theologians. Some others are Elisabeth Schüssler Fiorenza, *In Memory of Her* (New York: Crossroad, 1983), chap. 4; Patricia Wilson-Kastner, *Faith, Feminism, and the Christ* (Philadelphia: Fortress Press, 1983); Carter Heyward, "Jesus of Nazareth/Christ of Faith: Foundations of a Reactive Christology," in *Lift Every Voice: Constructing Christian Theologies from the Underside*, ed. Thistlethwaite and Engel, chap. 13; and Elizabeth A. Johnson, *She Who Is*, chap. 8. A valuable contribution is also being made by womanist theologians, notably Jacquelyn Grant, *White Women's Christ and Black Women's Jesus: Feminist Christology and Womanist Response* (Atlanta: Scholars Press, 1989).

17. Cone has in mind the work of William R. Jones, *Is God a White Racist? A Preamble to Black Theology* (Garden City, N.Y.: Doubleday, 1973). As opposed to a christocentric theism, Jones is led to a "humanocentric theism," which is really more humanocentric than theistic.

18. James H. Cone, *God of the Oppressed* (New York: Seabury Press, 1975), 121–22; see the whole of chap. 6.

19. Ibid., 134–37.

20. Theo Witvliet, *The Way of the Black Messiah: The Hermeneutical Challenge of Black Theology as a Theology of Liberation* (Oak Park, Ill.: Meyer Stone Books, 1987), 217–18, 224–25. The work by Mofokeng is *The Crucified among the Crossbearers* (Kampen: J. H. Kok, 1983).

21. Mercy Amba Oduyoye, "The Christ for Africa: Observations and Reflections," American Academy of Religion, Currents in Contemporary Christology Group Papers (1987); and Elizabeth Amoah and Mercy Amba Oduyoye, "The Christ for African Women," *International Christian Digest* 2, no. 8 (October 1988): 14ff. See Oduyoye's book *Hearing and Knowing: Theological Reflections on Christianity in Africa* (Maryknoll, N.Y.: Orbis Books, 1986), chap. 8.

22. James H. Evans, Jr., *We Have Been Believers: An African-American Systematic Theology* (Minneapolis: Fortress Press, 1992), chap. 4. Evans draws on the work of Eric Auerbach for the concept of figural interpretation, and on that of John W. Roberts for a study of the African American folk hero. He also provides a good summary of African American christology from Howard Thurman to Jacquelyn Grant. Evans's concept of "figura" is closely related to the concept of "gestalt" as employed in the present work. It is interesting to note that Ernst Troeltsch pointed toward the possibility of "many Christs." See Sarah Coakley, *Christ without Absolutes: A Study of the Christology of Ernst Troeltsch* (Oxford: Clarendon Press, 1988), chap. 6.

23. Rosemary Radford Ruether, "Jewish-Christian Relations in the Theology of Paul van Buren," *Religious Studies Review* 16 (October 1990): 320–23.

24. Paul M. van Buren, *A Theology of the Jewish-Christian Reality*, 3 vols. (San Francisco: Harper & Row, 1980, 1983, 1988).

25. See Rosemary Radford Ruether and Herman J. Ruether, *The Wrath of Jonah: The Crisis of Religious Nationalism in the Israeli-Palestinian Conflict* (San Francisco: Harper & Row, 1989); and Rosemary Radford Ruether, *Faith and Fratricide: The Theological Roots of Anti-Semitism* (New York: Seabury Press, 1974).

26. Peter Haas, "Toward a Post-Holocaust Christian View of Judaism," *Religious Studies Review* 16 (1990): 316–20.

27. John Pawlikowski, *Christ in the Light of the Christian-Jewish Dialogue* (New York: Paulist Press, 1982), 3.

28. Ibid., 114–15.

29. Ibid., 115.

30. Ibid., 121–22.

31. Ibid., 152.

32. Peter Haas, in *Religious Studies Review* 16:319.

33. William Schweiker, "Prospects for Christology in the North American Context," American Academy of Religion, Euro-American Theology Seminar (1992). The three directions reflect what Mark K. Taylor describes as a "postmodern trilemma," namely, appropriating Christian tradition while celebrating plurality and critiquing domination. See *Remembering Esperanza*, chap. 1. This book concludes with two excellent chapters on christology (chaps. 5–6).

34. On demythologizing, see Rudolf Bultmann, *Jesus Christ and Mythology* (New York: Charles Scribner's Sons, 1958). On fictional reference, see Paul Ricoeur, *Time and Narrative*, vol. 2, trans. Kathleen McLaughlin and David Pellauer (Chicago: University of Chicago Press, 1985).

35. Maurice Wiles, "Myth in Theology," in *The Myth of God Incarnate*, ed. John Hick (Philadelphia: Westminster Press, 1977), 154.

36. Johnson, *She Who Is*, 168.

37. The following analysis of the four patterns depends on Reginald H. Fuller, *Foundations of New Testament Christology* (New York: Charles Scribner's Sons, 1965); and especially John Knox, *The Humanity and Divinity of Christ: A Study of Pattern in Christology* (Cambridge: Cambridge University Press, 1967).

38. John Hick, who instigated the myth-of-God-incarnate debate, relies on a version of kenoticism; see his "Inspiration Christology for a Religiously Plural World," in *Encountering Jesus: A Debate on Christology*, ed. Stephen T. Davis (Atlanta: John Knox Press, 1988). In what follows I make use of it too.

39. For historical resources I rely on Aloys Grillmeier, *Christ in Christian Tradition: From the Apostolic Age to Chalcedon*, trans. J. S. Bowden (London: A. R. Mowbray, 1965); and J. N. D. Kelly, *Early Christian Doctrines* (London: Adam & Charles Black, 1958), chaps. 6, 11, 12. The most thorough recent study of classical christology and modern (Enlightenment and post-Enlightenment) critiques of it is by John Macquarrie, *Jesus Christ in Modern Thought* (Philadelphia: Trinity Press International, 1990), parts 1–2.

40. The christology sketched in this section draws on several of my earlier works: *Jesus—Word and Presence: An Essay in Christology* (Philadelphia: Fortress Press, 1971), chaps. 3–4; *New Birth of Freedom: A Theology of Bondage and Liberation* (Philadelphia: Fortress Press, 1976), chap. 5; *God in History:*

Shapes of Freedom (Nashville: Abingdon Press, 1989), 194–215. But the whole has been revised and rethought in light of new materials and new problems.

41. See John Macquarrie's discussion of "What Would Be Required in a Christology Today?" in *Jesus Christ in Modern Thought*, chap. 15. This is followed by Macquarrie's own christological reconstruction (chaps. 16–20), with which my approach is compatible although it has not been specifically influenced by his.

42. Wiles in *The Myth of God Incarnate*, ed. Hick, 161.

43. Ibid., 162–63.

44. This argument was first developed in *God in History*, 194–215, and in what follows I draw directly on that work, while at the same time revising my approach in certain respects, especially on the matter of understanding the bodily aspect of incarnation. Used by permission of the publisher.

45. Hegel used the term *Gestalt* in this sense, having borrowed it from Goethe. See Robert R. Williams, *Recognition*, 126, 136 (nn. 29, 30). I am also influenced by Ernst Troeltsch's use of the category *Gestaltung*. See my *God in History*, 138–40, 206–8.

46. Paul Tillich speaks of the "picture" of the New Being in Jesus as the Christ, meaning by this not an "essential picture" but an "expressionist portrait." The German words behind "picture" for Tillich are *Bild* and *Gestalt*. See *Systematic Theology*, 2:103, 115–16, 134–35.

47. This theme is strongly emphasized by Hegel, who understood incarnation to be "the consummate form of divine-human community" and the "speculative midpoint" of philosophy. See Hegel, *Lectures on the Philosophy of Religion*, 1:245; 2:475–77; 3:110–15, 124–25, 131–32, 211–15, 310–15, 324–26, 370; and Williams, *Recognition*, 224, 229–30, 237.

48. As Johnson puts it: "The living God is *capax hominis*, capable of personal union with what is not God, the flesh and spirit of humanity. Here divine immanence or universal presence through the indwelling Spirit takes on an intensely clear gestalt in divine embodiment, enabling God to dwell in a small segment of historical time. Bodiliness opens up the mystery of God to the conditions of history, including suffering and delight. She becomes flesh, choosing the very stuff of the cosmos as her own personal reality forever. She thereby becomes irrevocably, physically connected to the human adventure, for better or worse. Far from functioning as the index of creaturely separation from the divine, human bodiliness is manifest as irreplaceable sacrament of mutual communion between heaven and earth, not only in Jesus' case but ontologically for all." Johnson, *She Who Is*, 168.

49. Taylor, *Remembering Esperanza*, 168–75.

50. Ibid., 171. He is referring to *God in History*, 209–10.

51. Ernst Troeltsch argues the same point on psychological and sociological grounds. See "The Significance of the Historical Existence of Jesus for Faith," in *Writings on Theology and Religion*, trans. and ed. Robert Morgan and Michael Pye (Louisville, Ky.: Westminster/John Knox Press, 1990), 182–207. See also Coakley, *Christ Without Absolutes*, chap. 5.

52. William Schweiker, "Prospects for Christology in the North American Context," American Academy of Religion, Euro-American Seminar Papers (1992). Schweiker is attempting to relate the sort of christological thinking

represented by Hans Frei (*Types of Christian Theology* [New Haven, Conn.: Yale University Press, 1992]) and Robert Scharlemann (*The Reason of Following: Christology and the Ecstatic I* [Chicago: University of Chicago Press, 1991]) to the concerns of feminist and liberation theologians.

53. See James M. Robinson, "Very Goddess and Very Man: Jesus' Better Self," in *Encountering Jesus*, ed. Stephen T. Davis, 115–16.

54. Johnson, *She Who Is*, 86–90 (quotation from 87).

55. Ibid., 91.

56. Ibid., 82–86.

57. See ibid., 94–100, and the works cited in the next note.

58. For the following I rely on Robinson, "Very Goddess and Very Man," *Encountering Jesus*, ed. Davis, 116–21; Johnson, *She Who Is*, 98–100, 156–59, 165–69; Elisabeth Schüssler Fiorenza, *In Memory of Her*, 130–40; and Antoinette Clark Wire, "The God of Jesus in the Gospel Sayings Source," in *Reading from This Place: Social Location and Biblical Interpretation*, vol. 1, ed. Fernando F. Segovia and Mary Ann Tolbert (Minneapolis: Fortress Press, 1994).

59. The translation of *basileia tou theou* as "God's project" is suggested by Sharon H. Ringe (n. 65), and as "God's inheritance" by Antoinette Wire (n. 58).

60. Johnson, *She Who Is*, 159.

61. Robinson in *Encountering Jesus*, ed. Davis, 122.

62. John B. Cobb, Jr., "Christ Beyond Creative Transformation," in *Encountering Jesus*, ed. Davis, 152–53, 157–58.

63. At this point I disagree with Robinson's interpretation, *Encountering Jesus*, ed. Davis, 112.

64. See chap. 18, p. 295.

65. Sharon H. Ringe reports that the phrase *el proyecto de Dios* is used as a translation of *basileia tou theou* by Central American liberation theologians. See her "Solidarity and Contextuality: Readings of Matt. 18:21–35," in *Reading from This Place*, ed. Segovia and Tolbert.

66. The literature on the parables and the hermeneutical questions they raise is enormous. I have been influenced in various ways by Karl Barth, Ernst Käsemann, Gerhard Ebeling, Eberhard Jüngel, Paul Ricoeur, Amos Wilder, Norman Perrin, Robert W. Funk, Dan O. Via, John Dominic Crossan, Elisabeth Schüssler Fiorenza, to name a few. For more detailed discussion and references see my earlier work, *Jesus—Word and Presence*, 160–66; and *New Birth of Freedom*, 227–33. On the theory of liminality, I am indebted to Mark K. Taylor, "In Praise of Shaky Ground: The Liminal Christ in a Culturally Plural World," *Theology Today* 43 (1986): 36–51.

67. The Parable of the Great Supper (Luke 14:12–24; Matt. 22:1–10) is paradigmatic of the parables on this theme.

68. See *New Birth of Freedom*, 216–27. The following is a *theological* construal of the identity of Jesus as the radically free person (i.e., the Christ). I have been influenced by theologians as diverse as Karl Barth, Dietrich Bonhoeffer, Gerhard Ebeling, Jürgen Moltmann, Hans Frei, Karl Rahner, Gustavo Gutiérrez, Dorothee Sölle, Rosemary Radford Ruether, and Rita Nakashima Brock. The construal is also based on such historical evidence as is available from critical analysis of the Gospel traditions. Here the work of Rudolf Bultmann, Norman

Perrin, Martin Hengel, and especially Ernst Käsemann has been helpful. See Käsemann's "The Problem of the Historical Jesus," *Essays on New Testament Themes*, trans. W. J. Montague (London: SCM Press, 1964), 15–47; and *Jesus Means Freedom*, trans. Frank Clarke (Philadelphia: Fortress Press, 1970).

69. Paul Tillich speaks of the "essential humanity" of Jesus, which means the same thing as "essential God-manhood"; the latter expression is redundant since relatedness to God is an essential though broken aspect of being human. Tillich's name for essential humanity is the "New Being," which means the reestablished unity between God and humanity. The New Being is in Jesus as the Christ; it is what makes him the Christ. See *Systematic Theology*, 2:94, 135, 148.

70. The New Testament never predicates an *identity* of God and Jesus but rather a relationship. Typical is the Pauline expression, "God was *in* Christ, reconciling the world to himself" (2 Cor. 5:19), to which may be compared the Johannine statement, "I am *in* the Father and the Father is *in* me" (John 14:10). The Lukan Jesus asks, "Why do you call me good? No one is good but God alone" (Luke 18:18).

71. See Edward Farley, *Good and Evil*, chap. 16.

72. There is abundant evidence for this; see my *New Birth of Freedom*, 233–45.

73. E.g., Wolfhart Pannenberg and his followers.

74. See my *New Birth of Freedom*, 245–53; and *Jesus—Word and Presence*, 202–17. My interpretation has been influenced by Jürgen Moltmann, *The Crucified God: The Cross of Christ as the Foundation and Criticism of Christian Theology*, trans. R. A. Wilson and John Bowden (New York: Harper & Row, 1974), 126–59; and Eberhard Jüngel, *God as the Mystery of the World*, trans. Darrell L. Guder (Grand Rapids, Mich.: Wm. B. Eerdmans Publishing Co., 1983), 210–22, 317–20, 326–29. The interpretation of the death of Jesus as the death of God goes back to Hegel, *Lectures on the Philosophy of Religion*, 3:122–31. See Williams, *Recognition*, 232–40.

75. Hegel, *Lectures on the Philosophy of Religion*, 3:131–41. See also Johnson, *She Who Is*, 158–59.

Chapter 16. Christ Risen

1. Mark K. Taylor, *Remembering Esperanza*, 175–93.

2. Ibid., 185–89. The term "redemption" is similarly based in legal relationships: To redeem is to "buy back" (*re-emere*) by payment of a price. "Redemption" has commonly been used in religious discourse to refer to God's salvific or liberating action, whereas "emancipation" has had a more secular connotation.

3. Ibid., 176.

4. For a more detailed discussion of the topic of this and the next section, see my *Jesus—Word and Presence*, chap. 5; and *New Birth of Freedom*, chap. 6, sec. 4. I rely on the critical scholarship of Rudolf Bultmann, Ernst Käsemann, Gerhard Koch, Willi Marxsen, and Paul Schubert, among others. Theologically, my reflections on resurrection have been assisted by Dietrich Bonhoeffer, Karl Rahner, Gerhard Ebeling, Jürgen Moltmann, Wolf-Dieter Marsch, and Hans Frei.

5. See *Theological Dictionary of the New Testament*, ed. Kittel and Friedrich, 1:368ff.; 2:334ff.

6. This is one of the central themes in Ernst Troeltsch's dogmatics: "Redemption cannot . . . be a simple, unrepeatable interruption of the world-order at a single point. . . . It must rather be *the upraising of the divine Spirit in human history as a whole*." This upraising entails liberation and rebirth on the part of humanity. Redemption construed as rebirth is the essence of Christianity and the hallmark of the Spirit. *The Christian Faith*, 263, 271.

7. H. Richard Niebuhr, *Faith on Earth* (New Haven, Conn.: Yale University Press, 1989), 87–93.

8. Ernst Käsemann says it eloquently: "The power of Christ's resurrection becomes a reality, here and now, in the form of Christian freedom, and only in that. That reality is opposed on earth by anything that stands in the way of Christian freedom, and only by that. . . . The earth has no scarcity of lords, and they all demand obedience. . . . Christ differs from the other lords in that he effects freedom. He does not just call to it; that would be the law of which there are innumerable characteristic forms. Jesus *gives* freedom. That is what makes him unmistakably Lord and inseparably unites the earthly with the exalted Lord." *Jesus Means Freedom*, 154–55.

9. Elizabeth Johnson refers to this as "a transformation of [Jesus'] humanity so profound that it escapes our imagination." *She Who Is*, 163. The transformation is signified in the Fourth Gospel by a body that appears and disappears, passes through solid objects, can be touched and not touched, seen and not seen (John 20).

10. Karl Rahner, *On the Theology of Death* (New York: Herder & Herder, 1965), chap. 1.

11. Ibid., 22.

12. Julia Esquivel, *Threatened with Resurrection*, trans. Maria Elena Acevedo et al. (Elgin, Ill.: Brethren Press, 1982), 59–63. Copyright 1982 by Brethren Press. Used by permission. Mark Taylor called my attention to this passage; see his *Remembering Esperanza*, 244–45.

13. Elizabeth Johnson writes: "While Jesus is named the Christ in a paradigmatic way, multiple redemptive role models are available within the community and may inspire and guide by their example, however strong, however fragile. The heritage of the saints, including Mary of Nazareth, embodies this insight in an ongoing way. In a word, the story of the prophet and friend of Sophia, anointed as the Christ, goes on in history as the story of the whole Christ, *christa* and *christus* alike, the wisdom community. . . . The inevitable limitations of Jesus' humanity are completed in the wholeness of the human race anointed with the Spirit, women and the elderly included. Maleness is not constitutive of the essence of Christ but, in the Spirit, redeemed and redeeming humanity is." *She Who Is*, 162–64.

Chapter 17. The Spirit and Freedom

1. See Johnson, *She Who Is*, 128–31.

2. Joel Kovel, *History and Spirit: An Inquiry into the Philosophy of Liberation* (Boston: Beacon Press, 1991), 2, 5–13.

3. Krister Stendahl wrote a helpful study guide for the Assembly, *Energy for Life: Reflections on the Theme "Come, Holy Spirit—Renew the Whole Creation"* (Geneva: WCC Publications, 1990). The theme is based on the text of Ps. 104:30: "When you send forth your Spirit, they are created; and you renew the face of the ground." Korean theologian Chung Hyun Kyung concluded her address to the Assembly with these powerful words: "Dear sisters and brothers, with the energy of the Holy Spirit let us tear apart all walls of division and the culture of death which separate us. And let us participate in the Holy Spirit's political economy of life, fighting for our life on this earth in solidarity with all living beings and building communities for justice, peace, and the integrity of creation. Wild wind of the Holy Spirit blow to us. Let us welcome her, letting ourselves go in her wild rhythm of life. Come Holy Spirit, renew the whole creation. Amen!" *Christianity and Crisis* 51 (15 July 1991): 223.

4. Jürgen Moltmann, *The Spirit of Life: A Universal Affirmation*, trans. Margaret Kohl (Minneapolis: Fortress Press, 1992), 1–2, 34–37. Other recent theological works include, in addition to Stendahl (preceding note), José Comblin, *The Holy Spirit and Liberation* (Maryknoll, N.Y.: Orbis Books, 1989); and Michael Welker, *Gottes Geist: Theologie des Heiligen Geistes* (Neukirchen: Neukirchner Verlag, 1992; English translation forthcoming from Fortress Press). Johnson's *She Who Is* makes a valuable contribution to pneumatology, as does Sallie McFague's ecological theology of the Spirit in *The Body of God* (Minneapolis: Fortress Press, 1993). Volume 3 of Paul Tillich's *Systematic Theology* remains an important resource, as do earlier studies by Yves Congar, George Hendry, George Lampe, and Regin Prenter. Noteworthy among recent philosophical works are Steven G. Smith, *The Concept of the Spiritual: An Essay in First Philosophy* (Philadelphia: Temple University Press, 1988); Joel Kovel, *History and Spirit*; and Robert R. Williams, *Recognition* (Albany: State University of New York Press, 1992). These and other works serve as resources of my reflection in this chapter.

5. Smith, *The Concept of the Spiritual*, 9–11; Moltmann, *The Spirit of Life*, 278–79; McFague, *The Body of God*, chap. 5.

6. Hegel, *Lectures on the Philosophy of Religion*, 2:136. Hegel described both Judaism and Zoroastrianism as "religions of light" and viewed light as an image of the "sublimity" of God.

7. Hegel's famous allusion to Schelling's philosophy of identity in *Phenomenology of Spirit*, trans. A. V. Miller (Oxford: Clarendon Press, 1977), 9.

8. On the images of fire, light, and water, see Moltmann, *The Spirit of Life*, 279–84.

9. Stendahl, *Energy for Life*, viii. On Spirit as vital force or spirit-power, see Kovel, *History and Spirit*, 22–24.

10. In these "free spaces of life," writes Moltmann, "the multifarious *configurations of life* come into being." *Life in the Spirit*, 274–78. The term used here by Moltmann is *Gestalt*, and the suggestion is that Spirit is the *Gestalt* that configures, forms, shapes (*gestaltet*).

11. Tillich, *Systematic Theology*, 3:21–22, 26–28, 111.

12. On the linkage of *ruach* and *dabar*, see Moltmann, *The Spirit of Life*, 41.

13. The linkage of spirit, reason, and nature is seen in ancient Greek philosophy, which, Stephen Smith says, "presents us with no fewer than four important spirit-words, each offering a distinguishable sense to the assertion that

humans are spiritual beings: they are enfolded and sustained by cosmic *pneuma*; they are ruled by a universally operative faculty of rational cognition, *nous*; each is vivified by an individual *psyche*; each has an emotional attraction to the right, the noble, and the good, *thumos*." Human beings participate in a universal life force as well as a structure of rationality that transcends finite minds; they take on an individual identity as an embodied psyche, soul, or self; and they are drawn by passions or desires (*thumoi*) that are both sensual and intellectual. *The Concept of the Spiritual*, 21; cf. 11–21.

14. Smith, *The Concept of the Spiritual*, 223; Kovel, *History and Spirit*, 197. On the relationality and sociality of spirit, see Smith, 49–65, 67ff.; Kovel, 18–21; and Williams, *Recognition*, 191ff. I return to this theme below in the discussion of ecclesial community (chap. 18, pp. 293–95).

15. In Elizabeth Johnson's eloquent words: "Since what people call God is not one being among other beings, not even a discrete Supreme Being, but mystery which transcends and enfolds all that is, like the horizon and yet circling all horizons, this human encounter with the presence and absence of the living God occurs through the mediation of history itself in its whole vast range of happenings. To this movement of the living God that can be traced in and through experience of the world, Christian speech traditionally gives the name Spirit." *She Who Is*, 124.

16. Ibid., 83. The reference is to Jerome's *Comm. in Isaiam* 11.

17. Johnson, *She Who Is*, 82–86, 148–49 (quotation from 83); see also Letty M. Russell, *Human Liberation in a Feminist Perspective—A Theology* (Philadelphia: Westminster Press, 1974), 102.

18. This text was used in the nineteenth century to justify "preaching women." Guardians of the (male-dominated) Word against the Spirit argued that prophesying is not the same as preaching—to which the appropriate rejoinder is that anyone who can prophesy can preach, but not everyone who can preach can prophesy. See Rosemary Radford Ruether and Rosemary Skinner Keller, eds., *Women and Religion in America*, vol. 1: *The Nineteenth Century* (San Francisco: Harper & Row, 1982), chap. 5.

19. Johnson, *She Who Is*, 141–43; Moltmann, *The Spirit of Life*, 280–81. The references are to Augustine, *De Trinitate* 5.11.12; 15.17.27; 15.18.32; 15.19.33–37; Thomas Aquinas, *Summa Theologica* I, qq. 20.a.1; 36.a.1; 37.a.1–2; 38.a.2; Hildegaard of Bingen, *Carmina* no. 19.

20. For exegetical details, see my *New Birth of Freedom*, chap 7. The phrase "a new birth of freedom" is from Lincoln's Gettysburg Address. See also Moltmann, *The Spirit of Life*, 120–22.

21. The Belgian-Brazilian theologian José Comblin makes just this point in *The Holy Spirit and Liberation*, 49, 61ff. He also remarks on the triumph of atheism that seems to go hand-in-hand with a decline in the theology and practice of the Spirit (40, 42). Gustavo Gutiérrez has woven together the themes of spirituality and liberation in *The Power of the Poor in History* (Maryknoll, N.Y.: Orbis Books, 1983) and *We Drink from Our Own Wells* (Maryknoll, N.Y.: Orbis Books, 1984).

22. Michael Welker, "The Holy Spirit," *Theology Today* 46 (1989): 5–20; *Gottes Geist*, chaps. 5–6 (see n. 4); Marjorie Suchocki, "John Cobb's Trinity," *Theology and the University: Essays in Honor of John B. Cobb, Jr.*, ed. David Ray Griffin and Joseph C. Hough, Jr. (Albany: State University of New York Press,

1991), esp. 155–62; and a discussion with Welker and Suchocki at the Euro-American Theology Seminar of the American Academy of Religion (1990). The quotation is from Suchocki. Welker argues that *we* help to generate the Spirit through our multiform perspectives on and responses to Christ, in the process of which there are formed communal domains of resonance, which have the character of being a public or social person, a "polycontextual" as distinct from a self-referential person.

23. Moltmann, *Life in the Spirit*, quotations from 287, 289; on innertrinitarian personhood, see 10–14 and chap. 12. My discussion of this issue is found in chap. 11, pp. 152–53.

24. See Robert E. Hood, *Must God Remain Greek? Afro Cultures and God-Talk* (Minneapolis: Fortress Press, 1990), chaps. 7–8.

25. Hood describes it as follows: The God of African traditional religions "manifests a many-sided relationship with humankind, earth, and nature through divinities and spirits without ceasing to be the divine supreme and sovereign deity. Spirit and divinities have their jurisdiction and their mandates on assignment from God as intermediaries and subordinates, even though within their own jurisdictions and spheres they are supreme and sovereign. . . . The dynamics of everyday culture as well as articulated concepts testify to the varied relationships between God and the spirits." *Must God Remain Greek?*, 197.

26. Troeltsch, *The Christian Faith*, 175, 186–87, 207; see also 28, 120, 129–30.

27. G. W. F. Hegel, *Lectures on the Philosophy of World History*, Introduction: *Reason in History*, trans. H. B. Nisbet (Cambridge: Cambridge University Press, 1975), 30, 52–53, 63, 76, 82, 92, 124, 213–14. Hegel did not shrink from those religions that understand Spirit in the form of the natural. He even saw a connection between them and the highest of the spiritual religions, Christianity. See *Lectures on the Philosophy of Religion*, vol. 2: *Determinate Religion*, esp. 293.

28. Kovel, *History and Spirit*, chap. 4, "Spirit and Desire." The approach here is informed by Hegel's concept of *Begierde*.

29. Tillich, *Systematic Theology*, 3:111–12.

30. Ibid., 3:114ff. See also Kovel, *History and Spirit*, 29–32.

31. Tillich, *Systematic Theology*, 3:294.

32. Ibid., 3:125–26, 138–39.

33. José Comblin, *The Holy Spirit and Liberation*, 20–23.

34. Ibid., 20–31. These, he says (31), "are not five partial experiences of the Spirit, but one overall experience. This experience has one single object: God and creation united. It is experience of God in creation and of creation in God. . . . There is no separation between the experience of acting and the experience of the Spirit who acts, between experiencing the Spirit and experiencing 'me' and 'us.'" See also Moltmann, *The Spirit of Life*, 34–35, 73–77, 83–84; Johnson, *She Who Is*, 131, 136–37; Kovel, *History and Spirit*, 13, 25–28.

35. Moltmann, *The Spirit of Life*, 58ff.

36. See Tillich, *Systematic Theology*, 3:144–47; Moltmann, *The Spirit of Life*, 58, 60–62; Johnson, *She Who Is*, 140; and above, chap. 15, pp. 246, 255–59.

37. Stendahl, *Energy for Life*, 25.

38. George Hendry, *The Holy Spirit in Christian Theology* (Philadelphia: Westminster Press, 1956), 23; cf. 21–25.

39. Ibid., 37–42; Comblin, *The Holy Spirit and Liberation*, 167.

40. Tillich, *Systematic Theology*, 3:148–49.

41. Moltmann, *The Spirit of Life*, 308; cf. 71–72, 306–8.

42. Ernst Troeltsch, *Writings on Theology and Religion* (Louisville, Ky.: Westminster/John Knox Press, 1990), 193–96.

43. See David Burrell, "The Spirit and the Christian Life," in *Christian Theology*, ed. Hodgson and King, 311–12.

44. Kovel, *History and Spirit*, 36–39; and Jack Forstman, *Christian Faith in Dark Times: Theological Conflicts in the Shadow of Hitler* (Louisville, Ky.: Westminster/John Knox Press, 1992).

45. This is the limitation in the strictly Barthian response to Nazism, which, despite its prophetic power and political courage, is based on the sole authoritative revelation of the Word of God in Christ and thus in the final analysis comes down to pitting one authority against another. It is worth noting that, in Germany during the twenties and thirties, Jews rather than Christians were by far the more perceptive critics of Nazism. And during the war, regrettably, only a few theologians and pastors were involved in the organized resistance against Hitler. Dietrich Bonhoeffer was the great exception. In other words, it was possible to recognize Nazism for what it was without confessing the Lordship of Jesus Christ. Such a confession is certainly a legitimate basis for criticism and resistance, but it is not the *only* basis, even for Christians. See Forstman, *Christian Faith in Dark Times*, 11–20, 243–61.

46. Maintenance of the critical principle against uncritical enthusiasm is "what it's all about," argued Tillich in his debate with Hirsch and the German Christians; see Forstman, *Christian Faith in Dark Times*, chap. 14.

47. Illumination is one of the major themes in Augustine's understanding of revelation. See his *Lectures on the Gospel According to St. John* in *Nicene and Post-Nicene Fathers of the Christian Church*, First Series (New York: Christian Literature Co., 1886–90), 7:20–21.

48. Kovel, *History and Spirit*, chap. 6, esp. 215.

Chapter 18. The Liberation of the World

1. See Williams, *Recognition*, 191–93 (the quotation in the last sentence is from Nicolai Hartmann). This outstanding study has been of help to me in a number of ways. Hegel first developed the social concept of *Geist* in chap. 6 of *Phenomenology of Spirit*.

2. Hegel, *The Science of Logic*, trans. A. V. Miller (London: Allen & Unwin, 1969), 603. The passage as quoted is translated by Williams.

3. Williams, *Recognition*, 198–99, 206–11 (quotation from 211).

4. Ibid., 254–56, 265–66, 270, 286, 297–301. Steven G. Smith attempts to mediate between what he regards as Hegelian totality (no radical otherness) and Levinasian philosophy of absolute otherness. His own proposal is to define spirit as "the intentional togetherness of beings who are for themselves 'I' and for others 'You,' that is, other to each other." The "intentional togetherness" is the We that relates the I and the You without destroying their otherness. Smith thinks it is better to describe spirit as "togetherness-with-others" rather than as "unity in difference." But his proposal is not far from Williams's reading of Hegel. See *The Concept of the Spiritual*, 27–30, 35–43, 49–71, esp. 63–65.

5. Tillich, *Systematic Theology*, 3:162ff.

6. Josiah Royce, *The Problem of Christianity*, with an Introduction by John E. Smith (Chicago: University of Chicago Press, 1968), 298–307.

7. Ibid., 318–19, 339–41.

8. In this and the following two subsections, I draw upon my book *Revisioning the Church: Ecclesial Freedom in the New Paradigm* (Philadelphia: Fortress Press, 1988). Used by permission. For what immediately follows, see 28–35. In fashioning an ecclesiology I have been helped especially by the works of Paul Minear, Eduard Schweizer, Eric Jay, Ernst Troeltsch, Dietrich Bonhoeffer, Paul Tillich, H. Richard Niebuhr, James Gustafson, Edward Farley, Peter Paris, Yves Congar, Hans Küng, Edward Schillebeeckx, Bernard Cooke, Gustavo Gutiérrez, Leonardo Boff, Elisabeth Schüssler Fiorenza, Francis Schüssler Fiorenza, Rosemary Radford Ruether.

9. On the church as the communion or fellowship of the Holy Spirit, see Jürgen Moltmann, *The Spirit of Life*, chap. 9.

10. See Küng's discussion of "The Church as the Creation of the Spirit" in *The Church* (New York: Image Books, 1976), 215–36.

11. See *Revisioning the Church*, 53–55, 58–59. Friedrich Schleiermacher argued that the church is formed by "the communication of the Holy Spirit," and defined the latter as the "common Spirit of the new corporate life founded by Christ." See *The Christian Faith*, ed. H. R. Macintosh and J. S. Stewart (Edinburgh: T. & T. Clark, 1928), §§ 121–25. Tillich developed his ecclesiology of spiritual community in *Systematic Theology*, 3:149–245.

12. *Lectures on the Philosophy of Religion*, 3:133–62, 223–47, 328–47; see esp. 135–42, 328–33, 339–42.

13. This definition and the comments that follow are from *Revisioning the Church*, 103–7. The material has been slightly revised.

14. For the following I draw on materials contained in chap. 3 of *Revisioning the Church*, 97–102.

15. Thus Edward Schillebeeckx in the book of this title: *Ministry: Leadership in the Community of Jesus Christ* (New York: Crossroad, 1981); reissued in a revised and expanded version as *The Church with a Human Face* (New York: Crossroad, 1985). Leadership is essentially what H. Richard Niebuhr has in mind when "for want of a better phrase," he develops the idea of the minister as "pastoral director" in *The Purpose of the Church and Its Ministry* (New York: Harper & Bros., 1956), 79–91. "Leadership," in my view, is a better term since it is not burdened by administrative and managerial associations.

16. See Bernard Cooke, *Ministry to Word and Sacraments: History and Theology* (Philadelphia: Fortress Press, 1976), chaps. 1 and 2; Schillebeeckx, *Ministry*, chaps. 1 and 2; and *The Church with a Human Face*, parts 1 and 2.

17. Rosemary Radford Ruether, *Women-Church: Theology and Practice of Feminist Liturgical Communities* (San Francisco: Harper & Row, 1985), 75.

18. See Mary Jo Weaver, *Springs of Water in a Dry Land: Spiritual Survival for Catholic Women Today* (Boston: Beacon Press, 1993).

19. James M. Gustafson, *Treasure in Earthen Vessels: The Church as a Human Community* (New York: Harper & Bros., 1961); see esp. the appendix. See also Edward Farley, *Ecclesial Man: A Social Phenomenology of Faith and Reality* (Philadelphia: Fortress Press, 1975), chaps. 4–7; and *Revisioning the Church*, 66–67.

20. Paul Ricoeur, *The Symbolism of Evil*, trans. Emerson Buchanan (Boston: Beacon Press, 1969), 19, 352.

21. See Stephen W. Sykes, "The Sacraments," in *Christian Theology*, ed. Hodgson and King, chap. 10.

22. See Dieter T. Hessel, *Social Ministry* (Philadelphia: Westminster Press, 1982).

23. See Michael Welker, "The Holy Spirit," *Theology Today* 46 (1989): 5–20.

24. See Walbert Bühlmann, *The Coming of the Third Church: An Analysis of the Present and Future of the Church* (Maryknoll, N.Y.: Orbis Books, 1978); and *The Church of the Future: A Model for the Year 2001* (Maryknoll, N.Y.: Orbis Books, 1986).

25. Gavin D'Costa, ed., *Christian Uniqueness Reconsidered* (Maryknoll, N.Y.: Orbis Books, 1990), chaps. 9, 13, 14.

26. In a conversation with the author, spring 1992.

27. Paul J. Griffiths, *An Apology for Apologetics: A Study in the Logic of Interreligious Dialogue* (Maryknoll, N.Y.: Orbis Books, 1991).

28. Mark K. Taylor quoting Paul Rabinow, "In Praise of Shaky Ground: The Liminal Christ in a Culturally Plural World," *Theology Today* 43 (1986): 36–51; see also Taylor's *Beyond Explanation: Religious Dimensions in Cultural Anthropology* (Macon, Ga.: Mercer University Press, 1986).

29. Both approaches are well-represented by Raimundo Panikkar: the trinitarian approach in "The Jordan, the Tiber, and the Ganges," in *The Myth of Christian Uniqueness*, ed. John Hick and Paul F. Knitter (Maryknoll, N.Y.: Orbis Books, 1987), 89–116 (see above, chap. 8, pp. 109–10), and in *The Trinity and the Religious Experience of Man* (London: Darton, Longman & Todd, 1973); the apophatic approach in *The Silence of God: The Answer of the Buddha*, trans. Robert Barr (Maryknoll, N.Y.: Orbis Books, 1989), chap. 9.

30. Paul F. Knitter, *No Other Name? A Critical Survey of Christian Attitudes toward the World Religions* (Maryknoll, N.Y.: Orbis Books, 1985), chap. 10. See David J. Krieger's description of Raimundo Panikkar's steps for conducting interreligious dialogue, which include a faithful and critical understanding of one's own tradition, a conversion to the other, and a meeting of the two within oneself, a personal synthesis, which then issues in genuine dialogue with a representative of another religion. Krieger, *The New Universalism: Foundations for a Global Theology* (Maryknoll, N.Y.: Orbis Books, 1991), 45-75. On passing over and coming back, see also John B. Cobb, Jr., *Beyond Dialogue: Toward a Mutual Transformation of Christianity and Buddhism* (Philadelphia: Fortress Press, 1982), chaps. 4–5. I have been helped by a conversation on this subject with Julius J. Lipner and by his lecture "Seeking Others in Their Otherness: Incommensurability and the Study of Religion," presented to a graduate colloquium in religion at Vanderbilt University, fall 1992. See also the discussion above of dialogue and difference, chap. 8, pp. 99–101.

31. Paul Tillich, *The Future of Religions*, ed. Jerald C. Brauer (New York: Harper & Row, 1966), 80–94. See the helpful commentary by Krieger in *The New Universalism*, 37–43.

32. Krieger, *The New Universalism*, 43.

33. See Wilfred Cantwell Smith, "Idolatry in Contemporary Perspective," *The Myth of Christian Uniqueness*, ed. Hick and Knitter, chap. 4.

34. See Krieger, *The New Universalism*, 150–59; John Hick, "The Non-Absoluteness of Christianity," in *The Myth of Christian Uniqueness*, ed. Hick and Knitter, chap. 2 (esp. 18–20, 29–30); Joseph Mitsuo Kitagawa, *The Quest for Human Unity: A Religious History* (Minneapolis: Fortress Press, 1990), 4; N. Ross Reat and Edmund F. Perry, *A World Theology: The Central Spiritual Reality of Humankind* (Cambridge: Cambridge University Press, 1991), 22–23, 311.

35. I am grateful to both Julius Lipner and Aloysius Pieris for sharing their ideas on this subject with me in conversation. In addition, Lipner's lecture, "Seeking Others in Their Otherness: Incommensurability and the Study of Religion" (see n. 30), is a very helpful discussion of these issues.

36. See especially Wilfred Cantwell Smith's *Towards a World Theology: Faith and the Comparative History of Religion* (Philadelphia: Westminster Press, 1981). His writings on this subject go back to the 1960s; see *The Meaning and End of Religion: A New Approach to the Religious Traditions of Mankind* (New York: Macmillan, 1963).

37. Raimundo Panikkar, *The Unknown Christ of Hinduism*, rev. ed. (Maryknoll, N.Y.: Orbis Books, 1981); *The Silence of God; The Cosmotheandric Experience* (Maryknoll, N.Y.: Orbis Books, 1989). John B. Cobb, Jr., *Beyond Dialogue*. John Hick, *Problems of Religious Pluralism* (New York: St. Martin's Press, 1985); *An Interpretation of Religion* (New Haven, Conn.: Yale University Press, 1989). Knitter, *No Other Name?* Aloysius Pieris, *An Asian Theology of Liberation* (Maryknoll, N.Y.: Orbis Books, 1989); *Love Meets Wisdom: A Christian Experience of Buddhism* (Maryknoll, N.Y.: Orbis Books, 1989).

38. Robert Neville, *Behind the Masks of God: An Essay toward Comparative Theology* (Albany: State University of New York Press, 1991).

39. Reat and Perry, *A World Theology*. This work does not fall into the essentialist trap although it veers in that direction. The authors identify the formal characteristics of the central spiritual reality that all religions seek as undeniability, desirability, and elusiveness. The specific ways that religions symbolize and express these characteristics differ widely. The elusiveness of the central reality accounts for and justifies the existence of different religions. Each religion is valid on its own terms, and the commonality of religions can be expressed only in highly formal, abstract terms.

40. Krieger, *The New Universalism*.

41. Ibid., 102–24.

42. Ibid., 48–49, 124–52 (esp. 150–52).

43. Ibid., 152–55.

44. The nonviolent power of Spirit, writes Krieger, "reaches into the realm of violence and broken communication and performs there a gesture which binds this realm back (*re-ligare*!) to a truly universal community and thus opens up the possibility of transforming violence into discourse, meaninglessness and irrationality into meaning and truth. We come to see the world anew and through the language of this vision the world itself becomes a 'new creation.'" See ibid., 156–61.

45. Cobb, *Beyond Dialogue*, chaps. 4–5.

46. In John B. Cobb, Jr., and Christopher Ives, eds., *The Emptying God: A Buddhist-Jewish-Christian Conversation* (Maryknoll, N.Y.: Orbis Books, 1990), 3–65 (esp. 59–61).

47. I have found the responses of John Cobb, Catherine Keller, and Schubert Ogden to be especially helpful; *The Emptying God*, part 2, chaps. 2, 4, 6.

48. Charles R. Strain, "The Open Kingdom: Peter Hodgson's *God in History* in the Light of Interreligious Dialogue," paper presented at the 1992 Annual Meeting of the American Academy of Religion. In what follows I incorporate portions of my response to Strain. My views on history and eschatology are rethought and summarized below, but they are also scattered throughout chaps. 6–8 above. See also *God in History: Shapes of Freedom* (Nashville: Abingdon Press, 1989), esp. chap. 5.

49. Gary Snyder, *The Practice of the Wild* (San Francisco: North Point Press, 1990), 5.

50. Hodgson, *God in History*, 234.

51. See Jürgen Moltmann, *The Spirit of Life*, 228; and Sallie McFague, *The Body of God*, 79. McFague borrows the image from Stephen Jay Gould, *Wonderful Life: The Burgess Shale and the Nature of History* (New York: Norton and Co., 1989), 14.

52. See my *God in History*, 237–38.

53. Tillich, *Systematic Theology*, 3:107–10, 357–61.

54. This section makes use of materials from *God in History*, 237–49. Used by permission of Abingdon Press. The sources for the theology of history developed in that book are too numerous to mention here. For the ideas presented below, I am especially indebted to G. W. F. Hegel, Ernst Troeltsch, Paul Tillich, Paul Ricoeur, Karl Jaspers, and John Cobb. Feminist, African American, and Latin American liberation theologies have also been helpful, especially the works of Rosemary Radford Ruether, James Cone, and Gustavo Gutiérrez (see chap. 6 above).

55. These images have a Hegelian provenance. See G. W. F. Hegel, *Lectures on the Philosophy of World History*, trans. H. B. Nisbet (Cambridge: Cambridge University Press, 1975), 58–63, 149; and William Desmond, *Art and the Absolute: A Study of Hegel's Aesthetics* (Albany: State University of New York Press, 1986), 67–71, 75.

56. Joel Kovel, *History and Spirit*, 2–3.

57. Tillich points to the rhythmic character of history and introduces the category of "kairos" (the Greek word for time in the sense of a qualitatively significant moment). *Systematic Theology*, 3:362–72, 419–20.

58. I am thinking of the black spiritual:

De gospel train's a-coming',
I hear it jus' at han',
I hear de car wheels movin',
An' rumbling thro de lan'.

De fare is cheap, an' all can go,
De rich an' poor are dere,
No second class a-board dis train,
No difference in de fare.

Git on board, little chillen,
Git on board, little chillen,
Git on board, little chillen,
Dere's room for many a mo'.

See James H. Cone, *The Spirituals and the Blues: An Interpretation* (New York: Seabury Press, 1972), 94. Here the train is an eschatological image, but the gospel train is also a freedom train, the one that runs on the Underground Railway. One thinks too of the freedom rides of the civil rights movement.

59. I have been helped by papers presented to the Theology and Science Group of the American Academy of Religion (1992) on the theme "Redemption of Humanity and Nature," especially those by Holmes Rolston III and Joel E. Haugen. On tragedy, see above, chap. 14, pp. 209–10.

60. See above, chap. 13, pp. 195–96. This is an idea that Robert C. Calhoun introduced into his lectures on systematic theology at Yale Divinity School. He said something like this (from my lecture notes, spring 1958): The world was created with a principle of indeterminacy and "waywardness," so that humans could have an environment in which freedom is genuinely possible. The world did not consciously rebel against the ground of its being; no consciousness and will are found in the natural creation. But the world in its waywardness falls into evil to the extent that in disorder it ceases to function as it was created to function. The disorder takes the form of encroachment and destruction. Mosquitoes are good—except when they are unduly encroaching on other creatures. God does not eliminate the waywardness and indeterminacy of the world. Rather God redeems the world, restores it, by constantly acting so as to produce order, direction, and purpose. God does not eliminate the indeterminate backdrop against which human freedom is possible. Rather God keeps the backdrop from getting out of hand. Thus God does not eliminate mosquitoes but enables humans to control malaria. The world is "good" insofar as it *is*, but "evil" insofar as in its waywardness it has fallen into encroachment, destruction, and disorder. The world in its condition of unsteadiness per se is not evil, precisely because God chose to create an otherness that could be related to God in freedom.

61. Tillich, *Systematic Theology*, 3:30–106 (quotation from 91).

Chapter 19. The Perfection of God

1. Tillich, *Systematic Theology*, 3:283–84, 292–94 (quotation from 284).

2. See Martin Heidegger, *Being and Time*, trans. John Macquarrie and Edward Robinson (New York: Harper & Row, 1962), 499; and Paul Ricoeur, *Time and Narrative*, trans. Kathleen McLaughlin and David Pellauer, vol. 1 (Chicago: University of Chicago Press, 1984), part 1.

3. This is an Hegelian concept. See *Lectures on the Philosophy of Religion*, 3:77, 186–87, 327–28. See also Walter Jaeschke, "World History and the History of the Absolute Spirit," in *History and System: Hegel's Philosophy of History*, ed. Robert L. Perkins (Albany: State University of New York Press, 1984), 106–8, 111–12; and my *God in History*, 66–67, 250–51.

4. Tillich, *Systematic Theology*, 3:429.

5. Ibid., 3:421.

6. Ibid., 3:403–6 (quotation from 405).

7. John B. Cobb, Jr., *Process Theology as Political Theology* (Philadelphia: Westminster Press, 1982), 77–81.

8. Tillich, *Systematic Theology*, 3:415–18. Robert Calhoun came to a position

similar to Tillich's. As opposed to the doctrines of double predestination, universalism (all are saved immediately at the end of present life), absorption into God, and salvation on the basis of merit, he favored the idea of an eventual salvation for all—if God remains merciful and manifests mercy toward us in power. Lectures on Systematic Theology, Yale Divinity School, spring 1958. Ernst Troeltsch wavered on this question, struggling with the tension between the universality and particularity of grace. *The Christian Faith* (Minneapolis: Fortress Press, 1991), 288, 304.

9. Tillich holds the eternal and the temporal in a delicate balance. He says that the eschaton, which is a symbol of the "transition" from the temporal to the eternal, does not refer to a far or near catastrophe in time and space but is "an expression of our standing in every moment in face of the eternal, though in a particular mode of time. . . . Past and future meet in the present, and both are included in the eternal 'now.' But they are not swallowed by the present; they have their independent and different functions. . . . In this way the *eschaton* becomes a matter of present experience without losing its futuristic dimension: we stand *now* in face of the eternal, but we do so looking ahead toward the end of history and the end of all which is temporal in the eternal." *Systematic Theology*, 3:395–96.

10. See Krister Stendahl, *Energy for Life* (Geneva: WCC Publications, 1990), 44–47.

11. Tillich, *Systematic Theology*, 3:396–98.

12. Ibid., 3:398–401.

13. See John Cobb, "On the Deepening of Buddhism," in *The Emptying God*, ed. Cobb and Ives, 91–101.

14. Tillich, *Systematic Theology*, 3:401–3.

15. Ibid., 3:409–11.

16. Ibid., 3:406–9, 412–14.

SELECT BIBLIOGRAPHY

The bibliography identifies the principal works consulted for this project; it is not a complete list of authors and titles cited in the notes.

Barbour, Ian. *Religion in an Age of Science*. San Francisco: Harper & Row, 1990.

Barth, Karl. *Church Dogmatics*. Edited by G. W. Bromiley and T. F. Torrance. 12 vols. Edinburgh: T. & T. Clark, 1936 ff.

Vols. 1/1, 1/2: *The Doctrine of the Word of God*, Parts 1–2. 1936, 1956.

Vol. 2/1: *The Doctrine of God*, Part 1. 1957.

Vol. 3/2: *The Doctrine of Creation*, Part 2. 1960.

Vol. 4/2: *The Doctrine of Reconciliation*, Part 2. 1958.

Baur, Ferdinand Christian. *On the Writing of Church History*. Edited and translated by Peter C. Hodgson. New York: Oxford University Press, 1968.

Bernstein, Richard J. *Beyond Objectivism and Relativism: Science, Hermeneutics, and Praxis*. Philadelphia: University of Pennsylvania Press, 1983.

Berry, Thomas. *The Dream of the Earth*. San Francisco: Sierra Club Books, 1988.

Birch, Charles, and John B. Cobb, Jr. *The Liberation of Life: From the Cell to the Community*. Cambridge: Cambridge University Press, 1981.

Birch, Charles, William Eakin, and Jay B. McDaniel, eds. *Liberating Life: Contemporary Approaches to Ecological Theology*. Maryknoll, N.Y.: Orbis Books, 1990.

Bonhoeffer, Dietrich. *Creation and Fall: A Theological Interpretation of Genesis 1—3*. London: SCM Press, 1959.

Brock, Rita Nakashima. *Journeys by Heart: A Christology of Erotic Power*. New York: Crossroad, 1988.

Brown, Robert McAfee. *Kairos: Three Prophetic Challenges to the Church*. Grand Rapids, Mich.: Wm. B. Eerdmans Publishing Co., 1990.

Bultmann, Rudolf. *Theology of the New Testament*. Translated by Kendrick Grobel. 2 vols. New York: Charles Scribner's Sons, 1954-55.

Chopp, Rebecca. *The Praxis of Suffering: An Interpretation of Liberation and Political Theologies*. Maryknoll, N.Y.: Orbis Books, 1986.

Chopp, Rebecca, and Mark K. Taylor, eds. *Reconstructing Christian Theology*. Minneapolis: Fortress Press, 1994.

Cobb, John B., Jr. *Beyond Dialogue: Toward a Mutual Transformation of Christianity and Buddhism*. Philadelphia: Fortress Press, 1982.

______. *God and the World*. Philadelphia: Westminster Press, 1969.

______. *Process Theology as Political Theology*. Philadelphia: Westminster Press, 1982.

Cobb, John B., Jr., and Christopher Ives, eds. *The Emptying God: A Buddhist-Jewish-Christian Conversation*. Maryknoll, N.Y.: Orbis Books, 1990.

Collingwood, R. G. *The Idea of History*. Edited by T. M. Knox. Oxford: Clarendon Press, 1946.

______. *The Idea of Nature*. Oxford: Clarendon Press, 1945.

Comblin, José. *The Holy Spirit and Liberation*. Maryknoll, N.Y.: Orbis Books, 1989.

Cone, James H. *A Black Theology of Liberation*. Philadelphia: Lippincott, 1970.

______. *God of the Oppressed*. New York: Seabury Press, 1975.

______. *The Spirituals and the Blues: An Interpretation*. New York: Seabury Press, 1972.

Cooke, Bernard. *Ministry to Word and Sacraments: History and Theology*. Philadelphia: Fortress Press, 1976.

Davies, Paul. *The Cosmic Blueprint: New Discoveries in Nature's Creative Ability to Order the Universe*. New York: Simon & Schuster, 1988.

Davis, Stephen T., ed. *Encountering Jesus: A Debate on Christology*. Atlanta: John Knox Press, 1988.

D'Costa, Gavin, ed. *Christian Uniqueness Reconsidered: The Myth of a Pluralistic Theology of Religions*. Maryknoll, N.Y.: Orbis Books, 1990.

Ebeling, Gerhard. *Introduction to a Theological Theory of Language*. Translated by R. A. Wilson. Philadelphia: Fortress Press, 1971.

______. *The Study of Theology*. Translated by Duane A. Priebe. Philadelphia: Fortress Press, 1978.

Ellis, Marc, and Otto Maduro, eds. *The Future of Liberation Theology*. Maryknoll, N.Y.: Orbis Books, 1989.

Evans, James H. *We Have Been Believers: An African-American Systematic Theology*. Minneapolis: Fortress Press, 1992.

Fackenheim, Emil L. *God's Presence in History: Jewish Affirmations and*

Philosophical Reflections. New York: New York University Press, 1970.
Farley, Edward. *Ecclesial Man: A Social Phenomenology of Faith and Reality*. Philadelphia: Fortress Press, 1975.
———. *Ecclesial Reflection: An Anatomy of Theological Method*. Philadelphia: Fortress Press, 1982.
———. *Good and Evil: Interpreting a Human Condition*. Minneapolis: Fortress Press, 1990.
———. *Theologia: The Fragmentation and Unity of Theological Education*. Philadelphia: Fortress Press, 1983.
Fiorenza, Elisabeth Schüssler. *In Memory of Her: A Feminist Theological Reconstruction of Christian Origins*. New York: Crossroad, 1983.
Fiorenza, Francis Schüssler. *Foundational Theology: Jesus and the Church*. New York: Crossroad, 1984.
Forstman, Jack. *Christian Faith in Dark Times: Theological Conflicts in the Shadow of Hitler*. Louisville, Ky.: Westminster/John Knox Press, 1992.
Foucault, Michel. *Power/Knowledge*. New York: Pantheon Books, 1980.
Fuller, Reginald H. *Foundations of New Testament Christology*. New York: Charles Scribner's Sons, 1965.
Gadamer, Hans-Georg. *Truth and Method*. 2d ed. Translation revised by Joel Weinsheimer and Donald G. Marshall. New York: Crossroad, 1989.
Gilkey, Langdon. *Message and Existence: An Introduction to Christian Theology*. New York: Seabury Press, 1980.
———. *Society and the Sacred: Toward a Theology of Culture in Decline*. New York: Crossroad, 1981.
Gill, Jerry H. *Faith in Dialogue: A Christian Apologetic*. Waco, Tex.: Word Books, 1985.
Gleick, James. *Chaos: Making a New Science*. New York: Penguin Books, 1987.
Gore, Al. *Earth in the Balance: Ecology and the Human Spirit*. New York: Houghton Mifflin, 1992.
Griffiths, Paul J. *An Apology for Apologetics: A Study in the Logic of Interreligious Dialogue*. Maryknoll, N.Y.: Orbis Books, 1991.
Grillmeier, Aloys. *Christ in Christian Tradition: From the Apostolic Age to Chalcedon*. Translated by J. S. Bowden. London: A. R. Mowbray, 1965.
Gustafson, James M. *Treasure in Earthen Vessels: The Church as a Human Community*. New York: Harper & Bros., 1961.
Gutiérrez, Gustavo. *The God of Life*. Translated by Matthew J. O'Connell. Maryknoll, N.Y.: Orbis Books, 1991.
———. *The Power of the Poor in History*. Translated by Robert R. Barr. Maryknoll, N.Y.: Orbis Books, 1983.
———. *A Theology of Liberation: History, Politics, and Salvation*. 15th anniversary edition. Translated and edited by Caridad Inda and John Eagleson. Maryknoll, N.Y.: Orbis Books, 1988.

______. *The Truth Shall Make You Free: Confrontations*. Translated by Matthew J. O'Connell. Maryknoll, N.Y.: Orbis Books, 1990.

Habermas, Jürgen. *Communication and the Evolution of Society*. Translated by Thomas McCarthy. Boston: Beacon Press, 1979.

______. *The Theory of Communicative Action*. 2 vols. Translated by Thomas McCarthy. Boston: Beacon Press, 1984, 1987.

Harris, Errol E. *Cosmos and Anthropos: A Philosophical Interpretation of the Anthropic Cosmological Principle*. Atlantic Highlands, N.J.: Humanities Press International, 1991.

Hart, Kevin. *The Trespass of the Sign: Deconstruction, Theology and Philosophy*. Cambridge: Cambridge University Press, 1989.

Hegel, Georg Wilhelm Friedrich. *Encyclopedia of the Philosophical Sciences*. Translated by William Wallace and A. V. Miller. 3 vols. Oxford: Clarendon Press, 1970, 1971, 1975.

______. *The Encyclopaedia Logic*. Translated by T. F. Geraets, W. A. Suchting, and H. S. Harris. Indianapolis: Hackett Publishing Co., 1991.

______. *Lectures on the Philosophy of Religion*. 3 vols. Translated and edited by Peter C. Hodgson et al. Berkeley and Los Angeles: University of California Press, 1984, 1985, 1987.

______. *Lectures on the Philosophy of World History*. Introduction: *Reason in History*. Translated by H. B. Nisbet. Cambridge: Cambridge University Press, 1975.

______. *Phenomenology of Spirit*. Translated by A. V. Miller. Oxford: Clarendon Press, 1977.

______. *Philosophy of Nature*. Edited and translated by M. J. Petry. 3 vols. London: Allen & Unwin, 1970.

______. *Philosophy of Right*. Translated by T. M. Knox. Oxford: Oxford University Press, 1952.

______. *Science of Logic*. Translated by A. V. Miller. London: Allen & Unwin, 1969.

Heidegger, Martin. *Being and Time*. Translated by John Macquarrie and Edward Robinson. New York: Harper & Row, 1962.

______. *On the Way to Language*. Translated by Peter D. Hertz. New York: Harper & Row, 1971.

______. *Poetry, Language, Thought*. Translated by Albert Hofstadter. New York: Harper & Row, 1971.

Hendry, George. *The Holy Spirit in Christian Theology*. Philadelphia: Westminster Press, 1956.

Hick, John, ed. *The Myth of God Incarnate*. Philadelphia: Westminster Press, 1977.

Hick, John, and Paul F. Knitter, eds. *The Myth of Christian Uniqueness: Toward a Pluralistic Theology of Religions*. Maryknoll, N.Y.: Orbis Books, 1987.

Hodgson, Peter C. *Children of Freedom: Black Liberation in Christian Perspective*. Philadelphia: Fortress Press, 1974.

———. *God in History: Shapes of Freedom*. Nashville: Abingdon Press, 1989.

———. *Jesus—Word and Presence: An Essay in Christology*. Philadelphia: Fortress Press, 1971.

———. *New Birth of Freedom: A Theology of Bondage and Liberation*. Philadelphia: Fortress Press, 1976.

———. *Revisioning the Church: Ecclesial Freedom in the New Paradigm*. Philadelphia: Fortress Press, 1988.

Hodgson, Peter C., and Robert H. King, eds. *Christian Theology: An Introduction to Its Traditions and Tasks*. 3d ed. Minneapolis: Fortress Press, 1994.

Hood, Robert E. *Must God Remain Greek? Afro Cultures and God-Talk*. Minneapolis: Fortress Press, 1990.

Hopkins, Dwight N. *Shoes that Fit Our Feet: Sources for a Constructive Black Theology*. Maryknoll, N.Y.: Orbis Books, 1993.

Johnson, Elizabeth A. *She Who Is: The Mystery of God in Feminist Theological Discourse*. New York: Crossroad, 1992.

Jones, William R. *Is God a White Racist? A Preamble to Black Theology*. Garden City, N.Y.: Doubleday, 1973.

Jüngel, Eberhard. *God as the Mystery of the World: On the Foundation of the Theology of the Crucified One in the Dispute between Theism and Atheism*. Translated by Darrell L. Guder. Grand Rapids, Mich.: Wm. B. Eerdmans Publishing Co., 1983.

Käsemann, Ernst. *Essays on New Testament Themes*. Translated by W. J. Montague. London: SCM Press, 1964.

———. *Jesus Means Freedom*. Translated by Frank Clarke. Philadelphia: Fortress Press, 1970.

Kant, Immanuel. *Critique of Practical Reason*. Translated by Lewis White Beck. New York: Liberal Arts Press, 1956.

———. *Religion within the Limits of Reason Alone*. Translated by T. M. Greene and H. H. Hudson. New York: Harper & Bros., 1960.

Kaufman, Gordon D. *In Face of Mystery: A Constructive Theology*. Cambridge, Mass.: Harvard University Press, 1993.

Kelly, J. N. D. *Early Christian Doctrines*. London: Adam & Charles Black, 1958.

Kelsey, David H. *The Uses of Scripture in Recent Theology*. Philadelphia: Fortress Press, 1975.

Kierkegaard, Søren. *The Concept of Anxiety*. Edited and translated by Reidar Thomte. Princeton: Princeton University Press, 1980.

———. *Fear and Trembling* and *Repetition*. Edited and translated by Howard V. Hong and Edna H. Hong. Princeton: Princeton University Press, 1983.

———. *Philosophical Fragments*. Edited and translated by Howard V. Hong and Edna H. Hong. Princeton: Princeton University Press, 1985.

______. *The Sickness unto Death*. Edited and translated by Howard V. Hong and Edna H. Hong. Princeton: Princeton University Press, 1980.

Kirk, G. S., and J. E. Raven. *The Presocratic Philosophers: A Critical History with a Selection of Texts*. Cambridge: Cambridge University Press, 1957.

Kitagawa, Joseph Mitsuo. *The Quest for Human Unity: A Religious History*. Minneapolis: Fortress Press, 1990.

Kittel, Gerhard, and Gerhard Friedrich, eds. *Theological Dictionary of the New Testament*. Translated by Geoffrey W. Bromiley. Grand Rapids, Mich.: Wm. B. Eerdmans Publishing Co., 1964–74.

Knitter, Paul F. *No Other Name? A Critical Survey of Christian Attitudes Toward the World Religions*. Maryknoll, N.Y.: Orbis Books, 1985.

Knox, John. *The Humanity and Divinity of Christ: A Study of Pattern in Christology*. Cambridge: Cambridge University Press, 1967.

Kovel, Joel. *History and Spirit: An Inquiry into the Philosophy of Liberation*. Boston: Beacon Press, 1991.

Krieger, David J. *The New Universalism: Foundations for a Global Theology*. Maryknoll, N.Y.: Orbis Books, 1991.

Küng, Hans. *The Church*. New York: Image Books, 1976.

Levinas, Emmanuel. *Totality and Infinity: An Essay on Exteriority*. Translated by Alphonso Lingis. Pittsburgh: Duquesne University Press, 1969.

Lucas, George R. *Hegel and Whitehead: Contemporary Perspectives on Systematic Philosophy*. Edited by George R. Lucas. Albany: State University of New York Press, 1986.

McDaniel, Jay B. *Earth, Sky, Gods and Mortals: Developing an Ecological Spirituality*. Mystic, Conn.: Twenty-Third Publications, 1990.

______. *Of God and Pelicans: A Theology of Reverence for Life*. Louisville, Ky.: Westminster/John Knox Press, 1989.

McFague, Sallie. *The Body of God: An Ecological Theology*. Minneapolis: Fortress Press, 1993.

______. *Models of God: Theology for an Ecological, Nuclear Age*. Philadelphia: Fortress Press, 1987.

Macquarrie, John. *Jesus Christ in Modern Thought*. Philadelphia: Trinity Press International, 1990.

______. *Principles of Christian Theology*. New York: Charles Scribner's Sons, 1966.

Moltmann, Jürgen. *The Crucified God: The Cross of Christ as the Foundation and Criticism of Christian Theology*. Translated by R. A. Wilson and John Bowden. New York: Harper & Row, 1974.

______. *The Spirit of Life: A Universal Affirmation*. Translated by Margaret Kohl. Minneapolis: Fortress Press, 1992.

Monod, Jacques. *Chance and Necessity: An Essay on the Natural Philoso-*

phy of Modern Biology. New York: Vintage Books, 1971.

Musser, Donald W., and Joseph Price, eds. *A New Handbook of Christian Theology*. Nashville: Abingdon Press, 1992.

Nelson, James B. *Body Theology*. Louisville, Ky.: Westminster/John Knox Press, 1992.

Neville, Robert. *Behind the Masks of God: An Essay toward Comparative Theology*. Albany: State University of New York Press, 1991.

______. *A Theology Primer*. Albany: State University of New York Press, 1991.

Niebuhr, H. Richard. *Christ and Culture*. New York: Harper & Bros., 1951.

______. *Faith on Earth: An Inquiry into the Structure of Human Faith*. Edited by Richard R. Niebuhr. New Haven, Conn.: Yale University Press, 1989.

______. *The Meaning of Revelation*. New York: Macmillan, 1941.

______. *The Purpose of the Church and Its Ministry: Reflections on the Aims of Theological Education*. New York: Harper & Bros., 1956.

______. *Radical Monotheism and Western Culture*. New York: Harper & Bros., 1960.

Niebuhr, Reinhold. *The Nature and Destiny of Man*. 2 vols. New York: Charles Scribner's Sons, 1941.

Noll, Mark A., and David F. Wells, eds. *Christian Faith and Practice in the Modern World: Theology from an Evangelical Point of View*. Grand Rapids, Mich.: Wm. B. Eerdmans Publishing Co., 1988.

Oduyoye, Mercy Amba. *Hearing and Knowing: Theological Reflections on Christianity in Africa*. Maryknoll, N.Y.: Orbis Books, 1986.

Ogden, Schubert. *Is There Only One True Religion or Are There Many?* Dallas: Southern Methodist University Press, 1992.

Pailin, David A. *God and the Processes of Reality: Foundations of a Credible Theism*. London and New York: Routledge, 1989.

Panikkar, Raimundo. *The Cosmotheandric Experience: Emerging Religious Consciousness*. Maryknoll, N.Y.: Orbis Books, 1993.

______. *The Unknown Christ of Hinduism: Toward an Ecumenical Christophany*. Revised edition. Maryknoll, N.Y.: Orbis Books, 1981.

______. *The Silence of the God: The Answer of the Buddha*. Translated by Robert Barr. Maryknoll, N.Y.: Orbis Books, 1989.

Pawlikowski, John. *Christ in the Light of the Christian-Jewish Dialogue*. New York: Paulist Press, 1982.

Peacocke, Arthur. *Creation and the World of Science*. Oxford: Clarendon Press, 1979.

Peters, Ted, ed. *Cosmos as Creation: Theology and Science in Consonance*. Nashville: Abingdon Press, 1989.

Pieris, Aloysius. *An Asian Theology of Liberation*. Maryknoll, N.Y.: Orbis Books, 1988.

______. *Love Meets Wisdom: A Christian Experience of Buddhism*. Maryknoll, N.Y.: Orbis Books, 1988.

Polkinghorne, John. *One World: The Interaction of Science and Theology*. Princeton: Princeton University Press, 1986.

______. *Science and Providence: God's Interaction with the World*. Boston: Shambhala Publications, 1989.

Rahner, Karl. *Foundations of Christian Faith: An Introduction to the Idea of Christianity*. Translated by William V. Dych. New York: Crossroad, 1978.

______. *Hearers of the Word*. Translated by Michael Richards. New York: Herder and Herder, 1969.

______. *On the Theology of Death*. New York: Herder and Herder, 1965.

______. *The Trinity*. Translated by Joseph Donceel. New York: Herder and Herder, 1970.

Reat, Ross, and Edmund F. Perry. *A World Theology: The Central Spiritual Reality of Humankind*. Cambridge: Cambridge University Press, 1991.

Richardson, Alan, and John Bowdens, eds. *The Westminster Dictionary of Christian Theology*. Philadelphia: Westminster Press, 1983.

Ricoeur, Paul. *The Conflict of Interpretations: Essays in Hermeneutics*. Edited by Don Ihde. Evanston, Ill.: Northwestern University Press, 1974.

______. *Fallible Man: Philosophy of the Will*. Translated by Charles Kelbley. Chicago: Henry Regnery Co., 1967.

______. *Freedom and Nature: The Voluntary and the Involuntary*. Translated by Erazim V. Kohák. Evanston, Ill.: Northwestern University Press, 1966.

______. *Hermeneutics and the Human Sciences*. Translated by John B. Thompson. Cambridge: Cambridge University Press, 1981.

______. *History and Truth*. Translated by Charles A. Kelbley. Evanston, Ill.: Northwestern University Press, 1965.

______. *Interpretation Theory*. Fort Worth: Texas Christian University Press, 1976.

______. *The Rule of Metaphor*. Translated by Robert Czerny et al. Toronto and Buffalo: University of Toronto Press, 1977.

______. *The Symbolism of Evil*. Translated by Emerson Buchanan. Boston: Beacon Press, 1969.

______. *Time and Narrative*. 3 vols. Translated by Kathleen McLaughlin and David Pellauer. Chicago: University of Chicago Press, 1984, 1985, 1988.

Royce, Josiah. *The Problem of Christianity*. With an Introduction by John E. Smith. Chicago: University of Chicago Press, 1968.

Ruether, Rosemary Radford. *To Change the World: Christology and Cultural Criticism*. New York: Crossroad, 1983.

______. *Gaia and God: An Ecofeminist Theology of Earth Healing*. San Francisco: HarperSanFrancisco, 1992.

______. *Sexism and God-Talk: Toward a Feminist Theology*. With a new introduction. Boston: Beacon Press, 1993.

______. *Women-Church: Theology and Practice of Feminist Liturgical Communities*. San Francisco: Harper & Row, 1985.

Schillebeeckx, Edward. *Ministry: Leadership in the Community of Jesus Christ*. New York: Crossroad, 1981.

Schleiermacher, Friedrich. *The Christian Faith*. Edited by H. R. Mackintosh and J. S. Stewart. Edinburgh: T. & T. Clark, 1928.

______. *On Religion: Speeches to Its Cultured Despisers*. Translated by Richard Crouter. Cambridge: Cambridge University Press, 1988.

Smart, Ninian, and Steven Konstantine. *Christian Systematic Theology in a World Context*. Minneapolis: Fortress Press, 1991.

Smith, Steven G. *The Concept of the Spiritual: An Essay in First Philosophy*. Philadelphia: Temple University Press, 1988.

Sölle, Dorothee. *Thinking about God: An Introduction to Theology*. Philadelphia: Trinity Press International, 1990.

Stendahl, Krister. *Energy for Life: Reflections on the Theme "Come, Holy Spirit—Renew the Whole Creation."* Geneva: WCC Publications, 1990.

Swimme, Brian. *The Universe Is a Green Dragon: A Cosmic Creation Story*. Sante Fe, N.Mex.: Bear & Co., 1984.

Swimme, Brian, and Thomas Berry. *The Universe Story*. San Francisco: HarperSanFrancisco, 1992.

Tanner, Kathryn. *The Politics of God: Christian Theologies and Social Justice*. Minneapolis: Fortress Press, 1992.

Taylor, Mark C. *Erring: A Postmodern A/theology*. Chicago: University of Chicago Press, 1984.

Taylor, Mark K. *Remembering Esperanza: A Cultural-Political Theology for North American Praxis*. Maryknoll, N.Y.: Orbis Books, 1990.

Thistlethwaite, Susan Brooks, and Mary Potter Engel, eds. *Lift Every Voice: Constructing Christian Theologies from the Underside*. San Francisco: Harper & Row, 1990.

Tillich, Paul. *Christianity and the Encounter of the World Religions*. New York: Columbia University Press, 1963.

______. *The Courage to Be*. New Haven, Conn.: Yale University Press, 1952.

______. *The Future of Religions*. Edited by Jerald C. Brauer. New York: Harper & Row, 1966.

______. *Systematic Theology*. 3 vols. Chicago: University of Chicago Press, 1951, 1957, 1963.

______. *Theology of Culture*. New York: Oxford University Press, 1959.

Tracy, David. *The Analogical Imagination: Christian Theology and the Culture of Pluralism*. New York: Crossroad, 1981.

______. *Blessed Rage for Order: The New Pluralism in Theology*. New York: Seabury Press, 1975.

______. *Plurality and Ambiguity: Hermeneutics, Religion, Hope*. San Francisco: Harper & Row, 1987.

Trefil, James S. *The Moment of Creation: Big Bang Physics from Before the First Millisecond to the Present Universe*. New York: Macmillan, 1983.

Troeltsch, Ernst. *The Christian Faith*. Translated by Garrett E. Paul. Minneapolis: Fortress Press, 1991.

______. *Christian Thought: Its History and Application*. Translated and edited by Baron F. von Hügel. London: University of London Press, 1923.

______. *Writings on Theology and Religion*. Translated and edited by Robert Morgan and Michael Pye. Louisville, Ky.: Westminster/John Knox Press, 1990.

White, Hayden. *Metahistory: The Historical Imagination in Nineteenth-Century Europe*. Baltimore: Johns Hopkins University Press, 1973.

Williams, Robert R. *Recognition: Fichte and Hegel on the Other*. Albany: State University of New York Press, 1992.

INDEX OF BIBLICAL REFERENCES

INDEX OF NAMES AND SUBJECTS

Notes of a purely referential character are not indexed if the authors to whom they refer are named in and indexed from the text.